Psychology in the Brain

Psychology in the Brain

Integrative Cognitive Neuroscience

Leon Kenemans
Utrecht University

Nick Ramsey
University Medical Centre
Utrecht University

First published 2013 by
PALGRAVE MACMILLAN

Palgrave Macmillan in the UK is an imprint of Macmillan Publishers Limited, registered in England, company number 785998, of Houndmills, Basingstoke, Hampshire RG21 6XS.

Palgrave Macmillan in the US is a division of St Martin's Press LLC, 175 Fifth Avenue, New York, NY 10010.

Palgrave Macmillan is the global academic imprint of the above companies and has companies and representatives throughout the world.

Palgrave® and Macmillan® are registered trademarks in the United States, the United Kingdom, Europe and other countries

ISBN: 978–0–230–55324–8 hardback
ISBN: 978–0–230–55325–5 paperback

This book is printed on paper suitable for recycling and made from fully managed and sustained forest sources. Logging, pulping and manufacturing processes are expected to conform to the environmental regulations of the country of origin.

A catalogue record for this book is available from the British Library.

A catalog record for this book is available from the Library of Congress.

10 9 8 7 6 5 4 3 2 1
22 21 20 19 18 17 16 15 14 13

Printed in China

Contents

List of Figures

List of Plates

Preface

Psychology has yielded many relevant and fascinating insights, which in some cases have even resulted in Nobel Prizes. Many of these advances have addressed the exact nature of human behaviour when it is analysed in a sufficiently rigorous quantitative and objective way. However, for really understanding the underlying mechanisms of behavioural phenomena one has to resort to studying the brain. There is no behaviour without brain function and no variation in behaviour without variation in brain function. At a more principal level, the classical psychology textbook structure involves chapters named 'Perception', 'Attention', 'Memory', 'Emotion', and so on. These terms refer to abstract concepts which cannot be touched, measured or manipulated in any physical manner, and this prevents eventual ultimate understanding. To move forward, psychology has to be taken into the brain. For example, instead of stating that 'task A involves more perceptual than action mechanisms', while 'task B affects more action than perceptual mechanisms', we refer to different brain substrates, one of which is more involved in task A, whereas the other is more involved in task B. This is a first aim of the book: translating psychological terminology into a neuro-scientific treatise.

This book carries the aim of cognitive neuroscience in general, and in that it is therefore not new. However, even the few available cognitive-neuroscience textbooks maintain a chapter structure featuring first 'Perception', then 'Motor system', then 'Memory', and so on. We argue that these terms refer not only to abstract, non-existing entities but also to predominantly arbitrary categories which mainly reflect the terminological perspective that individual researchers happen to have taken. To transcend these arbitrary distinctions we adopt an integrative approach. We discuss how traditionally distinct concepts or the associated mental functions such as Perception and Memory converge on common brain substrates. We evaluate how a given brain substrate combines with other brain substrates in contributing to various mental functions. For example, activation of the secondary visual cortex is involved in perception, in attention, as well as in certain forms of memory. At the same time, when the visual cortex contributes to memory, it does so in combination with the activation of frontal and medial-temporal cortical areas.

The integrative approach immediately translates in the titles of the chapters, which read 'Perception and action', 'Attention and memory', Emotion and action', and so on. Furthermore, many of these chapters contain an exploration of the psychopharmacology of the various integrated systems. Distinct brain areas each contribute to multiple mental functions. Mental functions are realized by interactions (integration) between distinct brain areas. These interactions are fuelled by pharmacological processes.

The envisaged readership assumes completed core undergraduate courses on Biological Foundations of Behaviour (working of nerve cells etc.) and Cognitive Psychology. Courses for which this book would be suitable would be 'Cognitive Neuroscience', 'Cognitive Psychology and Neuroscience', 'Neurobiology of Mental Processes', '(Neurobiology of) Attention', and similar variations. Such courses are preferably at an advanced undergraduate or postgraduate level.

In sum, this textbook should bring the reader a coherent insight in human brain-function and its relation to behaviour. This goal is accomplished by using an integrated approach as outlined above. This approach presents interesting challenges for the reader. For example, readers are strongly encouraged to no longer stick to questions like, 'Is it memory or is it attention?' Rather, they should try to understand the function of brain substrate X in relation to its interaction with other brain processes and learn that, depending on the viewpoint of the researcher, these brain processes are discussed sometimes under 'attention' and sometimes under 'memory'.

Acknowledgements

The publisher and authors would like to thank the organizations listed below for permission to reproduce material from their publications:

The American Psychological Association for Figure 2.6, taken from Miller, J., & Hackley, S. A. (1992). Electrophysiological evidence for temporal overlap among contingent mental processes. *Journal of Experimental Psychology: General, 121*(2), 195–209; Figure 4.3 taken from De Jong, R., Wierda, M., Mulder, G., & Mulder, L. J. M. (1988). Use of partial stimulus information in response processing. *Journal of Experimental Psychology: Human Perception and Performance, 14*(4), 682–692.

Oxford University Press for Figures 2.9 and 2.10 taken from Gallese, V., Fadiga, L., Fogassi, L., & Rizzolatti, G. (1996), Action recognition in the premotor cortex. *Brain, 119*(2), 593–609; Figure 3.25 taken from Veldhuizen, M. G., Bender, G., Constable, R. T., & Small, D. M. (2007). Trying to detect taste in a tasteless solution: Modulation of early gustatory cortex by attention to taste. *Chemical Senses, 32*(6), 569–581; Figure 5.14 taken from Wheeler, M. E., Shulman, G. L., Buckner, R. L., Miezin, F. M., Velanova, K., & Petersen, S. E. (2006). Evidence for separate perceptual reactivation and search processes during remembering. *Cerebral Cortex, 16*(7), 949–959; Figure 7.5 taken from Gerwig, M., Dimitrova, A., Kolb, F. P., Maschke, M., Brol, B., Kunnel, A., et al. (2003). Comparison of eyeblink conditioning in patients with superior and posterior inferior cerebellar lesions. *Brain, 126*(1), 71–94; Figure 9.5 adapted from Lee, T., Dolan, R. J., & Critchley, H. D. (2008). Controlling emotional expression: Behavioral and neural correlates of nonimitative emotional responses. *Cerebral Cortex, 18*, 104–113.

John Wiley and sons for Figure 2.11 taken from Heiser, M., Iacoboni, M., Maeda, F., Marcus, J., & Mazziotta, J. C. (2003). The essential role of Broca's area in imitation. *European Journal of Neuroscience, 17*(5), 1123–1128; Figure 2.12 taken from Curio, G. N., Jussi Numminen, Veikko Jousmäki, & Riitta Hari (2000). Speaking modifies voice-evoked activity in the human auditory cortex. *Human Brain Mapping, 9*(4), 183–191; Figure 5.9 taken from Kimura, M., Katayama, J., Ohira, H., & Schröger, E. (2009). Visual mismatch negativity: New evidence from the equiprobable paradigm. *Psychophysiology, 46*(2), 402–409; Figure 9.12 taken from Vollstädt-Klein, S., Wichert, S., Rabinstein, J., Bühler, M., Klein, O., Ende, G., et al. (2010). Initial, habitual and compulsive alcohol use is characterized by a shift of cue processing from ventral to dorsal striatum. *Addiction, 105*, 1741–1749.

Wolters Kluwer Health for Figure 5.8 taken from Kenemans, J. L., Grent-'t Jong, T., & Verbaten, M. N. (2003). Detection of visual change: Mismatch or rareness? *NeuroReport., 14*, 1239–1243.

Elsevier Limited for Figure 2.13 taken from Ford, J. M., & Mathalon, D. H. (2005). Corollary discharge dysfunction in schizophrenia: Can it explain auditory hallucinations? *International Journal of Psychophysiology, 58*(2–3), 179–189; Figure 3.11 taken from Woldorff, M. G., & Hillyard, S. A. (1991). Modulation of early auditory processing during selective listening to rapidly presented tones. *Electroencephalography and Clinical Neurophysiology, 79*(3), 170–191; Figures 3.12 and 3.13 taken from Mangun, G. R., Hinrichs, H., Scholz, M., Mueller-Gaertner, H. W., Herzog, H., Krause, B. J., et al. (2001). Integrating electrophysiology and neuroimaging of spatial selective attention to simple isolated visual stimuli. *Vision Research, 41*(10–11), 1423–1435; Figures 3.20

and 3.21 taken from van der Lubbe, R. H. J., Neggers, S. F. W., Verleger, R., & Kenemans, J. L. (2006). Spatiotemporal overlap between brain activation related to saccade preparation and attentional orienting. *Brain Research, 1072*(1), 133–152; Figure 3.24 taken from Giesbrecht, B., Woldorff, M. G., Song, A. W., & Mangun, G. R. (2003). Neural mechanisms of top-down control during spatial and feature attention. *Neuroimage, 19*(3), 496–512; Figures 4.8 and 11.10 taken from Abdullaev, Y. G., & Posner, M. I. (1998). Event-related brain potential imaging of semantic encoding during processing single words. *NeuroImage, 7*(1), 1; Figure 4.16 adapted from di Michele, F., Prichep, L., John, E. R., & Chabot, R. J. (2005). The neurophysiology of attention-deficit/hyperactivity disorder. *International Journal of Psychophysiology Electrophysiology in Attention-Deficit/Hyperactivity Disorder, 58*(1), 81–93; Figure 4.18 taken from Kenemans, J. L., Bekker, E. M., Lijffijt, M., Overtoom, C. C. E., Jonkman, L. M., & Verbaten, M. N. (2005). Attention deficit and impulsivity: Selecting, shifting, and stopping. *International Journal of Psychophysiology, 58*(1), 59–70; Figure 5.12 taken from Farah, M. J. (1989). The neural basis of mental imagery. *Trends in Neurosciences, 12*(10), 395–399; Figure 5.15 taken from Gilbert, C. D., Sigman, M., & Crist, R. E. (2001). The neural basis of perceptual learning. *Neuron, 31*(5), 681–697; Figure 5.16 taken from Seitz, A., & Watanabe, T. (2005). A unified model for perceptual learning. *Trends in Cognitive Sciences, 9*(7), 329; Figure 6.14 taken from Toichi, M., & Kamio, Y. (2002). Long-term memory and levels-of-processing in autism. *Neuropsychologia 40*, 964–969; Figure 8.3 taken from Stark, R., Zimmermann, M., Kagerer, S., Schienle, A., Walter, B., Weygandt, M., et al. (2007). Hemodynamic brain correlates of disgust and fear ratings. *NeuroImage, 37*(2), 663–673; Figure 8.4 taken from Eimer, M., & Holmes, A. (2007). Event-related brain potential correlates of emotional face processing. *Neuropsychologia, 45*(1), 15–31; Figures 9.1 and 9.2 taken from Feinstein, J. S., Adolphs, R., Damasio, A., & Tranel, D. (2011). The human amygdala and the induction and experience of fear. *Current Biology, 21*, 34–38; Figure 9.9 taken from Ernst, M., & Fudge, J. L. (2009). A developmental neurobiological model of motivated behavior: Anatomy, connectivity and ontogeny of the triadic nodes. *Neuroscience & Biobehavioral Reviews, 33*(3), 367–382; Figure 11.1 taken from Hermans, E. J., Putman, P., & van Honk, J. (2006b). Testosterone administration reduces empathetic behavior: A facial mimicry study. *Psychoneuroendocrinology, 31*(7), 859–866; Figure 11.3 taken from Baumgartner, T., Heinrichs, M., Vonlanthen, A., Fischbacher, U., & Fehr, E. (2008). Oxytocin shapes the neural circuitry of trust and trust adaptation in humans. *Neuron, 58*(4), 639–650; Figure 11.9 taken from Crepaldi, D., Berlingeri, M., Paulesu, E., & Luzzatti, C. (2011). A place for nouns and a place for verbs? A critical review of neurocognitive data on grammatical-class effects. *Brain and Language, 116*(1), 33–49; Figure 11.11 taken from Ullman, M. T., Pancheva, R., Love, T., Yee, E., Swinney, D., & Hickok, G. (2005). Neural correlates of lexicon and grammar: Evidence from the production, reading, and judgment of inflection in aphasia. *Brain and Language, 93*(2), 185–238; Figure 11.12 taken from Lavie, N. (2005). Distracted and confused? Selective attention under load. *Trends in Cognitive Sciences, 9*(2), 75–82.

Macmillan Publishers for Figures 2.14 and 2.15, Sommer, M. A., & Wurtz, R. H. (2006). Influence of the thalamus on spatial visual processing in frontal cortex. *Nature, 444*(7117), 374–377; Figure 2.18 from Moore, T., & Armstrong, K. M. (2003) Selective gating of visual signals by microstimulation of frontal cortex. *Nature, 421*(6021), 370–373; Figure 3.2 taken from Zorzi, M., Priftis K., & Umilta, C. (2002). Brain damage: Neglect disrupts the mental number line. *Nature, 417*(6885), 138–139; Figure 3.8 taken from Roelfsema, P. R., Lamme V. A., & Spekreijse, H. (1998). Object-based attention in the primary visual cortex of the macaque monkey. *Nature, 395*(6700), 376–381.

IOP Publishing for Plate II, taken from Hermes, D., Vansteensel, M. J., Albers, A. M., Bleichner, M. G., Benedictus, M. R., Mendez Orellana, C., Aarnoutse, E. J., & Ramsey N. F. (2011). Functional MRI-based identification of brain areas involved in motor imagery for implantable brain-computer interfaces. *Journal of Neural Engineering*, 8(2), 025007.

Christian Keysers for kindly supplying the photographs in Figures 9.4 and 11.1.

Material is acknowledged individually throughout the text of the book. Every effort has been made to trace all copyright holders but, if any have been inadvertently overlooked, the publisher will be pleased to make the necessary arrangements at the first opportunity.

We would also like to thank Dennis Schutter, Tineke Grent-'t Jong and Floris Klumpers for their valued suggestions to improve the manuscript.

List of Abbreviations

5HT	5-hydroxytryptamine
AB	attentional blink
ACC	anterior cingulate cortex
ACh	acetylcholine
ADAN	anterior directing attention negativity
ADHD	attention deficit hyperactivity disorder
AIP	anterior intra-parietal sulcus
aMMN	auditory mismatch negativity
ANG	angular gyrus
BESA	brain electrical source analysis
BOLD	blood-oxygen level-dependent
BOLD-fMRI	blood-oxygen level-dependent functional magnetic resonance imaging
BRN	biasing related negativity
CNS	central nervous system
CS	conditional stimulus
CSRT	continuous serial reaction time
DA	dopamine
dACC	dorsal anterior cingulate cortex
DCS	D-cycloserine
DLPFC	dorsolateral prefrontal cortex
EBT	exposure-based therapy
ECoG	Electrocorticography
EDAN	early directing attention negativity
EEG	electroencephalography/electroencephalogram
EMG	electromyogram
EPN	earlier posterior negativity
ERF	event-related field
ERN	error-related negativity
ERP	event-related potential
FEF	frontal eye fields
FFA	fusiform face area
fMRI	functional magnetic resonance imaging
fNIRS	functional near-infrared spectroscopy
FPC	frontal polar cortex
fTCD	functional transcranial Doppler
GABA	gamma-aminobutyric acid
HPA	hypothalamus–pituitary–adrenal
IAPS	International Affective Picture System
IFG	inferior frontal gyrus
IPS	intra-parietal sulcus
IT	inferior temporal

LAN	lateral anterior negativity
LC	locus cereleus
LDAP	late directing-attention positivity
LOC	lateral occipital complex
LORETA	low-resolution brain electromagnetic tomography
LPD	late positive deflection
LPP	late positive potential
LRP	lateralized readiness potential
M1	primary motor cortex
MDD	major depressive disorder
MEG	magnetoencephalography
MMN	mismatch negativity
MNI	Montreal Neurological Institute
MNS	mirror neuron system
MRF	midbrain reticular formation
MT+	middle temporal complex
NB	nucleus basalis
NE	norepinephrine
NMDA	N-methyl-D-aspartate
OCD	obsessive–compulsive disorder
OFC	orbitofrontal cortex
OR	orienting response
PAG	peri-aqueductal grey
PCC	posterior cingulate cortex
Pe	error positivity
PET	positron emission tomography
PFC	prefrontal cortex
PMC	premotor cortex
PPA	parahippocampal place area
PPC	posterior parietal cortex
PTSD	post-traumatic stress disorder
R IFG	right inferior frontal gyrus
REM	rapid eye movement
RF	receptive field
RIR	reinstatement induced recovery
RRN	rareness-related negativity
RSVP	rapid serial visual presentation
RT	reaction time
SAM	synthetic aperture magnetometry
SC	superior colliculi
SCR	skin conductance response
SMA	supplementary motor area
SMG	supramarginal gyrus
SNN	social neural network
SNpc	substantia nigra pars compacta
SNS	sympathetic nervous system
SOA	stimulus onset asynchrony

SQUIDS	superconducting quantum interference device
SSRI	selective serotonin reuptake inhibitors
SSRT	stop signal reaction time
STN	subthalamic nucleus
TEO	occipital–temporal
TMS	transcranial magnetic stimulation
TPJ	temporal–parietal junction
UBT	unified brain theory
UR	unconditional response
US	unconditional stimulus
V1	primary visual cortex
V5	visual area 5
VM	ventromedial
VMFC	ventromedial frontal cortex
vMMN	visual mismatch negativity
VMPFC	ventromedial prefrontal cortex
VSC	visual–spatial cuing
VTA	ventral tegmental area

1 PRINCIPLES AND METHODS

1.0 INTRODUCTION

The basis of all mental processes lies in the signalling within and between neurons. The basic chain of events involves synaptic transmission, de- or hyperpolarization, and possibly action potentials which lead to further synaptic transmission. De- or hyperpolarization, the graded potentials, are believed to underlie non-invasively recordable signals like fMRI (functional magnetic resonance imaging) and EEG (electroencephalography).

Whatever mechanism is initiated, there is always a compensatory response: transmitters are synthesized and metabolized by specialized enzymes. They are released pre-synaptically, but immediately subjected to reuptake, and they also activate pre-synaptic autoreceptors resulting in reduced release. All these mechanism, including postsynaptic receptor binding, can be influenced by external substances (drugs) that cross the blood–brain barrier and interact more or less specifically with the various neurotransmitter systems (e.g. dopamine, acetylcholine, glutamate, anandamide).

The sequence of neurotransmitter–postsynaptic–receptor interaction, followed by postsynaptic potentials, and possibly action potentials is also referred to as the direct pathway. The direct pathway should be distinguished from so-called indirect pathways, which modulate signalling in the direct pathway. An important mechanism here is metabotropic transmission, which induces relatively slow second messenger effects in the postsynaptic neuron. The second messengers modulate the direct chain of events, such as the extent to which action potentials result in transmitter release. This is a basic model for the way top–down factors like attention, emotion, and memory modulate perception–to–action pathways.

For some reason, evolution has favoured those human brains in which multitudes of neurons with identical connections, and therefore identical functions, are both immediate neighbours as well as activated in synchrony. Given the current state of technology, this is why neuroimaging in humans yields meaningful results. There is a useful correspondence between what neuroimaging can tell us (e.g. resolution) and the way the brain is organized.

The classic method to delineate functional brain networks in humans involves patients with focal brain damage. However, these experiments of nature are badly in need of complementary methods that allow for more systematic experimental manipulation. These methods have become available in recent decades in the form of neuroimaging techniques such as fMRI, EEG, and PET (positron emission tomography), and related methods like TMS (transcranial magnetic stimulation). Especially powerful is the convergence of results from lesion methods with those from imaging. Such convergence has been established for diverse cognitive processes, as discussed in later chapters, such as the suppression of unwanted actions, selecting between multiple response options or sources of information, and modulation of long-term memory by short-term memory as implemented in a specific brain area. Recent developments aim to integrate results from animal single-neuron recording with human neu-roimaging by applying the principle of adaptation to fMRI or event-related potentials (ERP), enabling a more specific identification of the neural populations in cognitive processes.

In the remainder of this chapter, the basic principles behind these methods are addressed as a suitable background for subsequent chapters and terms like blood-oxygen level-depend-ent (BOLD) response, voxel, signal–to–noise ratio and source localization are clarified. The complementary value of these techniques is especially important. For example, the high temporal resolution of EEG, complementing the high spatial resolution of fMRI, is needed to further reveal the temporal dynamics in a network of distinct, active brain areas. Modern neuroimaging (like fMRI) in humans also reveals the localized effects of psychoactive sub-stances on brain activity that mediate their effects on behaviour. Other techniques (such as PET receptor occupancy tests) clarify whether these effects directly involve receptors in the brain area concerned, or follow indirectly from direct effects in other areas.

Box 1.1   The father of neuroscience

René Descartes is often considered the founding father of neuroscience, perhaps because he was the first to explicitly state that human behaviour is at least partly determined by connections between sensory organs, central nervous system, and muscles. 'No one before Descartes had ever seriously proposed that phenomena as complex as human behavior could be viewed as the product of purely physical interactions in physiological systems' (Glimcher, 2003, p. 7). In 1637 Descartes was convinced that it was just a matter of time until science would fully understand, and therefore be able to predict and manipulate, reflex-like behaviour that is evoked when, for example, one burns a foot in a fire and retracts the foot, while at the same time touching it with a hand and looking at it by directing head and eyes. As he put it: '... pulling the little thread cc... open(s) the entrance to the pore (d, e) where this thread terminates ... (and) the animal spirits from cavity F enter and are carried through it – partly into the muscles that serve to withdraw this foot from the fire, partly into those that serve to turn the eyes and head to look at it, and partly into those that serve to advance the hands and bend the body to protect it.' This citation is from *L'homme*, a work completed by 1637, but not published during his lifetime, perhaps out of fear that it might get into trouble with the church-dominated authorities. Indeed, it has been asserted that Descartes was a essentially a materialist, perhaps even a monist, who concealed his real ideas out of fear of persecution (La Mettrie, *L'homme machine*, 1748). In a later work (*Les Passions de l'ame*, 1649), he described these processes as involving the spirits being *reflected* from the image of the stimulation, hence the term 'reflex'; he appeared not to have been familiar with the notion of spinal reflexes.

Nowadays, current reflex pathway descriptions are generally accepted, but at the time such notions were sufficient for Descartes and his work to be banned. In the city and university of Utrecht his work was excluded from both pro or con argumentation in 1641. In 1667, seven years after his death, the catholic church declared all Descartes' work as forbidden despite his further reasoning that part of human behaviour should be conceived of as volitional, controlled by free will, therefore undetermined and unpredictable. These complex forms of behaviour reflect the interaction between the sensory–motor pathway and the soul. The soul is ethereal and therefore not accessible to scien-tific methods. The best we can do is determine the seat of the interaction between soul and reflex pathway, which in Descartes' view was the pineal gland.

Descartes' pineal-gland doctrine was a specific version of an older and more general idea that worm-like organs in the brain controlled, by their motion, the flow of animal spirits through and among the ventricles, as well as through nerves, afferently and efferently. Pineal-gland motion could result from sensory stimulation, or from intrinsic forces originating from the soul. The pineal gland was especially fit for this function, because it resided right in the middle of the brain, and was undivided across the hemispheres. The efferent motion of animal spirits to muscles would involve the opening of valves, an idea presaging our current knowledge of the opening of ion channels due to neuro-transmission. In *Les Passions de l'ame* (1649), he also surmised that movement of the pineal gland could be induced by animal spirits from the 'lower part...of the soul', and that this would compete with oppositely directed signals from the soul, as if the latter was attempting to suppress, or avoid giving into, certain desires.

1.1   IMAGING METHODS

When neurons are active they display three types of processes: electrical, chemical and metabolic.

The best known property of neurons is the electrical discharge called the action potential, which is the result of chemical events in and around the neuron. This, and other electrical properties of neurons, allows brain activity to be measured with EEG or MEG (magnetoen-cephalography). An important limitation of these methods is that the sensors are far away from the neurons, and that it is difficult to pinpoint exactly where in the brain neurons are active. Moreover, the orientation of neurons relative to the sensors strongly affects the meas-urements, to the point that some brain regions are invisible to the sensors. Sensors placed directly on or within the cortex only measure electric activity in their immediate vicinity, so they cover a limited part of the brain.

Many different chemical processes take place within and outside a neuron. These are fast and very subtle, making them difficult to detect and to distinguish from each other. A lot of effort is currently put into imaging these molecular events, but methods for use in humans are still very crude.

Metabolic processes deal with energy. When a neuron increases its firing rate it will use more energy, which is supplied by chemical reactions in and around the neuron. This in turn increases demand for the basic fuels: glucose and oxygen. The change in demand can be detected from the outside because it changes the amount of blood that flows to the region of the brain requiring it. Bloodflow in the brain is highly controlled and regulated and acts as a marker for neural activity. This chapter explains how these signals can be detected, and the strengths and weaknesses of different techniques.

1.1.1   What are the important properties of neuroimaging techniques?

The ability to detect is a prerequisite for any imaging technique. Ideally we would like to capture every event in every neuron with an imaging technique, but that is far from being realizable. Three types of processes can be measured with current techniques but how well depends on the properties of both the type of process and of the technique. What we aim for is twofold: high spatial detail and high temporal detail. Figure 1.1 shows the resolution properties for the most commonly used techniques in measuring brain activity.

Molecular (chemical) imaging is still quite insensitive because the processes are very subtle (since the quantity of molecules is small). A few chemicals can be imaged with PET using specially manufactured markers that need to be injected. Both spatial and temporal detail are poor compared to imaging of the other two neural processes: it takes up to half an hour to make one rather grainy picture of the brain, with each point about 5 mm cubic in size.

The imaging of electrical processes can be very detailed given that one can detect and distinguish two events separated by tens of milliseconds in the same brain region. However,

Figure 1.1

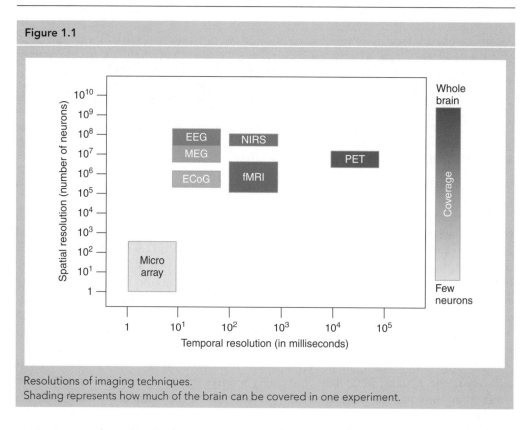

Resolutions of imaging techniques.
Shading represents how much of the brain can be covered in one experiment.

electricity is very hard to pinpoint within the brain. It is easily deflected by less conductive materials like thick membranes and the skull, leading to uncertainty about where the electrical signals come from. As a result, the pictures are quite grainy (each point is about 1–2 cm).

Metabolic processes are the focus of the most recently developed imaging techniques, those that track changes in bloodflow. Here, spatial detail is good, ranging from 5 mm to less than 1 mm per point. Temporal detail is moderate, even though the speed of the 'cameras' can be very high. Pictures can be made in less than half a second, but changes in blood flow are much slower: it takes about 2 seconds before a blood vessel reacts to increased oxygen demand, and it takes another 12 seconds for blood flow to slow down after peaking.

The choice of technique, be it electrophysiological or bloodflow, is determined by the question one wants to address. If one wants to assess whether the brain processes two stimuli differently, EEG may reveal subtle differences at a subsecond timescale. If one is interested in associating brain regions with functions, then fMRI would be the method of choice.

1.2   ELECTROPHYSIOLOGICAL IMAGING TECHNIQUES

Electroencephalography is the most widely used technique for measuring electrical correlates of brain function. In 1929 Hans Berger first reported EEG recordings and since then the technique has evolved continuously (Berger, 1929). Several inherent properties of the technique imposed some difficult limitations, notably the ability to localize active brain tissue. This prompted the development of MEG, which measures the magnetic fields that accompany electrical fields generated by neural activity. Magnetic fields are not affected by the electrical conductivity of tissue and therefore MEG is, in principle, a more accurate localizing technique. Nevertheless, it also suffers from low sensitivity since the signal strength, very weak to start out with, rapidly declines with distance (at about the square of the distance). Empirical evaluations indicate that actual localization accuracy does not differ significantly between the two techniques (Cohen & Cuffin, 1991). EEG and MEG do differ in their sensitivity to the directionality of the electromagnetic field generated by neuron populations: whereas EEG detects potentials in both the radial and tangential direction of a dipole (i.e. orthogonal or parallel to the surface of the scalp), MEG only detects the tangential component and therefore does not detect activity very well in the grey matter facing the inside of the skull (the 'crown' of the gyrus).

1.2.1   Electroencephalography

EEG measures electrical events in the brain. This can be achieved with a set of sensors (electrodes) connected to the scalp, and amplifiers that strengthen the signal so that it can be analysed. The sensors pick up electrical signals generated by large populations of neurons. When neurons fire, an exchange of electrically charged molecules takes place across the membrane of the cell. The exchange starts at the dendrites and travels to the cell body, or it starts at the cell body and travels along the axon. If, and only if, a large enough number of neurons generates electrical fields in the same orientation, with parallel dendrites and axons, is the combined electrical field strong enough to be detected by sensors on the scalp. When they are not aligned, or when the potentials of neighbouring patches of neuronal tissue are in opposite directions, they may not be detectable with EEG. The signals that are recorded consist of potentials (voltage differences) between each electrode and an internal ground in the amplifier. The environment contains various electrical fields that can contaminate the EEG signal. Therefore, additional electrodes are attached to the skin at positions away from brain or muscle (usually the earlobes or the bone behind the ear called the mastoid), but close to the scalp electrodes to minimize contributions from ambient fields. These additional electrodes serve as reference sensors for the scalp electrodes.

1.2.2   Origin of the EEG signal

Neurons at rest maintain a potential across the membrane where negatively charged ions dominate inside the cell resulting in an intra-extracellular voltage difference (polarity) of -70 mV. When the cell is stimulated by other cells, positive ions (sodium Na+) enter specific ion channels and cause a decline in the polarity. When the influx of sodium reaches a critical threshold, the influx increases drastically and the polarity briefly turns positive (20 mV), an event called depolarization or spiking. At this point potassium (K+) ions leave the cell, effectively preparing the cell for a new depolarization. The whole cycle (described and modelled in detail by Hodgkin and Huxley (1952)) takes about 1 ms, limiting the maximum spike rate to about 500 per second, depending on the type of neuron. Once a cell fires, the depolarization travels along the axon to the axon terminal where it causes a release of neurotransmitters. The electrical fields generated by axons are strong but the rapid membrane recovery makes them difficult to detect from outside the skull with EEG. Instead it is input to the cells that EEG measures, the result of the release of neurotransmitters by upstream axons onto the synapses on the dendrites. These cause small depolarizations which, when delivered in enough numbers, will cause a spike in the receiving cell. These stimulations are referred to as causing excitatory postsynaptic potentials, but other cells and their neurotransmitters serve to inhibit rather than stimulate the receiving neuron. They cause an inhibitory postsynaptic potential and are vital for regulating neural activity. Postsynaptic events are slower and more abundant than spikes, and are therefore the dominant contribution to what EEG measures (Buzsaki, 2006). For EEG to detect a neuronal event, the potentials need to be generated by tens of thousands of neurons with the same spatial alignment, close to each other and they need to do this synchronously (Murakami & Okada, 2006).

1.2.3 Features extracted from EEG

Computer software is used to analyse the EEG signals, usually in several steps. First, artefacts are removed from the signals by filtering (removing unwanted fluctuations), re-referencing and removal of movement-related artefacts. From this point, signals can be analysed in various ways, each of which addresses a different feature of brain activity. Most straightforward is the voltage signal (potential) from an electrode dominated by brain tissue underneath (several centimetres of cortical surface). Typically, the potential is a combination of fluctuations at multiple timescales, ranging from seconds to about 40 per second, and large deflections, both caused by neurons. By comparing the brain response (in technical terms the

Figure 1.2

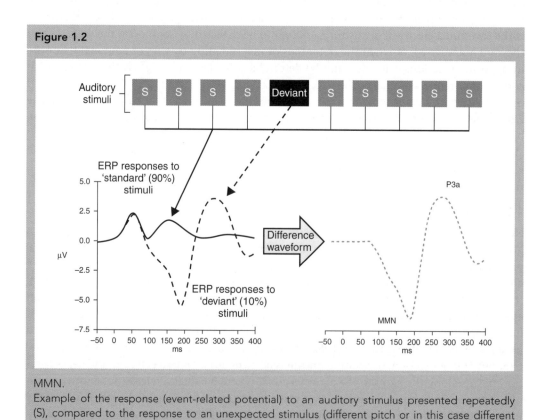

MMN.
Example of the response (event-related potential) to an auditory stimulus presented repeatedly (S), compared to the response to an unexpected stimulus (different pitch or in this case different duration). The differences becomes clearer after subtraction (bottom right).
Source: Light et al. (2010).

waveform) to two different stimuli, or to one stimulus in two different conditions, one can identify differences in the temporal evolution of the signal, the event-related potential. If one stimulus requires different processing, this may result in smaller fluctuations or an earlier or later deflection (Figure 1.2). As the EEG signals are rather noisy it requires multiple repeats and time-locking of responses to the stimuli to detect the differences. Averaging typically requires 50 responses or so, which then allows for a statistical comparison of the two average responses at every time point after the stimulus. ERPs often exhibit typical peaks or troughs at specific time points which signify particular brain events. For this, several descriptions are used, such as the P300 for perception of unexpected stimuli (denoting a positive deflection at about 300 ms after stimulus onset), or the N1 following visual stimulation (denoting the first clear negative deflection) (Figure 1.3). Other descriptions are less specific in terms of the exact deflection, but are based on the specific cognitive event they are evoked by, such as mismatch negativity (MMN) that occurs in response to an unexpected stimulus (similar to P300). The ERPs can be determined for each electrode, and displayed as a potential over time, and the difference between responses to different stimuli can be displayed as a difference potential (Figure 1.2). With multiple electrodes on the scalp, one can also display topographical maps, where the potential for each electrode is averaged (sometimes for a particular period after the stimulus onset), and the resulting value is translated to a colour, or an iso-contour line, on that position on the scalp. Interpolation of colours between electrodes then yields colour maps indicating the distribution of potential over the head, for each time window (Plate I).

Another prominent feature in the brain is the strength or amplitude of oscillations. The brain exhibits strong regular fluctuations in electrical potential with a preference for several frequencies, known as frequency bands such as alpha, theta, delta and beta waves, and whose power can be quantified. Some of these correlate with behaviour, such as alpha which changes with awareness and alertness, or theta which changes with mental effort (Gevins et al., 1995). These rhythms have been identified as essential components of homeostasis

Figure 1.3

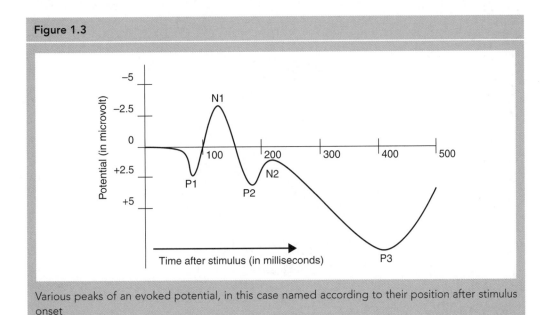

Various peaks of an evoked potential, in this case named according to their position after stimulus onset

(Buzsaki, 2006). For an example of a topographical map of changes in power in the mu band (typical frequency band for motor cortex) during a motor and an imagery task, see Plate II.

1.2.4   Estimating the generators of an EEG signal

In most experiments, multiple electrodes are placed on the skull, typically in a standardized configuration such as the International 10–20 system (Figure 1.4). Electrodes can be placed sparsely (about 32 electrodes), or densely (up to 128 or more). Whether placing more than 64 electrodes improves the measurements is debatable, since at some point two electrodes will be measuring from the same brain tissue. With multiple electrodes one can also estimate deeper sources of EEG signals. Whereas each electrode records from the immediately under-lying brain tissue, all electrodes also detect from more distant tissue, although that contri-bution is very small. By combining electrodes one can estimate those more distant sources based on similarity of the waveform. A deeper source of an event-related potential will gener-ate the same waveform to all the surface electrodes, but the polarity will differ across the elec-trodes depending on the orientation of the source. Although the signal is weak it is possible to estimate its source if many electrodes detect it and if the exact position of all the electrodes is known. Various techniques are available, the complexity of each is related to the number of sources one assumes is contributing to the EEG signals. For classical dipole modelling (Scherg & Von Cramon, 1985) one starts by assuming a single source, and calculating how many of the set of electrode signals it explains. Then one adds sources until the improve-ment in explained signals (more accurately the variance) becomes negligible, at which point one stops adding. Typically only a few sources are meaningful. Other approaches, such as LORETA (Pascual-Marqui et al., 1994), analyse the data with a large number of sources and

Figure 1.4

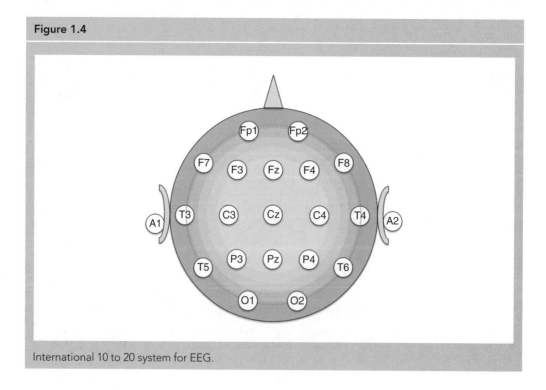

International 10 to 20 system for EEG.

place more dependence on certain assumptions about the data. A major drawback with these approaches is the inverse problem. One can calculate what a source would look like on the scalp electrodes, but from that data one cannot determine with certainty where a source is. This is because there are many possible source configurations that can generate the same set of EEG signals on the scalp. Moreover, given the fact that electrical signals are diverted from a straight line linking the origin and the electrode by conductivity changes between tissue, bloodvessels, dura and skull, localization accuracy is not very good (of the order of centimetres).

1.2.5 Magnetoencephalography

The magnetic fields created with neuronal activity are extremely weak (about one hundred-millionth of the earth's magnetic field, or 10^{-8} Tesla). As with EEG, MEG can only detect synchronous activity generated by tens of thousands of neurons with similar directionality and in close proximity to each other. A MEG scanner consists of a set of magnetometers called

Figure 1.5

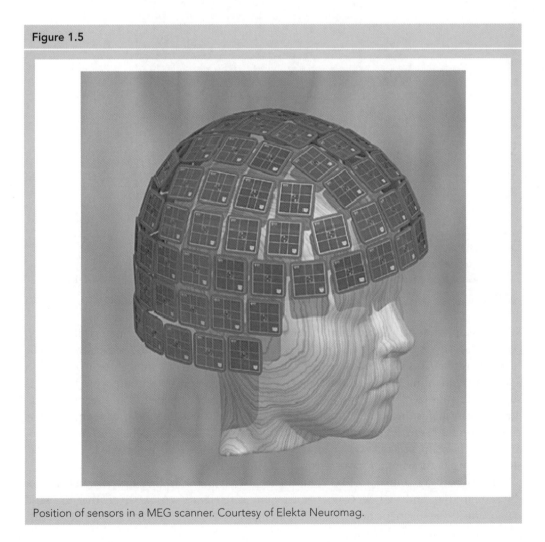

Position of sensors in a MEG scanner. Courtesy of Elekta Neuromag.

Figure 1.6

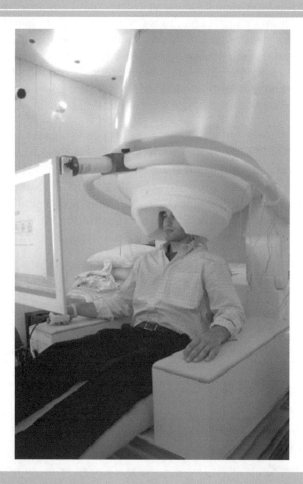

MEG scanner.
The subject is positioned in the array of sensor. The task is presented on a video screen and responses to the task can be made using a button device (subjects right hand). Courtesy of NIMH, Bethesda USA.

SQUIDS (superconducting quantum interference device) laid out in a helmet configuration (Figure 1.5). Given the extremely weak field generated by neurons, the sensors need to be highly sensitive. This is achieved by supercooling the sensors to a temperature of −269 °C in a housing containing liquid helium (Figure 1.6), at which point electronic wiring becomes superconducting (zero resistance). The scanner needs to be shielded from magnetic background noise and is therefore positioned in a magnetically shielded room. Modern scanners contain some 300 sensors covering the whole head. As MEG does not detect currents perpendicular to the scalp, unlike EEG, the most recent scanners also make it possible to record EEG simultaneously, allowing for more sensitive measurements.

MEG signals are similar to EEG signals except that the sampling rate is much higher (by several kHz), and that MEG does not require a reference sensor. Given that the skull hardly affects the magnetic fields, it is more straightforward to model the sources of activity, although it is not quite clear whether accuracy in localizing the sources is significantly better than with EEG (Cohen & Cuffin, 1991). Signals from sensors can be evaluated directly as event-related fields (ERFs). By using all sensors and their exact locations relative to the brain, one can apply spatial filtering techniques such as synthetic aperture magnetometry (SAM) to estimate sources of brain activity, much like source modelling in EEG (Hillebrand et al., 2005). The brain is then divided into a set of cubes (voxels) where the response to a stimulus is estimated and can be displayed and statistically evaluated. One drawback of MEG is that it is rather poor at detecting highly correlated sources. An advantage MEG has over EEG is that it can detect oscillations at frequencies over 40 Hz, making it possible to examine relationships between low and high frequency bands and the link with behaviour, one of the more recent fields of research (e.g. Osipova et al., 2008).

1.3   BLOOD-DYNAMICS IMAGING TECHNIQUES

Currently, there are four techniques for imaging changes in bloodflow and in related processes in humans. One method is functional transcranial Doppler (fTCD), which measures changes in bloodflow in the arteries that enter the brain (Stroobant & Vingerhoets, 2000). fTCD is quite sensitive but can only measure differences between left and right hemispheres so it offers virtually no spatial detail. A second method, Functional near-infrared spectroscopy (fNIRS), tracks changes in haemoglobin by the use of infrared light that passes through the skull (Boas et al., 2004; Villringer et al., 1993). Spatial detail is low (in the order of centimetres), but temporal detail is reasonable. PET is also used to track bloodflow but it requires the injection of radioactive compounds and is quite slow (it takes minutes to make a picture). The most sensitive and detailed technique, and the most widely used, is fMRI, which measures blood by tracking haemoglobin. PET and fMRI are explained in more detail in Sections 1.3.2 and 1.3.3.

1.3.1   Cerebral blood flow and brain activity

One of the key functions of blood is transportation of oxygen. It is pumped from the heart through the arteries, passes through organs and muscles throughout the body and returns to the heart via the veins. From the heart the venous blood is cycled through the lungs where it becomes fully oxygenated. It then returns to the heart and the cycle starts again. Each cycle takes about 1 minute. The transport of oxygen is conducted by haemoglobin, a molecule that contains iron and complex proteins and that can absorb oxygen. Passing through the lungs, it picks up 4 oxygen atom pairs (there is no free oxygen in the blood) and thereby becomes oxyhaemoglobin. When it passes through organs or muscles, it releases the oxygen, becomes devoid of it, and changes to deoxyhaemoglobin. The colour of haemoglobin is different in each state. When releasing oxygen it changes from light-red to dark-red, or even blue. It also changes with respect to its magnetic properties: when it is oxygenated it has no magnetic properties, but when it is deoxygenated it will react to a magnetic field. The importance of this will be explained later.

When a brain region increases in activity it consumes oxygen. The supporting cells around it, the glia cells, can provide it in some form but after a second or so, it will start obtaining oxygen from the capillaries (the smallest blood vessels in the brain). They respond by widening to allow more fresh blood to flow. Then three things happen: oxyhaemoglobin changes into deoxyhaemoglobin as it delivers the oxygen; the amount of blood (blood volume) in the immediate vicinity increases; and the speed (blood flow) increases. The haemodynamic changes all return to normal once the brain region returns to a baseline activity. The blood flow imaging techniques make use of one or more of these three phenomena.

Oxygen-rich blood is present everywhere in the brain, from the main arteries to the minute arterioles, to the capillaries. Oxygen-poor blood is present in the downstream part of the capillaries, passing through the venules and collecting in the larger veins, the largest of which runs between the hemispheres directly outside the brain. When a particular brain region increases its activity to perform a task, it alters the amount of oxygen present in its immediate vicinity, as it takes oxygen from the blood vessels. The exact mechanisms of the regulation of blood flow, which is very closely coupled to neuronal activity (Siero et al., 2011), is rather complex and is highly dependent on neurotransmitter release of both astrocytes and neurons (Attwell et al., 2010; Hyder et al., 2006). Importantly, the haemodynamic changes are most pronounced on the postsynaptic side of neurons, corresponding to where the potentials originate in EEG and MEG (Attwell & Iadecola, 2002; Logothetis, 2008).

1.3.2   Positron emission tomography

Positron emission tomography is used for imaging chemical as well as metabolic processes (Cherry & Phelps, 2002). Except for applications where bloodflow is imaged, PET is rather slow: it takes many minutes to get one image. PET makes use of the radiation generated by injected radioactive compounds. These compounds are synthesized in a cyclotron and radioactivity decays fast enough to avoid harmful effects to the human body. In the cyclotron, a radioactive atom is inserted in specific molecules. These molecules attach to specific cells in the body, carrying the radioactive marker with them. After infusing the compound, the subject goes into the PET scanner, where the radiation is detected with a ring of special cameras. After a while, enough radiation has been collected to reconstruct an image, which displays the distribution of radiation density over the brain (Plate III). For bloodflow imaging, oxygen −15 is inserted into water molecules, making radioactive water (Fox et al., 1984), which, when injected into the bloodstream, passes through the brain. Virtually all the water in the blood is then exchanged with water in the brain (it passes through the blood–brain barrier), and it does so proportional to the local level of bloodflow. So, in active brain regions bloodflow is increased and more radioactive water is deposited. The cameras pick that up and an image is generated where the active areas display a high density of radioactivity. To build one image, it takes at least 40 seconds, so temporal resolution is moderate. Accuracy is in the order of 4–5 mm.

A PET scanner is rather expensive because, apart from the PET camera, a cyclotron is needed in the immediate vicinity. This is because radioactivity of the water decays very fast (with a half life of about 2 minutes). This does mean that a subject can be scanned safely multiple times within one scan session, which makes it possible to map brain functions within one individual. Nevertheless, the use of radioactive compounds is always a matter of concern, so when functional MRI entered the scientific arena in the early nineties, researchers quickly lost interest in water PET.

An important application of the PET technology is to reveal the distribution of drug and neurotransmitter binding spots throughout the brain. For example, raclopride is a dopaminergic antagonist that can be labelled radioactively. When it is inserted into the blood and enters the brain, it stops for a while at the spots where there are dopamine receptors with which raclopride can bind. Thus, relatively enhanced radioactivity is detected at locations that contain a relatively high number of dopamine receptors, and these locations light up in the PET images.

Figure 1.7

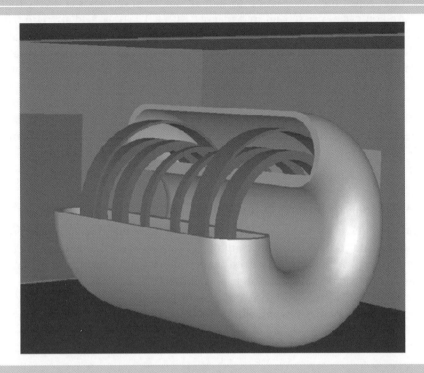

Schematic of an MRI main magnet.
Grey circles (inner six rings) indicate the wire bundles generating the main field inside the tunnel.
The external 2 rings generate a countering magnetic field to reduce the field outside the scanner,
allowing for installing an MRI in a hospital.
Source: http://www.wordsun.com.

1.3.3 Functional magnetic resonance imaging

Functional MRI saw first daylight in 1990 (Kwong et al., 1992; Ogawa et al., 1990), and has evolved so fast since then that it is now one of the most widely used techniques for imaging brain function in the neuroscience community; it is also one of the most complicated. A significant reason for its wide use is because it runs on an MRI scanner; the machine of choice for radiology departments in the western world because it has many applications for clinical imaging (see McRobbie et al., 2007, for a detailed explanation of MRI).

1.3.3.1 The MRI magnet

The MRI scanner contains a large magnet, usually two metres long with a 60 cm wide tunnel running through it. The magnet consists of special wire (Niobium-titanium embedded in copper) spun around the tube to form several rings (Figure 1.7). More wire makes a stronger magnetic field, the B_0 field, when an electric current is run through it. The wire is immersed in a casing containing liquid helium with a temperature of −269 °C (4 degrees Kelvin). At that temperature, the special wire becomes superconducting, which means it has no resistance to electric currents. This makes it possible to run a very strong current through it without the wire heating up, which creates a strong magnetic field inside the tunnel. Human tissue is not magnetic, but it does react to the field in a subtle way. Protons in hydrogen notice the magnetic field, and adjust their orientation to spin around their own axis at a very high speed (about 64 million cycles per second in a magnet with a 1.5 Tesla field strength, compared to about 1 cycle per second outside the scanner). Protons have a positive charge, and when this charge spins it creates a small magnetic field perpendicular to the axis of rotation. The human body is rich in hydrogen and protons, whose magnetic fields normally cancel each other out because their axis of rotation is random. However, in an MRI scanner a proportion of protons align their axes to the B_0 field, so technically, the human body turns into a weak magnet, albeit far too weak to be felt. The strongest magnets currently used for humans have B_0 fields of 11.7 Tesla. Most modern hospitals have a 3-T MRI scanner for clinical diagnosis and research, and most neuroscience research is conducted on scanners of that field strength.

1.3.3.2   Additional components of the MRI scanner

The second component is a radiofrequency transmission antenna which can send brief pulses into the head, again too small to notice anything. These pulses transfer extra energy to the protons in the body. When protons absorb that energy, it causes them to 'wobble', in other words their axis of rotation starts to rotate *around* their original axis (Figure 1.8). The pulse stops after a few milliseconds, and then the protons immediately get rid of the extra energy by returning to their original axis and emit a radiofrequency wave.

Figure 1.8

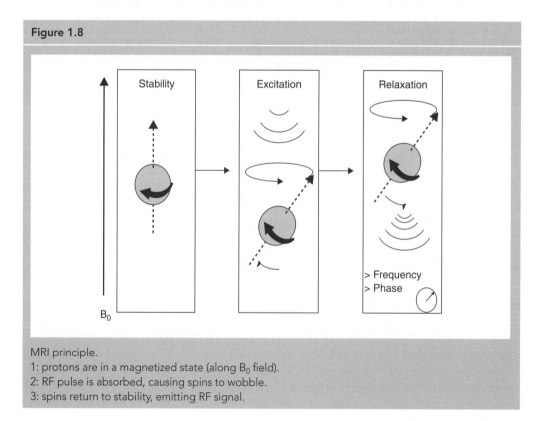

MRI principle.
1: protons are in a magnetized state (along B_0 field).
2: RF pulse is absorbed, causing spins to wobble.
3: spins return to stability, emitting RF signal.

This wave is recorded by the third component of the MRI scanner, the receiver antenna. It collects all the waves emitted by the protons and sends the signals to an image reconstruction computer where the signals are processed to produce an image of the brain. However, the reconstruction needs more than those waves to determine where the signals come from in the brain.

This brings us to yet another major component of the scanner: the extra magnets, which are hidden in a tube between the main magnet and the tunnel, called the gradient coils (Figure 1.9). These extra magnets are weak compared to the main magnet, but they can create extra fields on top of B_0.

One important feature of the spinning protons is that the B_0 field affects not only their axis of rotation but also the speed at which they spin. The spin speed is determined by the strength of the magnetic field and is called the Larmor frequency (see McRobbie 2007). A second important feature is that these protons will only absorb a specific radiofrequency wave, the one that matches its rotation speed. When a head is in the scanner all the protons spin at the same speed and will absorb only one frequency. If one of the extra magnets is switched on, the part of the brain that is exactly in the middle of the magnet will still absorb the main frequency. Its neighbours however feel a slightly different field because of the extra magnet, so they spin at different speeds and absorb different radio waves. If we now send a radiofrequency pulse with a range of waves (i.e. range of frequencies), each part of the brain will absorb a different wave, depending on their local magnetic field, and will emit a different wave to the receiver coil. The reconstruction computer is provided with the exact distribution of the magnetic fields relative to the centre of the tunnel, and it will then be able to determine where the different waves came from.

Finally, to build a complete image, a series of pulses and recordings is required, with a range of gradient settings. These schemas, called pulse sequences, determine what kind of image is obtained, and they make use of the fact that protons have slightly different

Figure 1.9

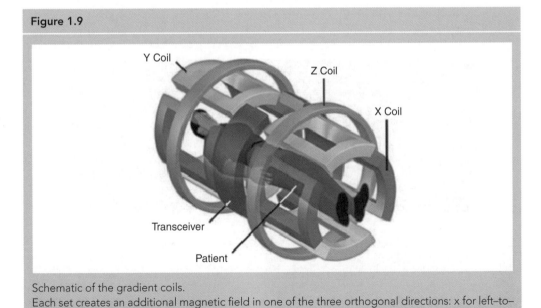

Schematic of the gradient coils.
Each set creates an additional magnetic field in one of the three orthogonal directions: x for left–to–right, y for front–to–back and z for foot–to–head.
Source: http://www.magnet.fsu.edu.

properties in different types of tissue (grey and white matter, cerebrospinal fluid, blood, fat, etc.). These differences can be magnified with pulse sequences that have been developed over the years, generating images of anatomy, blood flow, tumours, oedema, among others.

1.3.3.3   Blood-oxygen level-dependent signal change

Functional MRI essentially maps the haemodynamic response to brain activity, making use of the effect that deoxyhaemoglobin has on the magnetic field. It is called the blood-oxygen level-dependent signal change functional MRI technique (BOLD-fMRI), first presented by Ogawa and colleagues (1990). It utilizes that property of haemoglobin where deoxyhaemoglobin reacts to magnetic fields whereas oxyhaemoglobin does not. Deoxyhaemoglobin changes the strength of the magnetic field in its immediate vicinity, which affects the strength of the signal locally. An important feature of fMRI scans is that they are very fast: it takes less than a few seconds to make an image of the whole brain. This makes it possible to make a movie of blood flow. When a brain area starts to increase in activity (performing a particular task), it changes the amounts of oxy- and deoxyhaemoglobin in its immediate vicinity. At first, deoxyhaemoglobin increases, causing a darkening of that area in the image. However, the vascular system responds quickly to make sure that downstream brain regions are not left without oxygen, and supplies more oxygen-rich blood than is necessary. Importantly, in a resting state (before the subject performs a task) there is always some neuronal activity so there is always a certain amount of deoxyhaemoglobin and therefore local darkening in the image. When an increase in activity causes a surge of fresh blood, the presence of deoxyhaemoglobin effectively drops, causing the local darkening in the image to disappear. Hence, in spite of an initial darkening after activity starts, the brightness increases and in proportion to the strength of brain activity (Figure 1.10).

Figure 1.10

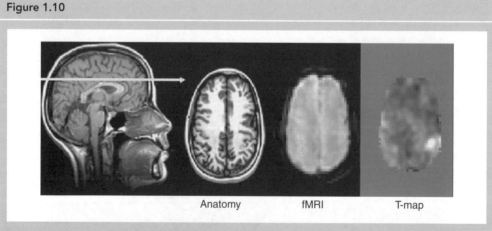

Anatomy   fMRI   T-map

Scans of an individual volunteer.
The first picture indicate the location of the slice imaged for fMRI (arrow indicates the imaged plane). Second picture shows the anatomical scan used for display of activation. Third slice shows a functional scan. Fourth slices shows the T-maps for a motor task. Grey values in this slice represent the strength of activation (white is increase in activity, black is decrease in activity, during fingertapping with the right hand). Left side of the pictures is the right side of the brain (radiological orientation).

1.3.3.4 Localizing a brain function

The main goal of functional neuroimaging is to discover which part of the brain performs a particular function. The brain is always active, even during sleep or under anaesthesia . When a task such as reading a book is performed many brain regions are involved. In this instance the language network is active, but visual, memory and even motor systems participate as one reads, comprehends, interprets text, moves the eyes back and forth, and flips pages. Most experiments are focussed on specific brain functions, which requires a way of removing contamination from other functions. Importantly, a single scan is not informative because the brain is always active. Many events take place in the brain that cannot be controlled, so active regions cannot be interpreted properly. The same principle applies here as to EEG and MEG, namely that brain function can only be measured in relative terms, i.e. as an increase or decrease in activity relative to a control state. When administering a task that evokes specific actions in the brain in a particular sequence, one can assume that when certain brain regions exhibit a change in signal that correlates with that sequence, those brain areas must be involved in the task. Other regions may be active but they are unlikely to correlate by pure chance with the task. To further remove confounding activity (such as visual processing in the reading task), an additional task can be administered which evokes all the functions that are evoked by the experimental task, except for the function of interest. By comparing the brain activity patterns correlated with the experimental task to the pattern

Figure 1.11

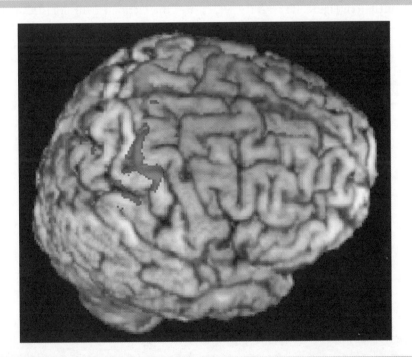

Example of a simple finger movement task (left hand).
Significant activity is projected in grey, onto the anatomy of a healthy volunteer.

of the control task, any remaining difference will be associated with the function of interest. The regions that are associated with a function can then be projected onto an anatomical scan (Figure 1.11).

The reason for acquiring many scans is that the BOLD effect is subtle, and the scans contain a lot of 'noise' due to head movements, respiration and pulsation of blood vessels. Various software packages are available to conduct the fMRI data analysis. They all generate brain activity maps based on statistical measures such as t- or F-statistics. Usually, for an individual subject the activity maps are called T-maps, where every pixel has a value that reflects the amount of signal change due to the task together with the variability of that value. The higher a t-value, the stronger the activity stands out from the noise. Analysis of fMRI data has evolved significantly over the past decade. Improvements have been made in removing artefacts and modelling the BOLD response, thereby improving the quality of the resulting activity maps. A variety of software packages are available for fMRI data analysis. The most widely used programs are SPM (http://www.fil.ion.ucl.ac.uk/spm/), AFNI (http://afni.nimh.nih.gov/afni), FSL (http://www.fmrib.ox.ac.uk/fsl/) and the commercial program Brainvoyager (http://www.brainvoyager.com/).

1.4   ANIMALS, LESIONS AND VIRTUAL LESIONS

The classic method to delineate functional brain networks in humans involved patients with more or less focal brain damage. In the 19th century the French neurologist Paul Broca described a patient with an extensive speech production deficit. After his death the patient's brain was isolated and turned out to have marked damage in the inferior prefrontal left hemisphere (see Figure 1.12). A few years later the German neurologist Carl Wernicke identified an individual with a pronounced speech comprehension problem. His brain later turned out to be damaged at the junction of the left hemisphere temporal and parietal

Figure 1.12

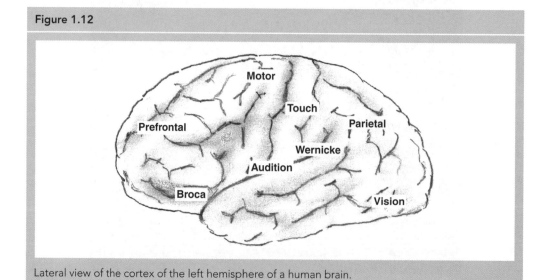

Lateral view of the cortex of the left hemisphere of a human brain.
Broca's and Wernicke's area are depicted, as well as some other specialized functional regions. Prefrontal and parietal refer to cortical areas with less specific specialization, the so-called association cortex.

cortex (Figure 1.12). Together these cases present a so-called double dissociation (explained in Chapter 2) between two functions (production and comprehension), each associated with a different brain region (frontal versus temporal–parietal).

Accidental brain damage differs widely between individuals, which hampers the systematic association between focal brain regions and specific psychological functions. One possible solution is the lesion-overlap method. For an arbitrary number of individuals with brain damage, all characterized by more or less the same cognitive deficit (for example, an inability to reproduce telephone numbers of more than 2 digits), the whole brain is divided into volumes of about half a cubic centimetre. For each volume (or voxel), the extent of overlap between the individual subjects with respect to damage is counted (for example, all subjects have damage in that voxel, or just half of them, or only one of them). The set of voxels found to be damaged in the highest number of subjects is then concluded to be most specifically associated with the cognitive deficit (for a language production problem this could well be an area in the vicinity of Broca's area).

Another approach is to produce a, so-called, virtual lesion in humans. This is accomplished by a technique called transcranial magnetic stimulation. Briefly, TMS is induced by holding a coil against the skull over the brain region that is hypothesized to be associated with a function (and always compare the results with those of TMS at a dummy location, or of a dummy TMS at the same location).

Figure 1.13

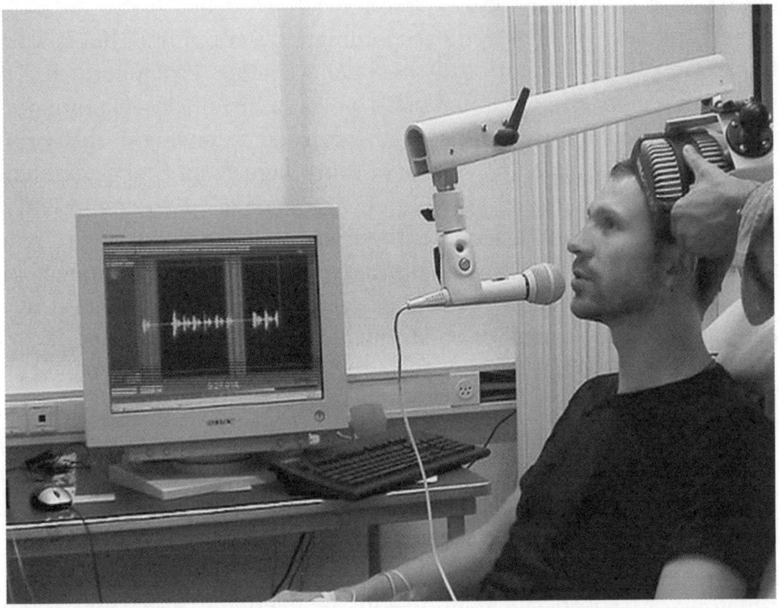

Set up for a transcranial magnetic stimulation procedure to induce speech arrest by interfering with neuronal activity in Broca's area. Courtesy of Dr Dennis Schutter and Dr Sylco Hoppenbrouwers.

A modest electrical current through the coil induces a magnetic pulse which swiftly transverses the skull and reaches cortical tissue (just as the magnetic signals from the brain do that can be recorded using MEG). Just like an electric current concurs with a change in magnetic field, a change in magnetic field induces an electric current, also in the brain, which then interferes with the electric component of neural signalling. In the example shown in Figure 1.13, TMS above Broca's area results in an interruption of the ability to produce speech. Depending on exactly how the TMS procedure is applied, it may either induce a disturbance or actually enhance the function.

The importance of human lesions and TMS techniques is that they reveal causal relations, this is in contrast to methods like EEG and fMRI. Specifically, if messing with A (a brain region) turns out to affect B (a function), and A precedes B in time, then there must be a unidirectional causal relation between A and B. Lesions and TMS of the human brain can be seen as an extension of lesions in animal brains. Lesions in animals can be made much more precise and in a limited space, they can be reversible (cooling) or irreversible (cutting), and several techniques can be used to create them (for example, cutting out a particular brain region or inserting a drug). Whichever technique is used, the problem is always that of generalizing conclusions to the function of the human brain. This depends on the assumption that the animal brain is sufficiently comparable to the human brain. Another widely used procedure in animals is that of recording the action potentials of a single neuron, or small groups of neurons. The same generalization problem arises, but the advantage is that spatial resolution currently achievable cannot be surpassed by methods for functional imaging of the human brain.

1.5   STANDARDS IN TOPOGRAPHY AND COORDINATES

To facilitate exchange of imaging results, researchers have relied first on already available reference frames, and later on an empirical coordinate system. Initial, but still widely used, reference frames are the Brodmann and the Talairach atlas. Brodmann, in 1909, distinguished grey matter regions of the human brain based on histological staining for determining neuronal cytoarchitecture. He mapped out regions on a drawing of the cortical surface. Each region was given a number, and several of those were given functional significance in later years. With advancing imaging capabilities, a more detailed 3D coordinate system was needed. Initially, the Talairach atlas served this purpose well. However, since it relied on only a few brains, and the match with individual healthy brains was rather limited, an empirical system was devised. Using a carefully processed set of 305 MRI scans of healthy subjects, a standardized system was developed for obtaining coordinates, based on specific methods for bringing individual brains or activity maps into the common system ('MNI space'). This was later expanded with more detailed anatomical information, allowing for probabilistic matching of individual data to an average brain ('ICBM152'). Most image processing packages can operate in MNI space and allow one to report on positions of active regions, and use coordinates from literature to examine specific regions in one's own data. Talairach coordinates can be translated to MNI coordinates, although with some degree of mismatch remaining. For both systems, atlases have been developed to facilitate naming of active regions.

3D coordinates (x, y, z) of specific brain regions are referred to every now and then in the remainder of this book. X refers to the lateral–medial (midline (zero)) versus extreme left (negative) or right (positive) position; y to posterior–anterior; and z to inferior–superior (or ventral–dorsal).

1.6 CONCLUDING REMARKS

Current imaging techniques have matured over the last decades but new developments continue to emerge. We have only explained task-related activation so far. As measures of brain activity became more quantitative (albeit in terms of per cent change in signal strength), correlations between regions became interesting. With fMRI several techniques have made it possible to extract meaningful information from scans without a task (task free or resting state experiments). Correlations (connectivity) between regions can be determined reliably, and networks that exhibit coherent fluctuations can be extracted and mapped onto known functional networks (Damoiseaux & Greicius, 2009). This mapping can be achieved with advanced signal analysis, in this case Independent Component Analysis, that considers the whole dataset at once. In another step forward, global measures of connectivity have been extracted using an approach from graph theory, a discipline concerned with mathematical representations of complex networks (Bullmore & Sporns, 2009). Here the correlations between all voxels in the brain are computed, and the structure of these correlation distributions reveals something about the efficiency of the organization. Studies are currently evaluating the utility of the key measures of graph analysis for research in clinical populations (van den Heuvel et al., 2010). Connectivity analyses have also uncovered a network of regions that appear to be active during rest, the default mode network. The function of this system is heavily debated, but it is clear that task-related brain activity is but a fraction of the total amount of brain activity in terms of metabolic demand (Raichle, 2010).

Finally, mathematical algorithms from the field of data mining have yielded exciting results in decoding brain activity. The key element of decoding is that mental processes, for instance seeing a face, are associated with a distinct and reproducible pattern of activity in the brain (Norman et al., 2006). Subjects perform tasks in the scanner that evoke specific mental events, and by analysing all the data combined (using multivoxel pattern analysis), the activity pattern for each specific type of event is obtained. Then the experiment is inverted and the challenge becomes identifying which mental event occurred, from brain activity data alone, not knowing what was presented to the subject. Good results have been reported, particularly with visual stimuli and patterns in the visual cortex (Miyawaki et al., 2008), and even with natural scenes in video clips (Nishimoto et al., 2011).

In summary, EEG and fMRI are the most widely used techniques for imaging the human brain. Both fMRI and MEG are relatively expensive techniques, but MEG is not widely used because the scanner does not have an established place in hospitals. Each technique has its well-characterized strengths and weaknesses. Data analysis techniques have moved the field of cognitive neuroscience forward at a fast pace, and have led to new ways of thinking about the brain. In addition, both classic (lesions of the human brain) and modern (TMS) approaches are available to disclose causal relations between brain function and psychology.

2 PERCEPTION AND ACTION

Key Points
• A typical question in psychology is: can action start before all relevant information has been perceived? Only by recording human brain potentials can this question be answered; partial perception may activate motor cortex areas, even though complete perception results in no overt reaction.
• Many neurons are not strictly tied to either perception or action; visuomotor neurons do both and mirror neurons are involved in perceiving specific actions.
• Preparing an act (e.g. speaking or eye movement) entails sending a copy of the expected outcome of the act to brain regions concerned with perception as a signal for the brain to anticipate a change in the environment as the result of the behaviour.
• Action intentions modulate the perceptual processing of visual features as a function of the relevance of those features to the intended action (e.g. shape is relevant for grasping, not for pointing). The signals from action centres to perception centres that implement these modulations have recently been visualized in both animal and human brains.

2.0 INTRODUCTION

How do we proceed from perception to action? One out of many possible answers is that action dictates the way we perceive. A generally accepted distinction is that between recognition-related object perception and action-related object perception. One patient (D.F.) has been described with a lesion in the occipitotemporal cortex (Figure 2.1) who presents a profound deficit in the recognition of objects (visual agnosia). She is hardly able to name common objects such as fruits or clothes (Goodale et al., 1991), or to make explicit judgements about the orientation or the size of an object. Yet, when asked to grasp such an object, she has no trouble preshaping her hand to match its orientation and size and performing this task. Hence, she cannot recognize orientation or size, but she can still use that information for motor actions directed at the object.

In contrast, another patient has been described with parietal lobe damage, who is very well able to name or describe objects and their characteristics such as orientation and size, but does not preshape at all during grasping and, in general, approaches objects 'like someone trying to find a light switch in the dark'. This double dissociation (see Box 2.1) indicates that different parts of the visual cortex process form information, depending on what has to be done with the information (e.g. naming it as opposed to grasping (Goodale & Milner, 1992)). This distinction elaborates on an earlier one, first proposed by Ungerleider and colleagues

Figure 2.1

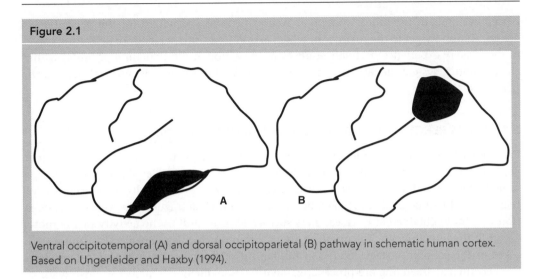

Ventral occipitotemporal (A) and dorsal occipitoparietal (B) pathway in schematic human cortex.
Based on Ungerleider and Haxby (1994).

(Ungerleider & Haxby, 1994), between a ventral visual 'what pathway' – concerned with processing form, colour and other 'non-spatial' properties – and a dorsal visual 'where pathway', concerned with where objects are located, where they are going and how fast. Goodale and Milner (1992) argue that the 'where system' is more justly conceived of as a 'how system': it translates object properties, especially the spatial properties, into corresponding action parameters.

Box 2.1   The usefulness of double dissociation

A double dissociation ensues when in one condition performance on task A is compromised but performance on task B is not (single dissociation), *and* there is a second condition in which performance on task B is deficient but that on task A is not. With only a single dissociation, it is possible that A performance is worse than B performance in *any* condition, for example because task A is more complex and therefore more sensitive to changes in condition. Traditionally, double dissociation is associated with the effects of brain damage and the quest to relate specific brain regions to specific cognitive functions or tasks. Section 2.0 discusses a double dissociation between dorsal versus ventral visual pathways and object recognition versus actions on objects. Another example is that if the region named Broca's area is damaged, there are problems with syntactic but not semantic processing, whereas damage in another region, Wernicke's area, results in the opposite pattern (detailed in Chapter 11). The principle of double dissociation is not limited to brain region/function relations, but can be applied to any experimental manipulation or state variable (for example, the cognitive effects of different drugs). Strictly speaking, it need not only refer to deficiencies in performance but may also address improvements, and this holds not only for task performance, but also for other reflections of brain activity.

Two perceptual systems each feed into the action system, the balance between their relative contributions being determined by the action requirements. Patients with damage to either system fail to carry out the corresponding action appropriately. In the following sections we discuss the transition from perception to action in healthy individuals. We then look at perceptual units in the motor system, as well as neurons specialized for the perception *of* action. Finally, we get to the manner in which action feeds into perception: delivering copies of the sensory experience that will result from the action and modulating priorities within the perceptual system, depending on what perceptual information is most relevant to the planned action.

2.1   FROM PERCEPTION TO ACTION IN THE HUMAN BRAIN

Psychologists have long wondered whether action can start before perception is complete. Suppose certain information has to be perceived and identified in order to determine whether or how to respond. If only part of this information has been processed by the perceptual system, can that part be used to activate the motor system? Unambiguous answers to this question were only obtained after researchers succeeded in recording the activity of the motor cortex in the human brain. The question about action starting before perception finishes was asked in the context of stage models of human information processing. Many stages have been postulated, including pre-processing, identification, memory search, response decision, motor preparation and motor execution. Whatever stages are assumed in the various models of information processing, the central question always was, and still is, how a given input (perception) is transformed into an adequate output (an overt action). The output is usually measured in terms of the accuracy and speed (reaction time) in choice–reaction time tasks: in any given moment (trial) one of several alternative stimuli is presented and the human subject has to choose the one and only action that is appropriate, given that stimulus.

Theories about how stages of information processing proceed can be divided into two categories. In terms of perception and action, serial–discrete models (Sanders, 1990; Sternberg, 1969) postulate that perception has to finish completely before action can start. Suppose a task requires that subjects base their response on both the shape of a visual stimulus (such as is it 'S' or 'T', see Figure 2.2), and on its size (large or small). According to a serial–discrete

Figure 2.2

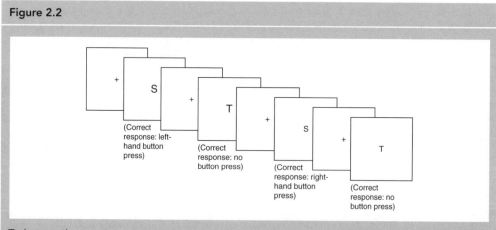

Task example.
On each subsequent trial (usually with a total number of hundreds of trials) a single letter is presented, in this case either a smaller S, a larger S, a smaller T, or a larger T, in an unpredictable alternation. Task instructions as indicated in the figure dictate the correct response.

Figure 2.3

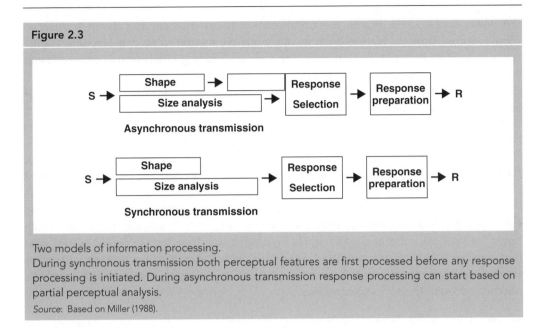

Two models of information processing.
During synchronous transmission both perceptual features are first processed before any response processing is initiated. During asynchronous transmission response processing can start based on partial perceptual analysis.
Source: Based on Miller (1988).

model, both the shape and the size have to be identified (perceived) completely before any of this information is transmitted to the response system, which determines what the adequate response is, and the response is prepared. In contrast, *parallel–continuous models* postulate that part of the stimulus information (such as size or shape) can be transmitted to the response system (and used there) before the stimulus has been identified (perceived) completely. An influential parallel–continuous model is Miller's theory of *Asynchronous Discrete Coding* (ADC; see Miller, 1988). According to Miller, transmission between stages can occur asynchronously. That is, different parts of the information transformed in a stage are transmitted as output at different times; and therefore processing in a succeeding stage begins before the preceding stage is complete. Transmission could still be reasonably discrete; this would depend on the grain size of information transmission. In the form/size example, the inferred grain size would be just one order smaller than in the maximally discrete case. That is, transmission takes place in two steps, rather than in one (see Figure 2.3).

To decide between these two classes of theories, many experiments using behavioural performance measures have been conducted. All these experiments suffer from the same problem: to arrive at a conclusion about transmission between (perception and action) stages in the human brain, assumptions have to be made about that transmission between stages and those assumptions may not be correct. For example, Figure 2.3 refers to a situation in which shape analysis is easier than size analysis. It is probably also easier to choose between using one hand or the other, than it is to choose between two fingers of the same hand. Furthermore, it turns out that using the easy shape information to determine which hand to use and using the difficult size information to determine the finger, yields faster responses than when it has to been done the other way around (Miller, 1988). This result is easily explained by the asynchronous model in Figure 2.3: the shape is analysed relatively fast and this information is transmitted immediately to the response system, which decides which hand to use, and the response with this hand is prepared. However, other researchers have demonstrated that the result can also be interpreted in terms of Synchronous transmission

(Proctor & Reeve, 1985). Briefly, this interpretation is based on the fact that it is easier to couple an easy stimulus feature (such as shape relative to size) to an easy response feature (such as hand relative to finger), than it is to couple an easy stimulus feature and a difficult response feature, or the other way around.

So, to interpret the above result in terms of asynchronous transmission, it has to be assumed that easy stimulus information is transmitted immediately to the response system or, in other words, that transmission is asynchronous (however, that was the conjecture to be proven). An obvious way to break this tie is to look in the brain for direct manifestations of the stages (perception, action) that are postulated in Figure 2.3. Here we focus on one of the major accomplishments in searching for such a manifestation: the lateralized readiness potential (LRP).

Brain activity in the primary and secondary motor cortices, preceding an overt response, varies as a function of what the response is going to be: which limb, which hand, which finger; and also the pattern of response, for example, a simple versus a threefold button press (see also Box 2.2). The preparation of a response with the right hand concurs with more activity in the motor area of the left hemisphere than in the right motor cortex; and the other way around for left hand responses.

Box 2.2 A recap of sensory and motor cortex, contralateralization and receptive fields

The primary visual cortex in the occipital lobe is the part of the cortex where signals from the retinas first enter the cortex, via the thalamus. From the primary visual cortex further signals are transmitted to the secondary visual cortices along dorsal and ventral pathways (see Section 2.0 and more details in Chapter 5). Similar principles hold for the primary and secondary auditory cortices in the temporal lobe, and the primary and secondary touch (somatosensory) cortices in the anterior parietal lobe. In reverse, the primary motor cortex, in the posterior frontal lobe, is the final common pathway for signals from the cortex to the spinal cord and the muscles, and anterior to the primary cortex are the secondary motor cortices, the more dorsal medial supplementary motor area, and the more ventral lateral premotor cortex. The visual, somatosensory, and motor systems are especially characterized by dominant contralateral connections. That is, the left hemisphere primary visual cortex receives signals primarily from the right side visual half field, and the right hemisphere primary visual cortex receives signals primarily from the left side visual half field. Analogously, the left hemisphere primary motor cortex sends signals primarily to the right side of the body (via the spinal cord), and the right hemisphere primary motor cortex sends signals primarily to the left side of the body. This contralateralization provides a first crude map for the brain to represent the body or the outside world, in the sense that there is a one–to–one correspondence between a part of, for instance, the visual environment and a part of the visual cortex. In the visual system, this map is actually far more fine-grained. In the primary visual cortex, adjoining patches of about a half square millimetre of neurons represent similarly adjoining regions of the vision field of less than a square degree of arc. The exact portion of the visual field that activates a certain neuron when light is reflected from it, is called the receptive field of that neuron.

The human scalp electroencephalogram (EEG) reflects postsynaptic potentials occurring in thousands of neurons at about the same time and in the same way. It has been known for quite some time that when the EEG is recorded over the motor areas of the human brain, it reflects a gradual increase in postsynaptic potentials in the time interval just preceding a motor response. This increase, which may last for seconds before the response is eventually issued, is termed the Readiness Potential.

When the Readiness Potential precedes an action exerted by one half of the body (like the left hand), it becomes more pronounced over the contralateral motor cortex (like the right hemisphere). This is the Lateralized part of the Readiness Potential, or the LRP. In every known application of the LRP, it starts to develop only a few hundred milliseconds before the overt response is visible (for instance a button press with one finger). Now consider a simple choice–reaction experiment, in which a subject has to respond to an S by pressing a button with his left index finger, and to a T using his right index finger. At the time point at which the LRP starts to evolve, we can be sure that the part of the motor cortex (the contralateral part) associated with one of the fingers (left or right) has become active. In other words, it can be inferred that at that time point, one of the two possible responses has been selected over the other, even if it is a preliminary selection. Typically in such experiments, overt reactions have a latency (time point of onset relative to stimulus onset) of about 400 or more milliseconds. Also typically, LRPs in such conditions start to evolve at about 200 ms latency. Now refer back to Figure 2.3. Given that the LRP signifies that one response option has been selected over the other, it can be inferred that when the LRP starts, the stages of response selection, preparation and execution have been initiated. In other words, we have a tool to track the initiation of action on-line, long before it is revealed in an overt response. This tool is based on the fact that different actions involve the preceding activation of different parts of the brain, in particular the motor cortex.

Figure 2.2 illustrates the logic of an experiment in which subjects had to press a button (Go) in response to the letter S (large or small), and refrain from responding (Nogo) in response to the letter T. Reaction times in the case of S were about 400 ms (relative to stimulus onset, time point 0). Figure 2.4 shows the LRP results (Kenemans et al., 1995). In this set-up, a relatively easy discrimination (is it S or T?) determines whether or not to respond, and the harder to discriminate dimension (large or small?) determines which hand to use

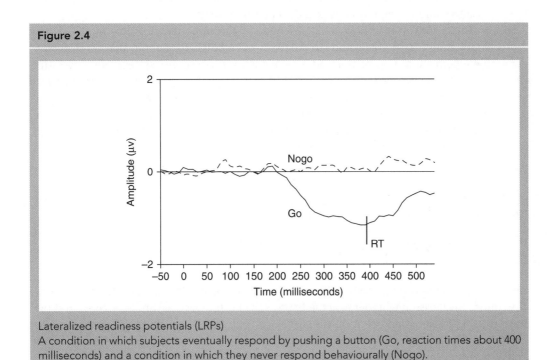

Figure 2.4

Lateralized readiness potentials (LRPs)
A condition in which subjects eventually respond by pushing a button (Go, reaction times about 400 milliseconds) and a condition in which they never respond behaviourally (Nogo).

Figure 2.5

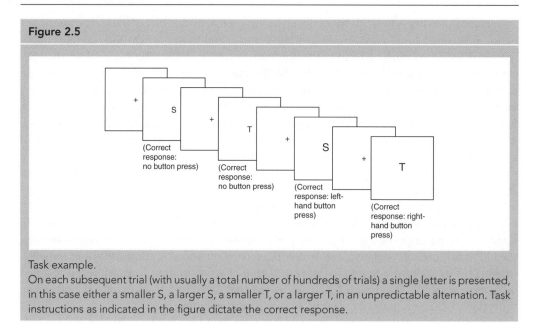

Task example.
On each subsequent trial (with usually a total number of hundreds of trials) a single letter is presented, in this case either a smaller S, a larger S, a smaller T, or a larger T, in an unpredictable alternation. Task instructions as indicated in the figure dictate the correct response.

(if there is a response). With this arrangement we only see LRPs to Go stimuli, not to Nogo ones. Note that the LRPs starts to evolve at about 200 ms latency. Thus, 200 ms after a stimulus and 200 ms before any overt reaction can be observed, the brain (especially the motor cortex) has selected one response option over the other. In this case, this selection simply proceeds up until the overt response, whereas there is no trace of a similar response selection in response to stimuli (Nogo) that eventually elicit no response.

These results make sense in a serial–discrete synchronous–transmission model (Figure 2.3). For Go stimuli, after shape and size analyses have finished, the information needed to determine whether and how to respond is available for the response system. For Nogo stimuli, the information processing sequence can be truncated after shape analysis. However, to see whether it always works like this, we have to make it more tempting for the brain to select a response option without knowing whether a response is needed at all.

Figure 2.5 shows a slight modification of the design in Figure 2.2 (Miller & Hackley, 1992). Stimulus response relations can be summarized as follows:

Response hand:	Left		Right	
Respond at all?	Nogo	Go	Nogo	Go
Stimulus	S	S	T	T

Here, the easy dimension (shape) determines which hand, and the difficult dimension (size) determines the decision whether to actually press the button or to withhold. Figure 2.6 shows the results. LRPs were significant on Go and Nogo trials. The Nogo LRPs had the same onset latencies as did Go LRPs; but they collapsed well before the Go LRPs reached their maxima, and were not eventually followed by overt responses.

Figure 2.6

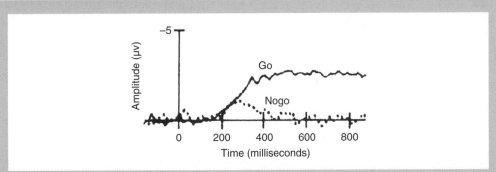

Lateralized readiness potentials (plotted upwards)
A condition in which subjects eventually respond by pushing a button (Go, reaction times about 500 milliseconds) and a condition in which they never respond behaviourally (Nogo). From Miller & Hackley, 1992. Copyright © [1992] by the American Psychological Association. Reproduced with permission.

To appreciate this evidence, consider what happens in the most obvious explanatory scenario. The conjunction of letter form and letter size contains two relevant pieces of information: which hand to respond with and whether to respond or not. A serial–discrete model predicts that both pieces of information are evaluated completely prior to any transmission of information to the response stage. Thus, in this scenario selective preparation on Nogo trials would be unlikely, because form and size would have been completely processed before selective response preparation could occur. Instead, we find that selective responses (one hand over the other, as reflected in LRPs) are, in fact, prepared, independently of whether the overt response is eventually going to be executed. The simplest explanation for this result is that available shape information is immediately transmitted to, and used in, the response stage. In other words, partial information is transmitted from the perceptual stage to the motor preparation stage (see Figure 2.3, upper panel).

When action starts before perception has finished, response options can be selected (producing motor cortex activation) without any eventual overt response. Is it also possible that one response option is selected, but another becomes visible as the overt response? To address this question, researchers use the flanker task, the simplest version of which is illustrated in Figure 2.7.

The response should be based on the central (target) letter. Flankers are irrelevant, but can be classified as either response–congruent or response–incongruent. In such set-ups, researchers found that, even on trials without behavioural errors, incongruent flankers elicited LRPs that were initially positive but then became negative. So, flanker-based response activation occurred at the cortical level without any ensuing peripheral activation.

In this scenario where does action start before perception finishes? Incongruent–flanker information results in the selection of an incorrect response (action) before completion of the stimulus processing (perception), including target processing. After incorrect response selection has started, information about target identity is transmitted from the perception to the action stage. As a result, the preparation of the incorrect response is aborted in favour of the correct one.

Figure 2.7

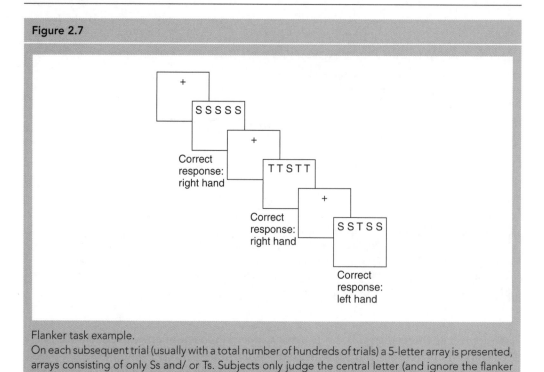

Flanker task example.
On each subsequent trial (usually with a total number of hundreds of trials) a 5-letter array is presented, arrays consisting of only Ss and/ or Ts. Subjects only judge the central letter (and ignore the flanker letters) in each trial, and task instructions as indicated in the figure dictate the correct response.

What determines whether action starts before perception is completed? One factor is what the configuration of perceptual events makes possible, in other words how well can the different perceptual dimensions be separated, or which one is processed faster. Another, more general, factor is strategic, involving a trade-off between speed and accuracy. Starting motor preparation before perception is completed yields the potential benefit of a relatively fast response, once the final piece of perceptual information arrives in the motor system. It also has a potential disadvantage in that preliminary motor preparation may erroneously exceed a threshold and thus result in erroneous behaviour.

2.2   VISUOMOTOR AND MIRROR NEURONS

The preceding discussion is consistent with a simple script in which neurons in the perceptual cortex connect in many ways to neurons in the motor cortex; depending on the context some connections are stronger than others, which determines how we respond to a given stimulus in a certain situation.

This basic idea still seems tenable, but in a far more multi-layered way than suggested above. To begin with we have primary and secondary perceptual cortices, as well as primary and secondary motor cortices. Take, for example, a secondary perceptual area in the parietal cortex and a secondary motor area in the precentral premotor cortex. Both areas contain many visuomotor neurons that respond to the presentation of visual objects but also preceding movements by the observer. Often, there is also a high degree of congruence in that a given neuron only responds to objects that afford the kind of movement (e.g. grasping) that the neuron is specialized for. For example, monkeys were taught to grasp a ring by inserting a finger into it, while they used their thumb to get hold of a plate. Neurons specifically activated in relation to the finger insertion movement also responded specifically to the presentation of the ring, even when no movement was required. The same held for neurons specifically activated in relation to thumb use, which were also then activated simply on presentation of the plate (Raos et al., 2006).

Box 2.3 Brain controlled computers

Neuronal spiking in a monkey's premotor cortex has some fascinating potential applications. One group of researchers (Santhanam et al., 2006) used it as input for a prosthetic brain–computer interface design device. An electrode grid spanning just a few millimetres was placed on the surface of an exposed monkey premotor cortex, between the central sulcus and the spur of the arcuate sulcus, the anterior boundary of the precentral gyrus. The monkey was trained to hold one hand on the middle square (see Figure 2.8, Home). A second square in one of the locations shown in Figure 2.8 always lit up subsequently, but the monkey was only to move his hand to that square when the middle square dimmed (the Go signal), which did not always happen. Neurons in the premotor cortex specifically coded the location where the hand might move to. For example, one group of neurons responded strongly when square 1 lit up, less strongly for 2 and 6, and weakly or not at all for the other squares. Another group of neurons responded strongly when square 4 lit up, less strongly for 3 and 5, and weakly or not at all for the other squares. This coding response was contingent on the stimulus that occurred some hundreds of milliseconds before the Go/Nogo signal. In Nogo trials the brain–computer interface used this coding response to place a cursor on the location where a square lit up, as if by an invisible arm.

Figure 2.8

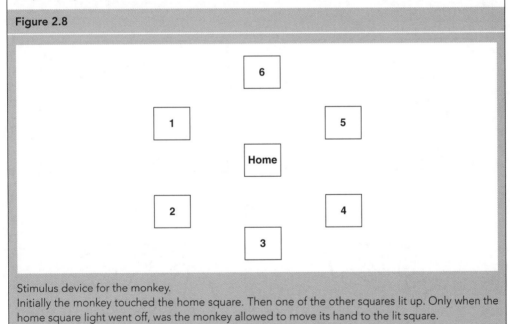

Stimulus device for the monkey.
Initially the monkey touched the home square. Then one of the other squares lit up. Only when the home square light went off, was the monkey allowed to move its hand to the lit square.

In the early nineties a group of Italian researchers aimed to further investigate the properties of visuomotor neurons in the secondary motor cortex of monkeys. Accidentally, they observed that some of the putative visuomotor neurons responded to the experimenter's action, rather than to a stimulus or in preparation of their own actions (Di Pellegrino et al., 1992). More systematic exploration revealed that these mirror neurons, as they were dubbed, exhibited a high degree of congruence between their response to observed actions and the kind of self-emitted action they are specialized for. In addition, the activity of any mirror neuron in the precentral gyrus was determined by the goal of the action (such as putting something in your mouth), rather than exactly how that goal was achieved (for a review, see Iacoboni & Dapretto, 2006).

Figure 2.9 shows the location in the monkey brain where mirror neurons were identified in one of the early studies (Gallese et al., 1996). This area is monkey F5. Its human analogue consists of ventral area 6 (precentral gyrus, premotor cortex), plus posterior area 44 (inferior frontal gyrus, frontal operculum, Broca's area). Figure 2.10 shows the typical response to observed actions, as well as the activity preceding and during self-emitted actions. It makes sense that the response to observed actions is smaller; otherwise we would be copying other individuals' behaviour all of the time. It is also conceivable that, with repeated observation of the same action, at some time the threshold for instigation of the action *by* the observer is exceeded, which results in imitation.

Studies in humans have looked for brain areas containing the human analogue of monkey mirror neurons. The experimental logic is that areas containing mirror neurons should display the greatest activity when action is executed and simultaneously observed in another

Figure 2.9

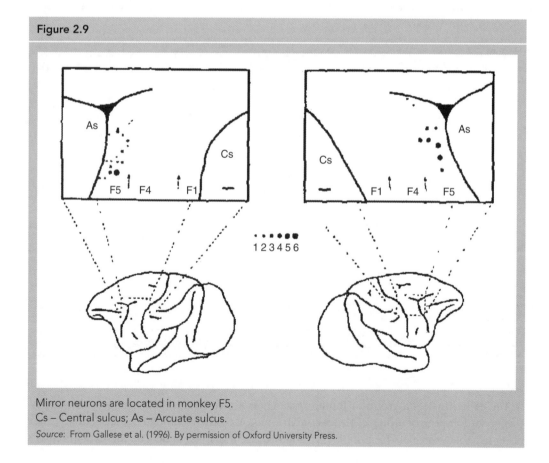

Mirror neurons are located in monkey F5.
Cs – Central sulcus; As – Arcuate sulcus.
Source: From Gallese et al. (1996). By permission of Oxford University Press.

agent; second greatest when it is self-executed; and third greatest when it is only observed in another agent (Iacoboni & Dapretto, 2006; Iacoboni et al., 1999). Following this logic, two relatively focal cortical regions were identified as likely to contain mirror neurons, in the inferior frontal cortex (BA 44; Figure 2.11), and in the rostral, but still posterior, parietal cortex. These findings mirror those obtained for monkey single neurons, which revealed mirror properties not only in the premotor cortex, but also in the parietal cortex. It has been suggested that while premotor neurons are more involved in coding the target of the movement, the parietal neurons are relatively more concerned with the precise motor parameters.

In a subsequent study the causal involvement of area 44 was investigated (Heiser et al., 2003). This was done using transcranial magnetic stimulation (TMS), in which a magnetic field is applied through the human skull to modulate the electrical signals in the cortical tissue just beneath the location of the TMS. Subjects viewed video clips of sequences of moving fingers simultaneously with the TMS stimulation, and in the imitation condition had to copy those movements exactly. Relative to a control task, as well as relative to a control TMS on the occipital cortex, right and left hemisphere TMS of area 44 (Figure 2.11), resulted in an increase in errors of imitation.

Some interesting consequences of human mirror neuron activity were suggested in a study by Hari and colleagues (Hari et al., 1998). These researchers looked at the burst of 15–25 Hz oscillations in the magnetoencephalogram (MEG), the so-called beta rhythm (remember that the MEG is the magnetic counterpart of EEG). Normally this beta rhythm is elicited within

Figure 2.10

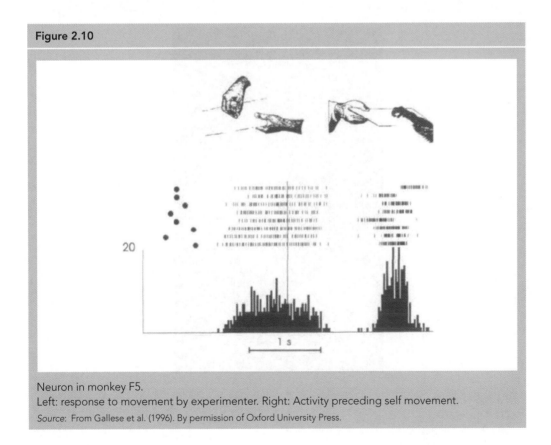

Neuron in monkey F5.
Left: response to movement by experimenter. Right: Activity preceding self movement.
Source: From Gallese et al. (1996). By permission of Oxford University Press.

a few hundred milliseconds by somatosensory stimulation (e.g. mild electric shocks to the wrist). This beta burst originates from the primary motor cortex and is thought to reflect widespread inhibition of the neurons in this area. If subjects manipulated an object during the somatosensory stimulation, the beta burst was almost completely absent. A significant reduction of the beta burst was also found when subjects observed object manipulation by another agent. The authors conclude that the beta burst reduction reflects a disinhibition of primary motor cortex neurons, due to synaptic inputs from mirror neurons in the premotor cortex.

Another rhythm that is commonly suppressed during motor activity is the mu rhythm, ranging from 8 Hz to 13 Hz. Like the MEG beta rhythm, the mu rhythm is most strongly suppressed when subjects execute goal-directed movements, like grasping an object, but it is also significantly reduced during observation of the action (Muthukumaraswamy et al., 2004). Action–observation related mu suppression can be observed in children as young as 52 months (Lepage & Theoret, 2006).

In individuals suffering from autism or autistic spectrum disorders mu suppression is disturbed (Oberman et al., 2005). Also, the severity of the autistic symptoms bears a strong negative correlation with the activation of the human frontal mirror system, as recorded with fMRI (Dapretto et al., 2006). A core symptom in autism is abnormal social behaviour.

Figure 2.11

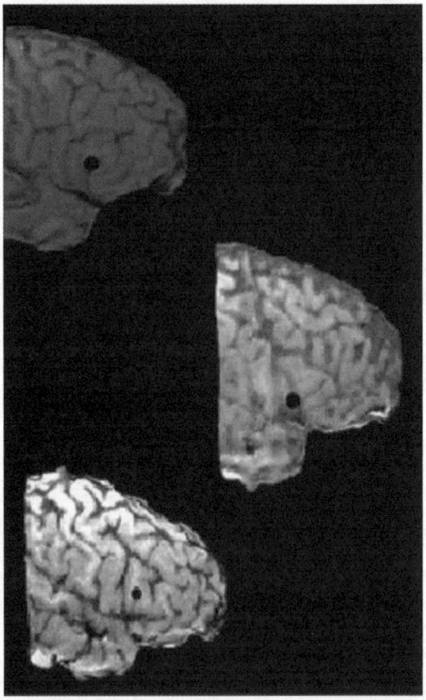

The approximate average location in the human brain where TMS was applied to disturb mirror neuron functioning: area 44 in the inferior frontal gyrus.

It is thought that this social deficit may be related to dysfunctional mirror neurons. Mirror neurons enable us to experience what others feel by imitating their actions (like emotional facial expressions; covered in detail in Chapter 9). This kind of imitation could be the basis for empathy, which is crucial for adequate social interaction.

In sum, at a very young age children are equipped with the ability to imitate, based on a specialized system for action observation and execution. This forms the basis for developing the myriad skills and abilities that characterize normal development. On the other hand, failures of this system may lead to pathological development, such as seen in autism.

2.3 LOOPING BACK: EFFERENCE COPY

Suppose you are scrutinizing a group of trees right in front of you. You fix your eyes on one of them, then move your eyes to a second one just a few degrees to the left. You still perceive the first one as if nothing has changed, at least not in the outside world. The same invariance occurs when you then fix your eyes on a third tree, to the right of the first one. The crucial point is that, whereas nothing changes in the outside world, the pattern of stimulation across your retina does, in fact, change. Each time you move your eyes, light reflecting from the first tree activates a different set of retinal receptors. Therefore, by virtue of the specific connections between retinal receptors and higher brain centres, the reflected light activates different neurons in the thalamus and in the visual cortex; this corresponds to the notion of very small (< 1 degree of arc) receptive fields of neurons in these brain areas. However, although different neurons are activated, the first tree is still perceived as the same first tree.

Similar problems are faced in numerous other situations. For example, we can imagine or anticipate all kinds of events, objects, features (e.g. colours), sound bites and so on. In doing so we almost certainly activate corresponding representations in various sensory cortices (elaborated upon in Chapter 5). Yet healthy individuals are able to distinguish the subjective

Figure 2.12

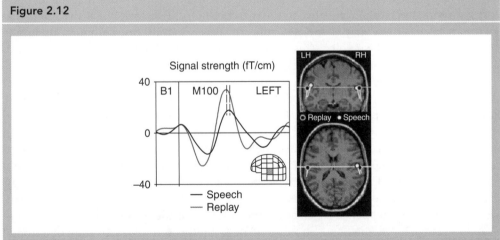

MEG response from auditory cortex at 100 ms post-stimulus to either self-spoken vowel ('speech') or intensity-matched playback ('replay').
Black and white dots in right panel denote estimated equivalent dipoles sources for the MEG response in left (LH) and right (RH) auditory cortex.
Source: From Curio et al. (2000). Reprinted with permission from John Wiley and Sons.

results of these internally driven activations from those driven externally. Another example concerns speech: we somehow have to distinguish our own utterances from those made by others. Let's dwell on that problem for a while. Researchers have addressed the issue by recording responses of the human brain to its own-speech sounds as they were uttered versus when these same sounds, matched for intensity, were played back on a tape-recorder (Curio et al., 2000). Figure 2.12 presents a typical result, showing the response from the auditory cortex (ERP N1 or N100, or MEG M100) to a speech stimulus when the stimulus is self-generated, relative to when it originates from an external device. As can be seen, the response to self-generated speech is smaller.

This finding has been interpreted as resulting from an activated feedback loop in the speech condition, e.g. from a frontal speech centre to the auditory cortex. It has attracted considerable interest because of the possibility that this feedback loop may be disturbed in certain hearing or speech disorders, and especially in schizophrenia, a population in which the disturbance may be causal in the induction of hallucinations. Indeed, using a similar paradigm, the finding was replicated in a group of healthy control subjects, but completely absent in a parallel group of schizophrenic patients (Ford & Mathalon, 2005). However, a difficulty in interpreting the result of reduced responses to self-generated speech sounds is that they may still be qualitatively different from the same sounds recorded and played back, even when they are equalized in intensity. An older study assessed single-unit action potentials in the auditory cortex of squirrel monkeys in similar conditions (Müller-Preuss & Ploog, 1981). One argument made by these authors was that qualitatively different stimuli should activate different neuronal populations. However, this was not found, instead the same group of neurons responded to both recorded and self-generated vocalizations, but the response to the latter was generally weaker.

Another experimental approach in humans is to use non-speech probe stimuli (e.g. tones, noise burst) to probe the general sensitivity of the auditory cortex during a condition of listening to speech as compared to talking (Ford et al., 2001). N1s in response to probe stimuli were *not* different for talking versus listening, consistent with the idea that the auditory cortex was not differentially sensitive in the two conditions. However, it is also possible that variations in sensitivity may specifically concern speech sounds, or even more specifically vocalizations in one's own voice. This interpretation would still be compatible with a feedback loop from higher or motor centres.

Another perspective is to search for the brain correlate of the feedback loop itself, rather than look at its consequences (the modulation of responsivity in auditory cortex). In 1950, Roger Sperry (a Nobel prize winner in 1981) coined the term corollary discharge to refer to the neuronal signal sent from a motor output centre (such as the frontal speech production centre) to a perceptual input centre (like the auditory cortex) that represents the expected sensory sequela of the prepared action (Sperry, 1950). Also in 1950, and probably independently, Von Holst and Mittelstaedt referred to the same putative mechanism as efference copy, defined as a copy of the efferent process that could be related somehow to the afferent consequences of the motor act. A schematic representation of the efference copy principle in relation to language production is shown in Plate IV. In this scenario, activation of a frontal speech area sends an efference copy to the auditory cortex, resulting in a corollary discharge which in turn results in suppression of the sensory experience brought about by the self-generated speech sounds (auditory reafference).

One way to investigate the connection through which the efference copy signals travel is to assess the connectivity between the area sending the efference copy and the one receiving it. Ford and colleagues used measures of EEG coherence for this. Briefly, coherence refers to the extent to which the EEG recorded above one area correlates with the EEG recorded over another area. For a given frequency component, the more the amplitudes (or power) and/or the phases of the two EEG signals resemble each other, the higher the coherence, which by definition ranges from 0 to 1. Higher coherence is assumed to reflect stronger connections between the two areas. This connectivity is also assumed to be flexible (depending on context or task demands), and may differ between populations. Depending on the exact experimental procedures (and perhaps also filter settings), Ford and colleagues found a higher coherence between frontal and temporal areas during talking than during listening, either in the theta band (4–7 Hz), or in the gamma range (20–50 Hz) (Ford et al., 2002; Ford & Mathalon, 2005). This higher connectivity during talking might reflect stronger signals from speech-output to auditory-input centres. These signals may carry the efference copy, which results in weaker auditory responses to the self-generated speech sounds during talking than during listening. In addition, Ford and colleagues found that these differences in theta and gamma coherence were absent in schizophrenic patients. For theta, the absence of higher coherence during talking was especially pronounced in hallucinating patients, less so in non-hallucinating ones. These findings do indeed suggest that the connection that carries the efference copy is disturbed in certain schizophrenic patients.

Frontal–temporal connectivity is probably just one way of realizing the generic efference copy principle. For other functions of the brain different pathways may be used. This is especially clear with respect to eye movement and stable visual perception. Analogous to the speech example, neurons have been found to change their response properties to one and the same stimulus, depending on self-emitted actions. Such neurons have been identified in the parietal as well as in the frontal eye fields (FEF) of monkeys (Duhamel et al., 1992); (Umeno & Goldberg, 1997). Note that from a more precise analogy with own-speech perception, we would predict them in the occipital cortex as well.

As discussed above, one question is how the visual system accomplishes that the outside world is subjectively still the same after a saccade, while the pattern of activity across the neurons in the visual cortex has changed due to the rather restricted receptive fields in the occipital and parietal areas. (To experience what it is like if this were not accomplished, gently push your eyeball and see how your perception of the outside world changes.) An obvious answer to this question is that certain neurons have flexible receptive fields that change so that after the saccade they are still stimulated by the same object, even though that object is now in a completely different location relative to the fixation point, and therefore completely outside the pre-saccadic receptive fields of these neurons.

Actually, neurons in monkey FEFs change their receptive fields just before a saccade, but not in the manner described above. Just before the saccade, the receptive fields of the neuron changes so that it exactly overlaps the anticipated post-saccadic receptive field (Plate V; Sommer & Wurtz, 2006). It is as if the neuron, prior to the saccade, already visualizes what the world will look like after the saccade. It remains somewhat enigmatic why this change in the receptive field before the saccade does not result in a subjective discontinuity of perception. It is conceivable that one neuron changes its receptive field from the apple to the green thing in the right upper corner, while, another neuron might do exactly the opposite, and both changes happen sufficiently gradually that no change is noticed. In addition, some neurons extend their receptive field to include the future field, rather than shift to it, which may also provide a sense of continuity.

Researchers think of the change in receptive fields as the result of a corollary discharge. The monkey models have also yielded information about the connections that carry the efference copy. Voluntary saccadic movements depend on a signal from the FEF to the sub-cortical superior colliculi (SC), which are in turn connected to the midbrain nuclei from which the cranial nerves originate that innervate the eye muscles. As is often the case, the FEF–SC connection is reciprocal. Since FEF neurons are known to use efference copies, and the SC are an obvious efferent output system, it could well be that the connection carrying the efference copy runs from the SC to the FEF. The causal role of this connection was dir-ectly tested in monkeys. The SC–FEF has a synaptic relay in the mediodorsal nucleus of the thalamus, and in one condition this nucleus was deactivated by a local infusion of musci-mol, an agonist of the inhibitory transmitter GABA. Under muscimol, neurons no longer, or to a lesser extent, changed their receptive fields in anticipation of a saccade (Plate VI). Thus, the changing receptive field that, presumably, reflects efference copy depends on an intact connection between SC and FEF. This is consistent with the idea that this connection implements the efference copy from an output centre (SC) to a more afferent centre (FEF). It is an interesting question whether neurons in parietal and occipital areas receive copies of the copy. Research results discussed in the next section strongly suggest that the necessary connections for such secondary copies exist.

2.4 LOOPING BACK: ACTION-GUIDED PERCEPTION

If you are still thinking exclusively in terms of feedforward processing from perception to action, consider the following possibilities. An observer could encounter a tasty looking red apple. This stimulus might elicit the decision to make a grasping response. Then it would be useful if this information were fed back to the perceptual system to amplify features relevant for grasping (e.g. size, form), relative to irrelevant features (e.g. colour). In another situation, it may be useful to make an eye movement to a certain location. Once this decision has been made, it would in turn make sense to feed back information about the target location to the perceptual system. This would enable increased focussing of the visual system on the target location, which in turn could result in enhanced accuracy of the saccade. This section is about whether we can identify such feedback connections as they implement action-guided perception.

First, we return to the two dissociable visual systems, where/how and what, in the dorsal occipital–parietal and the ventral occipital–temporal pathways, respectively. The patient research discussed in Section 2.0 suggested that the relative contributions are dictated by action requirements. An fMRI study shed more light on this issue (Culham et al., 2003). These researchers used a, so-called, grasparatus, a rotating octagonal drum that could be driven by compressed air, so that it was compatible with an fMRI setting. Plastic rectangles varying in size and shape were mounted on the drum and presented to the subject one by one through stepwise rotations of the drum. In one condition the subject had to grasp each object; in a second he or she needed only to reach for and touch it. In particular one area in the dorsal stream, called the anterior intra-parietal region (AIP, Figure 2.13), showed stronger activation in the grasping than in the reaching condition. Apparently, neurons in AIP are involved in translating spatial object parameters into action parameters, something which is more necessary during grasping than during reaching. AIP may be contrasted with a typical ventral stream region, namely the lateral occipital complex (LOC, also shown in Figure 2.13). LOC is perhaps the prototypical object recognition region, identified in

Figure 2.13

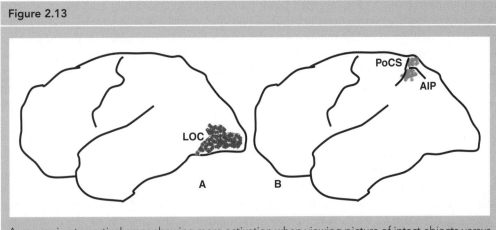

A: approximate cortical areas showing more activation when viewing picture of intact objects versus scrambled objects; B: approximate cortical areas showing more activation during grasping than during reaching.
LOC – lateral occipital cortex. PoCS – postcentral sulcus. AIP – anterior intra-parietal sulcus.

this study during a task with hardly any motor requirement by its stronger activation by intact objects (e.g. fruits, animals) than by scrambled counterparts. Although LOC was certainly activated, relative to baseline, during grasping and reaching, there was no difference between the two action conditions. In contrast, AIP was hardly activated by the intact or by the scrambled objects. Different kinds of objects then, activate both ventral lateral occipital areas and dorsal parietal areas. The relative contribution, especially of the latter however, is dictated by what has to be done with the information contained in the object: parietal activation is invoked more and more as we proceed from hardly any action, to global action (reaching), to global plus local adjustments that depend on the spatial layout of the object.

The behavioural consequences of such action-modulated perceptual processing are illustrated in a clever experiment by Bekkering and Neggers (2002). They made use of the fact that when observers detect an object relatively peripherally in the visual field and reach out to grasp it, they automatically make an eye movement to that object as well (gaze anchoring). Subjects were presented with three-dimensional multi-object displays. Each object had one of two possible orientations and one of two possible colours. There was always one unique target combination of orientation and colour that subjects had to either grasp (so the orientation was relevant) or point to.

During these tasks, subjects made a substantial number of saccade errors: about 30 per cent of the eye movements was directed at an object with a target colour but a non-target orientation (see Figure 2.14). However, these errors were much more frequent during pointing than during grasping. Apparently the information about object orientation that directs the saccades was of better quality, or more easily accessible, in a situation in which orientation was relevant for another action (grasping), compared to when it was not relevant (during pointing). This interpretation is supported by the fact that the percentage saccades directed to the wrong colour was not different for grasping versus reaching. This makes sense, because colour is equally irrelevant for both. As for the dorsal perception discussed above, this effect of motor requirements on orientation processing could be the result of a feedback signal from brain mechanisms implementing a specific action to perceptual regions; or a signal that strengthens the connections between certain perceptual input units and certain motor output units, like the ones that control eye movements. Just as improved quality of orientation information may lead to better grasping, more accurate or accessible information on the spatial layout of an object can lead to more accurate saccades to object. For example, Moore (Moore, 1999) reported a positive correlation between the number of action potentials of neurons in area V4, also a prototypical ventral form analysis area, and the accuracy of immediately subsequent saccades.

A similar feedback signal could originate from the eye movement system itself. Deubel and Schneider (Deubel & Schneider, 1996) reported on a situation in which subjects prepared and executed an eye movement to a certain target location. Shortly before the saccade was initiated (some 100 milliseconds), a target probe appeared, either at the exact target location of the saccade, or one or two degrees of arc to the left or right of the location. The target probe was the letter E appearing normally or mirrored. After the target probe the saccade was executed and after the saccade subjects reported the identity of the target probe (normal or mirror E). It turned out that probe discrimination was about 15 per cent to 30 per cent better when the probe was presented at the exact target location of the saccade, compared to when it was presented a few degrees away. Again, the generally accepted interpretation of these findings holds that neurons in the visual cortex become more sensitive to stimulation of the saccade target location just prior to the saccade, as a result of a signal from the saccade generating system to these neurons in the visual cortex.

Can we actually see these visual neurons being activated just prior to, and specifically due the preparation of, a saccade? We have already discussed V4 neurons that become more active prior to saccades and seem to have a positive influence on the accuracy of the saccades. Supèr and colleagues (Supèr et al., 2004) found cells in the monkey primary visual cortex (V1) that exhibit similar properties. Specifically, these cells responded to the onset of a visual stimulus at a certain location with a sharp transient increase in action potentials lasting about 50 milliseconds, after which they become silent again. After 100 or 200 milliseconds the visual stimulus is turned off and the monkey has to remember

Figure 2.14

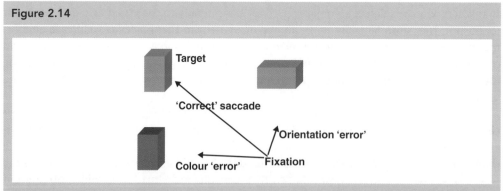

Subjects grasped (or pointed to) the object defined by a specific combination of colour and orientation.
Such actions are always accompanied by eye movements to the object. However, these saccades are often preceded by erroneous saccades, especially towards objects with the target colour, but the non-target orientation.

its location. After a delay of a second the monkey makes an eye movement. In the last hundred milliseconds before the saccade, the V1 cells become more active again. This is especially so when the saccade is directed to the location of the prior stimulus and that stimulus was in the neuron's receptive field. In short, saccade preparation activates V1 neurons that respond best to stimuli located in the target location for the saccade. It may be useful to stress that it is the saccade preparation that drives the visual neurons, not the other way around.

Given behavioural signs as well as macroscopic and microscopic neurophysiological indices of action-modulated perceptual processing, can we visualize the signal from the action centres to the perception centres that implements this modulation? The answer seems to be an increasingly loud and clear 'yes'. A typical action centre in relation to saccades consists of the FEFs. In one study (Moore & Armstrong, 2003), researchers electrically stimulated groups of neurons in monkey FEFs and assessed the effect on the responses of neurons in the ventral visual area V4 (Figure 2.15). In one condition FEF stimulation was sufficiently strong to elicit a saccade to a specific location. In a second condition the stimulation was too weak to elicit a saccade, but it still affected the response of the V4 neurons to appropriate visual stimuli. This modulation was only detectable when a V4 neuron was first activated by a visual stimulus,

Figure 2.15

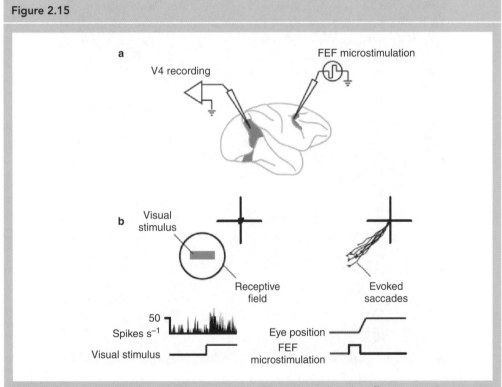

A: set-up for external stimulation of neurons in the FEF and recording the effects in visual cortex area V4. B, left: Response of V4 neuron to stimulus in its receptive field. See text for further explanation. B, right: From a separate condition where FEF stimulation was strong enough to evoke saccades to the receptive field of the visual stimulus (which was not presented in this condition).

Source: From Moore and Armstrong (2003). Reprinted by permission from Macmillan Publishers Ltd: Nature, 2003.

and only when the receptive field (RF) of the V4 neuron overlapped with the target location of the saccade elicited by the strong stimulation. When there was no such overlap, FEF stimulation resulted in suppression rather than enhancement of the V4 response. Specifically, the onset of the visual stimulus elicited a V4 response that adapted after a few 100 milliseconds (the visual stimulus remained on the screen), and it only recovered when RF matching FEF stimulation was applied. This effect was especially strong in the presence of distracting stimuli outside the RF. It was as if the V4 neurons, due to FEF stimulation, stated, 'Don't bother me, I'm still busy with this stimulus.'

Figure 2.16

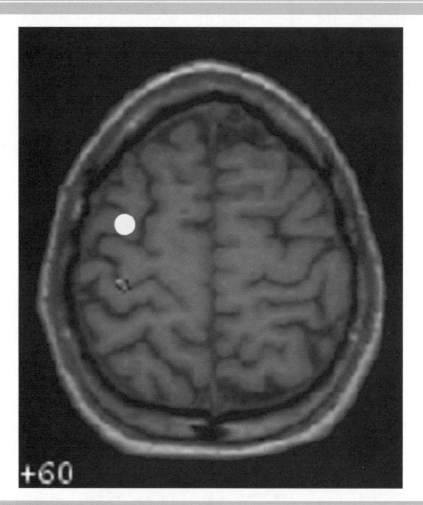

Approximate localization of the human FEF where activation was disrupted using TMS.
FEF is denoted by the white dot, flanked by the precentral sulcus (right below the dot) and the superior-frontal sulcus (to the right) of one of the authors. The grey blob indicates the area in primary motor cortex (M1) that is activated with right finger movements.
Source: O'Shea et al. (2004).

Is there something like a FEF signal with similar effects in humans? Yes, O'Shea and colleagues (O'Shea et al., 2004), using TMS, suppressed FEF activity some 40–80 milliseconds after presentation of a search array (Figure 2.16). This resulted in a significant reduction of sensitivity for potential targets in the search array. There are many possible interpretations of this effect, but a study by Silvanto and colleagues (Silvanto et al., 2006) provided more direct evidence for interactions between FEF and the visual cortex. In this study a TMS protocol was used that enhanced rather than suppressed FEF activity. A second TMS pulse was applied to visual area V5, the motion processing cortex. When the pulse exceeded a certain threshold it evoked the sensation of spots moving across the visual field (phosphenes). With appropriate FEF stimulation, the threshold for eliciting phosphenes was significantly reduced. The optimal timing of the FEF stimulation was 20 milliseconds prior to the V5 stimulus within each hemisphere. Hence, signals from the FEF modulate processing in visual cortex. More generally, signals from anterior areas involved in the preparation of specific motor activity (eye movement, grasping) modulate processing in perceptual centres, probably to enhance the analysis of sensory information that is relevant for an accurate execution of the motor act.

2.5 CONCLUDING REMARKS

By looking for answers to psychological questions in the brain it has become clear that perception and action overlap in terms of temporal organization, as well as with respect to the characteristics of individual neurons that appear to represent both perceptual and action aspects. Furthermore, the more obvious feedforward chain from perception to action is clearly supplemented by feedback signals from action-related parts of the brain to perception-related parts of the brain. The phenomenon of action-guided perception is well documented and is described further in the next chapter, which highlights the phenomenon of attention-modulated perception. While the last section of this chapter addressed how perception was driven by action intentions, Chapter 3 looks at the relevance of information and whether there is sufficient capacity for perceiving it.

Questions

1. See Section 2.1. Consider the Miller paradigm. Partial transmission of form information to the motor system predicts shorter LRP latencies (relative to the onsets of s, S, т or T) in the hand/name condition than in the other hand conditions, but this was not found. This may imply that the use of partial information about form was not used to prepare the response hand. What else could explain reaction times being shorter in condition 1 than in conditions 2 and 3?

2. In relation to Section 2.1, think about what may happen with respect to the timing of an action relative to perception in the case of a task in which there is just one stimulus feature that is emphasized to determine the behavioural response. For example, subjects are required to respond with one hand to (just a single) letter A and with the other to B. How could the results speak to the issue of synchronous versus asynchronous transmission?

3. See Section 2.2. How exactly can mirror neurons drive imitative behaviour? Are mirror neurons necessary for all learned behaviour?

4. In relation to Section 2.4, devise an experiment to test the idea that when subjects are required to grasp oriented objects (e.g. rods), their visual cortex becomes more sensitive to the orientation of objects. Think of how this would be manifest in behavioural performance as well as in brain recordings.

3 PERCEPTION AND ATTENTION

Key Points

- A mechanism termed selective attention imposes limits on perception, awareness, and other aspects of information processing
- Characterizing the more exact nature of such modulation by attention benefits from framing such questions in terms of activated brain areas
- Top–down signals from regions such as frontal and parietal cortex implement a bias in other brain areas such as sensory cortex as a basis for the attentional modulation
- There is good evidence for a separate brain mechanism dedicated to the detection of unexpected but potentially relevant events outside the current focus of attention.

3.0 INTRODUCTION

Patients with *hemispatial* neglect fail to initiate action of any kind with regard to events in the hemifield contralateral to their cortical lesion, especially when the damage is in the right hemisphere. They report no awareness for contralateral events, do not show any signs of orientation towards salient events in that half field, and often they keep their head and eyes turned to the ipsilateral field and never look in the contralateral direction (Parton et al., 2004). Some patients, when in bed, cling vehemently to the right side of the bed, 'as if responding to the irresistible magnetism of everything that is on the right' (Mesulam, 1999b). This is not due to a form of partial blindness at the level of the retina or even the primary visual cortex. For example, neglect patients, unlike patients with occipital damage (blindsight), show implicit semantic priming by objects in the neglected visual half field, whereas they cannot explicitly match this object to an identical one presented subsequently in the good field (Driver & Mattingley, 1998). Apparently, the impairment concerns some higher-order process that normally enables reporting awareness of these events as well as orienting to them and acting on them. We need this higher-order function at surprisingly high levels of information processing. One patient, when asked to imagine and describe a highly familiar square in Milan, would report only the half that was contralateral to his parietal–temporal lesion (see Figure 3.1) (Bisiach & Luzzatti, 1978).

One report on hemineglect patients with right hemisphere damage used a number bisection task, in which the midpoint value between two auditively presented numbers had to be reported, without making calculations (Zorzi et al., 2002). Compared to controls, the patients

Figure 3.1

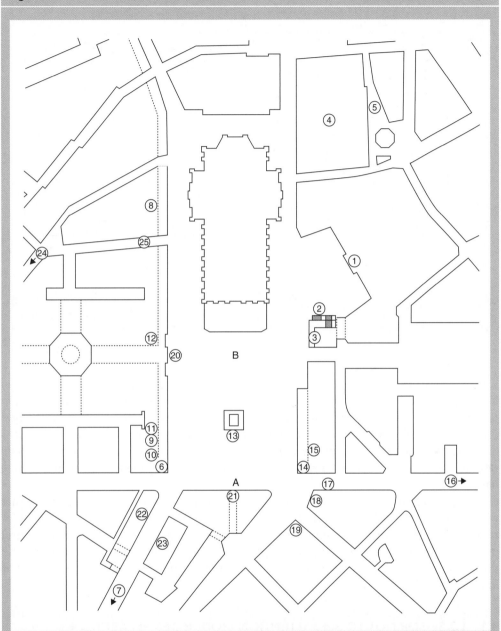

Imagining the Piazza del Duomo in Milan.
From perspective A, patient I.G. reports only the cathedral and items 1 to 5. Taking perspective B, she reports only items 6 to 12.

Source: Bisiach and Luzzatti (1978).

Figure 3.2

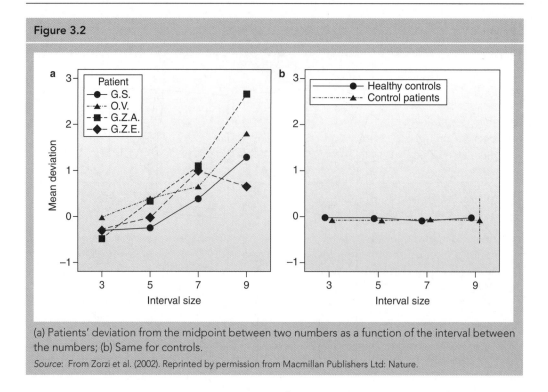

(a) Patients' deviation from the midpoint between two numbers as a function of the interval between the numbers; (b) Same for controls.

Source: From Zorzi et al. (2002). Reprinted by permission from Macmillan Publishers Ltd: Nature.

systematically overestimated the midpoint value, for instance stating that 15 was halfway between 11 and 17 (see Figure 3.2). This is consistent with the notion of an internal 'mental number line', which in the case of patients was scanned with a bias away from the part of the number line contralateral to the lesion (i.e. the part with the smaller numbers). It is important to note that the hemineglect patients performed normally in standard arithmetic tasks (e.g. subtraction), where performance may be severely impaired after left hemisphere damage.

It is generally believed that hemineglect patients fail to orient to specific parts of either real environmental or imaginary space. But what is this mechanism that makes us orient, or selectively attend to certain parts of space, or that makes us select one response from several options, or determines what gets into long-term memory and what does not? This chapter deals with this selecting mechanism, how it affects how we perceive the world, and how it is implemented in brain activity.

3.1   TO SEE OR NOT TO SEE: ATTENTION MODULATES PERCEPTION

Selective attention is the mechanism that makes us more sensitive or responsive to certain information, at the cost of processing other information. This variation in sensitivity or responsivity can take extreme forms. A telling case is 'inattentional blindness', when we are literally blind to certain, sometimes very salient, stimuli only because we are strongly focussed on other sources of information (Kim & Blake, 2005; Mack & Rock, 1998). The classic examples of inattentional blindness are particularly powerful in illustrating that what we perceive in a scene or a series of events can be completely dependent on how we direct attention to certain aspects of that scene or event, whereas the stimulus input itself is completely invariant.

Inattentional blindness is somewhat reminiscent of the classic 'cocktail party' phenomenon. In spite of the surrounding noise we manage to listen selectively to one speaker. Apparently, some quality enables us to select one stream of utterances among many others. In the laboratory this situation has been mimicked in what are called shadowing or dichotic listening tasks (Cherry, 1953). Two streams of information (prose passages, word lists) are presented to the subject, one to each ear. The subject has to straight away repeat the words presented to one ear, while the information presented to the other ear has to be ignored.

In another version of the task, the two information streams differ in an additional respect, such as one message being conveyed by a male voice, the other by a female voice. The task is to repeat all the words conveyed by one voice, even when the voice switches from one ear to the other. The task has now become more difficult: subjects take longer to repeat the words and they make more errors. Apparently directing attention is easier for some cues (e.g. ear or location), than others (e.g. voice type). In the split memory span task (Broadbent, 1958), the subject is presented with three consecutive pairs of digits to the two ears, (e.g. 3 left, 5 right; 7 left, 2 right; 4 left, 9 right). When asked to repeat the 6 digits, the subject will say 374 529, or 529 374. Thus, the subject first recalls the 3 numbers presented to one ear, and subsequently those presented to the other. If asked to follow a different strategy, such as repeat in the order of presentation, their performance deteriorates. It is as if after presentation the 6 digits reside in some memory buffer. The subject cannot pronounce 2 or more digits at one time so a selection has to be made as to which digit is pronounced first, which one second, and so on, from the information residing in the memory buffer. It appears to be convenient for the subject to use location in auditory space as a criterion for selection, much more than, for example, temporal position.

To summarize: (1) Attention involves a selection process. Not all stimuli can be processed at one and the same time, and not all responses can be issued at the same time. (2) Selection implies that there is a criterion with respect to which the selection is made. Some criteria appear to be more effective than others. In the above examples, the location in space of the source of an auditory message turned out be a relatively powerful criterion. As we will see, this is even more so in the case of visual information.

Box 3.1   Is selection perfect?

Is the attentional selection process perfect? The story about the cocktail party was not complete. When attending to one person at the party, we may be focussed on this one source for minutes and minutes; but, when we perceive our own name from another source, we see that attentional selection is not so complete as to prevent that perception. The question is, to what extent *do* we perceive such a supposedly ignored stimulus? In the standard shadowing task a word list is presented to each ear, using a male and a female voice, at a rate of one word per second. The subject's own name is presented just once, after 4 or 5 minutes of shadowing, in the to-be-ignored message. One or two minutes after presentation of the subject's name, the subject is asked whether she recalls hearing it. In a typical study, about 34 per cent of subjects (mostly psychology students) reported having heard their own names (Wood & Cowan, 1995). In contrast, none of the subjects recalled hearing the name of another subject, which was presented as a control. Furthermore, subjects who reported afterwards to have heard their name turned out to perform a bit worse on the shadowing task just after the presentation of their own name (in both speed and accuracy).

A lack of attention may prevent awareness of a stimulus (or rather, reporting awareness). At the same time, higher forms of processing, normally associated with extensive cortical activation, may be spared. A good example is the 'attentional blink', so termed because, similar to what happens during an eye blink, the ability to detect visual information is severely reduced for a brief period of time (Raymond et al., 1992). The original experimental paradigm is illustrated in Figure 3.3. Sequences of letters are shown in a rapid serial visual presentation (RSVP) format at a rate of one every 80 ms. Most of the letters are irrelevant, except for a single white target letter and, in some series, a probe letter (X). In the experimental condition, subjects must identify the white target letter. In addition, the subject has to detect the presence of probe letter X that may or may not appear once per series as one of the eight stimuli following the white target. Figure 3.4 shows the typical result: probe detection for post-target positions 2 to 5 (or 160 ms to 400 ms post-target) is severely impaired. Importantly, this result is not found when subjects view exactly equivalent streams but have to ignore the white target and only report on the X (as in the control condition). This rules out the possibility that the reduced probe detection reflects sensory interactions between the successive letters. Instead, it is as if attention to the target hampers attention to the subsequent probe, hence the term 'attentional blink'. Consistently, in a MEG study, using a similar RSVP series,

Figure 3.3

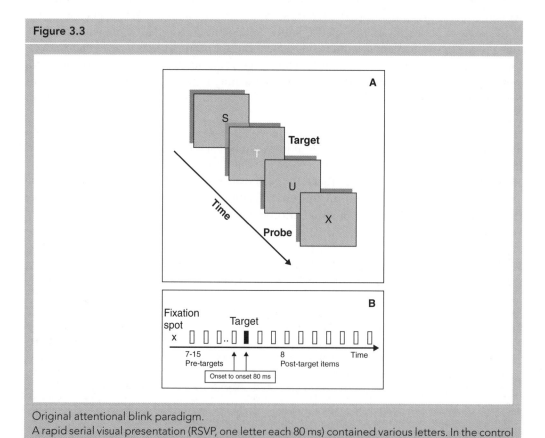

Original attentional blink paradigm.
A rapid serial visual presentation (RSVP, one letter each 80 ms) contained various letters. In the control condition the task was to detect the possible X in the series, which could be presented once per series at any of the 8 post-target positions, or replace the target itself. In the experimental condition the X was also to be detected, but in addition the white target letter had to be identified.

Figure 3.4

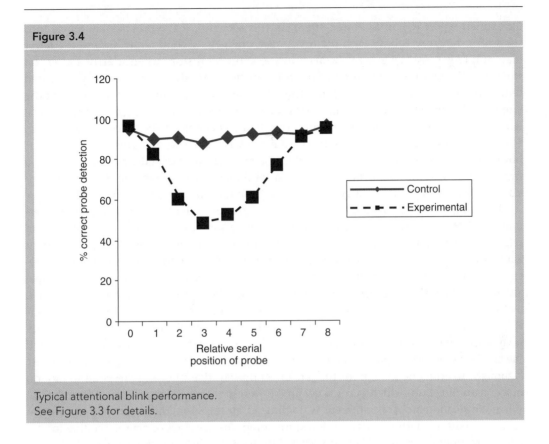

Typical attentional blink performance.
See Figure 3.3 for details.

all letters, including the probe, activated the occipital cortex equally, at about 100 ms post-letter. However, the MEG response at 300 ms post-probe above the frontal areas was significantly larger for detected probes than for non-detected probes (Hommel et al., 2006).

The attentional blink selects for awareness, but not for all forms of higher processing. Luck and colleagues used a variety of the original blink paradigm, in which the first target was a string of identical digits that had to be identified, and the second target was a word (Luck et al., 1996). The word could either match the semantic context that was provided before the RSVP started (e.g. context is 'food', second target is 'pizza'), or not (e.g. 'clothes' and 'pizza'). If midline ERPs to 'pizza' are compared, the main difference consists of an N400, the larger negativity at about 400 ms latency when the word is incongruent with the context. The crucial point is that the occurrence of this difference signifies that the eliciting word has been semantically processed, or in other words, its meaning has been identified. When the second target was presented three positions (249 ms) later than the first one, a significant attentional blink resulted in the explicit report by the participant as to whether the word matched the context or not. However, the N400 effect was equally large, irrespective of whether there was a performance blink or not (there was no blink at later positions relative to the first target, or in a control condition when the first target was ignored). Hence, semantic information can be available (N400 effect), but the attentional blink blocks it from explicit report.

What exactly is the use of information that is blocked by the attentional blink? One possibility is that the information is entered in a system termed 'short-term memory', which allows the information to be temporarily stored so that it can be used later (after the RSVP) for explicit report (Chun & Potter, 1995). In this scenario, if the process that stores into short-term memory is busy with the first target when the second target arrives, the latter may simply get lost, whereas it *is* saved in the short-term store when it arrives after the storage of the first target has been dealt with. Furthermore, short-term memory is limited in the amount of items it can store, but this is probably not instrumental in producing the attentional blink. Di Lollo and colleagues used an RSVP consisting of digits that were to be ignored, and letters on positions 5 and 7 that had to be identified (Di Lollo et al., 2005). The classical attentional blink was observed for letters on position 7. This blink effect was however completely annihilated by simply replacing the non-target digit at position 6 by a third letter target. Although the load on short-term memory was higher in the latter condition, processing of the third target in this condition did not suffer from the blink.

The examples of inattentional blindness discussed above refer to selective attention determining what we consciously perceive. Whereas these were extreme cases, the influence of selective attention on the perceptual experience can be more subtle. This is especially evident when the task for which selective attention is needed is made more taxing. In that case, perception of irrelevant, potentially distracting, stimuli can be substantially reduced, a principle also referred to as the 'load theory of attention' (Lavie, 2005). A telling example was reported by Chaudhuri (Chaudhuri, 1990), who investigated the motion aftereffect. The motion aftereffect (for an example, see http://www.michaelbach.de/ot/mot_adapt/index.html) had already been described by Aristotle. A well-known version involves staring at a movie of a waterfall. If the movie is suddenly stopped after some time, the water appears to stream upward. The effect is thought to arise due to neurons that are direction-sensitive (they only respond to motion in a certain direction) which become adapted (less responsive) upon prolonged stimulation. When stimulation stops, the percept is dominated by the spontaneous activity of motion-sensitive neurons. Without prior motion stimulation, the activities of neurons coding for different directions cancel out. After the waterfall stimulation, the neurons coding for downward motion have adapted, and those coding for upward motion dominate the percept, resulting in perceiving motion in the opposite direction. Chaudhuri used an 'optic flow field' stimulus, a full field of dots that move radially to the screen edge (also quite well-known as a computer screen saver). He found that directing attention away from the optic flow, by visually superposing and imposing a moderately demanding task, significantly reduced the aftereffect once the field stood still. This can be interpreted as indicating that the direction-sensitive neurons were now in a less adaptive state, presumably due to the fact that the impact of the optic flow was diminished as a result of attention being directed to the demanding task.

This experiment was replicated by Rees and colleagues (Rees et al., 1997). In the behavioural version, participants were again exposed to optic flow for about a half minute. When the dots were frozen in their position, they appeared to contract radially (the aftereffect). During optic flow, within a modest ellipse drawn around the central fixation point, subjects viewed identical lists of words in two conditions: a low-load condition, presumably requiring less selective attention to the task (discriminating upper versus lower case); and a high-load condition, presumably requiring more selective attention to the task (determining the number of syllables). For all participants, the aftereffect lasted for a significantly shorter time in the high- than in the low-load condition, again indicating that the optic flow had evoked less activity in direction-sensitive neurons in the more attention-demanding condition.

In another version of the experiment participants were again presented with the two task conditions, with the dots either in optic flow (motion) or stationary (no motion). Comparing fMRI scans acquired during motion versus non-motion conditions revealed activity in typical

Figure 3.5

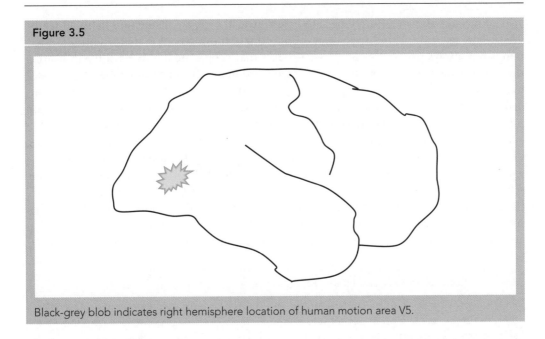

Black-grey blob indicates right hemisphere location of human motion area V5.

Figure 3.6

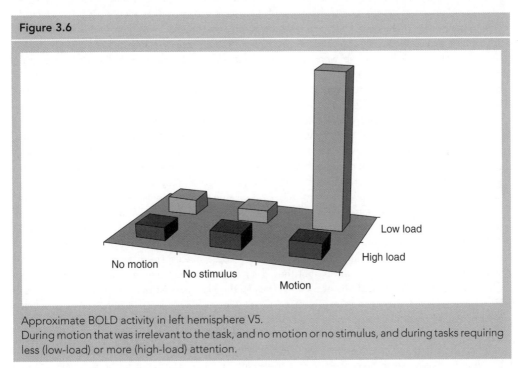

Approximate BOLD activity in left hemisphere V5.
During motion that was irrelevant to the task, and no motion or no stimulus, and during tasks requiring less (low-load) or more (high-load) attention.

motion areas like visual area 5 (V5), (see Figure 3.5). However, this motion-related difference was present only in the low-load, not in the high-load condition (see Figure 3.6). The obvious interpretation is that selective attention to another source of information suppresses the response of neurons in the visual cortex to the type of stimulation they are specifically sensitive to.

Findings like the above are especially relevant to the classic distinction between 'early' versus 'late' selection. This discussion was borne out of the observation that attentional selection is not always perfect (see Box 3.1). The fact that people are highly sensitive to hearing their own name makes it very likely that each word in a to-be-ignored message is processed to a certain extent. The extent of processing of 'unattended' stimuli has sparked a large-scale debate known as the 'early vs. late selection' discussion. According to the early selection principle, information is selected on the basis of very elementary features, like its location in auditory or visual space (Broadbent, 1958). Prior to selection, only a preliminary processing of all stimuli has taken place; more extensive processing (e.g. identifying what the stimulus was) takes place after selection, therefore only for attended stimuli. According to the late selection principle, the moment of selection is much later (relative to stimulus onset), and the criteria are much more complex (Deutsch & Deutsch, 1963). For example, the fact that subjects detect their own name in unattended conversation or speech would indicate that attentional selection takes place after the process through which the name is recognized.

Box 3.2   Reconciling early and late selection

Early selectionists point to perfect shadowing and the like as crucial evidence. Late selectionists likewise use the breakdown of perfect selection when the subject was appropriately probed. Early selectionists maintain that information is best selected based on 'simple' cues; and 'higher-order' processing is attenuated by attention to other stimuli. Late selectionists state that information is selected after 'higher-order' processing; 'higher-order' processing occurs without attention. Perhaps one could say that the early selectionists confused 'early selection' in the sense of 'a very simple feature as a criterion for selection' (which is true) with 'selection rejects the stimulus from any higher-order processing but the most preliminary, i.e. that processing needed to select' (which is not true). Likewise, late selectionists might be accused of confusing 'higher-order processing of to-be-ignored stimuli' (which is a fact) with 'attention never being based on low-order processing' (which is not correct).

In the eighties several papers appeared in which the early and late selection views were no longer seen as incompatible (Allport, 1989; Kahneman & Treisman, 1984; Van der Heijden, 1992). A key idea was the distinction between two concepts: that of building up a representation of external information on the one hand, and that of using that representation on the other. When two auditory or visual stimuli are presented at the same time (but at different locations), they may both be processed to a considerable extent, maybe even semantically. At the same time, subjects are perfectly able to use the location feature to govern selectivity of response, such as responding to all information delivered to one location, and not to information delivered to the other location. They may do so 100 per cent accurately, and very fast. Yet, when asked about the information presented at the unattended location, either explicitly or implicitly, it appears that they had devoted quite some processing to those stimuli. The crucial point is, however, that they did not use this information when performing the selection task (since there was no need for it). Thus, in this view at least two processes are at stake. First, there is 'selection for action' or 'selective cuing' (Allport, 1989). Selective cuing serves to select certain 'results' of stimulus processing to govern behaviour, in such a way that behaviour is coherent. The second process is 'selective processing'. Selective processing refers to, for instance, the extent to which the change of colour in the irrelevant traffic light is not processed (detected, perceived) at all. With decreasing selective processing, the irrelevant colour change is processed to an increasing extent; the fact that, in the end, it still does not govern behaviour is the consequence of selection for action. Referring back to the Rees et al. study (Figure 3.6), the extent to which selective processing (V5 activity) is reduced depends on the need for selection for action (which is presumably greater for the high-load task). An interesting question is whether selective (semantic) processing during the attentional blink is also sensitive to increasing task demands.

3.2   HOW EARLY IS THE ATTENTIONAL MODULATION OF BRAIN ACTIVATION PATTERNS?

Behavioural measures alone provide only indirect clues as to what exactly is modulated by attention. More direct indications may be derived by looking at the activation of the brain itself. For example, the 'early' versus 'late' dilemma can be translated into neurophysiological concepts: where in the brain, or where in a perception–action pathway (see Chapter 2), is the response to a stimulus being modulated by selective attention? The modulation of motion-related activity in V5, discussed above, is an example of an answer to this question. How early is selection? The answer is: as early as V5. Another example comes from the classic PET study by Corbetta and colleagues (Corbetta et al., 1991). When specifically attending to a change of colour from stimulus to stimulus, a change of motion speed, or a change of form, visual areas known to be specialized for these dimensions show elevated activation. This was measured relative to a condition in which all three dimensions had to be attended to. Thus, attention to colour or form was associated with more activation in ventral areas, attention to motion more with dorsal activation. In fact, attention-related activity was found in the same areas that were activated during 'passive' viewing of colour and motion, respectively (see Figure 3.7).

The statement 'as early as V5' should be qualified. It depends on the load (from the load theory of attention) how early irrelevant, potentially distracting, information is suppressed.

Figure 3.7

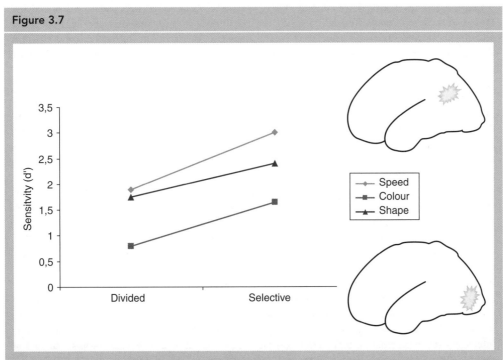

Results approximated from the Corbetta et al. (1991) study.
Selectively attending to a change in one feature results in better performance (higher sensitivity) than attending to a change in any feature (divided), even when the stimulus displays are identical in both conditions. Selective attention, relative to divided, also enhances activity in different occipital areas that are specific with respect to the selectively attended feature (speed in the upper, colour in the lower panel).

Furthermore, we are only looking at the suppression of irrelevant information; the story may be quite different for amplification of the neural representation of information that is *relevant* to the task at hand (see Box 3.3).

Box 3.3   The search for a neutral baseline condition

Separating suppression, or attenuation, of the irrelevant on the one hand, and amplification of the relevant on the other, requires an appropriate neutral baseline condition, in which information is neither attenuated nor amplified. Although this is perhaps a theoretical impossibility, a tremendous amount of research has been conducted on behavioural measures of attention, using an, at least intuitively, sound approximation of such a 'pure' neutral condition. For example, modern versions of the well-known Stroop task, in which the print colour of words or character arrays has to be named, include coloured words referring to an incongruent colour (e.g. 'red' in green), or coloured words referring to congruent colours ('green' in green), but, to obtain a neutral baseline reference, they also often include coloured words not referring to colour, or colour character arrays. Contrasting incongruent with neutral yields a measure of attenuation of the colour response by incongruent word information; contrasting congruent with neutral yields a measure of amplification of the colour response by congruent word information. A somewhat analogous neutral condition has been designed in the context of location cues that indicates the most likely location of an ensuing stimulus, so that attention can be directed to that location in advance; we will return to location cuing, or visual–spatial cuing (VSC) in the next section.

Like the Stroop task, in the Corbetta study (1991) one visual dimension had to be selectively attended to, while others had to be ignored. The three selective attention conditions (colour, speed, shape) were then compared to a neutral baseline condition, in which all three dimension were attended to (a divided attention condition). This seems an appropriate way to isolate at least the amplification part, because behaviourally a change in, say, the colour was detected much more quickly when colour was selectively attended to than when attention was divided. In this way we see the behavioural benefit of increasingly selective attention, and we can identify brain activity associated with selective attention by comparing scans from the selective condition to those from the divided condition. As this contrast reveals different areas for the different dimensions, we could go one step further and ask whether an area activated by attention to colour (relative to divided) is actually de-activated (attenuated) by attention to one of the other dimensions (again, relative to divided). (You may want to take a look at the original article to see whether the authors actually did this.)

The neutral baseline concept also illustrates two general problems in defining such a condition in imaging experiments. First, there is the general problem of the subtraction technique: how safe is the assumption that, with increasing selectivity and the associated behavioural benefits, only a limited set of brain areas increase in activity, without anything else happening? How sure can we be that the slower behavioural responses in the divided condition are not due to yet another brain process that is stronger in the divided condition and perhaps needed to perform the divided task? In fact, this is what Corbetta and colleagues found: a region in the anterior cingulate cortex was more active in the divided than in the selective condition. Second, how do we know that this is the best neutral condition? It could be that areas that are activated by attention to colour in the selective condition, are also activated in the divided condition, but to a lesser extent. It could also be that this colour-attention activity is actually attenuated as the result of competition between the representations of the three attended to dimensions. Perhaps a better neutral condition would be one in which none of the three dimensions had to be attended to, because there was no task at all…. But then again, this condition can be considered inappropriate because, in the absence of a task, the general level of arousal would be lower, which would result in lower activation in numerous areas that are not specifically involved in selective attention to a specific visual dimension. One way to go about this is to skip the idea of separating attenuation and amplification, and just to look at the sum of them, 'modulation'. Quite a number of classic studies have taken this approach.

Several studies have addressed the early/late issue not only in terms of space (where in the brain), but also in terms of time: when, relative to the onset of a stimulus, is the response of a brain area to that stimulus modulated by selective attention? There is no simple one-to-one relationship between spatial early and temporal early, in the sense of, for example, first primary sensory cortex at 50 ms post-stimulus, followed by secondary sensory cortex at 100 ms. Consider the following example from Roelfsema and colleagues (Roelfsema et al., 1998). Figure 3.8 shows traces representing firing rates in a group of monkey V1 neurons in response to the same visual stimulus, presented at time point zero. The black line represents the condition in which attention was directed to the location of the stimulus, the grey line the condition when attention was directed elsewhere. The initial volley, well before 200 ms latency, is not modulated by attention, but the part after 200 ms is. Researchers generally conclude that this shows that the earliest selection takes place in a more secondary visual area downstream from V1, and the resulting processing is then fed back upstream to the more primary area. Regardless of whether this is true, we can tell from Figure 3.8 that 'early selection' becomes an ambiguous term when we switch between the spatial and the temporal domain. Furthermore, to find out what is happening exactly, we need additional measures with high temporal resolution, such as intracranial recordings in animals and event-related potentials, fields or oscillations, in humans.

The bulk of the literature on animal studies agrees on attentional modulation in the secondary visual cortex. In an exemplary study (Moran & Desimone, 1985), two stimuli were presented simultaneously in the receptive field of a monkey V4 neuron. One of them, the preferred stimulus (e.g. a green rectangle), normally elicited a good response at about 100 ms latency, while the second one (e.g. a red rectangle) normally did not. When the animal's attention was directed to the location of the preferred stimulus, a sizable response was obtained. However, with exactly the same stimulus configuration, when attention was directed to the location of the non-preferred stimulus, the response was much smaller. It was as if attention made the receptive field shrink to match the location of the relevant stimulus. Furthermore, when attention was directed to a location outside the receptive field, the response to the same stimulus configuration was similar to the one with attention on the location of the preferred stimulus. From this, the authors concluded that attention

Figure 3.8

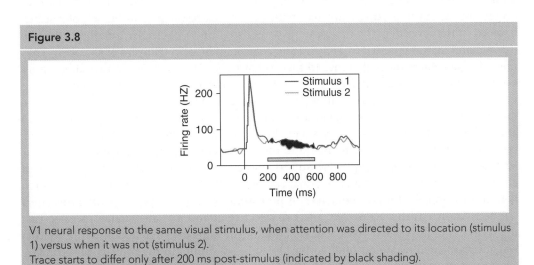

V1 neural response to the same visual stimulus, when attention was directed to its location (stimulus 1) versus when it was not (stimulus 2).
Trace starts to differ only after 200 ms post-stimulus (indicated by black shading).
Source: From Roelfsema et al. (1998). Reprinted by permission from Macmillan Publishers Ltd: Nature.

Figure 3.9

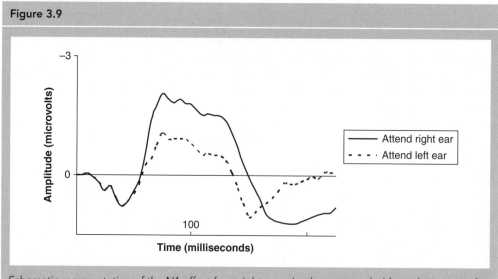

Schematic representation of the N1 effect for a right-ear stimulus as recorded from the vertex, after Hillyard et al. (1973).
Timescale in milliseconds since stimulus onset. For the left ear stimulus (not shown) the traces are swapped, as N1 amplitude is larger for attend left ear.

served to suppress the response to an irrelevant stimulus, but only when it competed with a relevant stimulus in the same receptive field, and that there was no evident facilitation by attention. Research like this answers a number of the questions posed above: selection was as early as V4 (similar results were obtained for the 'later', inferior–temporal area IT, but not for the 'earlier' area, V1), as early as 100 ms post-stimulus, and the mechanism was exclusively suppressive.

How does this work in humans? Event-related potential (ERP) studies in particular have yielded results that are not as detailed as those from animal research with respect to the exact location of the neurons involved, or the suppression versus facilitation balance. What they do present, however, is fairly consistent with the animal research. This branch of research boomed in the seventies. The first genuine demonstration of a selective attention effect on the human ERP was reported by Hillyard and colleagues in 1973 (Hillyard et al., 1973). They presented sequences of single tones to their subjects. The tones varied in two dimensions: ear of presentation (location: left or right) and pitch (high or low). In all, four kinds of tones were used, randomly alternating in a given sequence. The pitch difference was small and hard to discriminate relative to the location difference. Furthermore, one of the pitches had a large probability of being presented (e.g. 90 per cent), the other a small one (e.g. 10 per cent). Subjects were instructed to attend to the tones delivered in one ear (for instance the left) to detect the infrequent pitches, and to ignore the tones in the other ear. The earliest effect of location in the ERP was an enhanced negativity to tones at the 'relevant' location (left in this case), starting at about 100 ms post-stimulus (Figure 3.9). Since then this effect has been known as the 'N1'or 'Nd' effect of selective attention. Later studies revealed that the N1 effect at least partly reflects modulation of the obligatory N1 response (the N1 that was always elicited regardless of attention) to auditory stimuli in the primary or secondary auditory cortices (Woldorff & Hillyard, 1991).

Figure 3.10

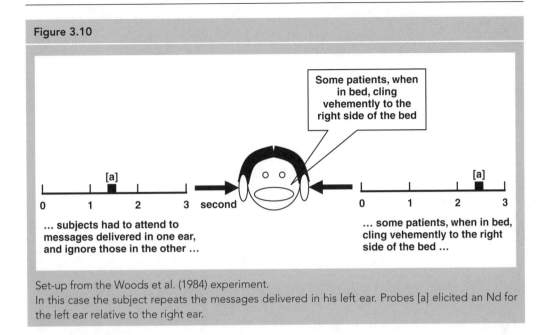

Set-up from the Woods et al. (1984) experiment.
In this case the subject repeats the messages delivered in his left ear. Probes [a] elicited an Nd for the left ear relative to the right ear.

Woods and colleagues (Woods et al., 1984) employed the classic shadowing task discussed above. As shown in Figure 3.10, subjects had to attend to messages delivered in one ear, and ignore those in the other. Task-irrelevant speech probes were mixed with the messages in both ears. Woods et al. reasoned that if shadowing entailed the kind of selective state that was also thought to underlie the Nd, as observed in the typical ERP design, then an Nd should be observed when comparing the ERPs to speech probes that were mixed with relevant messages, with those to speech probes presented in the irrelevant ear. This test was carried out and the Nd was observed. It can be concluded that the Nd as observed in the traditional ERP set-up reflects a selective state that also exists when subjects shadow messages in one ear over those in the other.

In 1991 Woldorff and Hillyard reported a selective attention effect that had a much shorter latency than ever reported before (it occurred between 20 ms and 50 ms post-stimulus; see Figure 3.11), and was qualitatively different, in that it had a different scalp topography and was recorded as a positivity, rather than a negativity, at standard electrode positions (Woldorff & Hillyard, 1991). To the authors it seemed that two factors might account for the fact that this effect had not been reported before. For one, they used an extremely high time pressure (intervals between successive stimuli of only a few hundreds of milliseconds). For the other, it was combined with relatively high task demands, with a difficult secondary discrimination that had to be made for stimuli satisfying the instructed primary, easily discriminable, attribute. In another study, MEG recordings were used to localize the sources of the early positivity and the later N1 (Woldorff et al., 1993). The results were consistent with a generator of the early positivity in the primary auditory cortex, and of the N1 in the secondary auditory cortex. The same held for their modulations by the selective attention manipulation.

In the meantime, what happened in the human visual domain? Also in the seventies, an experimental approach was applied similar to that for auditory attention (Mangun, 1995). A rapid sequence of single visual stimuli is presented, randomly to the left or the right of

Figure 3.11

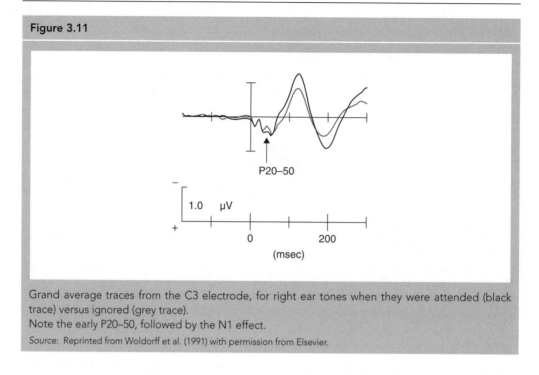

Grand average traces from the C3 electrode, for right ear tones when they were attended (black trace) versus ignored (grey trace).
Note the early P20–50, followed by the N1 effect.
Source: Reprinted from Woldorff et al. (1991) with permission from Elsevier.

fixation (say 5 degrees to 10 degrees). A small number of both left- and right-field stimuli deviate from the other stimuli. The subject is instructed to detect the deviants (targets), but only in the left field, and to ignore the right-field stimuli. In another sequence, the instruction is to detect right-field targets and ignore all left-field stimuli. In this way the response to one and the same stimulus (either left or right) can be compared across conditions in which the stimulus is attended or ignored, respectively. Figure 3.12 shows a typical result from two lateral occipital electrodes. Just after 100 ms post-stimulus, many visual stimuli evoke a pronounced positive peak over posterior areas, conveniently termed P1. As can be seen in Figure 3.12, the P1 is larger when the stimulus is in the attended location than when it is ignored. We have an answer yet again: selection is as early as 100 ms. Attempts to find shorter-latency effects have generally failed. ERP deflections preceding P1 are very sensitive to physical stimulus characteristics, like the location and the spatial frequency content of the stimulus, but not to typical manipulations of selective attention (Clark & Hillyard, 1996; Kenemans et al., 2002). Note also that the P1 effect is followed in time by an enhanced negativity and a later enhanced positivity for the attend condition, relative to the ignore condition. Apparently, early selection translates to modulated processing in later stages.

Although it is not very clear in Figure 3.12, the peaks of the P1 in each of the two attention conditions generally have the same latency, which is also the latency of the maximum effect of attention (temporal correspondence). The traces in Figure 3.12 are from recording sites contralateral to the stimulus (averaged across right and left field). The ipsilateral signals look basically the same, but everything is smaller: the P1 in the two conditions, as well as the P1 effect of attention. Stated differently, at a given recording site, say left occipital, right-field visual stimuli elicit a larger P1 than left-field stimuli do. Furthermore, the effect of attention at this site is also larger for right-field stimuli. In other words, there is a correspondence between the stimulus that evokes the largest P1, and the stimulus for which the attention

Figure 3.12

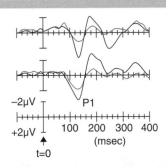

P1 effect. Traces are average ERPs recorded over two contralateral occipital electrodes.
Thick lines: lateral stimulus was attended. Thin lines: lateral stimulus was ignored.

Source: Reprinted from Mangun et al. (2001) with permission from Elsevier.

effect on P1 is largest (stimulus correspondence). Another way to view this is to look at one stimulus, for instance the one in the right-field. The P1 to right-field stimuli is generally larger over contralateral than over ipsilateral sites. If this is the case, then the attention effect on P1 for this stimulus is also larger contralaterally than ipsilaterally (spatial correspondence). Stimulus and spatial correspondence are illustrated in Plate VII: the P1 effect for right stimuli is larger over the left hemisphere, following the distribution of the P1 to right stimuli independent of attention, and the P1 effect for left stimuli is larger over the right hemisphere, also following the distribution of the P1 to left stimuli independent of attention. Note that, depending on exact stimulus characteristics, P1 scalp distributions may sometimes have an ipsilateral maximum (this depends on the orientation of the contralateral equivalent dipoles, see Chapter 1), but this does not affect the spatial-correspondence principle.

The properties of temporal, spatial, and stimulus correspondence are very much consistent with a theoretical notion that has been advocated numerous times under a variety of headers including sensory gain (Hillyard et al., 1998), neural specificity (Harter & Aine, 1984), or relative amplification (Posner & Dehaene, 1994). The notion basically holds that stimuli elicit a certain activity in the sensory cortex that is merely amplified when these stimuli are attended to (or attenuated when they are ignored, or both). That is, selective attention does not produce a qualitative change in the response to stimuli, but only a quantitative one. The sensory gain notion is rather similar to the idea discussed earlier in this chapter, that selective attention amplifies or attenuates the response of neurons in the visual cortex to stimulation they are specifically sensitive to. The P1 effect is an example of how this notion translates into specific predictions for at least three domains: the effect is largest at a specific time point, it is larger at a specific recording site, and it is larger for a specific stimulus.

How early is P1 in the spatial domain? Figure 3.13 shows a typical result from combined PET and ERP research (Heinze et al., 1994; Mangun et al., 2001). Note that the PET data are contrasted in terms of 'attend left greater than attend right', and vice versa. These contrasts reveal a lot more than just the P1 effect: other stimulus-evoked activity that is modulated by attention, as well as activity that is not stimulus-related but does contribute to the attentional effect (see next section). If we translate the PET results into theoretical generators of the P1-effect scalp distribution, we can examine which one of all the possible generators

Figure 3.13

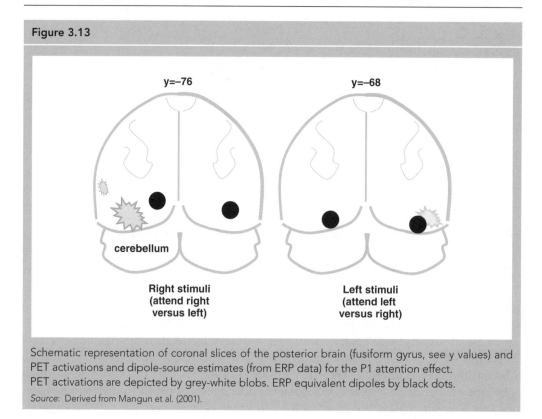

Schematic representation of coronal slices of the posterior brain (fusiform gyrus, see y values) and PET activations and dipole-source estimates (from ERP data) for the P1 attention effect.
PET activations are depicted by grey-white blobs. ERP equivalent dipoles by black dots.
Source: Derived from Mangun et al. (2001).

produces a model scalp distribution that best fits the recorded distribution. This procedure yields pictures like the one shown in Figure 3.13. The locations of the equivalent dipole sources were initially estimated from the PET data, and then both locations and orientations were optimized with respect to how well they fitted the ERP data. As can be seen, there is a fair overlap between the location of PET activity and the locations of the dipoles. This overlap is located in the posterior fusiform gyrus, a region at the base of the brain, generally considered to be a part of the ventral visual pathway. This also gives us a further clue as to what exactly spatial attention to a specific location is doing. It is modulating the strength of signals in a part of visual cortex generally believed to be involved in the processing of non-spatial, object- and form-related aspects of the stimulus. How it achieves that, is the topic of the next section.

Box 3.4   Attentional modulation in the dorsal occipital cortex

The story about the P1 effect in the spatial (anatomical) domain is actually a little more complicated, because spatial and stimulus correspondence apply not only along the horizontal but also along the vertical dimension (you may recall that upper field stimuli project to lower visual cortex and vice versa). The ventral occipital ERP sources were obtained when attended and ignored visual stimuli were presented above the fixation mark. Following visual retinotopy however, in another PET/ERP study, using stimuli below fixation, the sources of the P1 effect were found in the dorsal occipital cortex (Weissman et al., 2002). The question is, can dorsal occipital areas still be considered part of the ventral visual pathway?

3.3   SETTING THE GAINS: TOP–DOWN SIGNALS CREATING A BIAS IN PERCEPTUAL CORTEX

We have learned that selective attention can modulate perception in various ways; but how does this modulation come about? Suppose you are in front of a stereo audio device and someone asks you to pay particular attention to the left channel. What would you do? Given that information is already coming from both channels, a sensible action would be to turn the balance control to the left, up to the point that the right channel becomes inaudible; that puts you in a better position to process the relevant information from the left channel. You could do this after the music, or other kind of information to which you want to selectively pay attention, has already started. Importantly, you can also do it before the music starts, if you know in advance which channel is relevant and which one is not.

It is the latter possibility that we can use to investigate the process of adjusting the gains of different channels so that some are amplified and others are attenuated. In the experimental paradigms discussed above, subjects are instructed to attend to one category of information (e.g. everything in the left visual half field), and ignore other categories. Could they do this by increasing the gain in one channel, and/ or lowering it in others, before the information is actually presented? To elucidate this issue, researchers have to create a condition in which the a priori gain-setting, if it exists, can be made visible before the attentional modulation takes place. One way to ensure this is to look at the time period before the to be attended target, or the to-be-ignored non-target, is physically presented. Of course the subject needs

Figure 3.14

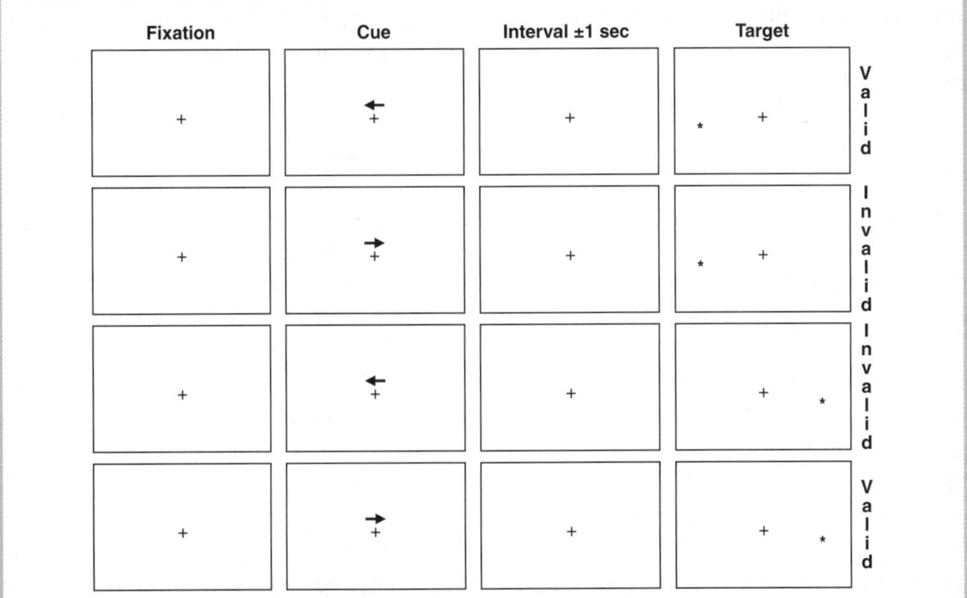

Valid and invalid conditions in the visual–spatial cueing (VSC) paradigm.
Invalid trials have a lower probability than valid ones. Subjects detect or discriminate the target stimulus. At all times they keep their eyes fixated on the '+'.

to be prompted to start adjusting the gains. This can be achieved by using an instruction, for example, in the form of a second stimulus, a 'cue' that tells the subject how to adjust the gains. Logically, at least two things are important about such a cue. First, to find out about how the cue is processed, and how the gain-setting process takes place, is to look at brain responses to the cue. Second, we should immediately realize that any cue stimulus elicits a lot of brain activation that is not specifically related to setting the gains (e.g. bottom-up determined activation; or a general attentional response because it contains relevant information). Therefore, there should always be some control cue stimulus, which matches the gain-setting cue in every respect, except that it does not inform the subject about a specific manner of setting the gains (see also box 3.3).

A classical experimental paradigm that separates cue and targets in time is the visual–spatial cuing task (VSC) (Posner et al., 1980). VSC involves a sequence of double-event trials, each consisting of a cue followed some seconds later by a target (see Figure 3.14). The cue (e.g. arrow or letter) signals the most likely location of the subsequent target; it is valid for a majority (e.g. 80 per cent) of the trials, and invalid for the rest. A proportion of the trials contains a neutral cue that is not spatially informative. The target has to be detected or discriminated. The main readout measure is the validity effect: speed and/ or accuracy of the response is better after valid than after invalid cues. One interpretation is that the validity effect positively reflects the selectivity of attention to a specific location, but this is very likely an over-simplification, as will be argued later. Neutral cues allow for a decomposition of the validity effect in costs and benefits, given certain assumptions about how they are processed.

Figure 3.15 shows typical results for a VSC experiment (van der Lubbe et al., 2006). In the detect version there was only one target form (for example, an asterisk), and upon detection the subject pressed a button. In the saccade version there was also only one possible target form, and the subject made a saccade to its location. In the discrimination version, the subjects pressed one button in response to the asterisk, and another to an alternative target. Regardless of the version, and of the overall reaction time values, valid targets are processed faster than invalid ones.

As described before, we see how some process commonly referred to as 'selective attention', modulates the behavioural response in various tasks. What can we say about VSC modulation at the level of the visual cortex? In their classical study, using a very similar VSC paradigm, Mangun and Hillyard (1991) identified a posterior positivity (P1) at a latency of about 100 ms which was larger to valid than to invalid targets. In trial-by-trial cuing then, in addition to the behavioural modulation, we observe a modulation of the brain response similar to the one discussed in the previous section, in relation to the 'streaming' experiments with rapidly presented series of letters. Now we can go one step further and ask whether we can observe brain activity triggered by the cue that is involved in setting the gains. At this point it may be useful to make an a priori conceptual distinction between two subprocesses that can, at least on logical grounds, be expected to embody a possible gain-setting process. One is the analogue to you when you actually turn the balance control to the left or the right. The other is analogous to what happens inside the amplifier: The adjustment of specific resistors in specific electronic circuits, some of them related to the left, and others to the right channel. Let us first turn to the latter, and especially the end result of the balance shift as it exists before a target (or the music) is presented.

Researchers addressing this issue reasoned that if the P1 modulation reflects a strong response in one visual cortex channel, and a weak response in another, then cue-elicited, pre-target activity in these channels might very well exhibit the same pattern. Perhaps the

Figure 3.15

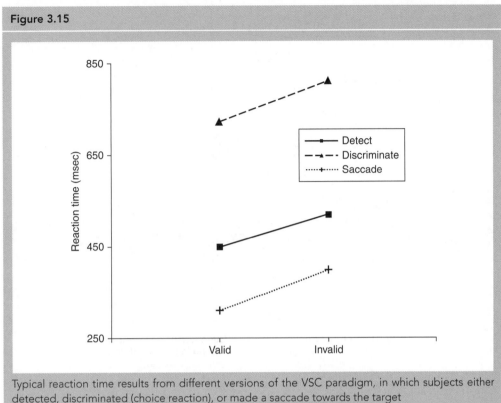

Typical reaction time results from different versions of the VSC paradigm, in which subjects either detected, discriminated (choice reaction), or made a saccade towards the target

Source: van der Lubbe et al. (2006).

most obvious instance of a visual cortex channel is the contralateral response to visual half field stimuli. As we have seen previously, P1 modulation also follows this lateralization. Would such a pattern also be visible before the target is presented, when the system, with its gains adjusted, is anticipating the target? Figure 3.16 presents an fMRI study on this topic by Hopfinger and colleagues (2000). Subjects were instructed that a cue would indicate which visual half field might contain a target (a checkerboard with a few gray checks). In all cases both half fields contained a checkerboard. (Think about this in terms of 'P1 logic': both left and right checkerboards would elicit a contralateral P1, but the P1 contraleral to the attended half field should be bigger.) Figure 3.17 presents the results. As may be expected, the fMRI response to the two checkerboards (targets) is larger contralateral to the cued direction of attention. As to the main question above, consider the fMRI responses to the cue: they basically show the same pattern! Hence, a centrally presented cue that, more or less symbolically, tells the subject which half field to attend to, activates an area in the secondary visual cortex, even before the lateral stimulus that normally evokes such activity has been presented. Returning to our metaphor: this is how the adjusted resistors in specific circuits may look in terms of brain activity. It is a typical example of how a group of neurons that is strongly sensitive to bottom-up (stimulus-driven) activation, can also be activated in a top–down fashion. Such top–down activation has also been described as a biasing mechanism that facilitates the responses of one group of neurons, representing a certain stimulus feature to that feature, over others. Finally, note how the data analysis by Hopfinger and colleagues solves

Figure 3.16

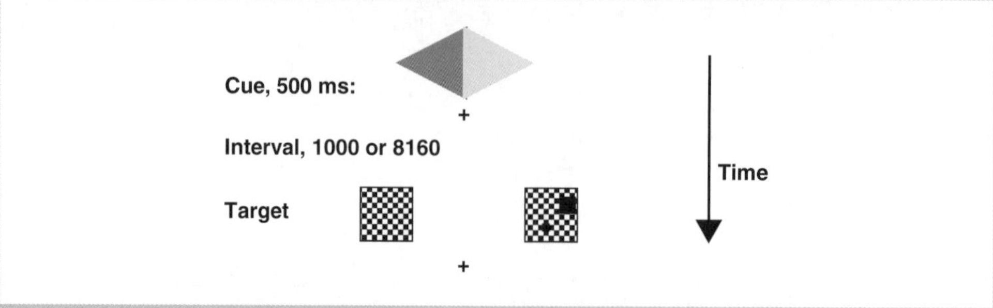

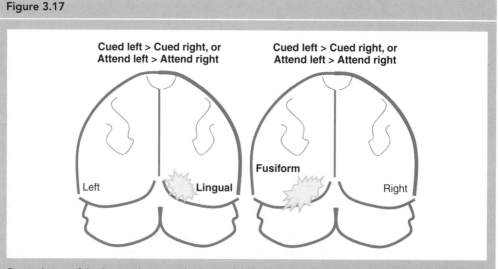

The Hopfinger et al. (2000) paradigm.
The dark part of the cue diamond signalled the to be attended half field. A flashing (4 Hz) subsequent target could contain additional grey checks. Only the long cue–target intervals were used for fMRI analysis.

Figure 3.17

Coronal view of the human brain, at the level of the occipital cortex.
Attend left versus attend right contrasts that yielded significant activations very similar to those for cued left versus cued right contrasts. The lingual gyrus is located medial relative to the fusiform gyrus. After Hopfinger et al. (2000).

the control cue problem: the contrasted cues may be considered equivalent in all respects except that one cues the left and the other the right half field.

Now it is time to go back one step further: the analogue to you when you actually turn the balance control to the left or the right, which we think produces the adjusted gains in the secondary visual cortex. The last decade or so has witnessed a number of studies addressing this question in the context of VSC, using cue-related fMRI responses and more or less adequate control cues (Corbetta & Shulman, 2002). The general pattern of results from these studies is fairly consistent: if we think of a little person in our head that adjusts the gains, then he resides in parts of the frontal and parietal cortex. Specifically, cue-related activity presumably implementing such 'attentional control' is commonly observed in and around the intra-parietal sulcus (IPS), and in or in the immediate vicinity of the frontal eye fields (FEF), located in the dorsal part of the precentral gyrus as well as in the middle frontal gyrus anterior to it (premotor cortex) (Darby et al., 1996). Figure 3.18 provides an overview of these areas. In addition to FEF and IPS there is also cue-related activity in typical secondary visual areas that we know as the target site for top–down activation and attentional biasing and modulation, as discussed above. According to Corbetta and Shulman these areas show a more transient response, as opposed to the more sustained nature of the FEF and IPS responses; this transient nature would be more compatible with an interpretation in terms of bottom-up, stimulus-driven activity, rather than of attentional control (Corbetta & Shulman, 2002).

Knowing *where* neurons are that implement attentional control, is not the same as knowing how they do it. Perhaps neurons in FEF and IPS signal to each other? In that case, cue-elicited activity in one area may precede activity in the other. Over the last 15 years many ERP studies have been devoted to cue-elicited activity related to attentional control, and perhaps the results of these studies can be used to address this issue. Following the paradigm first proposed by Harter and colleagues (Harter et al., 1989; Hopf & Mangun, 2000), van der Lubbe and colleagues (2006) reported a sequence of cue-elicited ERP components, using a logic of analysis that selectively reveals activity that is greater contra- than ipsilaterally to the cued visual field (pooled over left versus right cues). Let us examine this study in greater detail. Specifically, for each time point and pair of homologous electrodes (e.g. F3 [left hemisphere] and F4 [right hemisphere], C3 and C4, P3 and P4, and so on), the double subtraction (Left Cue(E_{right} minus E_{left}) minus Right Cue(E_{right} minus E_{left})) was made, where E_{right} and E_{left} refer to right and left hemisphere electrodes, respectively. This double subtraction yields the difference between contra- and ipsilateral activity, relative to the cued half field, averaged over left and right cues. Note that this subtraction logic is equivalent to the one used to derive the LRP, as discussed in Chapter 2.

Figure 3.18

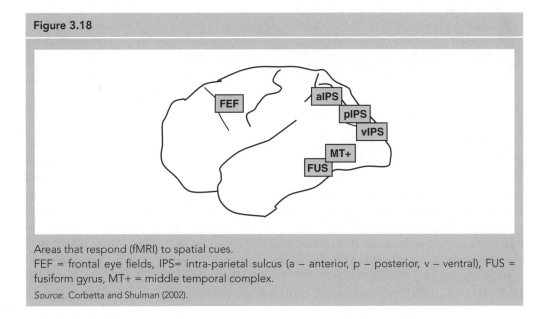

Areas that respond (fMRI) to spatial cues.
FEF = frontal eye fields, IPS= intra-parietal sulcus (a – anterior, p – posterior, v – ventral), FUS = fusiform gyrus, MT+ = middle temporal complex.
Source: Corbetta and Shulman (2002).

Figure 3.19

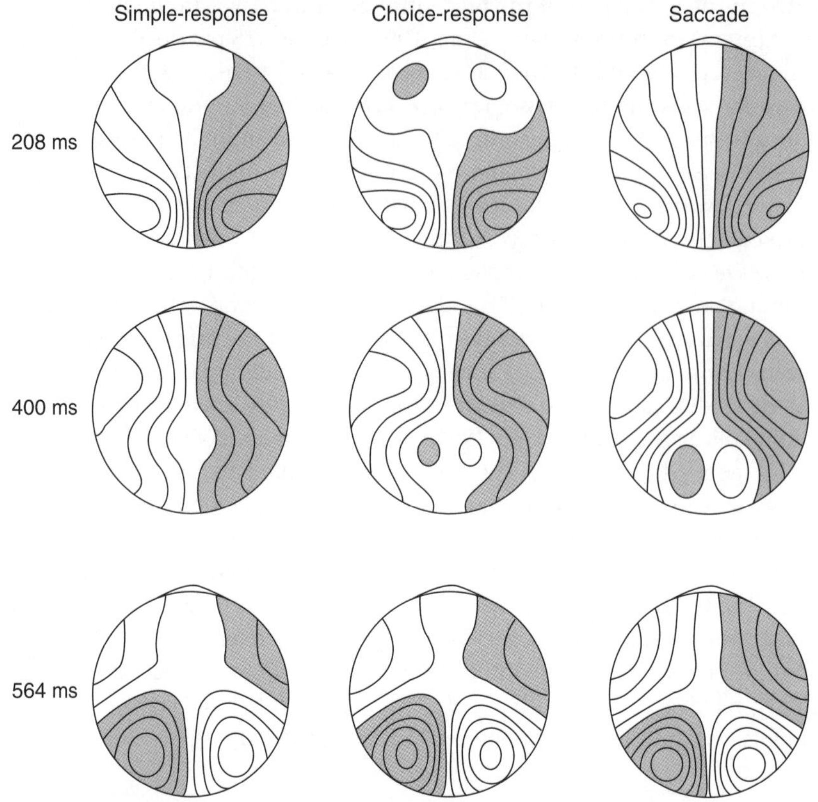

Scalp topographies of cue-direction-sensitive difference (contralateral minus ipsilateral) potentials, at successive latencies (208 ms EDAN; 400 ms ADAN; 564 ms LDAP) relative to cue onset.
Radial top view, front of the head is up. Isopotential line spacing is 0.1 μV. The artificial symmetry is inherent to the subtraction technique (see text).

Source: Reprinted from Van der Lubbe et al. (2006) with permission from Elsevier.

The resulting difference potentials are shown in Figure 3.19 for different tasks in relation to the targets that followed the cue–target interval (see explanation in relation to Figure 3.15). In each task, the typical sequence of activations that has by now been reported many times is visible. It consists of a posterior negativity at about 200 ms latency commonly termed EDAN (early directing attention negativity) (Harter & Anllo-Vento, 1991), an anterior negativity around 400 ms latency (ADAN, anterior directing attention negativity), and a posterior positivity (LDAP, late directing attention positivity). Figure 3.20 shows an equivalent dipole model for this sequence of scalp distributions, seeded by fMRI coordinates representing FEF and ventral IPS. The right panels show the time courses, relative to cue onset of the activity in the two cortical areas. IPS appears to activate first, followed

Figure 3.20

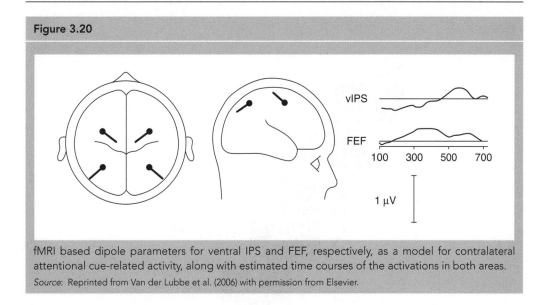

fMRI based dipole parameters for ventral IPS and FEF, respectively, as a model for contralateral attentional cue-related activity, along with estimated time courses of the activations in both areas.
Source: Reprinted from Van der Lubbe et al. (2006) with permission from Elsevier.

by FEF, and again by a polarity reversal in IPS activity, corresponding to respectively EDAN, ADAN and LDAP.

This pattern of results might be taken to suggest that attentional control originates in IPS, then involves a signal to FEF, and finally back to IPS. However, the interpretation of EDAN as a true component of attentional control has been questioned on good grounds. Van Velzen and Eimer argued that EDAN does not so much reflect directing attention, but rather the detection of relevant information (like the attentional cue) to the left or the right of fixation (van Velzen & Eimer, 2003). For example, in Figure 3.16, the relevant part of the diamond is to the left of the fixation cross. When van Velzen and Eimer presented the relevant part (i.e. the right pointing arrow) to the right of fixation, while it still signalled that attention be directed to the left visual half field, EDAN reversed polarity, consistent with the idea that it is related to the location of relevant information, rather than to attentional control. As such, EDAN could be an instance of the, so-called, N2pc (Luck & Hillyard, 1994). The N2pc is a negativity with a maximum over the hemisphere that is contralateral to the visual half field that contains a task-relevant target among distracters. It is thought to reflect the process of directing attention to a stimulus that is already there.

Although ERP studies have revealed mechanisms of adjusting the gains, we have thus far not seen an ERP correlate of the adjusted gain itself, or the bias, as it was previously termed. Recently, Grent-'t-Jong and Woldorff (2007) used yet another variety of the visual–spatial cue–target paradigm. As illustrated in Figure 3.21, letter cues that indicated the direction of attention (or not) preceded subsequent targets for detection by 900 ms or 1900 ms. Over the last second or so of the 1900 ms cue–target interval a prolonged negativity that was maximal over the hemisphere contralateral to the cued visual half field was observed. Because this activity increased gradually up to, or even beyond, the moment of target onset, and because its scalp distribution was very similar to the one observed for the post-target attentional modulation, it was termed biasing related negativity (BRN): the adjusted gain proper.

Figure 3.21

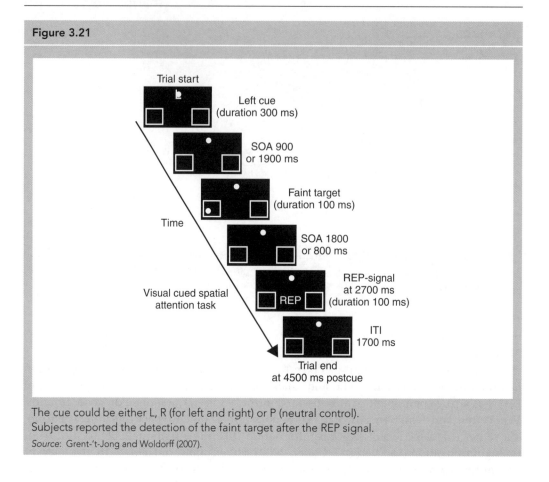

Trial start

Left cue
(duration 300 ms)

SOA 900
or 1900 ms

Faint target
(duration 100 ms)

Time

SOA 1800
or 800 ms

REP-signal
at 2700 ms
(duration 100 ms)

Visual cued spatial
attention task

REP

ITI
1700 ms

Trial end
at 4500 ms postcue

The cue could be either L, R (for left and right) or P (neutral control).
Subjects reported the detection of the faint target after the REP signal.
Source: Grent-'t-Jong and Woldorff (2007).

A further interesting aspect of the Grent-'t-Jong and Woldorff study concerns the issue of lateralization. Remember that EDAN, ADAN, LDAP (as well as BRN) all refer to activity in the (contra-) lateral part of the attentional cue. In the fMRI studies discussed before, similar lateralization was observed for the cue-related FEF and IPS activation, but also a substantial activation ipsilateral to the cued half field (Corbetta et al., 2002). Similarly, Grent-'t-Jong and Woldorff looked primarily at the difference between left and right cues on the one hand, and neutral cues on the other (see Figure 3.21). In other words, they focussed on the non-lateralized part. Also, the specific nature of their cue stimuli may have reduced the possibility of observing EDAN-like activity. The results of this procedure are shown in Plate VIII. ERP difference waveforms (average of (L, R) minus neutral) revealed a leading frontal negativity, followed by a parietal one (Plate VIII A). Furthermore, an otherwise identical fMRI version had revealed activations in the medial frontal and parietal areas, although not with major foci in FEF and IPS. Using the fMRI coordinates to seed the dipole model for the time-varying ERP scalp distribution yielded a very good fit, as well as source time courses that again featured a leading frontal, followed by a parietal signal (Plate VIII B).

In summary, attentional control during VSC appears to be implemented as partially lateralized signalling between medial frontal and parietal areas, with frontal areas taking the lead, and resulting in biased activity over the secondary visual cortex.

Box 3.5   Covert spatial attention and the suppression of overt saccades

Another conspicuous feature is that the frontal–parietal activity observed during the anticipation of a to be detected or discriminated target, is quite similar to the activity observed when the target signals the target location for an eye movement. In other words, when subjects prepare (but suppress up until target presentation) an eye movement to the most likely location, the same brain mechanisms become active as when they covertly direct their attention to that location. At first sight this seems significant support for the premotor theory of selective attention, which essentially asserts that directing spatial attention to a certain location is equal to preparing an eye movement to that location (Rizzolatti et al., 1987) (recall also the discussion about feedback signals from FEF to the visual cortex in Chapter 2). However, on closer examination things may be different. Van der Lubbe and colleagues, in their previously discussed study, conducted a second experiment in which the cues told subjects the direction of a saccade; subjects had to make this saccade after an estimated delay of about a second, without any specific target. The cue elicited ADAN and LDAP, but these components were not observed preceding the voluntary saccades. Instead, a positivity was observed, with a topography and underlying source model very similar to ADAN (van der Lubbe et al., 2006). One interpretation is that this is a FEF-generated saccadic 'go' signal, and that ADAN, with its reverse polarity, actually reflects suppression of a saccade in response to the cue. Spatial attentional and saccadic preparation would then only overlap to the extent that the saccade has to be suppressed in both cases (as with saccades that have to be delayed until after a target, or a self-estimated time period).

Given what we have learned about attentional modulation and control thus far, how does this work for domains other than visual space? Specialized regions are known to exist in the primate visual cortex for the analysis of face-like stimuli (fusiform face area, FFA) as well as for other categories such as spatial orientation (e.g. parahippocampal place area, PPA) (Epstein & Kanwisher, 1998; Kanwisher et al., 1997). The response from these areas to competing stimuli (such as overlapping transparencies of a face and a house) depends strongly on attention. The FFA has been shown to respond more strongly when face information is attended to, whereas the PPA response is stronger when the houses are attended to (O'Craven et al., 1999). We see something similar for simple features like colour and shape, which also activate specific areas in the visual cortex dedicated to the processing of these features. Again, selectively directing attention to one of these features results in modulation of the activity in the area that is specialized for that feature (Corbetta et al., 1991).

With respect to attentional control, recent studies suggest significant overlap between the areas controlling selective attention in space and those involved in controlling non-spatial attention (e.g. to a specific colour). Plate IX shows the results of a comparative analysis of attention to a location and attention to a specific colour. Similar overlap between spatial and colour attentional control was reported by Slagter and colleagues using ERPs (Slagter et al., 2005). It should be noted that, in the Slagter study, the estimated cortical generators were different from the IPS–FEF network discussed above, in that a posterior cortical region was identified located much more ventrally than the IPS. This could be taken as a first indication that the cortical implementation of attention control may not be completely invariant across meta-conditions (although an alternative explanation holds that these differences mainly reflect differences in the reference condition). Another example concerns the dorsolateral prefrontal cortex, which is associated with executive control, and has also been linked to attentional control based on functional neuroimaging research (MacDonald et al., 2000).

Figure 3.22

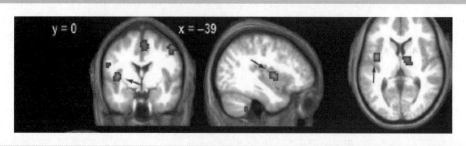

The insular region (indicated by an arrow) responds to physical taste, as well as to the expectation of a taste when it is physically absent (note: z = 6).

Source: Reprinted from Veldhuizen et al. (2007) with permission from Oxford University Press.

These topics will be taken up further in Chapter 6, where we address the interface between selective attention and working memory.

Comparable mechanisms appear to operate in other perceptual modalities, even the more primitive ones. The gustatory cortex is defined as mainly right hemisphere parts of the insula and frontal operculum (Fisher et al., 2002). Activity in these areas is also higher in the absence of taste stimulation, but merely as a consequence of selective attention to the expected occurrence of taste stimuli (relative to when no such occurrence is expected, see Figure 3.22) (Veldhuizen et al., 2007). The same researchers also found that cues instructing taste detection activated the canonical spatial attention network (IPS and FEF), and that activity in the IPS correlated with that associated with taste anticipation in the gustatory cortex. Although cues and taste targets were not separated with respect to activation patterns, these data are consistent with a logic of higher mechanisms biasing activity in lower sensory areas. So, we can speculate about what is actually going on and, based on previous discussions, we can expect IPS–FEF and sensory cortex biasing in response to the cue, and sensory cortex modulation in response to the target.

In summary, the cortical implementation of attentional control takes on identical forms (notably the IPS and FEF) across a wide variety of features, objects, and even perceptual modalities. On the other hand, even subtle changes in task demands may promote the involvement of other cortical areas. The next section addresses a mechanism that triggers attentional control in a much more bottom-up stimulus-driven fashion, and that seems to have a specific anatomical and neurochemical substrate.

3.4   BREAKING THE CIRCUIT: A DEDICATED VENTRAL SYSTEM FOR PROCESSING UNEXPECTED EVENTS

Visual–spatial cuing (VSC) is an interesting paradigm in relation to psychopathology and brain damage, because certain populations and states are associated with abnormal validity effects. Moreover, for other populations, such as people with schizophrenia or ADHD, validity effects seem to be far less robust (Huang-Pollock & Nigg, 2003). A classic result has been found in individuals with damage in the vicinity of the parietal and temporal cortex, who display the symptoms of hemispatial neglect as discussed in the beginning of this chapter.

Figure 3.23 shows that targets presented in the visual half field contralateral to the (unilateral) lesion are detected more slowly than those presented contralateral to the intact hemisphere, especially, or even only, when the target has been cued invalidly (Posner et al., 1984). This applies mainly to right hemisphere damage, and significantly less to left hemisphere lesions. It appears that an intact right hemisphere can help the left hemisphere to process right visual field targets normally, but not vice versa. The abnormal validity effect is also consistent with the clinical symptoms of hemispatial neglect. The failure to initiate action of any kind with regard to events in the hemifield contralateral to the parietal–temporal lesion, is much more prominent with right- than with left hemisphere damage.

Posner and colleagues (1984) interpreted their results as indicating that the contralateral damage resulted in an incapacity to disengage attention from the cued location. This disengagement is presumed to be followed by a movement of attention to, and a subsequent engagement with, the location of the incorrectly cued target. Stated differently, a cue induces a shift of spatial attention from the fixation point to the cued location, where attention is subsequently engaged. A subsequent target at the uncued location induces the same processes, but now they are preceded by a special disengagement operation, to uncouple attention from the cued location. It is this disengagement mechanism that was thought to be specifically impaired in hemineglect patients.

It has been argued that the assumption of a separate disengagement mechanism is not necessary on logical and computational grounds. Specifically, Cohen and colleagues (Cohen et al., 1994) constructed a computational model of spatial attentional control and modulation, using only a bias principle (bias being induced by the cue), as well as bottom-up activation by validly and invalidly cued targets. The bias mechanism was implemented as two or more attentional modules (e.g. left hemisphere/right visual field and right hemisphere/ left visual field) that were mutually inhibitory and amplified the corresponding bottom-up activations by reciprocal excitatory connections between the bottom-up pathway and the

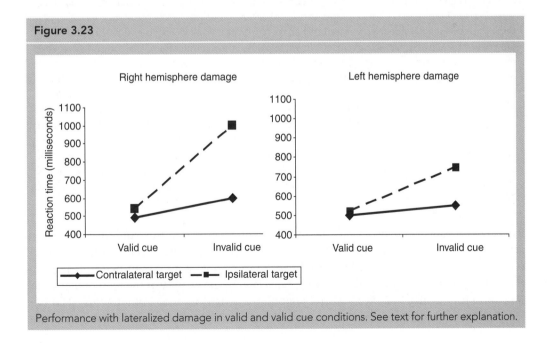

Figure 3.23

Performance with lateralized damage in valid and valid cue conditions. See text for further explanation.

corresponding attentional module. Destruction of a specific attentional module (e.g. the right hemisphere) produced a pattern of reaction times as in Figure 3.23, consistent with the idea of a dedicated disengagement mechanism. However, such a dedicated mechanism was not explicitly incorporated in the model, and the observed pattern of reaction time results can be considered as reflecting an emergent property of a system for which only cue-elicited bias and target-evoked bottom-up activation were assumed.

There are, however, a number of empirical findings that suggest strongly that some special mechanism handles the processing of invalidly cued target stimuli. This need not be a disengagement mechanism, as described above, but could be viewed as a more general system for the prioritized processing of novel, unexpected, or otherwise intrinsically salient events (like a target stimulus unexpectedly appearing outside the focus of attention). As to the exact nature of validity costs, neuroimaging and ERP studies have provided strong evidence for a dedicated circuit breaker system that breaks into the current attentional settings and captures attentional control whenever there is an event outside the focus of attention that has sufficient potential biological relevance (Corbetta & Shulman, 2002). Stated differently, there seems to be a specialized network for the processing of (external) events that are not anticipated within the current context but are nevertheless relevant to adaptive behaviour in a more general sense. This is because they contain relatively novel, but potentially relevant information. Consider driving a car in smooth traffic, until suddenly brake lights flash up ahead, or a child jumps onto the road from behind a parked car.

Box 3.6   Disengagement in depression

Increased validity effects, similar to those observed for patients with parietal–temporal damage, have been observed in relation to negative emotion. In a nonclinical sample, larger validity affects were observed for individuals with a relatively large increase in negative affect in response to a distressing film (Compton, 2000). Recently, Jongen and colleagues reported a positive correlation in bipolar patients between the depth of depression (as assessed by a depression inventory scale) and the size of the validity affect (Jongen et al., 2007). More specifically, this correlation was also present when the validity affect was computed as the contrast between invalid and neutral, reflecting the costs of an invalid cue. It was absent however, when the validity affect was computed as valid minus neutral, reflecting the benefits of a valid cue. This is particularly strong evidence for a specific deficit in disengagement. The disengagement deficit might underlie an apparently specific, mood-congruent attentional bias. The latter is observed when subjects are presented with two words, for instance one to the left and one to the right. One of the words is negatively affective (e.g. death), the other positive or neutral. A second or so after the words are presented, a dot is presented at either the negative or the positive/neutral location, which has to be detected as rapidly as possible. It turns out that depressed individuals have a stronger tendency for better detection at the negative, relative to the positive/neutral location, than controls do (Mathews & MacLeod, 2005; Mogg & Bradley, 2005). Again, this *could* reflect a failure of disengagement of attention from a location that contained mood-congruent information.

Based on an extensive review Corbetta and Shulman suggest that this kind of salient event activates a circuit breaker that *overrules* the settings of the attentional–control network (Corbetta & Shulman, 2002). The circuit breaker is a predominantly right hemisphere function, based in the temporal–parietal cortex, especially in the vicinity of the temporal–parietal junction (TPJ), acting in concert with a region in the right inferior frontal gyrus (IFG) (see Figure 3.24). A similar combination of cortical regions has been proposed previously as the

Figure 3.24

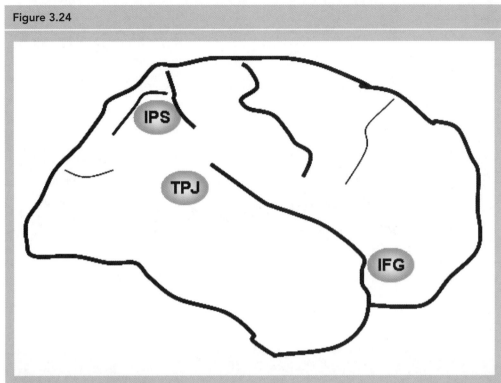

The putative circuit breaker network.
It consists of neurons in the right temporal–parietal junction (TPJ), together with neurons in the inferior frontal gyrus (IFG). Neurons in the IPS (intra-parietal sulcus) would belong to the dorsal attentional–control network, which could be triggered by the circuit breaker.

'vigilance network' (Posner & Petersen, 1990). The vigilance network was presumed to deal with highly infrequent target stimuli; even though they were relevant to a task, the rareness of the occasions on which they appeared could make it difficult for the dorsal attentional–control system to maintain the settings that favoured the processing of these rare target stimuli.

Figure 3.25 shows how areas respond more strongly to invalid than to valid VSC targets (Corbetta et al., 2002). As for the preceding cues, IPS and FEF are activated more strongly by invalid cues, consistent with the idea that attention has to be (re)directed after an invalid target. In addition to the cue-related activation, we also see activation in TPJ and IFG, consistent with the idea that an invalidly cued target activates a special dedicated system, the circuit breaker. The next logical step would be to show that activation of the dorsal IPS–FEF control network depends on, or is at least preceded by, activation in the ventral TPJ–IFG network. ERP study comparisons between invalidly and validly cued targets have also revealed activation that seems to be larger for the former than for the latter. Remember that Mangun and Hillyard (1991) found larger P1s to validly, relative to invalidly, cued targets. However, in that same study, a later positivity (termed late positive deflection or LPD), was actually larger for invalid than for valid targets. This then could be the ERP signature of a special reaction to an (unexpected) invalidly cued target, originating from a system dedicated to breaking the

Figure 3.25

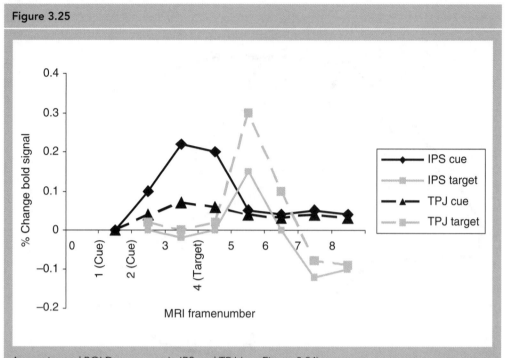

Approximated BOLD responses in IPS and TPJ (see Figure 3.24).
On IPS cue and TPJ cue trials there are no subsequent targets. TPJ target responses are especially strong for invalid, relative to valid, targets (this difference is not shown). MRI frames last about 2.5 seconds.

circuit of the current attentional settings. It remains to be seen whether this circuit breaker response is actually followed in time by something that reflects re-activation of the dorsal attentional–control system. One possible candidate here is the N2pc component discussed earlier in this chapter, which is thought to reflect the parietal attention-directing response to a just-detected, task-relevant stimulus (Luck & Hillyard, 1994).

The idea of a separate disengagement/circuit breaker mechanism may find some support in pharmacological research. According to Corbetta and Shulman, the TPJ–IFG network depends on noradrenergic transmission, whereas the IPS–FEF attentional–control system involves more cholinergic mechanisms (Corbetta & Shulman, 2002). These specific links were inspired mainly by animal research, using tasks in which top–down attentional control and circuit breaking are not easy to distinguish. Attentional control in particular may work quite differently in humans compared to animals such as rodents (Dalley et al., 2001). The scarce relevant evidence in humans supports some kind of dissociation between the two neurotransmitter systems on the one hand, and the two attention systems on the other. Clonidine is a noradrenergic agonist that mainly binds to pre-synaptic autoreceptors (Grilly, 2006), and therefore effectively antagonizes noradrenergic transmission. Like any other norepinephrine (NE) blocker, it generally slows down cognitive processes, resulting in generally longer reaction times (sedation). In two studies, clonidine has been found to reduce the validity effect (Clark et al., 1989; Coull et al., 2001). Additionally, in the Coull et al. study, clonidine also reduced parietal cortex activation specifically related to the processing of attention-directing cues. Nicotine is an acetylcholine (ACh) nicotine receptor agonist, mimicking the effects of acetylcholine itself which, like NE agonism, generally speeds up cognitive processes and reaction times (stimulation). One study has reported reduced validity effects due to nicotine (Witte et al., 1997). A similar effect has been reported for the stimulant methylphenidate (ritalin) (Nigg et al., 1997)). Thus, substances with stimulant effects on general information processing reduce the validity effect, while substances with generally sedating effects do the same. This apparent paradox can be resolved if we accept the dual process account of the validity effect, the two processes being attentional control (producing the bias) and circuit breaking (disengagement). From this viewpoint, clonidine (NE reduction) mainly reduces bias, thereby reducing the validity effect; nicotine (ACh enhancement) mainly facilitates circuit breaking, thereby reducing the validity effect. This would still be a double dissociation, but in a completely opposite direction to the one suggested by Corbetta and Shulman (2002). Consistent with the disengagement explanation for nicotine, early Alzheimer patients, with a cholinergic deficit, exhibit greater validity effects (Parasuraman et al., 1992).

It has been suggested that norepinephrenic or cholinergic medication could be useful in the treatment of hemispatial neglect (Parton et al., 2004). It is conceivable that the efficacy of such medication depends on exactly which anatomical–pharmacological mechanism is disturbed; is it more the parietally based biasing system (norepinephrine?) or more the temporally based disengagement system (acetylcholine?)? These matters are further complicated when we consider that any circuit breaker activation could trigger the attentional–control system, and a failure to orient may be due to disturbances in either phase. Such ambiguities may also underlie the repeated shifting of ideas about the exact anatomical location of the damage thought to be crucial for hemispatial neglect. The original candidate was the parietal cortex, perhaps even the superior region (that is, dorsal to the IPS) (Posner et al., 1984). In more recent years, it has been suggested that the crucial region is located in the supratemporal gyrus (Karnath et al., 2001); even more recently, the focus has shifted back to the posterior located angular gyrus (in between IPS and TPJ) (Mort et al., 2003). These inconsistencies may be due, at least partly, to the fact that behavioural impairments reflect one of a number of underlying mechanisms, each of which is based in different brain areas.

3.5 CONCLUSION

This chapter discusses how one and the same stimulus may be processed differently due to a top–down modulation generally referred to as attentional. This may even take the form of complete suppression of conscious perception of an otherwise perfectly perceivable event, if attentional bias away from it is strong enough. These modulations take place mainly in secondary sensory cortices and are due to biasing signals to these areas from other cortical areas involved in attentional control, most notably the dorsal IPS–FEF system. In turn, attentional–control operations can be triggered by more bottom-up mechanisms, one of them being the circuit breaker TPJ–IFG system that responds to potential biological relevance of novel, unexpected events. Other, somewhat analogous trigger systems will be discussed in later chapters covering emotion and attention. The IPS–FEF and the TPJ–IFG systems may be dissociable along the cholinergic/noradrenergic neurotransmission dimension, but the precise direction is unclear as yet. Patients failing to act on or orient to anything in a relatively lateral part of extra-personal space may have problems in either or both of these systems.

Questions

1. See Section 3.2, in relation to Figure 3.11. How do the results of the Woldorff & Hillyard study (1991) square with Lavie's 'load theory of attention', in light of the particulars of their experimental set-up?

2. See Section 3.2, Plate VII and related text. It is argued that, depending on exact stimulus characteristics, P1 scalp distributions may sometimes have an ipsilateral maximum (this depends on the orientation of the contralateral equivalent dipoles, see Chapter 1), but that this does not affect the spatial-correspondence principle. Explain the spatial-correspondence principle and provide arguments as to why it is not affected by the ipsilaterality of P1 scalp distribution.

3. Compare Figures 3.11 and 3.12. The global suggestion is that attentional modulation occurs earlier in the auditory than in the visual system. Why would this be the case? Think about the idea that the visual system is organized much more in terms of parallel processing compared to the more serial auditory system. Evaluate this idea and its possible implications for the issue of early versus late selection in auditory and visual cortices.

4. Consider the paradigm (Section 3.2) in which subjects are instructed to attend to one category of information (e.g. everything in the left visual half field), and ignore other categories. In Section 3.3, the question is raised whether subjects could do this by increasing the gain in one channel, and/or lowering it in others, before the information is actually presented. Please reason whether there could be alternative methods for such gain modulation.

5. Figure 3.17 and related text: Discuss the cued left versus cued right fMRI activations in terms of the principles of stimulus correspondence and spatial correspondence as discussed in Section 3.2.

6. In Figure 3.21, behavioural responses to targets in the cue–target set-up had to be delayed until after the representation of the REP (report) stimulus. What would have been the rationale for the delay? Try to reason in terms of the quest for an adequate control cue condition.

4 ATTENTION AND ACTION

Key Points

- Neural populations specifically dedicated to motor preparation can be selectively activated (biased) in anticipation of eventual imperative signals for overt responding. These anticipatory activations depend on intentional control signals from dorsal–prefrontal and parietal areas that resemble those that implement attentional control, although differences exist at a more detailed level.
- Overruling an existing motor set (motor circuit breaking) involves left hemisphere regions in parietal and lateral frontal cortices, and depends at least partly on dopaminergic transmission.
- Difficulties in selecting a specific motor set, resulting in the activation of conflicting response tendencies, even to the extent of erroneous behavioural output, activate a medially located region in the anterior cingulate cortex. How this activation is related to the various controlling mechanisms is something that still has to be worked out.
- A network involving the right hemisphere inferior frontal gyrus is crucial for inhibiting ongoing actions, a mechanism that is disturbed in numerous pathologies.

4.0 INTRODUCTION

Q.E. was a healthy man in his thirties without any history of pathological or illegal behaviour. One day while driving his car, he approached a junction, completely ignored the red traffic light, and bumped into another car that was crossing. Casualties were only mild, but there was substantial material damage. Q.E., being a psychologist himself, related what had happened in a rather detailed manner: 'I had to go the city of A. On the radio they'd said that there was a jam on the freeway to A, so I took the old road. As I approached this junction, I noticed that the red light was on and realized (at least for a brief moment) that I had to stop the car. Then suddenly I noticed a sign saying: "To A (freeway)". I was almost completely sure that the old road to A ran straight on, but there was no sign to confirm that... next thing I know I crashed into this car.'

Although there is no way of finding out whether this a valid description of the chain of events in Q.E.'s brain, the case illustrates important points. Staying focussed on a certain subgoal (stopping the car) is essential to governing your behaviour in such way that you achieve your global goal (a safe ride to A). This focussing is often associated with attention, and may very well involve a temporary representation of priorities (in this case, stopping the car rather then driving). However, this representation is vulnerable and may be interfered with by other information if the latter is sufficiently salient or potentially relevant (e.g. a cue where to go for A). To the extent that the temporary representation involves a kind of limited capacity memory buffer, these matters will be discussed in Chapter 6. The present chapter addresses primarily the way in which attentional selection processes control motor output (e.g. to go or not to go).

The interaction between attention and action may also concern the competition between two or more incompatible response options. Consider, for example, the classic Stroop task (Plate X) (MacLeod, 1991; Stroop, 1935). In Stroop's second experiment, 100 subjects each received two card versions for colour naming, one with incongruent colour words, and one with neutral colour patches. The time it took to name 100 colours was recorded and the results are depicted in Figure 4.1. The average difference between incongruent and neutral was 47 seconds, a highly significant effect that has since been replicated hundreds of times (see MacLeod, 1991). Stroop interpreted this result in terms of interference by the tendency to read the word with the colour naming task, this tendency being due to 'a difference in training' leading to a situation in which 'associations between the word stimulus and the reading response are ... more effective than those that have been formed between the colour stimuli and the naming response.' (Stroop, 1935, p. 660).

The original formulation by Stroop strongly hints at the coupling between certain kinds of perceptual information (colour, word) and certain kinds of response representations (name, read). Due to lifelong training, the coupling between specific words and specific reading responses is relatively strong, at least compared to the coupling between specific colours and specific naming responses. Task context however demands that the latter be strengthened and/or the former weakened, something that is commonly accomplished by human subjects, as they may be slower in incongruent than in neutral conditions, but nevertheless produce correct responses for the vast majority of incongruent items. What kind of mechanism

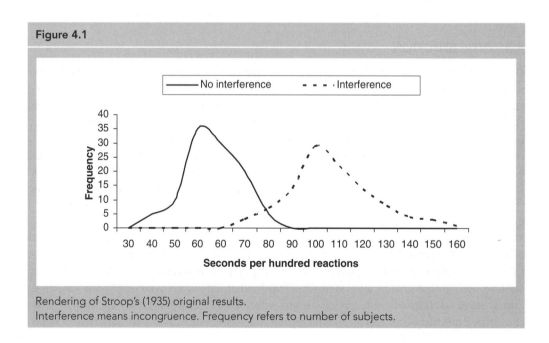

Figure 4.1

Rendering of Stroop's (1935) original results.
Interference means incongruence. Frequency refers to number of subjects.

could account for these adjusted couplings? Is adjusting couplings somehow similar to setting the gains, as discussed in the previous chapter, in relation to the mechanism of attentional control?

This chapter addresses the question of attentional control in relation to action, also termed intentional control. Is intentional control different from attentional control, and can action capture attentional or intentional control? We start off with a discussion of how attentional mechanisms that control covert attention (see Section 3.3) compare with those controlling actions. Other issues concern the possibility that control systems monitor the competition between different action tendencies (Section 4.3), and the notion that there are dedicated inhibition mechanisms that specifically suppress ongoing actions in response to changing, or otherwise difficult, task demands (Section 4.4). Referring to the story of Q.E., a monitoring system could sharpen intentional control for similar future events, and dedicated inhibition is instrumental when the red traffic light is recognized just in time after the temporary distraction.

Box 4.1   Attention deficit implies deficit in adjusting stimulus–response coupling?

Is adjusting couplings between colours or words and responses in the Stroop task somehow similar to setting the gains, as discussed in the previous chapter, in relation to the mechanism of attentional control? If some kind of attention plays a role here, then Stroop interference (the difference in performance between incongruent and neutral conditions) should be enhanced in individuals with attention deficit, as in ADHD. Indeed, although this a rather complicated field in itself, recent meta-analyses confirmed robust increases in Stroop interference across ADHD groups, relative to control groups (Lansbergen et al., 2007b). This chapter will discuss a number of issues regarding ADHD and the underlying brain mechanisms.

4.1   INTENTIONAL MODULATION AND CONTROL: THE ROLE OF NEURONS IN PARIETAL AND FRONTAL CORTICES

4.1.1   Greasing the motor pathway

Let us continue the logic from the previous chapter: can attention be directed to a motor response in a similar way as the bias in sensory areas? Part of the answer has been given in Section 2.1, where we saw motor and premotor activity that preceded overt motor responses, or occurred even without any succeeding overt action, in monkeys as well as in humans. In fact, one of the very first papers using the lateralized readiness potential (LRP) (De Jong et al., 1988) visualized such motor bias in a straightforward manner. Consider the visual–spatial cuing paradigm (VSC) as discussed in the previous chapter. Already in the original description of this paradigm (Posner et al., 1980), a variety was introduced in which the cue not only signalled the most likely location of the target, but also the most likely response (e.g. left hand over right hand), since the task demanded that the response be dictated by the target location. Now remove the visual–spatial component: targets will only appear at fixation, and the preceding cue tells the subject which of two (or more) targets is most likely to appear, and therefore which response (e.g. left or right hand) is the most likely to be required. In Section 3.3 we noted that the double subtraction technique to uncover bias-related activity in the visual cortex was formally equivalent to the calculation of the LRP. Using the LRP, De Jong and colleagues (1988) demonstrated significant selective activation of the motor cortex contralateral to the cued responses, in response to

Figure 4.2

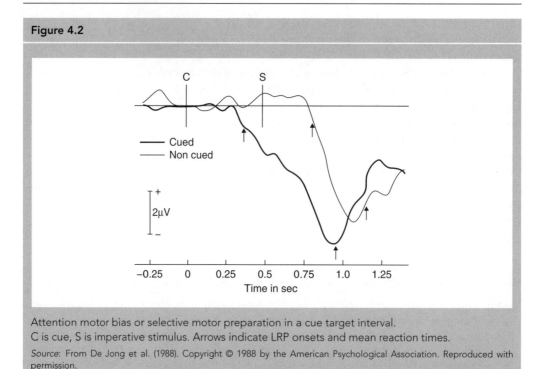

Attention motor bias or selective motor preparation in a cue target interval.
C is cue, S is imperative stimulus. Arrows indicate LRP onsets and mean reaction times.

Source: From De Jong et al. (1988). Copyright © 1988 by the American Psychological Association. Reproduced with permission.

the cue, and well before the target that signals that the eventual overt response should be issued (see Figure 4.2). Note that this kind of attentional motor bias is actually seldom sold under this heading, and the usual terminology is often something like selective motor preparation. It may be that such terminological distinctions become meaningless in the face of neural substrates.

One could argue that there is a logical distinction between sensory bias and motor bias: the former concerns a specific feature (e.g. spatial), but does not inform about shape, colour, etc., whereas the latter specifies the complete response. However, this is not a logical necessity as is shown, for example, in experiments in which subjects are pre-cued with respect to the hand to be used, whereas information on which finger to use is provided only by a subsequent event. Miller (1982) reported a reaction time experiment with the following mapping of stimuli on response alternatives:

(Miller paradigm)				
Response hand:	Left		Right	
Response finger:	Middle	Index	Index	Middle
Stimuli condition 1	S	S	T	T
Stimuli condition 2	S	T	S	T
Stimuli condition 3	S	T	T	T

He found first that reaction times (RTs) in condition 1 were faster than in conditions 2 and 3; and second, that RTs in conditions 2 and 3 did not differ. To understand this pattern of results, it should first be realized that in this set-up stimuli differed in 2 dimensions: form (S and s vs. T and t) and size (S and T vs. s and t). The dimensions were chosen in such way as to elicit faster discrimination of form than of size; this was verified in a separate experiment. Furthermore, Miller assumed that the motor system is organized in such way that it is possible to prepare a response with one hand without knowing the finger, but not the other way around. In condition 1 the easy dimension (form) determined which hand to respond with, and the hard dimension (size) which finger to use. In condition 2 it was the other way around. Apparently, in condition 1 the early information on which form had been presented could be used to partially prepare the response without complete information on which finger to use. In condition 2, finger information was available earlier than hand information, but could not be used without full hand information; therefore, RTs were slower in condition 2 than in condition 1. This was corroborated by the results in condition 3, in which neither form nor size could be used to prepare a particular hand or a particular finger, as for both full information on the conjunction of form and size was necessary. Nevertheless, RTs in condition 3 equalled those in condition 2; apparently, in condition 2 the finger information, even though it was available relatively early, could only be used in combination with hand information, just as in condition 3.

To Miller these data had a more far-reaching implication. He assumed that at least 2 stages of information processing were involved in this task. One was concerned with identifying the size and the form of the letter stimulus (perceptual stage); the other with preparing the appropriate response based on the size and form of the stimulus (motor stage). In conditions 2 and 3 both dimensions had to be identified before any response preparation could be made; in other words, the perceptual stage had to finish completely before the motor stage could start. In condition 1 however, partial information about the form of the stimulus was transmitted from the perceptual stage to the motor stage, and was used in the latter, before the former had finished; in this way, a benefit in RT was obtained in condition 1. Curiously enough, Miller's interpretation was heavily challenged when his findings were replicated and LRPs were also included (in the same De Jong et al. paper as discussed above). Briefly, partial transmission of form information to the motor system predicts shorter LRP latencies (relative to the onsets of S, s, T, or t) in the hand/name condition than in the other hand conditions, but this was not found.

Intentional modulation of motor cortex activation can be demonstrated. As discussed in Section 2.1, this modulation may proceed independently of the eventual overt behavioural outcome. Exactly how and when intentional modulation occurs is hard to predict from the results of behavioural experiments. In the above example, global hand areas were not activated without information on which finger to use, even though behavioural evidence suggested otherwise.

4.1.2 Setting the motor gains

It has been stated that changing a dominant stimulus–response mapping is associated with activation in a frontal–parietal network (Corbetta & Shulman, 2002), just like typical attentional control (Chapter 3). But what are the exact areas involved, in terms of dorsal–medial frontal versus more lateral prefrontal, or in the left versus the right hemisphere, and can we demonstrate causal links?

The answers to these questions depend on exactly how one looks at these matters, especially with regard to task parameters. Jiang and Kanwisher report a series of experiments in which response–selection demands were manipulated by varying congruence between response options and stimulus features (Jiang & Kanwisher, 2003b). In a first task variety, subjects had to indicate the spatial position of a unique line length using either a compatible (e.g. third key from left for the third line from left) or an incompatible response key (e.g. third key from left for the most left line). A similar logic was maintained in two other task varieties: report the temporal position of a unique auditory tone by pressing a specific key; and report vocally whether two subsequent colours were the same or different (by stating 'same' or 'different', respectively, in the congruent condition, and vice versa in the incongruent condition). For all three tasks, the contrast [incongruent minus congruent] revealed identical, bilateral, activations in parietal (IPS), prefrontal (FEF, as well as middle and inferior frontal gyrus), and cerebellar regions. This suggests a general purpose response–selection mechanism, which becomes particularly evident when human observers use visual or auditory information and must switch from a natural to an unnatural response to that information. The next question is how precisely the observed FEF and IPS regions overlap with the FEF and IPS regions associated with the attentional–control system (see Box 4.2).

Box 4.2   Comparing the coordinates (1)

An informal inquiry as to how identical the FEF/IPS regions associated with attentional and intentional control are can be based on the 3D coordinate systems commonly used in neuroimaging research, such as the Montreal Neurological Institute (MNI) system. Take the typical attentional–control MNI coordinates, as summarized by van der Lubbe et al. (2006; Section 3.3): x = 29, y = −55, z = 50 for vIPS, and x = 30, y = 0, z = 51 for FEF. For the incongruent–congruent contrast from Jiang and Kanwisher's first task variety, averaged across hemispheres, IPS coordinates are 39, −50, 44 (anterior IPS) and 30, −68, 47 (posterior IPS). Thus, the attentional–control region lies a centimetre more medial than the anterior IPS, and more than a centimetre more anterior than the posterior IPS, not strongly suggestive of a common area, however informal this comparison may be. The FEF in Jiang and Kanwisher's study is positioned at MNI 30, 3, 48, which resembles the attentional–control coordinates more closely (30, 0, 51). Thus, a preliminary conclusion would be that the Jiang and Kanwisher response–selection network partly overlaps (FEF region) with the attention–control network. Note also that Jiang and Kanwisher utilized a traditional blocked fMRI paradigm, and did not isolate the brain response to an instruction cue.

In a subsequent study these same authors (Jiang & Kanwisher, 2003a) compared the first and the third response–selection contrasts discussed above to one of perceptual discrimination difficulty. Following the logic of the load theory of attention (see Chapter 3), increasing the difficulty of identifying unique line length, or colour discrimination in the same–different task, should augment the selective attention to these visual attributes, and therefore be associated with stronger top–down control signals. All cortical regions that were activated in the response–selection contrast, also responded to the discrimination–difficulty contrast. However, from this one cannot conclude that the functional anatomy of top–down control is identical for (more perceptual) attentional control and (more action-related) response selection. In fact, the maps in Jiang & Kanwisher (2003a) that illustrate the overlap between attentional and intentional control, as well as the voxels that were activated for each control process, suggest that the number of non-overlapping voxels was actually substantial. Furthermore, it turned out to be difficult to exclude the possibility that all the common effects were in fact general effects of task difficulty.

A different approach was taken by Rushworth and colleagues (Rushworth et al. 2001b). In their response–selection task, a regularly recurring cue stimulus signalled whether the current stimulus–response mapping should be maintained (stay) or reversed (switch). This response–selection switch–stay contrast was compared to that from a visual–selection task, in which the cue signalled that either visual form (or colour) should be continued to be attended to, or that attention should switch to colour (or form). For the IPS, the results are summarized in Plate XI. Visual–selection activation is located lateral, anterior, and ventral, relative to response–selection activation, and more lateral and ventral relative to the IPS proper, compared to the more dorsal and medial IPS activations for response selection.

In conclusion, the cortical implementation of top–down control of attention, versus that of intention, may at first glance look quite similar. However, on closer examination, focussing on activation specifically elicited by cues that prompt a redefinition of stimulus–response mapping, subtle differences in the activated areas become visible, at least in the vicinity of the IPS.

4.2   BREAKING THE MOTOR CIRCUIT

4.2.1   Intentional versus attentional circuit breaking

If intentional modulation exists then we may expect not only mechanisms of attentional motor control, but also a dedicated motor circuit breaking mechanism, analogous to the attention–capture circuit breaker discussed in Section 3.4. Rushworth and colleagues (Rushworth et al., 2001a) compared the effects of disrupting transcranial magnetic stimulation (TMS) over two areas in both hemispheres: the angular gyrus (ANG, at the junction of the superior temporal sulcus and the inferior parietal cortex) and the supramarginal gyrus (SMG, see Figure 4.3). This was done with two tasks. The first was a visual–spatial cuing task as discussed extensively in Section 3.3, including valid and invalid cues. The second was a motor attention task: cues signalled the most likely target stimulus (either slightly above or slightly below fixation), and therefore the most likely response (index finger to one possible target, middle finger to the other). In both tasks, the cue was invalid on 20 per cent of the trials and the TMS was initiated 20 ms after a target. Note that the motor situation can be seen as quite Stroop-like, as the subject gets ready to issue a prepared, and therefore prepotent, response, but has to refrain from it after an invalidly cued target.

In both tasks clear validity effects were observed, although the effect was much larger in the motor attention task: invalid cues resulted in longer reaction times. These validity effects were presumed to correlate inversely with the ability to shift attention or intention in the invalid condition. They interacted with TMS so as to produce a double dissociation (refer back to Box 2.1). Validity effects in the visual–spatial cuing task were augmented by TMS of the right ANG only, whereas validity effects in the motor attention task were augmented by TMS of the left SMG only. These TMS effects are consistent with fMRI activations specific to conditions of invalid visual–spatial cues, as discussed in Section 3.4 (Corbetta et al., 2000). They are also consistent with PET activations as obtained in a motor attention task (Rushworth et al., 2001c) in relation to invalid cues. Together, these data indicate a motor circuit breaking mechanism analogous to the circuit breaking/

Figure 4.3

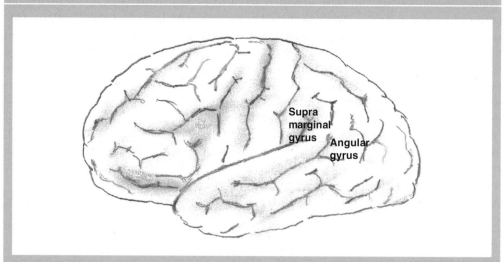

Supra
marginal
gyrus
Angular
gyrus

Breaking the orienting circuit occurs in the right hemisphere analogue of the angular gyrus, BA 37/39, Talairach coordinates 41, −69, 43. Breaking the motor circuit occurs in the left hemisphere supramarginal gyrus, BA 40, Talairach coordinates −52, −36, 56.
Source: From Gazzaniga et al. (2002).

disengagement mechanism described in Section 3.4, with a distinct location in left hemisphere parietal cortex.

A more recent study by Rounis and co-workers (Rounis et al., 2007) found a similar double dissociation with respect to motor versus visual–spatial attention for other cortical regions. Figure 4.4B illustrates there typical spatial–attention task, in which again the validity effect is presumed to correlate inversely with the ability to shift attention in the invalid condition. The validity effect was increased specifically by TMS inhibition of the right posterior parietal cortex (PPC), not by TMS over the left PPC, nor by TMS over the left or right dorsolateral prefrontal cortex (DLPFC, middle frontal gyrus), and especially for left visual targets. Note that this is the pattern of results typically seen for hemi-neglect patients (Chapter 3; Mesulam, 1999a). In contrast, inhibiting the left DLPFC specifically enhanced the motor attention validity effect (Figure 4.4A).

A further question is whether motor circuit breaking involves similar cholinergic mechanisms as the spatial–attention circuit breaker, or whether other neurotransmitters are involved. Remember that (Section 3.4), consistent with the disengagement explanation for nicotine, patients with early Alzheimer's disease (primarily cholinergic deficit) exhibit larger validity effects, reflecting larger Invalid–Neutral differences than Neutral–Valid ones (Parasuraman et al., 1992). In contrast, Parkinson patients (primarily dopaminergic deficit) exhibit smaller validity effects (Wright et al., 1990), exactly like those of dopaminergic antagonists (Clark et al., 1989). In the one study relevant to intentional control, Stillman and colleagues (Stillman et al., 1993) had endogenous cues indicate not only the most probable location of the target, but also the most probable response (e.g. left hand over right hand because the cue location is to the left). They found that acute cocaine resulted not only in an overall reduction of reaction times, but also in a reduced effect of the validity of endogenous spatial cues. Cocaine is characterized by basically the same mechanism of action as amphetamines: it enhances the synaptic availability of dopamine (DA) by blocking pre-synaptic DA reuptake. In terms of motor circuit breaking, this finding suggests that dopaminergic transmission aids in disengaging from a cued response option. The next question is whether this involves transmission in the supramarginal gyrus, or perhaps in more anterior regions, given the higher density of dopaminergic projections in anterior, relative to posterior, cortical areas (e.g. Purves et al., 2001).

In sum, motor circuit breaking (left SMG and/or left DLPFC) can be dissociated from intentional control (IPS–FEF). It can also be dissociated from attentional circuit breaking (R TPJ and R IFG). In Section 4.4 we will discuss additional mechanisms that are involved in more general braking of ongoing motor processes.

Figure 4.4

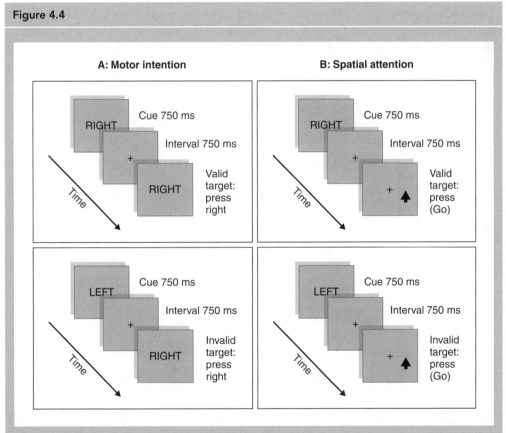

Logic for an experiment to compare aspects of motor intention and of spatial attention.
LEFT responses (A) and left-sided arrows (B) were used in the same amounts, preceded by either LEFT cues (valid) or RIGHT cues (invalid). In B, PRESS targets randomly alternated with NO PRESS (Nogo, downwards arrow) targets. See text for further explanation.
Source: cf. Rounis et al. (2007).

4.2.2 Action grabs attention

In Section 2.4 we discussed how specific action contexts (e.g. pointing versus grasping) triggered activity in specific parts of the visual cortex specialized in providing the information relevant for the particular action. We also noticed that when subjects reach out to grasp an object, they first move their eyes to the location of that object (gaze anchoring). A study by Handy and colleagues suggests that these mechanisms interact with the circuit breaking mechanisms as discussed in 4.2.1. (as well as in 3.4). These researchers demonstrated that the action that is afforded by an object concurs with directing covert attention to the location of that object (Handy et al., 2003). Subjects viewed combinations of two pictures, one a tool (e.g. cup, hammer), the other a non-tool (e.g. an animal). The tool and the non-tool appeared randomly in the left or right, or the upper or lower visual fields. Subjects were to ignore these pictures, but were to press a button in response to a target pattern that, after a 600–650 ms delay, was equally likely to be superposed on either the tool or the non-tool (see Figure 4.5). There was a strong P1 effect: targets over tools elicited (contralateral) P1s that were larger than the P1s to targets over non-tools. (If you do not know what the P1 effect is check Section 3.2).

Which mechanisms could bring about this P1 effect? In a subsequent fMRI experiment, Handy and colleagues found greater activation for tools than for non-tools in premotor areas (BA 6/8) and in, mainly right, inferior parietal cortex (BA 40). Like the P1 effect, this

Figure 4.5

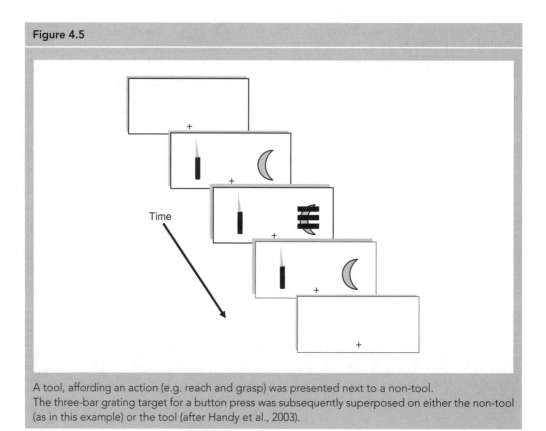

A tool, affording an action (e.g. reach and grasp) was presented next to a non-tool.
The three-bar grating target for a button press was subsequently superposed on either the non-tool (as in this example) or the tool (after Handy et al., 2003).

activation was present only, or was larger, for tools in the right visual field (all participants were right-handed). According to the authors, the parietal activation was '... more inferior and anterior to the parietal regions typically associated with the volitional control of spatial attention' (Handy et al., 2003, p. 425). Combined with the right hemisphere dominance of this inferior parietal activity, this could implicate a contribution of the circuit breaking mechanism as discussed in Section 3.4. The unfolding scenario then is that action affording objects, perhaps mediated by premotor visuomotor neurons (see Section 2.2), trigger a circuit breaking mechanism (in the temporal–parietal junction, Section 3.4) that signals the occurrence of a potentially relevant event outside the current task set. Perhaps supplemented by top–down attentional–control mechanisms, this results in a bias in the sensory cortex representing the location of the tool, which in turn interacts with the target so as to produce attentional modulation visible as a P1 effect. As the authors note, the enhanced processing as reflected in the P1 effect may in turn serve to improve the extraction of information about the object to which a specific action (e.g. grasping, including pre-shaping) is directed. This would be comparable to the saccade facilitation by enhanced signalling from the visual cortex due to feedback signals during the time period in which the saccade is being prepared (see Section 2.4).

4.3   ACTION MONITORING: THE ROLE OF THE ANTERIOR CINGULATE CORTEX

Cognitive neuroscience investigates how cognition is realized by neuro-activity. Sometimes researchers focus on a specific brain region to identify its specific function. This is certainly what has happened to the dorsal anterior cingulate cortex (or gyrus) (dACC) and it makes for an interesting piece of scientific history. This quest was almost exclusively based on correlative data from PET, fMRI and ERP. Older patient data indicated that damage in this region was associated with akinesia, the state of being without movement (Németh et al., 1988). One general picture emerging from the neuroimaging literature is that the dACC lights up in almost any contrast, provided that the stimulus or situation prompts some motor response (e.g. it is hardly seen in response to attentional cues). As most contrasts between experimental conditions involve a contrast in task difficulty, it could be that the dACC lights up whenever things get difficult, in the sense of deciding between one or more response options.

The omnipresence of dACC activation has probably inspired early theories on the function of the anterior cingulate cortex (ACC). Posner and Petersen viewed the ACC as the centre of attentional control, in a more meta-theoretical fashion than discussed in Chapter 3 (Posner & Petersen, 1990). ACC was thought to control other attention systems, like the orienting system and the circuit breaker or vigilance system (see Section 3.4), as well as the biasing of stimulus dimensions and the contents of working memory. These ideas were inspired by ACC activation in Stroop incongruent conditions, verb generation, and sensitivity of orienting to dual-task manipulation. Dual-task manipulation concerns the fact that validity effects could be reduced by loading the attentional–control centre, presumably the ACC, with a second, sufficiently involving, task (Posner et al., 1989). In the verb generation task, subjects generate uses for nouns (e.g. 'strike' in response to 'hammer'), and a simple reading of the noun is used as a control condition. Figure 4.6 depicts the ACC activation emerging from the contrast between the two conditions, in terms of both PET and ERP, at a latency of about 200 ms post-noun (Abdullaev & Posner, 1998; Petersen et al., 1989). This relative activation disappeared with repetitions of the task in which the same nouns were repeated over and over and the same verbs could be used for responses. This

Figure 4.6

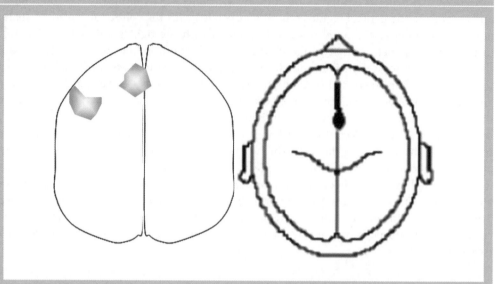

The medial PET activation (left) originates from the ACC, in the contrast verb generation minus read word.

The x, y, z stereotactic coordinates are −6, 24, 38 (Petersen et al., 1989). The ERP dipole source (200 ms post-noun latency) represents an unseeded minimum residual variance estimate (reprinted from Abdullaev & Posner, 1998, with permission from Elsevier). The ACC coordinates in the Stroop contrast were −10, 29, 30 (Pardo et al., 1990). The more left lateral activation originates from the left inferior frontal gyrus (Broca's area).

was interpreted as indicating that the ACC was activated in the face of competing response options (i.e. multiple valid verbs for one noun), a competition that was resolved by the repetition; once the high selection demands had disappeared, ACC was no longer involved. A similar logic was applied to the finding of increased ACC activity with incongruent, relative to congruent, Stroop stimuli (Pardo et al., 1990): incongruent stimuli impose higher selection demands. Note that a similar logic could be applied to the left inferior frontal gyrus activation shown in Figure 4.6; however, at that time, this was related to the semantic aspects of the verb generation task. As we will see in the next section, there are alternative possibilities.

These ideas, and others, about the ACC are summarized in Figure 4.7, from the Gazzaniga et al. textbook (1st ed.) (Gazzaniga et al., 1998; Posner & Raichle, 1994). It contains hypothetical projections from the ACC to control orienting in parietal cortex, as well as the biasing of different visual features and word forms. ACC projections also control the contents of different forms of working memory, the on-line representation of what is relevant and what is not. Now consider Figure 4.8, the analogous figure from later editions (Gazzaniga et al., 2002, 2008). ACC still informs working memory, but now the signals to the posterior areas and their functions, and the controllings from the ACC, have disappeared. Apparently, some hypotheses had been disconfirmed in the meantime. How did this come about? If the ACC is no longer the seat of every form of attentional control, what then is its function? One major inspiration for new insights about the ACC has been a series of studies by Cohen and colleagues, using fMRI.

4.3.1   From attentional control to action monitoring and back

First, event-related fMRI revealed that the ACC was not only activated by to-be-responded to targets, especially when the behavioural response was erroneous, but also when the correct response was improbable (Carter et al., 1998). Second, this latter result was also obtained in Stroop and flanker tasks (Section 2.1) from the contrast incongruent versus congruent, especially when incongruent stimuli were rare at a global level (Carter et al., 2000), or unexpected due to a preceding congruent stimulus (Botvinick et al., 1999). Figure 4.9 summarizes the loci of ACC activations in these studies. The general interpretation of these findings was that the ACC responds to the presence of competing response options, whether resulting in an error or not, rather than showing an activation pattern that would be typical for an attentional–control mechanism.

The distinction between responding to competing response tendencies on the one hand and attentional control on the other, in relation to the ACC, was underlined in particular by the results of a further study (MacDonald et al., 2000). Here, event-related fMRI was used

Figure 4.7

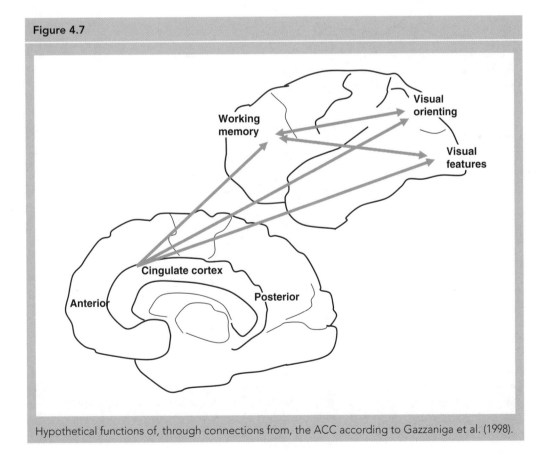

Hypothetical functions of, through connections from, the ACC according to Gazzaniga et al. (1998).

Figure 4.8

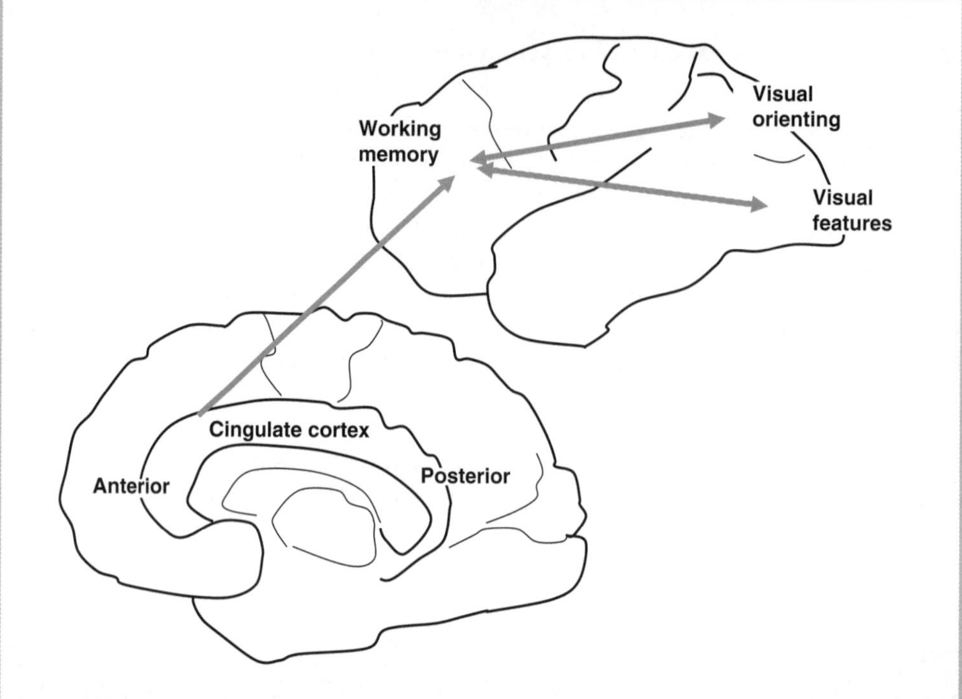

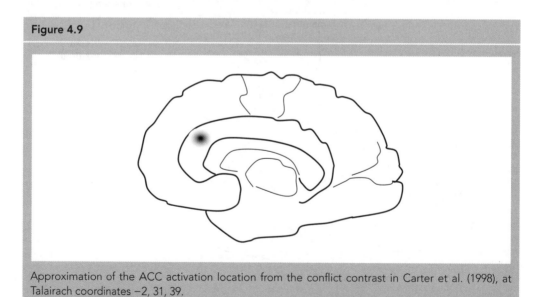

Hypothetical functions of, through connections from, the ACC.
Source: Gazzaniga et al. (2002) and Gazzaniga et al. (2008).

Figure 4.9

Approximation of the ACC activation location from the conflict contrast in Carter et al. (1998), at Talairach coordinates −2, 31, 39.
Analogous coordinates from other relevant studies were 4, 25, 43 (Botvinick et al., 1999) and 0, 15, 41 (Carter et al., 2000).

Figure 4.10

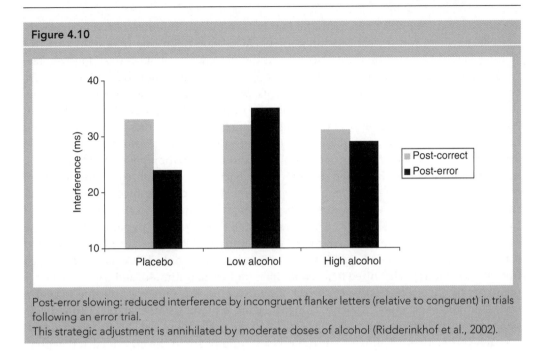

Post-error slowing: reduced interference by incongruent flanker letters (relative to congruent) in trials following an error trial.
This strategic adjustment is annihilated by moderate doses of alcohol (Ridderinkhof et al., 2002).

to separate cue-elicited from target-elicited activations (see Chapter 3). Specifically, cues told subjects to identify either Stroop colour or Stroop word, and targets could be Stroop incongruent or congruent. The ACC responded more to incongruent than to congruent targets, but there was no difference between colour and word instruction cues (colour instructions were assumed to invoke more attentional control; this did activate a part of the dorsolateral prefrontal cortex, a finding that will be discussed further in Chapter 6).

An additional idea is that conflict monitoring in the ACC generates signals to regions that do implement attentional control, at least in Stroop-like conditions, such as the prefrontal cortex (cf. Figures 4.7 and 4.8). One behavioural consequence of these signals would be the post-error (Ridderinkhof et al., 2002), or post-conflict adjustments of behavioural responding (Kerns et al., 2004). Although this is often referred to as post-error slowing, a general slowing of responses after an error has been committed, this general phenomenon turns out to be rather elusive, in that it is often not found (e.g. Jonkman et al., 2007). One factor here is that post-error adjustments are more subtle and manifest as a reduced sensitivity to irrelevant but compulsory information, such as Stroop words or flanker letters. These adjustments result in post-error slowing on congruent trials (less facilitation from the to-be-ignored information), but may also lead to speeded responses on post-error incongruent trials, because of less interference from incongruent words or flankers. An example is presented in Figure 4.10, in which there is significantly reduced flanker interference after an error, relative to after trials with correct responses. Of note, this behavioural adjustment largely disappears after moderate alcohol consumption (see Figure 4.10). This was paralleled by a significant reduction in an electrophysiological index (see below) of ACC-based error processing, consistent with a chain of events in which errors result in signals to and from the ACC, that are subsequently used to reduce the probability of interference and errors.

However appealing this scenario of error, or conflict, monitoring producing a signal to lateral prefrontal attentional–control areas may be, it has thus far been rather difficult to actually demonstrate this sequence of brain events in human volunteers. In one approach, using fMRI, there was a clear relation between ACC activity on one trial, and post-error slowing as well as lateral prefrontal activity on the next (Kerns et al., 2004). However, one would expect that conflict detection during a certain trial would, more or less immediately, be followed by attentional–control adjustments within the time frame of that same trial, so that the adjustment can take effect before the next stimulus appears. Several ERP studies have addressed this issue by examining Stroop effects (incongruent minus congruent or neutral) on the ERP. Indeed, this Stroop ERP generally consists of two major phases, the Stroop negativity at about 400 ms post-stimulus, and a later Stroop positivity at about 700 ms latency. Even better, the Stroop negativity has generally been localized in the vicinity of the ACC. But worse, indications for a lateral prefrontal origin of the subsequent Stroop positivity have been meagre, with most studies pointing to a generator in the posterior half of the head (Lansbergen et al., 2007c; Liotti et al., 2000; West, 2003). This pattern has become especially clear with respect to the Error-Related Negativity (ERN), first described by German (Falkenstein et al., 1991) and American researchers (Gehring et al., 1993). ERNs are derived from average ERPs synchronized to reaction times (rather than stimuli), and consist of a large negativity for incorrect, relative to correct, responses with this difference starting to evolve just before the behavioural response is made. Figure 4.11 shows an example. Using dipole source analysis, Dehaene and colleagues estimated the generator of the ERN to be in the ACC (Dehaene et al., 1994). Figure 4.11 also shows a second phase in the error-related potential, namely a positivity starting after 100 ms post-error, usually termed Pe (van Veen & Carter, 2002). Figure 4.12 shows a typical ERN scalp distribution. Whereas the early ERN has been modelled as originating from the ACC, the Pe appears to originate more from posterior areas,

Figure 4.11

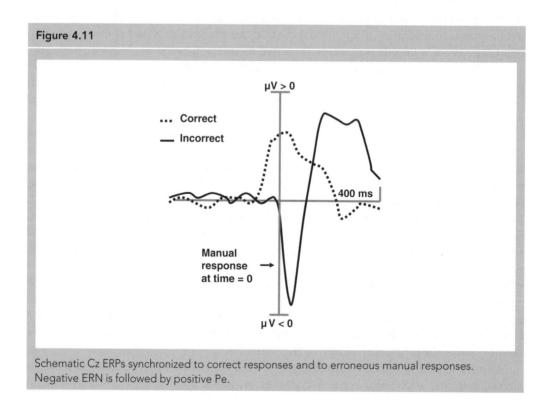

Schematic Cz ERPs synchronized to correct responses and to erroneous manual responses. Negative ERN is followed by positive Pe.

Figure 4.12

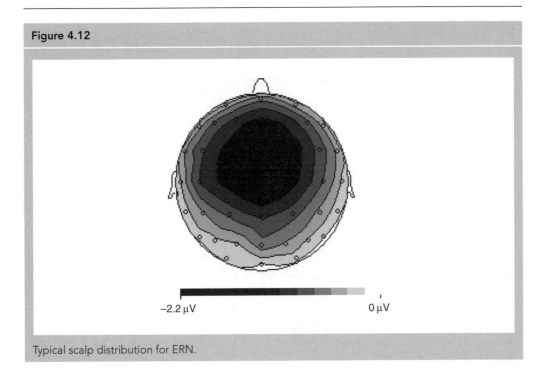

−2.2 µV   0 µV

Typical scalp distribution for ERN.

either in the precuneus, posterior-cingulate gyrus, or the parietal cortex (van Veen & Carter, 2002). In short, there is still a missing link with respect to the neuro-anatomical correlates between action monitoring and attentional adjustments.

As suggested before, ACC activation could be instrumental in adjusting performance after experiencing errors or conflict. Such adjustments should be relatively poor for individuals with damage to the ACC. However, the results of patient studies suggest that the causal role of the ACC in these processes is rather subtle, or at least not yet well understood. Fellows and Farah examined four patients with damage in the ACC (see Figure 4.13). Compared with controls, these patients did not show larger Stroop interference, nor a larger increase in Stroop interference in a high-conflict condition (in which there were many more congruent than incongruent Stroop stimuli). Apparently, an intact ACC is not necessary to keep Stroop interference at a normal level when viewed across a series of trials, even when occasional incongruent stimuli presumably invoke high levels of conflict (Fellows & Farah, 2005). Perhaps these patients would perform abnormally in relation to adjustment after an error on a specific trial? Post-error slowing was not observed in these patients, but nor was it in the controls. As discussed above, post-error adjustments are in themselves quite subtle. Rather than to a general adjustment, they pertain to the difference between congruent and incongruent conditions, and this was not analysed by these researchers. Only one of these four patients had bilateral damage, but, according to the authors, this patient's performance did not differ from that of the other three.

To summarize, there are good grounds for assuming a role for ACC neurons in the detection of error and response conflict. A causal role for ACC-based control has been found difficult to prove, especially in relation to the triggering of adaptive attentional control. Another possibility that has been raised is that the ACC triggers autonomic responses (Critchley et al., 2003), which are then fed back to cortical areas (Bechara, 2004; Hajcak et al., 2003). This

Figure 4.13

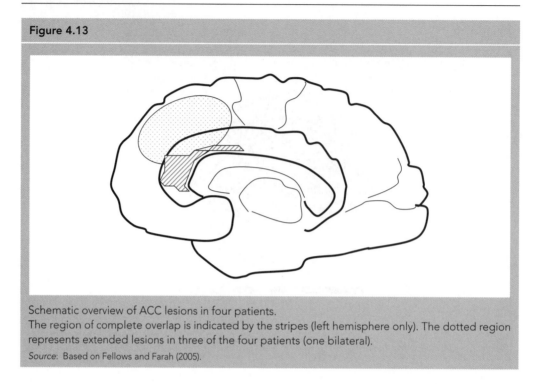

Schematic overview of ACC lesions in four patients.
The region of complete overlap is indicated by the stripes (left hemisphere only). The dotted region represents extended lesions in three of the four patients (one bilateral).
Source: Based on Fellows and Farah (2005).

'somatic marker' mechanism could continue for a considerably longer time than would a direct signal from the ACC to lateral prefrontal areas. The somatic marker model is extensively discussed in Chapter 10, as a form of emotional memory.

4.3.2   From reward processing to action monitoring

Based on what is known about functional connectivity, quite elaborate models have been presented on how the conflict signal in ACC depends on signals from other regions (Holroyd & Coles, 2002). Research in monkeys has revealed that dopaminergic neurons in subcortical structures such as the ventral tegmental area (VTA) and the substantia nigra pars compacta (SNpc) exhibit a transient decrease in their spontaneous firing rates in response to the omission of an expected reward (Schultz, 2000; Schultz et al., 1997b). These transient changes in firing rate would be transmitted as neural signals to various other structures, including the basal ganglia, as well as cortical regions, among which is the ACC (see Figure 4.14) (Di Michele et al., 2005). In the ACC, this transient DA dip is translated into the conflict- or error-related signal, recordable using EEG or fMRI as discussed above. This would make sense: whenever a human participant or an experimental animal detects self-generated erroneous behaviour, or experiences a high-conflict situation, this causes a neural signal that represents the opposite of reward and has the function of avoiding future exposure to the error- or conflict-generating situation. It is plausible that the strength of the transient DA dip depends on tonic DA levels: the higher the tonic, the more pronounced the transient dip can be. This is consistent with reports of DA antagonists reducing the ERN in humans (De Bruijn et al., 2004; De Bruijn et al., 2006).

Furthermore, a VTA–ACC network that has been implicated in producing these conflict signals has also been linked to the control and generation of theta oscillations. Theta waves are 4–7 Hz oscillations that can be recorded in the human EEG during diverse task conditions, as well as during rest. One proposed generator source for theta is the ACC, and the

Figure 4.14

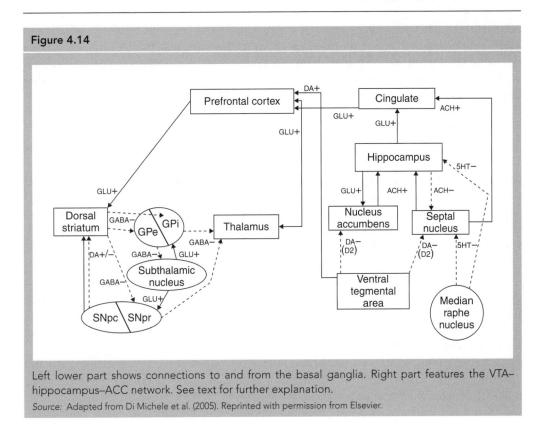

Left lower part shows connections to and from the basal ganglia. Right part features the VTA–hippocampus–ACC network. See text for further explanation.

Source: Adapted from Di Michele et al. (2005). Reprinted with permission from Elsevier.

generation of theta waves within the ACC would in turn be controlled by theta signals from the hippocampus (see Figure 4.14) (Gallinat et al., 2006). This suggests substantial overlap between the networks for conflict signals and theta generation, respectively. High theta states have traditionally been associated with drowsiness, and more specifically with strong control by subcortical of cortical regions (Schutter et al., 2006). In certain tasks, subjects gradually learn to make choices about what is rewarding to them and what is not (Bechara et al., 1994; discussed further in Chapter 10). In this typical error-learning situation, individuals characterized by high theta learn and perform worse (Schutter & van Honk, 2005). Thus, it seems that high theta in the hippocampus–ACC system is detrimental for learning from negative feedback. This is consistent with the idea that low tonic DA (associated with high theta) results in small transient DA dip error signals. Consistently, ADHD patients who mostly receive medication that enhances tonic DA (methylphenidate), are generally characterized by abnormally high theta levels when they are off medication (Snyder & Hall, 2006).

An intriguing possibility is that analogous subcortical–cortical networks exist for other neurotransmitter systems, such as the serotonin (5HT – 5-hydroxytryptamine) system. For example, it has been suggested that 5HT innervations from the raphe nuclei implement punishment signals analogous to the transient DA reward prediction–error signals (Cools et al., 2008), including a reciprocal relation between low tonic levels and a strong transient punishment signal. Thus, low tonic levels of 5HT make individuals more sensitive to negative feedback or punishment signals. This principle could be mediated by the same hippocampus–ACC network as discussed above, which receives innervations from the raphe nuclei (Figure 4.14, lower right).

In sum, the ACC may implement a monitoring system that responds to competing response tendencies or discrepancies between what is deemed appropriate and what has been achieved. This monitoring may very well depend on interactions between the ACC and subcortical structures. The monitoring hypothesis is consistent with its ubiquitous activation in diverse task conditions. At the same time, what the exact consequences of ACC activation are has remained rather elusive, for behavioural adjustments as well as for activity in other brain regions that receive signals from the ACC.

4.4   INHIBITING ACTIONS

Coherent, goal-directed, adequate behaviour results from an adequate balance between rigidity and flexibility. We sometimes need to be rigid, e.g. respond to the left traffic light, never to the right one, or keep up with the colours and always ignore the word; at other times some flexibility is needed, e.g. when one day, due to circumstances, we need to choose the right instead of the left hand lane. Flexibility can be captured in task switching paradigms, which more or less continuously demand a switch from one dimension (e.g. colour) to the other (e.g. word), and back. Such regularly invoked control processes, in the face of competing response options, involve the prefrontal cortex, and the general idea is that these control processes change the strength of association between certain stimulus feature representations and certain response representations. A different situation occurs when an ongoing (preparation for a) response suddenly has to be cancelled, either in favour of an alternative response (which suddenly has become more adaptive), or just like that.

Suddenly having to step on the brake, after a prolonged sequence of stepping on and retreating from the gas pedal, in response to a child that suddenly crosses the street, or to brakes that light up right in front of you, exemplifies the former situation. Or think of a bus driver in a bus loaded with school children, approaching a T junction where both traffic lights are green, desperately trying to figure out which direction to take, who, after finally deciding, notices that both lights have turned red.

For a long time researchers have wondered how an internal brake mechanism could work. Logically, there would be some connection in the brain activated by an external or internal brake signal which is instrumental purely in suppressing general or more specific overt actions. This brake signal/suppression connection activation idea has been captured in the stop task. In this task participants perform a go task, usually a choice RT task with respect to alternative stimuli. Occasionally, the go stimulus is followed, after a few hundred milliseconds delay, by a stop signal (sometimes a sound, sometimes another visual stimulus), which signals that, whatever you are doing, you should stop it (Logan & Cowan, 1984). One can guess that stopping success depends on the adequate perception of, and direction of attention to, the stop signal, as well as on the translation of these processes into a response suppressing signal. The stop signal is a potentially relevant signal occurring outside the current task set, and (in the laboratory as well as in everyday life) is a relatively rare signal. Therefore, stop signal processing could very well involve a kind of circuit breaking, as discussed in both Section 3.4 and the present chapter. To the extent that circuit breaking involves general behavioural arrest, or interruption of ongoing behaviour, it could also facilitate, or even embody, the brake function.

On a technical note, assessing the proportion of stop signal trials that result in successful stopping seems a straightforward way of quantifying stopping performance, but the situation is more complex. Stopping success depends not only on the efficacy of the internal brake signal/suppression mechanism, but also on the speed of the go process, and on the interval between go and stop stimulus. Combining these three variables, we can estimate the duration of the break/suppression mechanism, or the stop signal reaction time (for more details see Box 4.3).

Box 4.3   Stop signal reaction times and the build-up of motor activation

Stop signal reaction time (SSRT) is derived from the proportion of successful stops, combined with the go distribution, to identify a cut-off RT for which stopping is just successful, and a correction for the average go-stop interval (Logan, 1994). Simulation studies have shown that SSRT estimation proceeds most validly when stopping rates approximate to 50 per cent (Band et al., 2003); in experimental practice, therefore, go-stop intervals are continuously adjusted to maintain an approximately 50 per cent stopping rate. In average, healthy students, SSRTs are usually between 150 ms and 200 ms for the average auditory, and somewhat longer for the average visual, stop signal. Interestingly, SSRTs have been shown to be significantly shorter in simple stop conditions (refrain from any action), than in stop-change conditions (the ongoing action has to be changed to a physically different one, think of having to step on the brake pedal) (De Jong et al., 1995). This is consistent with the idea that stopping processes are different during simple stop versus stop-change conditions, perhaps even qualitatively different: simple stop responses may involve much more quick and dirty inhibition of action tendencies in general, affecting action signals at a relatively low level, much more towards the spinal cord and the muscles. If this is true, then the motor cortex activation that can eventually be stopped successfully, should be greater with simple stops than with stop changes. This has been found by De Jong and colleagues (1995), as illustrated in Figure 4.15.

Figure 4.15

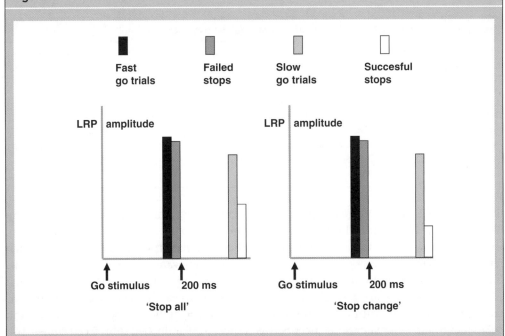

LRPs to go stimuli in different go/stop/change conditions.
Selective motor activation is larger and quicker on failed stop trials than on successful stop trials, reflecting the fact that fast motor cortex activation is less easily stopped from being translated into overt action. By definition, the corresponding parts of the go trials also differ in timing. Most importantly, the amount of selective motor activation that can be tolerated without leading to an overt action is larger for stop-all than for stop-change (compare successful-stop trials for these two conditions).

4.4.1   The electrophysiology of stopping

The common method of assessing SSRT depends on the assumption of independent progressions of go and stop processes, (stated differently, go and stop processes are assumed to race as independently driven horses). Logan and Cowan (1984) specified a number of validation criteria internal to the method for this assumption, but these turned out to be sensitive to other factors as well. This inspired the use of other sources of information about the stop process, the most obvious one being the brain response to a stop signal. The initial motivation may have been to back-up inferences of differences in stop processes between two conditions based on differences in SSRT; however, recording brain responses may also shed light on how the different components of the stopping process are implemented as activated brain areas and their mutual connections. The stop signal set-up is marked by a delicate temporal framework, which dictates the use of brain activity readout measures with high temporal resolution. The chain of processes initiated by the stop signal that are instrumental in producing inhibition must take place in only a few hundreds of milliseconds, and the stop signal itself is only a few hundreds of milliseconds away from the go stimulus. It should therefore not be surprising that ERPs, and possibly ERFs, have become a popular method to illuminate these mechanisms (more technical details on this in Box 4.4).

Box 4.4   Disentangling brain response to temporally close events

The use of ERPs in temporally tight designs such as the stop task creates its own problems, the major one being the biophysical overlap between the response to the go stimulus and that to the stop signal. Perhaps the best method to deal with this issue was introduced by Woldorff (1993), termed Adjar level 2, which stands for Adjacent Response Removal at a complex level. The original application by Woldorff was in the domain of streaming experiments (see Chapter 3), in which stimuli from different attention conditions are presented in rapid succession (intervals between successive stimuli of a few hundred milliseconds). A successful new application was reported in relation to exogenous visual–spatial cuing (see Chapter 3), to remove the brain response to the cue from that to the target (Hopfinger & Mangun, 1998).

Bekker and colleagues managed to disentangle ERPs to the go stimulus from those to the stop ERPs (Bekker et al., 2005a). The next question is how to separate stop signal-elicited activity that is somehow related to the stopping process from unrelated activity (such as that which reflects the mere detection of the stimulus, or its general relevance). One way to address this, is to compare stop ERPs for successful stops with those for failed stops, assuming that internal stopping mechanisms are generally recruited more vigorously in successful cases than in failed cases. In a set-up with visual choice RT stimuli and an auditory stop signal, Bekker and colleagues found two major differences between successful and failed stops (see Figure 4.16). One difference, stop P3, consisted of a larger frontal–central positivity to successful than to failed stops, at about 150 ms latency, which had been reported before using less sophisticated methodology (De Jong et al., 1990). The other difference, stop N1, was a new finding (and was not visible without go-ERP distortion correction). It consisted of a larger negativity (or N1 peak) at about 100 ms post-stop signal, again over frontal–central areas. Source localization confirmed that N1 originated from the auditory cortex.

As was noted in Section 3.2, auditory N1s are sensitive to whether attention is directed at the eliciting stimulus or not. Modulation of N1 may also play a role in the stopping process.

Figure 4.16

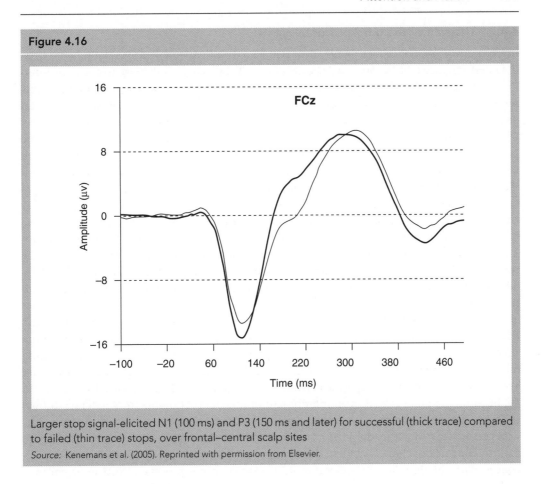

Larger stop signal-elicited N1 (100 ms) and P3 (150 ms and later) for successful (thick trace) compared to failed (thin trace) stops, over frontal–central scalp sites

Source: Kenemans et al. (2005). Reprinted with permission from Elsevier.

On some trials subjects are better prepared for the possible presentation of the stop signal than on others due to spontaneous fluctuations in attention. When they are better prepared stop signals have more impact in the auditory cortex, therefore other processes that depend on this impact also proceed better, inducing a higher probability of successful stopping. When stimuli are processed more thoroughly, then they have a higher chance of resulting in the desired outcome, in this case stopping.

How to interpret stop P3? In the simplest scenario, a larger N1 results in a better inhibitory signal (from the auditory cortex) to the motor cortex, and therefore a higher chance of successful stopping. In that case, no additional mechanism needs to be invoked to explain proficient stopping. One possibility is that stop P3 is actually a reversed ERN: failed stops are errors and may concur with enhanced ERNs (see previous section). One study found that within a group of healthy volunteers subjects who were fast at stopping did not differ in ERN from those who were slower (Lansbergen et al., 2007a). They did, however, have smaller stop P3s, but not smaller stop N1s. Note that if different individuals have different SSRTs but also different stop ERPs, then this answers the goal of recording stop ERPs in the first place: which is to confirm that stop signals are processed differently in certain individuals relative to others.

4.4.2   The role of the inferior frontal gyrus

In 2003, Aron and colleagues reported that, in a group of patients with frontal lesions, stopping performance (SSRT) correlated specifically with the extent of damage to the right inferior frontal gyrus (R IFG) (Aron et al., 2003b). That is, this area was the only one to show such a correlation, which was absent for more dorsal, medial, or left hemisphere frontal areas. How does this result fit in with the ERP results in the stop task, as discussed above, where such right-lateral frontal activity was not observed in response to the stop signal? One possibility is that the R IFG is instrumental in producing adequate stopping not by responding to the stop signal, but rather as a kind of top–down control mechanism. Specifically R IFG would, more or less continuously, send signals that amplify an inhibitory connection between the auditory cortex and the motor cortex, as outlined schematically in Figure 4.17. In this way, the connection between the R IFG and the auditory cortex (or its projection to the motor cortex) implements a context driven (auditory input should be translated into inhibition) selective potentiation of a specific inhibitory connection between the auditory cortex and the motor system. It is clear that such a potentiation mechanism should be flexible; in other situations, auditory inputs may be mere distracters, and should, preferably, *not* result in motor inhibition.

Is there any evidence for the involvement of IFG from research using the cue target logic that was extensively discussed in this and the previous chapter? Brown and Braver (2005, supplementary materials) isolated the fMRI response to cues that signalled whether stopping on the current trial would be hard or easy, from the fMRI response to go and stop stimuli. These researchers found cue specific activations of a right-lateral frontal area, in BAs 44 and 46, including the IFG as well as an inferior part of the DLPFC (middle frontal gyrus) (Brown & Braver, 2005). Furthermore, a large cue specific activation was found in right inferior parietal cortex, very much in the vicinity of the TPJ (coordinates 52, −48, 39, compare Figure 4.3). In conclusion, there is evidence for a top–down control role of the R IFG, perhaps in concert with the right TPJ, in relation to inhibition of motor processes. Notice the contrast with the analogous conclusions in relation to the control of orienting of attention and motor attention, which involved a more dorsal network; here the R IFG/TPJ network was implicated in disengaging from a previously established attentional set. One possibility, already alluded to above, refers to the intuitive inhibition component of the circuit breaker system: whatever you are doing, or wherever you are attending to, stop it, because something potentially urgent has come up.

Figure 4.17

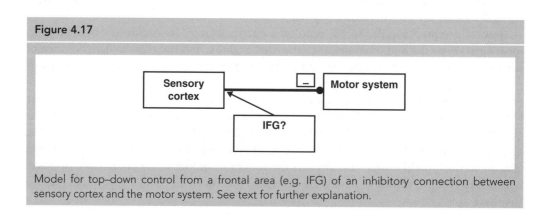

Model for top–down control from a frontal area (e.g. IFG) of an inhibitory connection between sensory cortex and the motor system. See text for further explanation.

4.4.3 Pathology and pharmacology

It may be surmised that impulsive individuals are not proficient stoppers, and that deficient stopping is characteristic for disorders generally associated with elevated impulsivity, such as ADHD (attention deficit hyperactivity disorder) and schizophrenia. While there are hardly any data with respect to the latter syndrome (Enticott et al., 2008), abnormal stopping in ADHD is an acknowledged fact, as demonstrated by several meta-analyses (Lijffijt et al., 2005; Oosterlaan et al., 1998). Using the same ERP logic as described above, Bekker and colleagues found that the stop N1 effect was completely absent in a sample of adult ADHD patients (Bekker et al., 2005b). Whereas healthy controls again showed a direct link between the impact of the stop stimulus and the probability of stopping, such a link was absent in ADHD patients. As discussed, this inhibitory link may be under the control of areas such as the R IFG, and this controlling connection may be malfunctioning in ADHD. Actually, a number of areas have been found to be structurally different, or functionally aberrant, in ADHD (Valera et al., 2007). Among these areas is the right inferior cortex, exhibiting reduced fMRI activity in ADHD (relative to controls) both during rest (Yu-Feng et al., 2007), and when comparing successful versus failed stop trials (Rubia et al., 2005).

If ADHD involves disturbed functionality of certain connections, perhaps because of degraded control signals from lateral frontal areas, what does medication do in relation to these deficiencies? Sixty to seventy per cent of ADHD patients taking methylphenidate show a positive clinical response (Spencer et al., 1995). Methylphenidate suppresses the reuptake of DA and norepinephrine (NE) from the synaptic cleft by blocking the reuptake transporter protein, effectively elevating levels of DA and NE that are available for synaptic transmission. As a fact, acute clinical dose methylphenidate improves stopping, and often more so than other performance parameters, such as go RT (Aron et al., 2003a; Bedard et al., 2003; Lijffijt et al., 2006; Scheres et al., 2003). Consistently, patients with Parkinson's disease, who have a DA deficiency in the basal ganglia (see below), but probably also in other areas, are slower at stopping, relative to matched controls (Gauggel et al., 2004). Furthermore, we recently found that methylphenidate restores the stop N1 effect (Overtoom et al., 2009; see also Pliszka et al., 2007). Based on correlations with blood levels of DA and NE metabolites, improved stopping has been related more to the DA than to the NE effect (Lijffijt et al., 2006a).

Box 4.5   Alternatives to methylphenidate

A more recently developed, specifically noradrenergic substance, atomoxetine, also improves stopping (Chamberlain et al., 2007; Chamberlain et al., 2006), as well as increases R IFG activation during stopping (Chamberlain et al., 2009). Atomoxetine selectively blocks the NE reuptake transporter, and thus the improvement in stopping would suggest that stopping does not depend on dopaminergic function. However, in the prefrontal cortex atomoxetine also increases available extra-cellular DA, which may additionally account for the improvement in stopping (Bymaster et al., 2002). Interestingly, this relation between the NE transporter blockade and DA holds only for the prefrontal cortex, not for the striatum or the nucleus accumbens; in contrast, methylphenidate enhances DA in all three regions, and therefore potentially induces motor effects (striatum) as well as effects on error learning (see previous section), and also reward sensitivity (accumbens). Although this might point to a lower likelihood for amoxetine to induce unwanted side effects (e.g. abuse potential), the flip side may be that methylphenidate also yields improvements in other domains (working memory, attentional shifting), in which atomoxetine is not effective (Chamberlain et al., 2007; Mehta et al., 2004; Turner et al., 2005).

4.4.4   Attention and action: a bigger picture

In discussing inhibition of actions or their representations, we have focussed on flexible connections between input and output systems, the control of these connections by other regions, in particular the IFG, and the involvement of dopaminergic and norepinphrin-ergic transmission. Of course, this is only a small part of the story. First, the IFG has been implicated not only in response inhibition, but also in other domains. Second, whatever it does, it does not do it on its own, but in concert with other brain regions to which it is heavily connected. Examples of the latter are found in the work of Aron and colleagues. Figure 4.18 shows areas activated in a visual–auditory stop task, contrasting the fMRI BOLD signals (synchronized to the go signal) for successful stop versus go trials. In addition to extensive R IFG (or inferior frontal cortex) activation, we note pre-supplementary motor area (pre-SMA)/ACC and temporal–parietal activation; the latter may be related to the circuit breaking aspect of stop signal-elicited activity, as discussed before (Aron & Poldrack, 2006). Furthermore, we see the auditory cortex response to the auditory stop stimulus (think of the stop N1 effect). Finally, besides some occipital activation that is hard to explain, we note activation in the (right) subthalamic nucleus (STN; see Figure 4.14), generally considered to be part of the basal ganglia. Because R STN and R IFG contrast activations were also significantly correlated across 13 subjects, Aron and Poldrack postulate a functional connection between these two regions in relation to stopping; one suggested possibility is the hyper-direct pathway, running from the (inferior) frontal cortex to the STN, to the internal globus pallidus that inhibits the thalamo-cortical activation (Aron & Poldrack, 2006). The IFG–STN connection was confirmed in another study

Figure 4.18

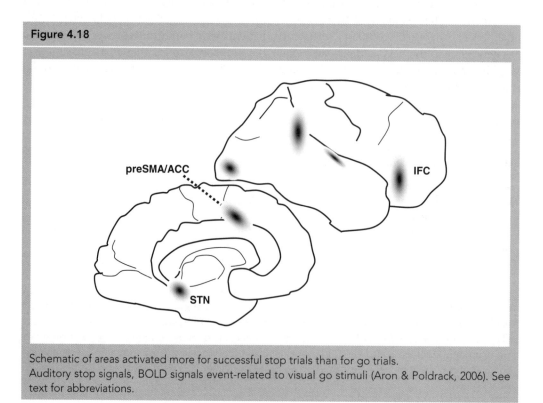

Schematic of areas activated more for successful stop trials than for go trials.
Auditory stop signals, BOLD signals event-related to visual go stimuli (Aron & Poldrack, 2006). See text for abbreviations.

using diffusion-weighted tractography. This relatively new method enables the tracking of white-matter fibres, and therefore connections between different regions, throughout the brain and it revealed triangular white-matter tracts between IFG, STN and pre-SMA (see Figure 4.19) (Aron et al., 2007). In a fascinating study, van den Wildenberg and colleagues showed that deep brain stimulation of the STN improved stopping in patients with Parkinson's disease (van den Wildenberg et al., 2006). Recall that Parkinson's patients off stimulation are poor stoppers, and stimulation of the hyper-direct pathway may benefit their stopping performance.

The successful stop minus failed stop fMRI contrast in the Aron and Poldrack (2006) study yielded no cortical activity worth mentioning, except for a blob covering the left middle and superior frontal gyrus (see Figure 4.20), and again, unexpectedly, in the occipital gyrus. In contrast to the ERP equivalent, there was no difference in the auditory cortex, perhaps due to the transient and subtle nature of the electrocortical N1 effect. This superior–frontal–gyrus activation in the successful minus failed stops contrast is interesting in light of a second lesion study. That study revealed a negative relation between stopping performance and the extent of superior–frontal, not inferior, damage (Floden & Stuss, 2006). These authors suggest that this superior–frontal system is (additionally) invoked when very rapid inhibitory signals are needed, which may capture response preparation even at a spinal level. Admittedly, the focus of lesion overlap in the superior–frontal patients was more in the right hemisphere than in the left, and was also more medial than the blob shown in Figure 4.20. Nevertheless, this is consistent with the idea that different regions and connections contribute to the inhibition of actions, either in concert, or separately, depending on what the exact task situation affords and how individuals adjust to it.

What other perspectives do we have on the (right) IFG and other structures involved in inhibition? Right and left IFG have been implicated in the computerized Wisconsin Card

Figure 4.19

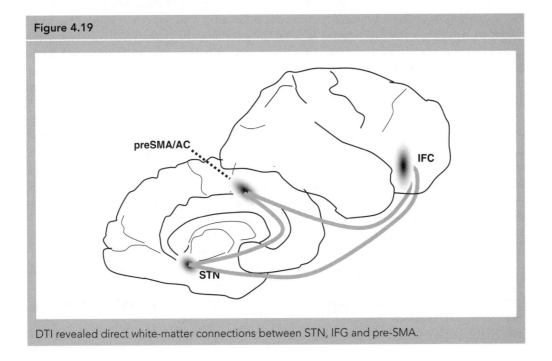

DTI revealed direct white-matter connections between STN, IFG and pre-SMA.

Figure 4.20

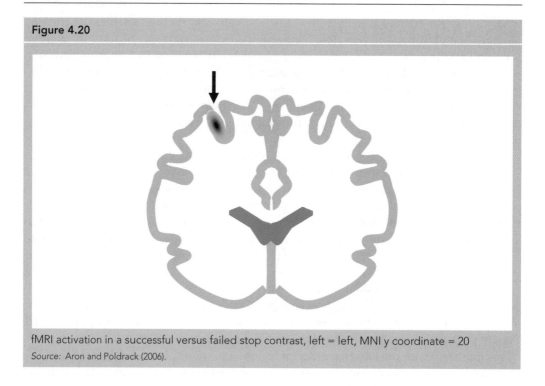

fMRI activation in a successful versus failed stop contrast, left = left, MNI y coordinate = 20
Source: Aron and Poldrack (2006).

Sorting Task during shifting to a new rule, as a function of how many alternative dimensions there are to choose between (Konishi et al., 1998), consistent with a role in suppressing some options in favour of others. Based both on imaging and on patient studies, left IFG activation has been implicated in the verb generation task, especially when the selection load is high, relative to when it is low (Thompson-Schill et al., 1999). That is, some nouns prime a larger number of verbs (high-load) than others (low-load), entailing larger demands on the inhibition of alternative interpretations. The left versus right hemisphere dominance may be related to the specific materials involved, such as verbal versus more visual–spatial stimuli. This is especially evident in tasks assessing working memory, the ability to maintain and use information for a limited, uninterrupted time period (D'Esposito et al., 1998). Interestingly, in adult ADHD patients a positive correlation has been reported between speed of stopping and spatial working memory performance (Clark et al., 2007). In that same study, both variables depended inversely on the extent of right IFG damage within a group of patients. One could surmise that signals from the IFG to other regions that implement specific stimulus information as well the desired consequences (e.g. an inhibitory signal), function to maintain this information in a prioritized state, which can manifest as working memory in one task situation, or as inhibition in another. On a slightly different level, Klingberg and colleagues had healthy subjects, as well as ADHD patients, doing visual–spatial working memory training day after day for weeks and found a resulting increased working memory capacity, as well as improved performance on other tasks, including the Stroop, and amelioration of clinical symptoms in the patients (Klingberg et al., 2005; Olesen et al., 2004).

Box 4.6   The inferior gyrus in language and in depression

Future research may well reveal a more fine-grained parcellation of functions in the IFG. For example, the left IFG, including Broca's area has been traditionally associated with language production. Poldrack and colleagues argued that the more ventral–anterior part of the L IFG (BA 47–45) is specifically involved in semantic processing, whereas the more dorsal–posterior part (BA 45–44) is more involved in syntactic or phonological processing (Poldrack et al., 1999). A similar distinction is conceivable in relation to functions such as inhibition, working memory, and disengagement. A related issue concerns the relative contributions from the left and right hemispheres. It has been suggested that mood and anxiety disorders are marked by a relatively overactive right hemisphere, and that this may result in excessive behavioural inhibition and hyper-vigilance (Davidson et al., 2002). This seems inconsistent with the finding discussed in Chapter 3, that depressed individuals are deficient in disengaging from a current attentional set, which is crucial for inhibiting ongoing actions that depend on an intact R IFG. Perhaps *the excessive* behavioural inhibition pertains more to the chronic attitude of depressed individuals, rather than to the dynamic, rapid and transient activation of an inhibition system that lends flexibility in the face of changing environmental demands.

4.5   CONCLUDING REMARKS

Neural populations specifically dedicated to motor preparation can be selectively activated (biased) in anticipation of eventual imperative signals for overt responding. These anticipatory activations must depend on intentional control signals from dorsal–prefrontal and parietal areas that resemble those that implement attentional control, although differences do exist at a more detailed level. Overruling an existing motor set (motor circuit breaking) seems to involve left, rather than right hemisphere, regions in parietal (supramarginal) and lateral frontal cortex, and depends, at least partly, on dopaminergic transmission. This holds true all the more for a network involving the right hemisphere IFG, which appears to be crucial for inhibiting ongoing actions, a mechanism that is disturbed in numerous pathologies. Difficulties in selecting a specific motor set, resulting in the activation of conflicting response tendencies, even to the extent of erroneous behavioural output, activate a medially located region in the anterior cingulate cortex. How this activation is related to the various controlling mechanisms is something that still has to be worked out.

Questions

1. See Section 4.3.1. To prove a causal link between conflict detection and ensuing cognitive control, could transcranial magnetic stimulation (TMS) be of use? Describe possibilities at the level of experimental design and of technical set-up (how to apply the TMS).
2. See Sections 4.2.1 and 4.4. Describe the resemblances and the differences between brain mechanisms of motor circuit breaking, and those of braking (inhibition) in terms of anatomical connections and of biochemical aspects.
3. See Section 4.4.1. It is stated 'that internal stopping mechanisms are generally recruited more vigorously in the case of a successful stop than in the case of a failed stop'. Are there any other factors determining the chance of successful stopping that you can think of?

5 PERCEPTION AND MEMORY

Key Points
• How we perceive features, objects and events depends to an important extent on how representations in the sensory cortex link to representations in memory, and these links are compromised in certain forms of agnosia.
• On short-term time scales, neural representations in the sensory cortex may be subjected to adaptation, habituation and dishabituation. These phenomena are discussed at a number of levels, ranging from single neurons in *Aplysia* to the human mismatch negativity and orienting response.
• Both the visual and the auditory modalities feature dedicated systems for the detection of unexpected change or novelty, even though the exact memory mechanisms involved may differ. The right hemisphere especially, in combination with cholinergic transmission, seems to be implicated in these systems, as well as in their interactions with a more non-specific circuit breaker system.
• Sensory memory is the huge capacity, very short-lived register of sensory inputs that affords sensory continuity. The mechanisms may differ, however, between different modalities, as do the characteristics of sensory memories.
• Sensory memory contents may or may not be transferred to more enduring storage, depending on factors like attention. Prefrontal neurons that are instrumental in representing relevant stimuli after the representations in the perceptual cortex have vanished, have response properties quite different from those in the perceptual cortex. In particular they exhibit tremendous flexibility, which rests in part on optimal, not maximal, stimulation of the dopamine receptors.
• Episodic retrieval processes, including imagery, involve interactions between perceptual cortex regions and higher control areas in prefrontal cortex and possibly hippocampus.
• More enduring representations in perceptual cortex itself form the basis of perceptual learning, the implicit and often unconscious modulation of later behaviour due to prior perception. Perceptual learning seems to depend on interactions with subcortical regions. Such interactions are contingent upon the detection of salient changes in the environment and involve activation in ascending subcortical cortical projections involving various neurotransmitters.

5.0 INTRODUCTION

In Section 2.0 we describe patients with visual agnosia, a deficit in reporting the identity of objects in the visual world. These problems with object recognition are associated

Figure 5.1

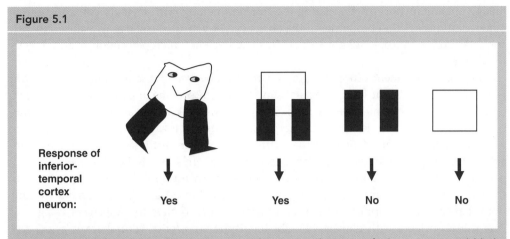

Neuron in the inferior–temporal cortex responds to a combination of white square and black rectangles, but not to the separate square or rectangles.
The latter may be presumed to elicit good responses from lower visual areas in the occipital cortex.

Figure 5.2

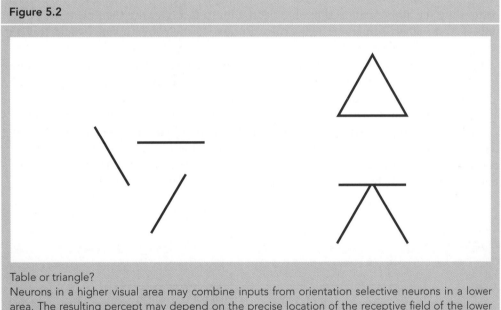

Table or triangle?
Neurons in a higher visual area may combine inputs from orientation selective neurons in a lower area. The resulting percept may depend on the precise location of the receptive field of the lower area neuron selectively sensitive to horizontal orientations.

predominantly with damage in the ventral visual pathway, and are dissociated from more action-related functional loss as seen with more dorsal lesions. Recognizing objects can be thought of as requiring two linking operations. First, a link (or binding) should be established between visual attributes, such as colour and shape. This link may be established by neurons in higher visual areas that integrate inputs from neurons in lower areas (see Figures 5.1 and 5.2), or by the coherent activity of neural populations responsive to specific colours, shapes, and so on, resulting in the neural representation of a coherent percept. The second linking operation concerns associating the coherent percept with memory contents, so that representations of other properties of the object can be activated (such as its name, semantic connotations or conceptual knowledge). This is a stage in which perception relates directly to memory.

One source of evidence supporting the distinction between these two linking operations is patients with different kinds of visual agnosia, which become apparent in differing patterns of deficits across multiple tasks. To certify that we are really dealing with visual agnosia, we need to rule out deficits in primary visual cortex or lower level visual structures, as well as general memory deficits. If that is the case, we can distinguish two or three variants of visual agnosia. In *apperceptive* agnosia, the problem seems to be forming a coherent percept. In *associative* agnosia there is no problem with forming a coherent percept, but there is trouble linking this percept to representations of information (e.g. of name or function) that have been formed in the past, in other words to memory. Apperceptive agnosia is mostly associated with damage in right hemisphere posterior ventral areas; associative agnosia mostly with lesions in left hemisphere posterior ventral areas (Gazzaniga et al., 2008). A third form of visual agnosia that is sometimes distinguished from the other two has been dubbed *integrative* agnosia, since the main problem seems to be the integration of parts of an object in a larger-scale structure; these patients appear unable to perceive an object at a glance. Consistent with our discussion in Chapter 2, these patients have no problem performing the appropriate action on objects and, in fact, viewing their own action with respect to an object sometimes helps them to retrieve the correct name (would this also work for associative patients?).

Figure 5.3 summarizes what different visual agnosia patients can (+) or cannot (-) achieve in certain tasks. Unusual views present objects from rare perspectives (e.g. a top view of a bike) and subjects have to detect that an object presented in two unusual views is indeed one and the same object. Overlapping figures require that one in a set of overlapping objects is singled out by being drawn. As can be seen, only when objects have to be named in either task do associative–agnosia patient reveal a deficit. Another task in which associatives fail is matching by function: a closed umbrella has to be matched to an open umbrella, not to a walking cane, although its physical resemblance with the latter is much closer.

Figure 5.3

	Unusual views	Overlapping objects	Naming
Apperceptive	-	-	-
Associative	+	+	-
Integrative	+	-	-

Task performance in different agnosia categories. See text for further explanation.

Figure 5.4

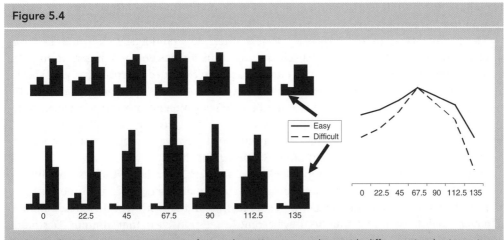

Left panels: approximate responses of a monkey V4 neuron to bars with different visual orientations (indicated at abscissa's) serving as sample stimuli that had to be compared to subsequently presented test stimuli.
The histograms represent the number of action potentials per unit of time (40 ms) and extend across a 200 ms stimulus duration. The comparison was either difficult (orientation difference between sample and test of 22.5 degrees) or easy (90 degrees). The neuron is more sharply tuned to 67.5 degrees orientation in the difficult, relative to the easy condition (Spitzer et al., 1988). Right panel: tuning curves derived by plotting the maximum response for each bar orientation in the two conditions, normalized for the maximum response in the difficult condition. The tuning curve for the difficult condition is much sharper.

Associative visual agnosia illustrates the importance of one of the many interactions between the global functional domains of perception and memory. Perception can be defined as the activation of a neural representation in the sensory cortex by an event external to the brain. A general definition of memory is not that different: it involves either the strengthening of existing connections within or between neural representations, or a change in the relative strengths in these connections. Especially when these memory mechanisms operate in the sensory cortex, perhaps the only difference concerns the relative dependence of the activated representation on the presence of the external event.

What do perceptual representations look like at the level of single neurons? Figure 5.4 shows an example. In the difficult condition, the neuron responds most vigorously to a bar oriented at 67.5 degrees, then gradually more weakly to different orientations. This pattern is often captured in a tuning curve, which represents that the neuron is tuned to 67.5 degrees, but not perfectly, because it also responds to other orientations, albeit more weakly. A labelled line perspective on perceptual representation emphasizes the specificity of the neural pathway from retina via thalamus and V1 to V4 for this specific orientation, although it does not exclude non-zero responses to other orientations. A slightly different perspective is referred to as vector summation, in which the pattern of responses from a neuron across orientation is captured in a vector with high values for some orientations, and low or even zero values for others. The actual representation then depends on the summed activity of multiple neurons, each with its own response vector.

Both perspectives emphasize, or allow for, the principle of gradual tuning curves. Figure 5.4 also illustrates that, depending on circumstances, tuning curves for a single neuron may vary. Both the overall level of responding, as well as the sharpness (specificity for certain orientations) are greatly reduced in the easy discrimination condition.

The essential point in the above example is that top–down influences may modulate over-all response levels as well as tuning specificity, and thus the perceptual representation of the same stimulus. Similar effects have been noted based on extended practice involving specific stimuli in various ways. These effects may involve enhanced specificity, for example, after training on a task in which vertical orientations are relevant a given neuron becomes tuned more sharply to that specific orientation, responding less to other orientations than it did before. These effects may also involve enhanced sensitivity, e.g. a larger set of neurons may become responsive to vertical orientations (Gilbert et al., 2001).

Merely being exposed to a stimulus without any task or training can also modify the response of, presumably perceptual, neurons. Desimone discusses neurons in monkey infe-rior–temporal cortex that shows repetition suppression, in that with repeated presentation of a (preferred) task-irrelevant stimulus they become less responsive to that stimulus (Desimone, 1996). Such phenomena are traditionally discussed in terms of adaptation, habituation or the formation of a memory trace and memory comparison. The next section is devoted to rendering the main issues in relation to these perceptual memory phenomena.

5.1   SHORT-TERM PERCEPTUAL PLASTICITY

5.1.1   Habituation and dishabituation

During the 1960s E. Kandel and colleagues studied the effects of stimulus repetition on the gill withdrawal reflex of the *Aplysia* or sea snail (Kandel et al., 1991). Stimulation with a jet of water of the aplysia's siphon elicited the reflex; and with repeated stimulation the reflex became less and less discernible. When another stimulus (i.e. electrical stimulation of the head) was applied between two successive repetitions of the siphon stimulation, the second of these two repetitions again elicited a relatively intense gill withdrawal. Kandel and col-leagues termed the decrement of the withdrawal reflex habituation, and its recovery after head stimulation, dishabituation. Dishabituation should not be confused with generaliza-tion. The latter refers to the response to a deviant stimulus presented after a sequence of repeated standard stimuli, whereas the former refers to the effect of the deviant stimulus on the response to a subsequent standard stimulus.

Kandel and colleagues also uncovered the complete neural circuitry underlying the reflex, which essentially consisted of a sensory neuron (from the siphon), an inter-neuron, and a motor neuron (to the gill). They observed that waning of the reflex was preceded by a decrease in the release of neurotransmitter (glutamate) from the pre-synaptic sensory neuron to the inter-neuron. So, there was no change in the activity of the motor neuron itself with-out a change in activity at the preceding level of the system (the inter-neuron); furthermore, there was also no change in the density of action potentials in the sensory neuron. Rather, pre-synaptic efficiency, that is the extent to which these action potentials caused a release of neurotransmitter (glutamate) from the pre-synaptic sensory neuron, was modulated and this seemed to mediate the behavioural effects. This pre-synaptic efficiency seemed to depend on the closure of channels for uptake of extracellular calcium.

Kandel et al. also uncovered the pathways that were activated via the head stimulation. One of these pathways branched off to contact the pre-synaptic ending of the sensory neu-ron that mediated the withdrawal reflex. Presentation of the dishabituating stimulus caused activity in the pathway to the pre-synaptic ending of the sensory neuron; thereafter, siphon stimulation resulted in a recovered release of neurotransmitter from the pre-synapse, to the inter-neuron, and in recovery of the withdrawal reflex. The increase of pre-synaptic efficiency appeared to be brought about by serotonin (a neurotransmitter) release from the terminals of the axon coming from the head. Serotonin, via a second messenger cascade, promotes opening of the calcium channels in the membrane of the pre-synaptic neuron.

These findings suggest that habituation of the withdrawal reflex does not reflect an absolute incapacity of the aplysia to respond to a stimulus already repeated many times. Rather, it is as if it did not feel like responding after a number of repetitions. It did feel like responding after dishabituation; dishabituation entailed the recovery of pre-synaptic resources. Habituation then, can be seen as being self-controlled (aplysia controlled). It can be considered as having an adaptive value. There was simply no need for the animal to keep responding when a possible threat, or an otherwise relevant event, was no longer detected. This kind of habituation is considered by many authors as a form of learning, a psychological process.

In fact, authors who have explicitly addressed the issue of habituation invariably define it as a higher-order process, as opposed to a reflection of built-in limitations of neural functioning (like adaptation). The ultimate criterion for true habituation then, is dishabituation. The appropriate experimental set-up for dishabituation involves an ongoing sequence of identical standard stimuli in which, at some point, a deviant stimulus is inserted without affecting the temporal structure of the standard sequence. Response decrement can be evaluated up to the point at which the deviant stimulus is inserted; dishabituation can be analysed by comparing the response to the standard stimulus presented after the deviant stimulus to the response to the standard preceding the deviant. Many experiments with this procedure have been conducted, almost invariably using micro-level recordings in various animal preparations. These studies have inspired a theory of habituation called dual process theory.

5.1.2   Dual process theory

Also in the 1960s, R. Thompson and colleagues formulated the dual process theory of habituation (Groves & Thompson, 1970; Thompson & Spencer, 1966). For the present discussion two features of the dual process theory are important: that it postulates a dual process and that it is based on a first-order principle. To begin with the latter, the first-order principle implies that:

(1) there is neural specificity, i.e. neurons have preferred stimulus features;
(2) neural specificity concerns a series of neurons, rather than a single one; that is, if the preferred stimulus is presented, a first neuron activates a second one and so on;
(3) a change of responsivity in a series of neurons is caused only by processes internal to that series.

The third property is of special importance. It implies, for example, that a decrease in responsivity with repeated stimulation is only caused by processes internal to neurons in the series of neurons that code the repeated features. In contrast, a second-order model would postulate an additional path, parallel to the coding path, which would contain, for example, a memory representation of past events that would play some role in the decrease of responsivity in the first path. Of course, a first-order model explains an increased response to a deviant after a repetition of standards simply as a lack of generalization.

The first-order principle in the dual process theory is illustrated in Figure 5.5 (dual process), which presents an account of skin conductance response (SCR) to habituation and generalization (the SCR is a relatively pure measure of sympathetic activation as elicited by any novel, or otherwise potentially relevant, event). Stimulus repetition response decrement occurs at both early (a) and late (f to i) levels of processing (synapses), and with respect to the eventual SCR. Presenting a deviant stimulus after a number of standard ones results in the activation of a set of neurons that is partially different from the one activated by the standard (a and c vs. c and d). This new activation is transmitted to higher levels of processing and eventually converges on f. Due to the preceding stimulus repetition f, and all other levels up to i, were in a state of low responsiveness; however, because there was also low responsiveness at earlier levels of processing, during the course of stimulus repetition the higher levels were eventually not stimulated anymore. Therefore, they recover from their state of low responsiveness (see the preceding section), and respond again to the stimulation they received from the alternative lower level pathways.

It may be clear that this model accounts for decrement–plus–recovery functions. The model features a single-stream pathway for stimulus processing in which modulation of responsiveness is an inherent property; as such it is based on a first-order principle. However, it embodies no criterion to discern true habituation from other forms of response decrement.

This brings us to the second principle postulated by dual process theory: sensitization. An example of sensitization was discussed in the preceding section as the effect of the dishabituating stimulus on the pre-synaptic mechanisms of the aplysia in the experiments of Kandel and co-workers. In general, sensitization is thought to be brought about by neurons other than the ones that exhibit intrinsic habituation.

Together then, dual process theory features the following principles:

(1) Habituation is a first-order process.
(2) Decreased neural responsiveness due to stimulus repetition can be counteracted by the activity of other neurons.

Figure 5.5

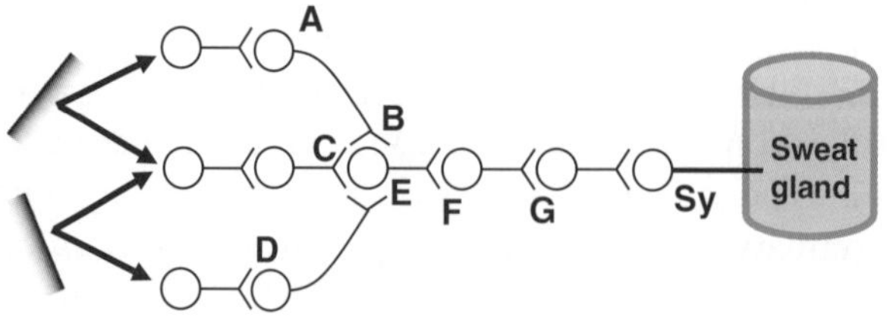

A dual process account of habituation and generalization of habituation of the SCR.
Oriented bars represent two stimuli with partly different features. A to G represent habituating synapses. Sy = sympathetic neuron; the condition of the sweat gland determines skin conductance level, and is modulated by input from the chain of synapses.
Source: Based on Thompson et al. (1979).

5.1.3 Model comparator theory

An influential concept in psychophysiology and cognitive neuroscience is that of the orienting response (OR). OR refers to that part of stimulus processing that entails preparation for optimal processing of whatever had not yet been optimally processed in the stimulus. For example, upon noticing the first indications of a door being opened, we might like to know whether: it is really being opened; who is coming in; whether we are to react behaviourally. So the OR prepares us for: extended sensory processing; for an increased ability to integrate stimulus information; for the possibility of action; and so on. In addition to changes in sensory and cerebral structures, orienting is also observed as adjustments in peripheral effectors. The presentation of a stimulus may cause changes in skin conductivity, in heart rate and in pupil diameter. It can also result in an explicit readjustment of the sensory organs (e.g. eye movements towards the perceived location of the stimulus) and in the arrest of any overt behaviour going on at the moment the stimulus was presented.

The experimental and theoretical work on this subject is to a considerable extent inspired by E.N. Sokolov. As early as 1960 he had formulated the basic principles of a theory on the OR (Sokolov, 1963). Sokolov focussed on two aspects: first, that elicitation of the OR was non-specific with respect to the kind of stimulus; second, that its habituation was stimulus-specific. The former implies that a response that is considered a manifestation of orienting should occur for any stimulus that is intrinsically salient; for example, a change in retinal activity would not qualify as an orienting response because it will not be elicited by a salient auditory stimulus. Stimulus specificity of habituation refers to the fact that a habituated response recovers after a change in stimulation. We have already discussed this kind of recovery in the context of generalization of habituation. However, according to Sokolov, a lack of complete generalization is not the only mechanism that contributes to the recovered SCR to a deviant stimulus. We will look at a possible second mechanism in the context of Sokolov's theory, which is therefore discussed first.

Sokolov's basic theory is illustrated in Figure 5.6. A first emergent feature is that an initial, novel stimulus directly activates a so-called amplifying system (arrow 2), in addition to activation of a system that is concerned with the neural representation (the model) of the stimulus (arrow 1). A candidate neurophysiological substrate for the amplifying system used to be the midbrain reticular formation (MRF). It was thought that the sensory organs had at least two projections that could be activated by an appropriate stimulus: one going to the primary cortical projection areas, the other to the MRF (Skinner & Yingling, 1976). It was also generally thought that MRF activation resulted in increased cortical arousal: an increase in the excitability of cortical neurons that could serve optimal processing of incoming stimuli (arrow 4). In recent years, however, the MRF is increasingly being viewed as specifically concerned with motor processes. In contrast, other brain stem structures are now more likely candidates to control the more or less diffuse activation of the cortex from down below. An example is the locus cereleus (LC), a relatively small area from which massive projections originate then diffuse throughout the cortex (although not completely a-specifically). The LC projections feature noradrenaline as a neurotransmitter. It is also possible that other brain stem areas that project in a similar way, but with other neurotransmitters, play a similar role in activating the cortex. The amplifying activity is thought to activate peripheral response systems like the one that governs the SCR (arrow 7).

Figure 5.6

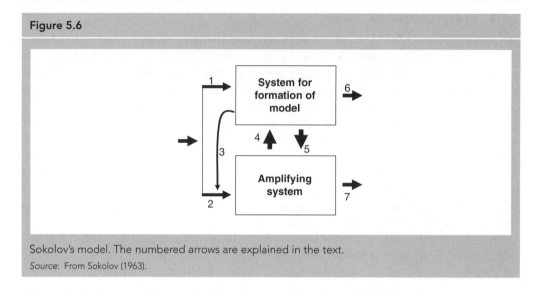

Sokolov's model. The numbered arrows are explained in the text.
Source: From Sokolov (1963).

Optimal cortical stimulus processing would entail the formation of a neural representation of the incoming stimulus (system for formation of model). It would also entail a comparison of this representation with representations of past events. Arrow 3 represents the possibility that cortical processing prevents the activation of the amplifier after stimulus presentation. So, stimulus-driven amplifier activity enhances cortical processing, which in turn inhibits amplifier activity. This amplifier activity inhibition would occur in particular when the outcome of cortical processing is that the stimulus does not contain further salient information, e.g. because it has a relatively complete neural representation due to preceding presentations. The one arrow (5) that has not yet been discussed refers to the possibility that cortical processing results in detection of a mismatch between representations of past events and the representation of the actual stimulus. Such a detection would result in excitation of the amplifier system by the system concerned with model formation, i.e. the cortex. Arrow 3 then, could represent a mechanism reflected in adaptation and generalization. Arrow 5 represents an additional mechanism.

In conclusion, Sokolov postulates that incoming information is compared to a neural model of information processed earlier. Depending on the degree of mismatch detected in the comparison process, the amplifier is activated, then the cortex is activated and peripheral responses are issued: the organism is orienting. The mismatch may occur after the first few presentations of a novel stimulus, when there may be no model to compare it with. It is very likely to occur after presentation of a deviant in a sequence of standards. If the deviant differs from the standard on a limited number of dimensions, e.g. when it differs in pitch or in colour, we have a well-specified deviation from a well-developed model. Sokolov asserts that it is a second-order process (arrow 5) which causes at least part of the difference between the response to the deviant and to that of the preceding standard.

In the next section we will turn to pertinent ERP evidence in this matter. A first-order principle may be simpler than, and therefore preferable to, a second-order principle. However, as we will see, the available experimental evidence on deviation effects on the ERP makes it hard not to invoke the second-order notion.

5.1.4   First-order and second-order deviation effects

Many simple learning phenomena can be explained by a first-order model: a decrease following repeated presentation of the same stimulus, and (a lack of) generalization which depends on the difference between the standard (the adaptation stimulus) and the deviant (the test stimulus). Therefore, we may call them first-order deviation effects. Now it is time to take a closer look at the ERPs to these various stimuli. Figure 5.7 shows ERPs recorded from a single representative subject at the Fz electrode. The ERPs were elicited by tones with different sequential and temporal probabilities. The deviants were infrequently presented stimuli with a lower intensity. At about 100 ms post-stimulus the ERPs to deviants and those to standards start to differ and the difference peaks at about 200 ms. Clearly, there is no temporal correspondence between the first negative peak in the standard ERP (the N1, just before 100 ms) and the peak in the difference; this is a first indication that the deviant ERP might contain more than just incomplete N1 generalization.

Now we look at the third condition: the deviant stimuli presented without intervening standards. The absence of standards results in a sequence of lonely deviants with relatively long intervals between successive stimuli (or stimulus onset asynchrony, SOA), or rare standard, if you want. If a given stimulus is repeatedly presented with relatively long SOA, response decrement with repetition will be slower than when SOA is relatively short. Thus, the average response across trials with long SOA will resemble the true response on the very first trial more than the average response with short SOA will. The long SOA average response then, can be taken as a relative estimate of what the response would look like on the first trial. The ERP to the deviant stimulus without intervening standards can be seen as a reasonable estimate of the single trial ERP to the deviant stimulus, had it been the very first in a sequence of standards. As Figure 5.7 shows, this ERP is marked by a very pronounced N1, as could be expected; but it lacks the subsequent protracted negativity that characterizes the difference

Figure 5.7

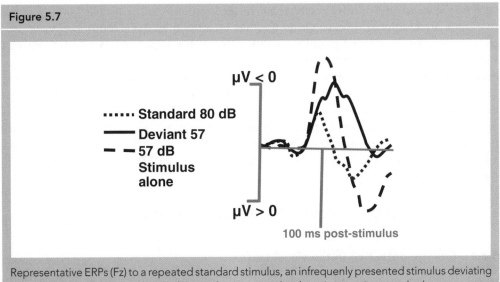

Representative ERPs (Fz) to a repeated standard stimulus, an infrequenly presented stimulus deviating in intensity (57 dB), and to the 57-dB stimulus presented without intervening standards.

between the ERP to the true deviant and that to the standard. So, there is a really strong suggestion that the true deviant evokes an activity that is not observed in response to the initial stimulus of a repetition of standards. The story is completed by taking into the account the difference between the topographies of the N1 and the protracted negativity: whereas the latter has a more frontal distribution, the former has a central maximum. This indicates that they reflect two different brain processes.

The protracted negativity discussed above is known as mismatch negativity (MMN). Since 1978 a myriad studies have been published on MMN, both inspired and conducted to a considerable extent by R. Näätänen and colleagues (Garrido et al., 2009; Näätänen, 1992). These studies have yielded a robust picture of MMN as a process that is very sensitive to, among other things, the difference between standard and deviant, the relative probabilities of standard and deviant, and to deviation on various auditory dimensions (pitch, intensity, location, phonetic properties, etc.). For a recent review the reader is referred to Garrido et al. (2009).

Näätänen recognized the implications of the fact that MMN was not elicited by first trial stimuli: stimuli that could be considered as more or less equivalent to the first stimuli presented in a habituation series after a period of relative silence. If anything, the MMN appears to depend strongly on prior exposure of the subject to the standard stimuli. Thus, information about the standard stimuli determines the amplitude of the MMN to the deviant. Therefore this information must be represented somehow in the information processing system. MMN depends on the difference between standard and deviant and this strongly indicates that it reflects the degree of mismatch that is detected between the neural representation of the standard and that of the deviant. In other words, MMN results from a comparison between a neural model of past events and incoming information. On the first trial there is no MMN because there is no well-defined neural model. It is hard to avoid the conclusion then, that MMN cannot be explained in terms of a first-order principle but that it reflects a second-order principle. Another argument in favour of this view is that MMN is elicited by intensity decrements (see Figure 5.7) and even unexpected stimulus omissions. In first-order terms, this involves only weaker, or even absent, stimulation of the same neurons that were stimulated by the standard. For this to activate a dedicated response to change like MMN, one has to assume an additional process. Other findings in support of the second-order view concern MMN to an unexpected stimulus repetition (see next section) and to relatively abstract stimulus features, such as infrequent changes in a single tone within a straightforward or broken (arpeggio) chord consisting of multiple tones. These lines of evidence are, in fact, quite important, because the rare standard effect described above is also open to an alternative interpretation. Consider, for example, the possibility that the ERP to rare standards is marked not so much by absent MMN but rather by a huge anteriorly distributed positivity (P2) that immediately follows the N1 and masks the MMN. In the next section we will meet an example of the reverse situation, in which there is a greater MMN-like response in the rare standard condition.

5.2   FIRST- OR SECOND-ORDER MEMORY AND CIRCUIT BREAKING

5.2.1   Change detection in the visual cortex

Given the strong evidence for second-order short-term plasticity in the auditory system, how does this work in other modalities, like the visual one? A study by Czigler et al.

(2002) seemed to settle this issue by demonstrating a negative wave between 100 and 200 ms post-deviant as elicited within a sequence of standards, predominantly above occipital cortex (Czigler et al., 2002). In this traditional standard–deviant set-up standards and deviants differed in colour (red versus green). Furthermore, in a separate condition, the deviant was presented among other deviants (i.e. the sequence was made up of 15 differently coloured stimuli). In this multiple-colour condition, a memory trace for a specific standard could presumably not be developed. Because the visual mismatch negativity (vMMN) was also observed when contrasting the traditional deviant ERP with the multi-colour–deviant ERP, Czigler and colleagues concluded that their vMMN was dependent on the context of constant standards, consistent with a second-order memory comparison scenario.

However, in 2003, Kenemans and colleagues applied the rare standard logic to vMMN and found that the occipital negativity between 100–200 ms was even larger in response to the rare standards (when contrasted with the traditional standard response) (Kenemans et al., 2003; Kenemans et al., 2010). These results are illustrated in Figure 5.8, showing the traditional vMMN waveform (deviant minus standard) for the Oz as well as for more lateral (T6=P8, and T5=P7) electrode sites. Note that after 150 ms, the vMMN has a relatively more lateral distribution. Furthermore, the black inset shows the isopotential scalp topography for deviance (traditional deviant standard contrast) as well as for rareness (rare standard minus traditional standard). If anything the rareness-related negativity (RRN) is much stronger than

Figure 5.8

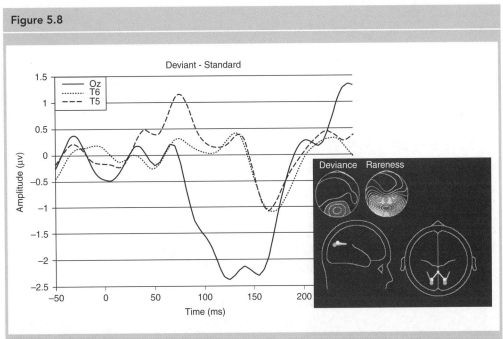

Visual cortex response to visual change: mismatch- or rareness-related?
Waveforms represent traditional (deviant minus standard) ERP. Note the stronger contribution at lateral electrodes just after 150 ms. Scalp topographies: grey is negative, black positive; isopotential line spacing is 0.8 µV. White dipoles for deviance, grey ones for rareness (Kenemans et al., 2003). See text for further explanation. Reprinted with permission from Wolters Kluwer Health.

the deviance-related negativity, and the locations of the corresponding equivalent dipoles were not statistically distinguishable. This is a pattern completely opposite to that presented in Figure 5.7 (auditory mismatch negativity, aMMN), and inconsistent with the results reported by Czigler and colleagues. In fact, even the larger effect for rareness, relative to deviance, is entirely consistent with a first model as illustrated in Figure 5.5 (think of the overlap in neural population for the two oriented bars; there is no such overlap for a rare standard, hence even less generalization).

So what was going on? The inconsistencies were even further emphasized by subsequent Czigler reports that vMMN could also be elicited by infrequent unpredictable stimulus omissions, as well as by infrequent unexpected repetitions, as in red–red–green–green– red–red–green–green– red–red–green–green–*green* (Czigler et al., 2006a; Czigler et al., 2006b). A first clue pertains to that the omission and repetition effects produced occipital negativities that were either relatively more lateral (no focus over medial occipital cortex), and/or, even over 200 ms latency. A second clue rests on noticing that the pseudo-standards in the multiple-colour condition in the Czigler et al. (2002) study deviated on average much less from the deviant than did the identical standards in the traditional sequence; therefore contrasting the traditional deviants with the multicolour deviants would still reveal

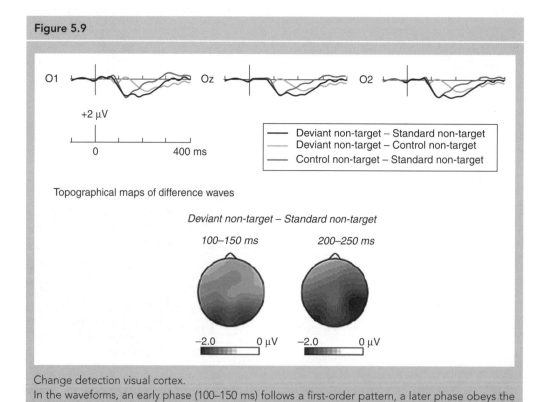

Figure 5.9

Topographical maps of difference waves

Deviant non-target – Standard non-target

Change detection visual cortex.
In the waveforms, an early phase (100–150 ms) follows a first-order pattern, a later phase obeys the second-order principle. Topographical maps show a much more right lateralized pattern for the later phase (Kimura et al., 2009). Non-target refers to the fact that the stimulus sequences also contained target stimuli, which are not relevant for the present discussion. Reprinted with permission from John Wiley and Sons.

an occipital negativity that can be explained in terms of difference in generalization (i.e. first-order).

In a recent study by Kimura and colleagues it was ascertained that the differences in deviation across multi-deviants and traditional standard blocks were effectively zero (Kimura et al., 2009). As can be seen in Figure 5.9 (e.g. Oz trace), a first deviant-related negativity between 100 ms and 150 ms is equally strong for the traditional deviant-standard contrast as for the multiple deviant-standard (control) contrast, and non-existent for the deviant minus control contrast. In contrast, around 200 ms, the traditional deviant-standard negativity enters a second phase, the control negativity returns to zero and, of course, the deviant minus control negativity starts to develop. This pattern is entirely consistent with an early (100–150 ms) first-order, rareness-related response, followed by a later, second-order true vMMN. Notice in the topographical maps that this later phase again shows much more lateralization, especially in the right hemisphere.

Given that at least the early vMMN is in fact a first-order phenomenon, or RRN, can something more precise be stated about the underlying mechanism? One point is that it can still be considered either as the result of physiological limitations (or adaptation), or as the result of primitive psychological learning (habituation). As discussed in Section 5.1.1. dishabituation is the criterion for habituation and such studies have not been performed yet. Another perspective comes from the timing of the rareness effect, the lower limit of which seems to be at about 100 ms post-stimulus. Shorter-latency activity has not been found to respond to manipulations of deviance, and therefore seems to be non-plastic. However, it does appear to be very sensitive to physical stimulus factors like the location of the stimulus and its dominant spatial frequency (Kenemans et al., 2000, 2002). Another point in case is the suspected location of the RRN generators, as indicated approximately by the equivalent dipoles in Figure 5.8. These locations appeared to be independent of the physical stimulus features that define deviance, whether these were high or low spatial frequencies, or red or blue colours. Another study using a distributed source modelling technique (LORETA) concluded that the most likely sources of the RRN (using motion–direction deviants) were anteriorly to BA 17, and perhaps even to 18 and 19 (Pazo-Alvarez et al., 2004). In contrast, the approximate locations for the generators of the preceding non-plastic activity are probably much closer to, or even within, BA 17 or the primary visual cortex. As said, the exact parameters of these dipoles are heavily dependent on physical parameters, notably the spatial frequencies of the eliciting stimuli. In fact, the experimental conditions that produced the results illustrated in Figure 5.8 involved an oddball sequence of either standard high spatial frequencies and deviant low spatial frequencies, or in additional sequences, the reverse. Such a stimulus configuration then yields a two-phase result: an early activation (between 50–100 ms), very specific to the physical stimulus parameters but highly non-plastic, and subsequent activation (between 100–150 ms), highly plastic, not at all stimulus-specific, and additionally clearly downstream in the visual projection pathways, relative to the first phase. This is clearly different from the principles illustrated in Figure 5.5, in which connections a to e represent both stimulus specificity and plasticity (if only by adaptation). In contrast, for the sequence of non-plastic, stimulus-specific activation followed by plastic, non-stimulus-specific activation as associated with visual rareness, the stimulus specificity would still be implemented in connections a to e, but the plasticity is now limited to somewhere between f and h. Perhaps we should call this two-stage first-order memory.

Box 5.1   Primitive memory as a tool to identify neurons

A conspicuous application of decrement recovery functions has been coined as fMRI adaptation (an ERP version exists as well). Here the memory phenomenon serves as a readout measure for characterizing some perceptual mechanisms. In fact, adaptation paradigms may be the only method to relate the result of macroscopic imaging (fMRI, ERP) to microscopic neuronal processes. Suppose that there are two conditions, repeated presentation of stimulus A and that of stimulus B. In either case, the repeated representation can be assumed to elicit adaptation somewhere in the brain of neurons preferring either stimulus A or stimulus B. After the adaptation we present stimulus C, under the hypothesis that the neurons activated by C are at least partly the same neurons that were activated by (and adapted to) stimulus A. Any physiological response then, that is smaller after repetition to A than after repetition to B, can be assumed to reflect the activity of neurons that respond more to A and C, than they do to B and C.

This may sound abstract and potentially uninteresting, but the principle has in fact found some conspicuous applications. Piazza et al. reported that fMRI adaptation in horizontal IPS to specific dot-coded numerosities is followed by recovery in response to a different numerosity coded as either dots or Arabic number symbols, and vice versa, suggesting that there are neurons responsive to both numerosity formats (Piazza et al., 2007). Lorteije et al. found that visual cortex ERP responses to implied motion (a static display depicting a moving agent or object) were significantly reduced when preceded by an adaptation to real motion, but only when the direction of the real motion was consistent with that of the implied motion (Lorteije et al., 2007). Again, the interpretation is that this large-scale response of the human brain is carried by single neurons that respond to both kinds of motion information. Thus, whatever the exact type of memory, it can help researchers to connect different domains of information processing.

5.2.2   Connecting to the circuit breaker

Is pure adaptation a form of memory? This seems to be merely a matter of definition. The fact is that it turns to out to provide a powerful methodology for identifying specific neural populations using macroscopic methods in humans (see Box 5.1); note that for that purpose, habituation or a second-order process would do equally well.

Of course, adaptation may make information from unadapted channels stand out, and therefore increase the salience of a stimulus, and result in it capturing attention. In the latter case we could say, in the terminology of Chapter 3, that the circuit breaking system has been activated, the ventral right hemisphere (TPJ, IFG) based system for the detection of biologically relevant change. It is possible that the circuit breaker is activated by relatively low-level first-order processes (adaptation, habituation). Such activation then could be the result of local processes in or close to the primary perceptual cortex, or in more upstream regions, such as the thalamus. These processes would involve stimulus-specific or feature-specific neural pathways (e.g. involving neurons that prefer a certain colour, pitch, etc.), that feed into the dedicated system for salience detection which in turn is not at all dependent on the specific characteristics of the salient stimulus or stimulus feature.

In addition, the more specialized second-order and two-stage first-order systems that we discussed above seem to be in an even better anatomical and neurochemical position to act in concert with the circuit breaker. As already indicated in the previous section, the later phase (after 150 ms latency) of the visual change detection response (RRN or vMMN) has a right hemisphere dominance. This would be consistent with visual salience activating cortical areas that are still specific for the visual modality (occipital cortex), but at the same time functionally connected to a right hemisphere higher-order system that generalizes across perceptual modalities. A similar story holds for aMMN: it has been known for a long time that for a majority of deviating auditory features the aMNN has a predominantly right hemisphere scalp distribution and a stronger contribution from right hemisphere generators. This holds even for features contributing to the linguistic quality of auditory–temporal streams of stimuli, such as subtle deviations in tone duration (De Sanctis et al., 2009).

Also, certain neurochemical findings point to a special relationship between higher-order modality specific and modality non-specific salience detectors. For both systems acetylcholine (ACh) seems to be a crucial neurotransmitter (see also discussion in Chapter 3), and fluxes in ACh may facilitate both systems in concert. Figure 5.10 shows a pertinent result from a study by Furey and colleagues (Furey et al., 2000). In this study, available ACh was manipulated by infusing physiostigmine, a substance that suppresses the effect of natural acetylcholine esterase, which breaks down ACh. As can be seen, increasing ACh levels are associated with an enhanced BOLD response to face stimuli especially during their first presentation, and not during a subsequent memory retrieval phase. The exact effect of ACh in the visual cortex that mediates such effects remains to be established; there are indications that it alters the balance between excitatory glutamatergic and inhibitory GABA transmission. As for the treatment of psychopathology, salience detection systems and their pharmacology form a promising lead in relation to schizophrenia and psychosis. One idea is that the positive symptoms of schizophrenia especially are related to a disturbance in the discrimination of salient, potentially important events from the ongoing background of innocuous events (Turetsky et al., 2007). In parallel, clinicians have recently become excited about the possibility of cholinergic substances, including both nicotinic and muscarinic agonists, as a new line of treatment for this disease (Lieberman et al., 2008).

In sum, both the visual and the auditory modalities feature dedicated systems for the detection of unexpected change or novelty, even though the exact memory mechanisms involved may differ. Especially the right hemisphere, in combination with cholinergic transmission,

Figure 5.10

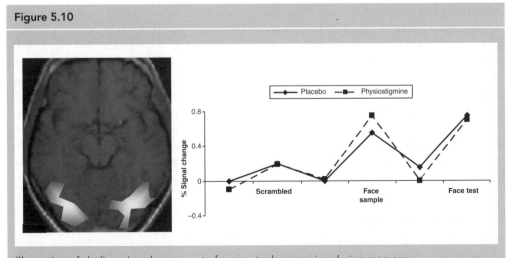

Illustration of cholinergic enhancement of perceptual processing during memory.
In ventral lateral visual cortex (MNI z = −12), physiostigmine (which boosts ACh transmission), specifically enhances the BOLD response to the first presentation (face sample, relative to same face test) of a specific face.

seems to be implicated in these systems, as well as with their interactions with a more non-specific circuit breaker system.

5.3 SHORT-TERM PERCEPTUAL MEMORY AND WORKING MEMORY

It is generally believed that there exists a special form of perceptual memory. Especially in vision, 'iconic memory' is thought to have a very short lifetime and a potentially unlimited capacity. The classical experimental paradigm to demonstrate iconic memory is the partial report task. Here, a multi-element display of, say, 12 different letters (3 rows of 4) is briefly flashed up on the screen. If the subject is immediately asked to report as many letters as possible from the display, the result amounts to about 4 out of 12; this is the whole report. However, if the subject is immediately asked to report one particular row that is spatially cued (afterwards!), no matter which location is cued the subject will always report correctly the 4 items. This means that:

(1) all information in the display resides in iconic memory for some time;
(2) something that is conventionally termed selective spatial attention (see Chapter 3) can be used to retain any information that is relevant for the report.

The partial report advantage (over whole report) disappears when the cue is delayed too long, about more than 200 ms. Apparently, this is the period that unselected information resides in the iconic buffer. Partial report performance declines with increasing complexity of the selection criterion. For example, with colour it is worse than with location, and with alpha-numeric category (report the digit among the letters) even worse. Apparently, with colour and alphanumeric category it is highly probable that a selected item has already vanished from the buffer.

For the auditory modality a similar system has been postulated. It may be the buffer you have access to when you're not paying attention to what someone is telling you until that person suddenly asks 'You're not listening, are you?' That is when you search your echoic memory and often succeed in retrieving the last twenty or so words spoken. Retrieval from echoic memory may be relatively easy because the echoic trace is thought to have a lifetime of several seconds. This is one reason why it may be related to the aMMN as described in the previous section, which also disappears when intervals between successive stimuli (standard and deviant) exceed several seconds (Cowan, 1995). Applying this logic to the vMMN, one would expect it to disappear with intervals longer than a few hundreds of milliseconds. Indeed, the studies into vMMN cited above used intervals up to 450 ms; but a systematic inquiry into inter-stimulus intervals and vMMN is lacking as yet. From the perspective of vMMN as a first-order mechanism, the effect of elongating inter-stimulus intervals is not so obvious: deviance detection responses would become larger, but so perhaps would responses to the standards.

5.3.1 Working memory

Results from partial report experiments are generally described as indicating that some selection mechanism allows partial information from sensory memory to enter more durable short term or working memory. Once it has entered this limited capacity system, it can be used to control behaviour, such as reporting the letter or digit (see discussion of the attentional blink in Chapter 3).

What does it mean when perceptual information has entered working memory in neuro-physiological terms? Desimone summarizes several mechanisms that become manifest in single neuron activity in the monkey brain. Perhaps of greatest importance, neurons in both the secondary visual cortex (inferior temporal or IT) and the lateral prefrontal cortex (PFC) show sustained action potentials, especially after a stimulus has disappeared, while the information it carried is still relevant (delay activity) (Desimone, 1996). Furthermore, introducing irrelevant but distracting stimuli during the delay interrupted the delay activity in IT, but not in PFC. In addition, Fuster et al. found that suppressing (by cooling) the activity of PFC neurons resulted in reduced stimulus specificity in IT, suggesting that PFC neurons support stimulus representations in IT (admittedly, the reverse effect of IT cooling on PFC activity was also found), and maintain these representations in the face of possible interference (Fuster et al., 1985).

A more detailed account of how PFC neurons represent information was provided by Duncan. While neurons in the perceptual cortex can show plasticity as a result of prolonged training (see later section on perceptual learning), PFC neurons change their stimulus specificity almost overnight as a function of changing task demands; they are not so much plastic as extremely flexible (Duncan, 2001). An extreme version of this view would assert that any neuron in the lateral PFC (say BAs 9 and 10, perhaps 45 and 46 as well) can represent features from any modality (a specific colour, pitch, location, or intensity of tactile stimulation), and shift to a different preferred stimulus an hour later, when task demands have changed. This, so-called, adaptive coding is probably not completely flexible; according to Duncan (2001), there is some statistical preference in specific groups of PFC neurons for specific features, especially across the hemispheres (e.g. right spatial, left verbal). This enormous flexibility of PFC neurons can only be explained by assuming that individual PFC neurons receive inputs from widely different perceptual modalities or from neural representations of a multitude of features within these modalities. A pertinent question then is: how do changes in goals and

Figure 5.11

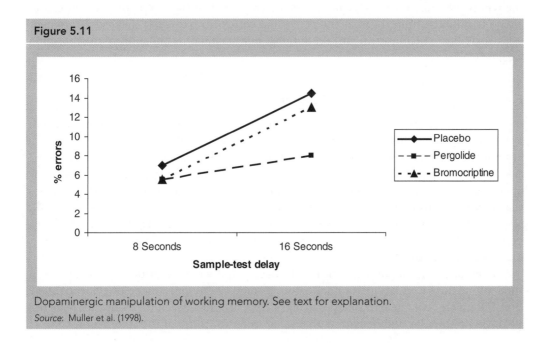

Dopaminergic manipulation of working memory. See text for explanation.
Source: Muller et al. (1998).

task demands modulate the strength of the connections from these neural feature representations to any given PFC neuron? This question is especially intriguing in the face of the idea that lateral PFC itself is often thought to be crucial in modulating the strength of connections throughout the brain.

To perform such tasks, PFC neurons need neurotransmitters, and the neurotransmitter traditionally viewed as crucial is dopamine (DA). More specifically, based on rodent research, working memory performance has been suggested to depend on optimal, rather than maximal stimulation of the D1 receptor, following an inverted U function relating working memory performance to levels of D1 stimulation (Robbins, 2000). This could be one reason why dopaminergic manipulation of human working memory function has produced mixed results (Mehta & Riedel, 2006), including improvements or nil effects under DA agonists, or even amelioration under DA antagonists (Mehta et al., 2004). Another factor could be the dependence of DA working memory effects on individual measures of basic information processing capacity (Mehta & Riedel, 2006). An example of the importance of D1 agonism in humans is shown in Figure 5.11. Healthy human volunteers performed a visual–spatial working memory task, in which the location of a test pattern of dots had to be matched to that of a preceding sample after an interval of either 8 s or 16 s (Muller et al., 1998). The task was performed after administration of either a placebo, the specific D2 agonist bromocriptine (2.5 mg per 80 kg body weight), or the mixed D1/D2 agonist pergolide (0.1 mg). As can be seen in Figure 5.11, the regular increase in matching errors with increasing delay was counteracted by pergolide but not by bromocriptine. The possibility that this was due to doses of bromocriptine that were too low was rendered unlikely by the parallel finding that the two substances did not differ in the extent to which they lowered levels of prolactin, a hormone that is sampled in blood. Although this suggests specific involvement of the D1 receptor, a more recent study indicates that bromocriptine may also improve working memory performance, but only in subjects selected for high self-reported impulsivity (Cools et al., 2007).

In sum, prefrontal neurons that are instrumental in representing relevant stimuli after the representations in the perceptual cortex have vanished have response properties that are quite different from those in the perceptual cortex. In particular they exhibit tremendous flexibility, which rests in part on optimal, not maximal, stimulation of the dopamine receptors.

5.4   RETRIEVAL FROM THE PERCEPTUAL CORTEX

Imagery is the covert act of perceiving something that is not present in the outside world, as it were with the mind's eye (while knowing that it is not actually there). It is a supreme example of interplay *and* overlap between mechanisms generally categorized under perception, or memory, or even attention. For example, Driver and Frith suggest that 'preparing to attend to a particular stimulus may be psychologically and neurally equivalent to imaging that stimulus, with both cases involving increased activity in those brain areas that would respond to the corresponding stimulus if it were represented.' This increased activity corresponds to the bias as discussed in Chapter 3, or 'baseline shift' in Driver and Frith's terminology (Driver & Frith, 2000).

Numerous studies support the idea that imagery and real perception overlap, at least at the level of the secondary perceptual cortex (Farah, 1989). One source of evidence stems from ERPs. One could imagine a topographical comparison between two contrasts, reflecting perceiving a stimulus and imagining that same stimulus (think of the comparison between

Figure 5.12

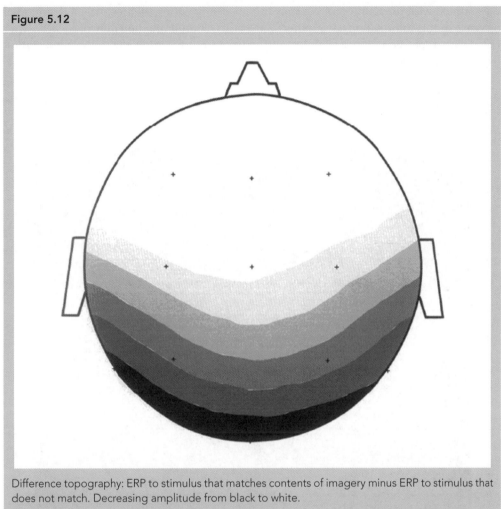

Difference topography: ERP to stimulus that matches contents of imagery minus ERP to stimulus that does not match. Decreasing amplitude from black to white.

Source: Reprinted from Farah (1989), with permission from Elsevier.

bias and attentional modulation as discussed in Chapter 3). The actual evidence for this issue is a little less straightforward however (see Figure 5.12). Another line of argument refers to patients with damage in their posterior cortex, who often report deficits in imagining visual scenes very similar to those of real perception. One example is patient I.G., (discussed in Figure 3.1, Chapter 3), who exhibited hemispatial neglect both when viewing a particular scene and when imagining it.

Pertinent evidence also stems from research on retrieval from (long-term) memory, the process of activating a representation of previously learned materials, so that they can be reported as part of a retrieval task. What exactly happens when people are cued to retrieve an item from memory? A fascinating view on this issue was provided by Wheeler and colleagues (Wheeler et al., 2000). Figure 5.13 not only shows an area of visual cortex activated by visual stimuli, but also that part of this area in the secondary visual cortex is activated when these stimuli are being retrieved from memory. Also illustrated is that similar findings were obtained for auditory stimulus materials. Hence, retrieving specific sensory information is associated with reactivation of neurons in the sensory cortex that responded to an initial presence of this information. In another study, visual stimuli that had previously been associated with a specific auditory stimulus, also activate auditory cortex upon later presentation (Nyberg et al., 2000).

Figure 5.13

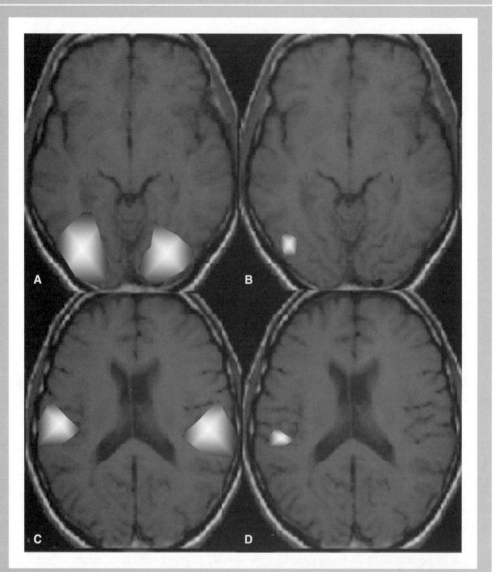

A: approximated visual cortex regions (MNI z = −6) showing more activation to pictures than to sounds; B: a subset of approximated secondary visual cortex regions showing more activation when cued to retrieve visual, relative to auditory, items; C: approximated auditory cortex areas (MNI z = 18) showing more activation to sounds than to pictures; D: a subset of approximated secondary auditory cortex regions showing more activation when cued to retrieve auditory, relative to visual, items.

A later study distinguished between the roles of ventral (inferior–temporal–fusiform as well as inferior–occipital areas) and dorsal (parietal) visual pathways in retrieving visual information (Wheeler et al., 2006) (Plate XII). The ventral areas responded more strongly to a label that previously, through learning, had been associated with visual information (a picture of an apple), than to one associated with a sound (of a train). The dorsal areas not only showed this same pattern, but also responded more strongly to a preceding cue that predicted that the label would signal visual retrieval, relative to one that predicted auditory retrieval. Thus, the hierarchy in the top–down modulation of visual processing encountered before (Chapter 3) can also be observed during memory retrieval processes, where dorsal areas implement expectation for visual retrieval in general, and ventral areas implement more the search for a specific visual item.

Are there any other signals, from other parts of the brain, which may be instrumental in retrieval from the perceptual cortex? Every now and then, brain activation maps reveal hippocampal activity during retrieval. This seems to be at odds with studies on hippocampal patients that have demonstrated predominantly anterograde amnesia, and only limited retrograde amnesia (see Chapter 6). One possibility is that the hippocampal activations during retrieval actually reflect consolidation mechanisms that are invoked along with the retrieval operation; this would indeed be consistent with the limited retrograde amnesia reported for hippocampal patients (as well as with dense anterograde amnesia). This issue is discussed in more detail in Chapter 10. A further classic view is that lateral prefrontal areas are crucial for episodic retrieval operations.

Another possibility was suggested by the famous taxi driver studies. While being scanned with PET, London taxi drivers recalled complete routes between two locations in the greater London area. Control conditions included one in which they imagined famous landmarks from all over the world that they had not actually visited. Compared to the control condition, route retrieval was specifically associated with activation of the posterior right hemisphere hippocampus (Maguire et al., 1997). This effect appears to be very specific for 'navigating in a large-scale spatial framework'; in contrast, landmark retrieval was associated with left lateral prefrontal activation, consistent with many other studies implicating this region in semantic retrieval. A follow-up study found a significant correlation between right posterior hippocampus volume and years working as a London taxi driver (Maguire et al., 2000). Such a correlation is generally taken as supportive of plasticity in the brain area concerned, as driven by long-term experience in certain environments. In other words, taxi drivers have a large right posterior hippocampus because of their history as a taxi driver, not the other way around. According to Maguire and colleagues, the right posterior hippocampus may even contain the neural population that implements the long-term representation or storage of topographical information. However, other studies suggest that the hippocampus is not necessary for imaginary navigating in well-known spatial layouts (Rosenbaum et al., 2005). It is hard to exclude that the larger hippocampus parts that come with navigating experience reflect the continuous re-encoding or consolidation that accompanies any retrieval operation.

In sum, episodic retrieval processes involve interactions between perceptual–cortex regions and, again, higher control areas. The latter are probably based in the prefrontal cortex, or perhaps, in relation to memory, also in the hippocampus. However, it is questionable whether interactions with the hippocampus actually support the retrieval operation, even in the case of spatial semantic information.

5.5   LONG-TERM PLASTICITY IN PERCEPTION

Neural representations in the sensory cortex sometimes turn out to be very plastic, in that their characteristics are affected by practice. One well-known example concerns string musicians, who show evidence of abnormally large representations in the somatosensory cortex of those fingers that are most important for playing the instrument. Another example consists of phantom experiences after amputation, which can be explained by the activity of somatosensory–cortex representations of the amputated limb having been taken over by projections from other parts of the body. Recent years have witnessed substantial research into renewed functionality of the occipital cortex in blind individuals. These results are often taken as indicative of plasticity in the strength of dormant connections between the occipital cortex and the rest of the brain, but given that most of these studies only included participants blind from birth, this conjecture may be hard to defend.

At a more subtle level is the phenomenon of perceptual learning. This is a form of implicit learning that involves 'improving one's ability, with practice, to discriminate differences in the attributes of simple sensory stimuli' (Gilbert et al., 2001). In the visual modality, perceptual learning is said to involve changes in the response characteristics of neurons in the inferior–temporal cortex as well as upstream to the primary visual cortex. As mentioned in the first section of this chapter, perceptual learning can entail enhanced sensitivity. Due to training on a task in which, for example, vertical orientations are relevant, a large number of neurons may become responsive to vertical orientations. Training may also enhance specificity: a given neuron becomes tuned more sharply to a specific orientation, responding less to other orientations than it did before. It has been proposed that perceptual learning involves a shift of representations that control action and subjective experience from secondary to primary sensory areas (Gilbert et al., 2001). For example, inferring a triangle from the individual lines in Figure 5.2 may initially require integration by the secondary visual cortex of signals from orientation-sensitive neurons with specific receptive fields (coding the locations of the

Figure 5.14

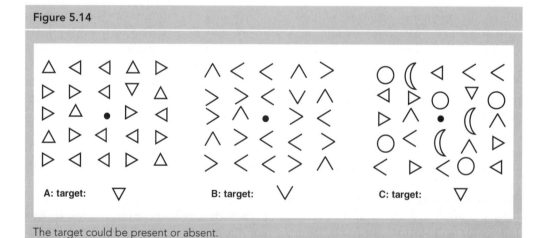

A: target: ▽   B: target: ∨   C: target: ▽

The target could be present or absent.
Long-term perceptual learning was observed for trained configurations (A, although locations for all orientations changed continuously), and also when there was a new background of non-targets during testing (C), but not when the target object changed (B).
Source: Gilbert et al. (2001). Reprinted with permission from Elsevier.

lines) in the primary visual cortex. With training, and through feedback from the secondary to the primary cortex, joint activation of the orientation- and location-specific neurons in the primary cortex may become sufficient to experience a triangle.

What exactly can be learned through these mechanisms? Sigman and Gilbert trained observers for four to six days to detect a specifically oriented triangle as a target in displays like the ones shown in Figure 5.14. Using ultra-fast presentation rates, observers improved their target detection rate from between 10 per cent and 20 per cent to over 70 per cent, and this performance level was retained in a one month follow-up (Sigman & Gilbert, 2000). This improvement was specific for the target object (triangle), its orientation (pointing downwards, for example, as in Figure 5.14), and the part of the visual field where the displays were presented (a 4 by 4 degrees square around fixation). Whereas learning pertained only to identically oriented triangles, it was completely independent of the background of non-target distracters.

Such results suggest that perceptual learning is quite independent of the context, but there actually appears to be quite a subtle limit to this independence. According to Gilbert et al. (2001), visual learning requires the active involvement of the observer. However, this notion is not consistent with the available evidence. According to Seitz and Watanabe, perceptual learning depends on temporal coincidence with task-relevant events (Seitz & Watanabe, 2005). Figure 5.15 depicts an example. Hardly detectable coherence of motion was paired with either a target (the white L and T) in a sequence of non-target distracters, or with one of the distracters. Only in the former case was there an improvement in the detection of coherent motion with training for the specific motion direction that was consistently paired with the target. Specifically, training extended over 20 days, with at least 960 trials per day. During training only 5 per cent of the dots moved coherently in the directions indicated by the dark arrows in Figure 5.15, a proportion that is too small for subjective awareness of a specific motion direction to occur. Nevertheless, this subliminal training yielded improvements after 20 days in the detection of 10 per cent coherent motion (not for 5 per cent), but only for the direction that had been paired systematically with the target letters.

Target detection, as opposed to distracter processing, has been associated with the diffuse release of several neurotransmitters (Aston-Jones et al., 1999), and this has, in turn,

Figure 5.15

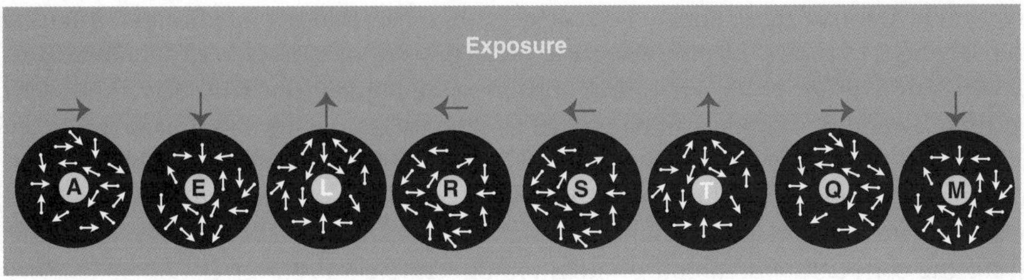

Hardly detectable coherence of motion paired with a target in a sequence of non-targets. See text for explanation.

Source: Reprinted from Seitz and Watanabe et al. (2005) with permission from Elsevier.

Figure 5.16

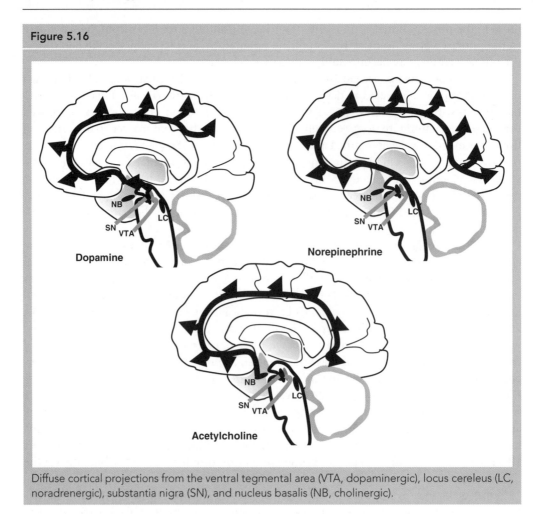

Dopamine

Norepinephrine

Acetylcholine

Diffuse cortical projections from the ventral tegmental area (VTA, dopaminergic), locus cereleus (LC, noradrenergic), substantia nigra (SN), and nucleus basalis (NB, cholinergic).

been associated with enhanced plasticity in cortical representations. In older rodent studies, stimulation of subcortical nuclei like the ventral tegmental area (VTA) (Bao et al., 2001) and the nucleus basalis (NB) (Kilgard & Merzenich, 1998), paired with specific auditory stimuli, resulted in altered cortical maps for these specific stimuli, relative to equal but unpaired auditory stimuli. A similar argument has been made with respect to norepinephrine (Gordon et al., 1988). Figure 5.16 shows the diffuse cortical projections from VTA, LC and NB. These projections mediate a diffuse cortical release of dopamine, norepinephrine and acetylcholine. Note that these ascending systems can be viewed as primary candidates to implement Sokolov's amplifying system (Figure 5.6), since they can be activated by any novel, or otherwise potentially relevant, stimulus (Aston-Jones et al., 1999; Redgrave & Gurney, 2006). Specifically, a dopamine gate implemented through such an ascending system has been suggested as crucial for the correct interpretation of attention-directing cues (Braver & Cohen, 1999) (see Chapter 3). Generally then, novel or otherwise relevant stimuli activate these amplifying systems, which in turn diffusely activate the cortex and therefore promote learning from that stimulus. This learning may relate to the fact that it is harmless or uninteresting, or to more subtle aspects discriminating it from other stimuli that more or less resemble it, as in typical perceptual learning. It remains to establish how these different ascending systems differ with respect to the exact form of modulation of perceptual processing and learning they cause. One clue is that dopaminergic stimulation paired with auditory stimulation promotes stimulus specificity (sharper tuning), while paired cholinergic stimulation seems to increase the strength of the stimulus-evoked activity. This may or may not be related to the fact that, in spite of their diffuseness, the various projections still differ in the exact pattern of their cortical targets. For example, the NE projections are more posterior on average compared to the DA projections.

A study by Dinge and colleagues beautifully underscores these principles. Here, subjects were exposed to three hour mechanical stimulation of an 8 mm diameter spot on the right index fingertip. Within this 8 mm spot, a number of overlapping receptive fields of cortical somatosensory neurons were stimulated in concert. This three hour stimulation training produced a marked reduction of the discrimination threshold for that fingertip (but not at all for the left index fingertip); the discrimination threshold was the just notable difference in millimetres between two stimulated points on the fingertip. Furthermore, this effect was obtained in a placebo condition, but was significantly enhanced after acute administration of a dose of amphetamine, which boosts the release of dopamine, and perhaps also of norepinephrine (see Figure 5.16). Even more spectacularly, the geometrical centre of somatosensory–cortical activation due to fingertip stimulation shifted from one location before training to a different one after training, for the right index finger but not the left one, and this effect was

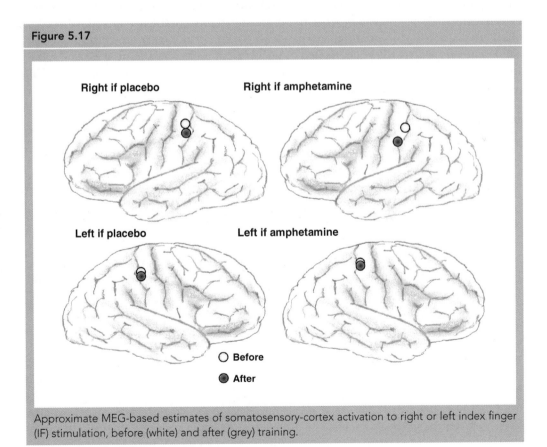

Figure 5.17

Right if placebo   Right if amphetamine

Left if placebo   Left if amphetamine

○ Before

● After

Approximate MEG-based estimates of somatosensory-cortex activation to right or left index finger (IF) stimulation, before (white) and after (grey) training.

also more pronounced under amphetamine than under a placebo (see Figure 5.17). Finally, there was also a clear correlation between change in the discrimination threshold and the extent of the shift in the somatosensory–cortex activation (Dinse et al., 2003). Note that this latter shift only indicates that the equivalent dipole, or geometrical centre of activation, has changed after training; it is possible that this reflects an increase in the cortical area that responds to finger stimulation. Even then, this pharmacological study demonstrates concurrent perceptual learning and changes in the response of the perceptual cortex, consistent with a mediating role for those changes of subcortical–cortical projections.

5.6   CONCLUDING REMARKS

Perception and memory interact at the level of the sensory cortex. In visual and auditory cortices, prior experience may induce several variants of short-term plasticity, that were summarized as modality specific, first-order (adaptation and habituation), two-stage first-order, as well as second-order learning processes, the latter involving parallel sensory–memory traces of past events. Such phenomena may form the neural basis of sensory memory, the huge capacity, very short-lived register of sensory inputs that affords sensory continuity. They may also be transferred to more enduring representations, either in the prefrontal cortex to constitute working memory, the on-line maintenance of relevant in formation, or in the perceptual cortex itself, where they form the basis of perceptual learning. The latter phenomenon seems to depend on interactions with subcortical regions. Such interactions are also instrumental in driving higher-order learning, and are in turn contingent upon the detection of salient changes in the environment, based on the results of higher-order learning. From a different perspective, the phenomenon of imagery can be seen as a form of explicit recall, which involves reactivation of (perhaps even the primary) sensory cortex, driven by signals most probably originating in higher control areas such as the prefrontal cortex.

Questions

1. In the introduction to this chapter (Section 5.0) it was stated that to certify that we are really dealing with visual agnosia, deficits in primary visual cortex or lower level visual structures, as well general memory deficits, need to be ruled out. How can this be accomplished?
2. Also in Section 5.0 it was stated that patients diagnosed with integrative agnosia have no problem performing the appropriate action on objects, and in fact viewing their own action with respect to an object sometimes helps them to retrieve the correct name. Would this also work for associative–agnosia patients?
3. See Section 5.4. Retrieving specific sensory information is associated with the reactivation of neurons in the sensory cortex that responded to an initial presence of this information. Would these really be the same neurons that were reactivated? Can we use the principles laid out in Box 5.1 to answer this question?

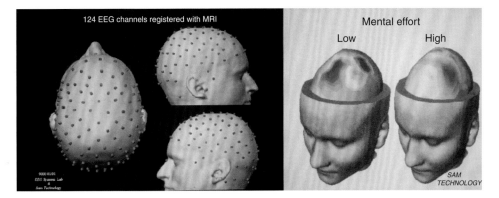

Plate I Left: accurate localization of electrodes (pink dots) based on an MRI scan of the head allows for optimal source localization.
Right: topographical display of brain activity in a working memory task with low effort trials and high effort trials. Colour indicates the evoked potential, after mathematical deblurring of the 124-channel EEG recordings and MRI-based projection onto the brain surface. Courtesy of EEG systems lab and Sam technology.

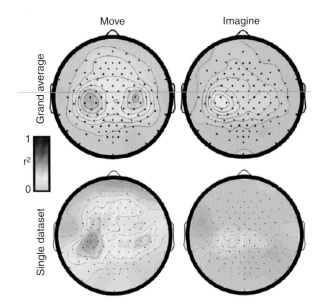

Plate II Topographical map of changes in the 8 to 24 Hz frequency band.
The top row shows the average for 12 healthy subjects, the bottom row shows a single subject. Subjects performed a finger tapping task with the right hand (left column), and a motor imagery tasks (right) where they imagined making the same movements. Power decreased with movement or imagery but is shown as a positive correlation for display purposes. Colour indicate the square of the correlation between power decrease and task (i.e. explained variance as a measure of activity). The figure shows an expected power decrease in the contralateral hemisphere.

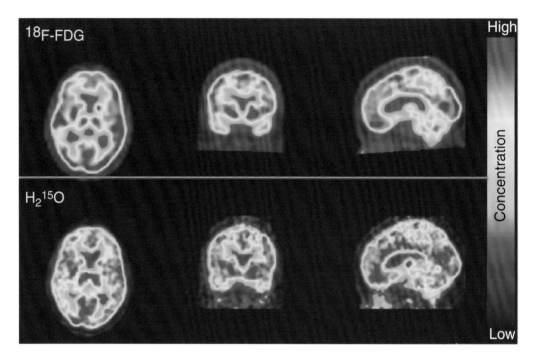

Plate III PET images of one person.
The top displays the distribution of a radioactive marker of glucose metabolism (^{18}F-FDG). One slice is shown in each direction: transaxial, coronal and sagittal. The bottom displays the distribution of a radioactive marker of cerebral bloodflow (^{15}O in water), reflecting brain activity. Courtesy of B.N.M. van Berckel, Free University Medical Center, Amsterdam, Netherlands.

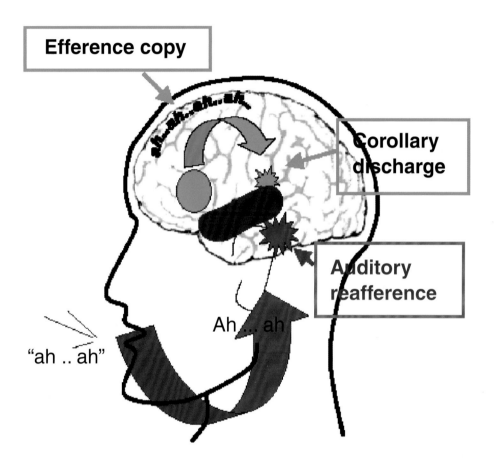

Plate IV Schematical outline of how speech intention would result in an efference copy to auditory cortex.
There the efference copy causes a corollary discharge that interacts with the auditory reafference signal from the speech sound.
Source: Reprinted from Ford and Mathalon (2005) with permission from Elsevier.

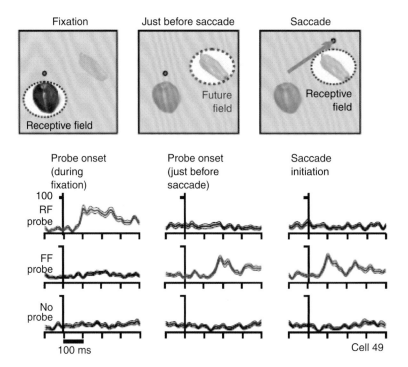

Plate V Action potentials per time unit for neurons in the FEF.
Peppers and apples are used as probe stimuli to define the receptive field. Just before a saccade, the receptive field changes to the one it would normally have (and has) after the saccade.
Source: From Sommer and Wurtz (2006). Reprinted by permission from Macmillan Publishers Ltd: Nature.

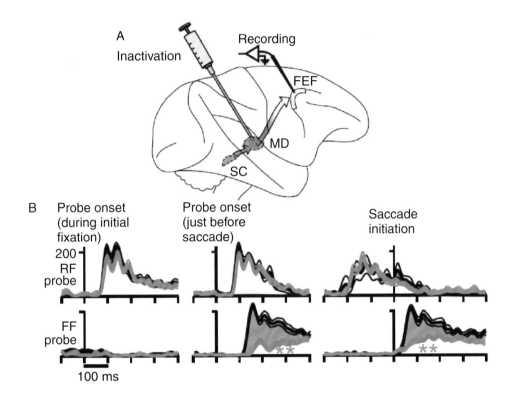

Plate VI A: SC – superior Colliculus, MD – mediodorsal thalamus, FEF – frontal eye fields.
Inactivating MD interrupts the SC-FEF connection; B: this results in loss of the 'future field' (FF) response (RF – original receptive field). Normally the neurons respond to new receptive field (FF) just before the saccade, but this shift is suppressed when the connection is lost. In contrast, the response tot the original RF is not affected, apparently because it is not dependent on the SC-FEF connection. Note also that this neuron, rather than shifting from RF to FF, extends its RF, adding FF to RF.

Source: From Sommer and Wurz (2006). Reprinted by permission from Macmillan Publishers Ltd: Nature.

P1 Attention effect

Right stimuli   **Left stimuli**

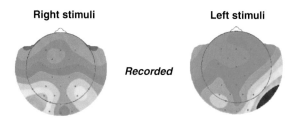

Recorded

Plate VII Recorded scalp topography of the P1 effect (ERP to stimulus when attended minus ERP to same stimulus when ignored).

Voltages range from slightly negative (blue), via intermediate values (green–yellow–orange), to pronounced positivity (red). A very similar topography was estimated from information from a PET version of the experiment.

Source: Reprinted from Mangun et al. (2001) with permission from Elsevier.

A   Attend-cue minus Interpret-cue difference waves: scalp channel activity

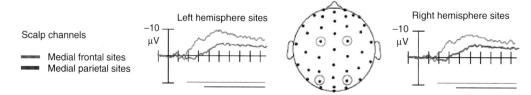

B   Attend-cue minus Interpret-cue difference waves: source activity of dippoles constrained to fMRI foci

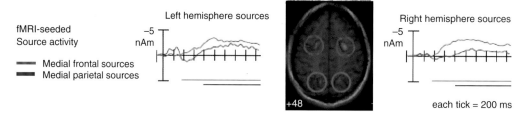

Plate VIII The interpret-cue was the neutral control cue.

See text for explanation. Tallairach Z coordinates for the fMRI hotspots ranged from 46 to 50. Front of the head up

Source: Grent-'t-Jong & Woldorff (2007).

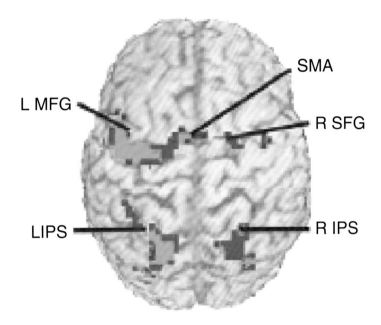

Plate IX Cortical areas that respond to cues that direct attention to a location in space (blue), or to cues that direct attention to a specific color (red), or to both kinds of cues (green).

Source: Giesbrecht et al. (2003). Reprinted with permission from Elsevier.

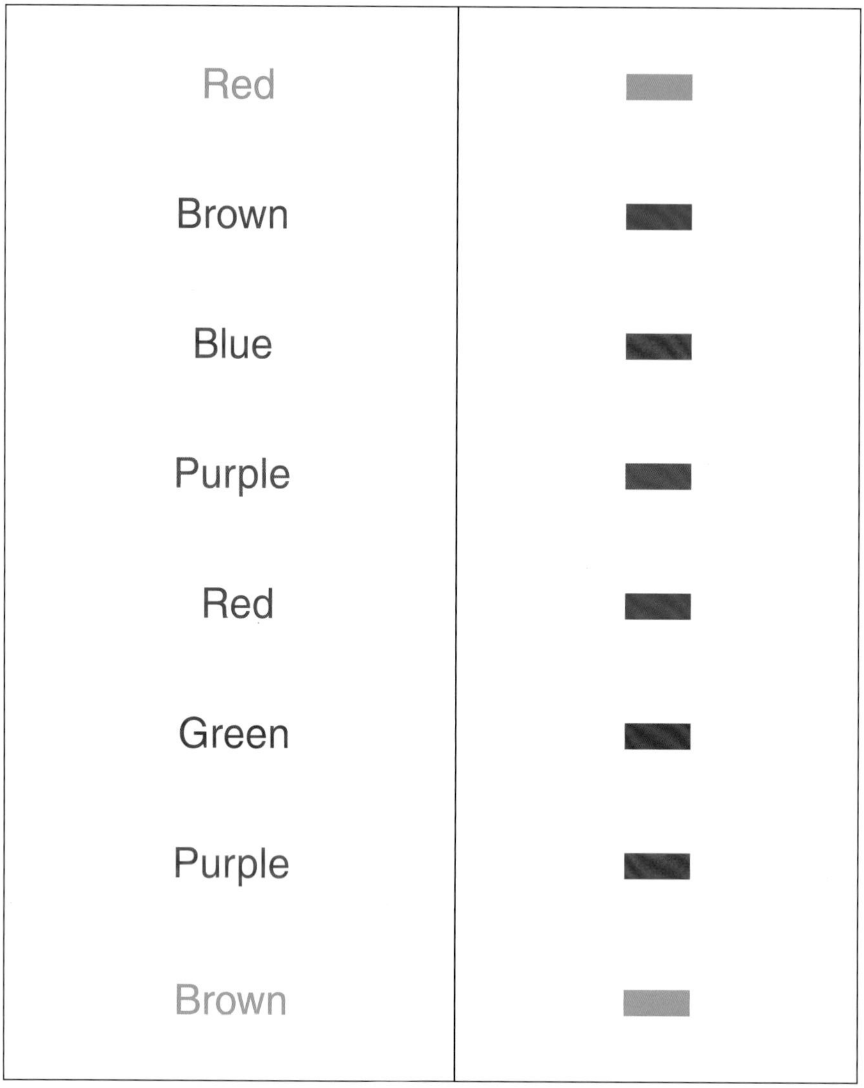

Red

Brown

Blue

Purple

Red

Green

Purple

Brown

Plate X Approximation of Stroop's (1935) original colour-naming stimuli, in the incongruent (left) and the neutral (right) condition.

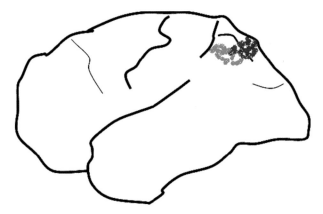

Plate XI Approximate results of the Rushworth et al. (2001) study.
Green: IPS activation related to selection of a visual dimension. Red: IPS activation related to selection of stimulus–response mappings.

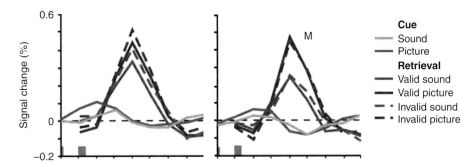

Plate XII Narrow grey bars on x-axis represent onset of preparatory cues ('expect sound retrieval' or 'expect picture retrieval'), which were mostly valid.
Preparatory cues were followed by retrieval cues (wide grey bars) that signalled what actually had to be retrieved. Left: intra-parietal sulcus responds stronger to 'expect picture retrieval', and to picture retrieval cues. Right: left fusiform gyrus (IT) responds differentially only to retrieval cues.
Source: From Wheeler et al. (2006) by permission of Oxford University Press.

Plate XIII The upper stimulus is from the well-known Stroop task ('name the colour in which the word is written').

The lower stimulus is from an alternative 'conflict' paradigm

Source: De Fockert et al. (2001).

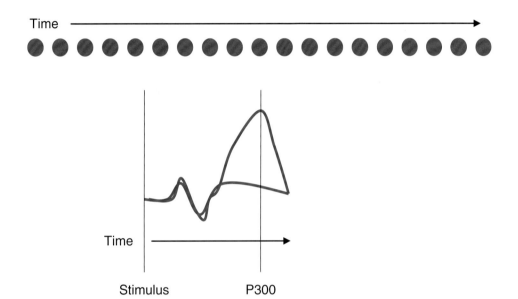

Plate XIV Typical P300 set-up and response.
Averaging the event-related brain potentials to successive frequent red dots and infrequent blue dots yields the average signals in the corresponding colours. The P300 peak occurs some 300 to 500 ms post-stimulus, mainly over parietal areas.

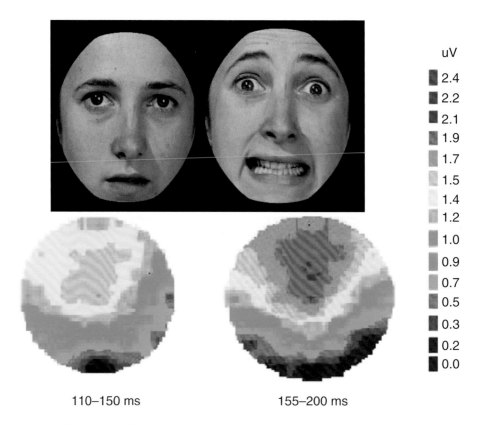

	uV
	2.4
	2.2
	2.1
	1.9
	1.7
	1.5
	1.4
	1.2
	1.0
	0.9
	0.7
	0.5
	0.3
	0.2
	0.0

110–150 ms   155–200 ms

Plate XV A: Illustration of emotional expressions used in experiments evaluating responses to fearfulness. Courtesy of prof. Christian Keysers.
B: topographies (back of the head below) represent the difference between the ERPs to fearful versus neutral stimuli at latencies from 110 to 200 ms post-stimulus.

Source: Reprinted from Eimer and Holmes (2007) with permission from Elsevier.

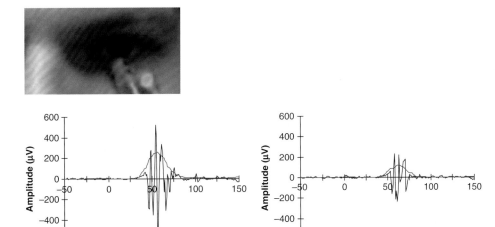

Plate XVI Upper panel: recording of the muscle activity through electromyography from the muscle that controls eyelid closure.

Lower panels: the blue traces represent a typical burst of muscle activity as evident in the electromyogram; the burst may be more (left) or less (right) intense. The pink trace is a transformation of the recorded signal to aid in quantification.

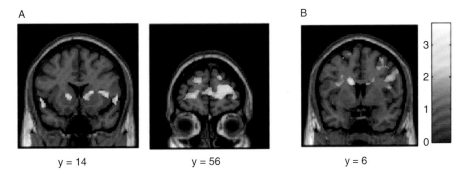

Plate XVII A: responses in likers. Left: ventral striatum/ nucleus accumbens (medial blobs) activation higher for alcohol cues than for neutral cues. Right: same contrast for prefrontal cortex.

B: same contrast for dorsal basal ganglia (part of the caudate nucleus dorsal to the ventral striatum) in wanters. Coronal slices at MNI y coordinates.

Source: From Vollstadt-Klein et al. (2010). Reprinted with permission from John Wiley and Sons.

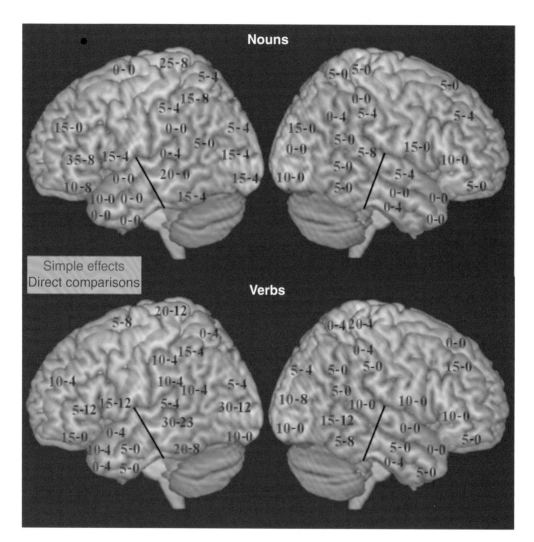

Plate XVIII Functional-neuroimaging derived cortical activations related to noun processing or verb processing.

Blue: noun or verb condition versus baseline. Red: Nouns > Verbs (above) or Verbs > Nouns. The black lines run from the fronto-ventral corner of Heschl's gyrus and orthogonally to the main axis of the superior temporal sulcus.

Source: Reprinted from Crepaldi et al. (2011) with permission from Elsevier.

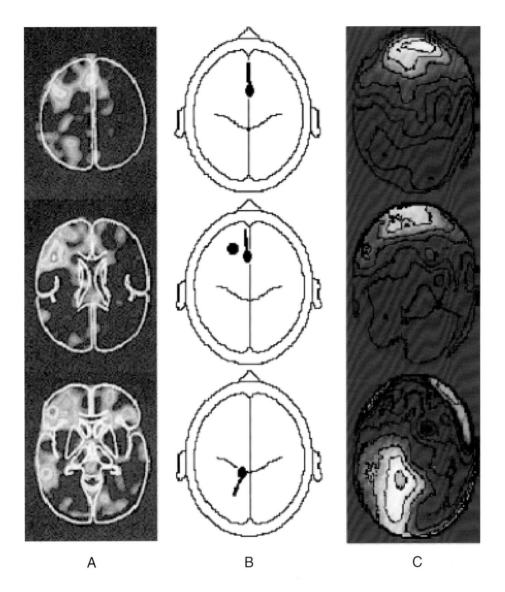

A   B   C

Plate XIX Complete set of activations for novel versus repeated verb generation (see Figure 4.6).
Middle and right columns depict dipoles and scalp distributions as function of time: 200 ms, 250 ms, and 650 ms.

Source: Reprinted from from Abdullaev and Posner (1998) with permission from Elsevier.

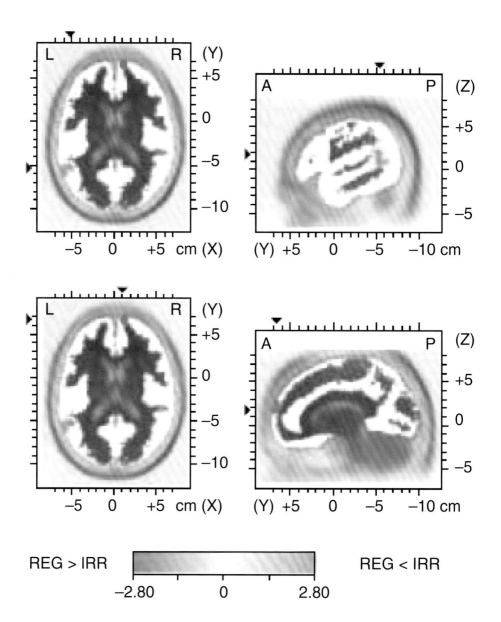

Plate XX Activations during production of regular (REG > IRR), green spots) and irregular (REG < IRR, orange) verb past tense.

Based on ERP recordings from healthy volunteers, latency 288 to 321 ms relative to verb–stem presentation.

Source: From Lavric et al. (2001a, b) reprinted with permission from Elsevier.

6 ATTENTION AND MEMORY

Key Points

- Attentional modulation and working memory maintenance converge on modulated sensory cortex responses, such as the P1 effect.
- Attentional control mechanisms and working memory operations overlap in dorsal parietal and frontal cortices. The additional recruitment of dorsal and ventral lateral prefrontal cortices may depend on additional working memory demands subserving extended maintenance or distracter suppression.
- Dopaminergic mechanisms subserve attentional control mechanisms and working memory operations.
- Attentional modulation influences later episodic long-term memory, involving a network of visual cortex, parahippocampal, and lateral prefrontal areas.

6.0 INTRODUCTION

Patients with bilateral damage to a brain structure called the hippocampus (Figure 6.1) have trouble forming new episodic memories, which are explicit and/or conscious memories of past events. For example, patient H.M. could learn procedural tasks (like mirror drawing) as skillfully as the average healthy person after a number of daily training sessions; yet he was unable to relate anything about the previous sessions. Another patient, C.W., would meet his wife and greet her quite cordially; if she then left the room to return a few minutes later, he would greet her as if it was for the very first time that day. From H.M.'s example, we learn that different forms of memory (episodic versus procedural, see Box 6.1) are probably based on different mechanisms. The incident of C.W.'s wife illustrates how memory interacts with other cognitive functions, like attention: episodic memory, and probably other forms, is a strong determinant of the amount and kind of attention we pay to certain events, in this case someone entering the room. This chapter is about a number of ways in which memory and attention interact, and how this maps onto overlapping and non-overlapping brain mechanisms.

Memory is a short- or long-lasting change in the pattern of neural activity or responsivity, which can be detected at a later stage. This concise, global, and rather technical, definition covers a wealth of phenomena and principles. As we know from experimental psychology, memories can be more or less enduring. We retain a phone number just long enough to dial it; other information we remember for a lifetime (e.g. a definition of memory). Memory, or learning, involves a neural trace, or an engram, a change somewhere in the brain. After learning, or after the memory has been formed, the pattern of neural activity across the whole brain must have changed. This neural trace makes us respond to information differently from

Figure 6.1

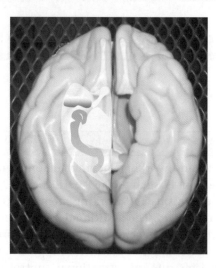

Illustration of the hippocampus in a ventral view of the brain.
Upper = anterior, right hemisphere to the left side. The right hemisphere hippocampus is projected as a seahorse-like structure, posterior to the more peanut-like amygdala.

Box 6.1 A brief overview of memory systems

Memory is commonly divided into very short-term, short-term and long-term systems. The very short-term system is discussed in Section 5.3. Short-term and working memory are discussed in this chapter. Long-term memory is commonly divided into a declarative or explicit system, and implicit systems. The creation (encoding and storing) and consolidation of explicit episodes, especially personal ones, into a long-term store that can be accessed for later use (retrieval) is believed to be dependent on structures of and within the temporal lobe (see discussion of hippocampal patients in this section). This system may largely overlap with that devoted to semantic explicit memory, which is concerned with factual information such as words and other language materials, and world knowledge. In both cases, the memory traces themselves are thought to be implemented in widespread cortical areas (more on this in Chapter 11). Also, in both cases, retrieving such memory depends on prefrontal cortex function. Generally, hippocampal patients are unable to create new explicit memories (they suffer from anterograde amnesia), but their retrieval of old information is not, or is far less, impaired (they have no, or limited, retrograde amnesia), and neither is their short-term or working memory. In addition, they do not show deficiencies in what is termed procedural memory. This kind of learning is important for skills such as driving or swimming, or for tasks such as learning to draw mirror images. Procedural learning mainly involves signals between motor cortical areas and basal ganglia, as will be discussed extensively in Chapter 7. Finally, there is also a perceptual variety of implicit learning and memory.

---

the way we responded to that same information before the change took place. For example, encountering a person for the first time will trigger a response different from the one after several encounters, both on the neural and the subjective levels (if there is not too much damage to the hippocampus). If at some time we are actually introduced to this person, on the next occasion a further difference will be evident: we are able to use this person's name. Upon being introduced, the change that has taken place concerns the link between the face information and the name information. This change can be detected at a later stage: by ourselves, when we call the name; and by a researcher, who records the naming response as evidence of prior learning.

What determines the quality of the neural trace, so that it changes responsivity? What else determines how well it can be detected at a later stage? This chapter addresses how neural traces come about and how their development is intertwined with processes commonly referred to as the concept of attention.

6.1   SPATIAL ATTENTION AND WORKING MEMORY CONVERGE ON A FRONTO-PARIETAL NETWORK

6.1.1   Working memory or working attention?

As we saw in Section 5.3, a distinction can be made between ultra short-term and short-term storage. Ultra short-term or sensory register traces may last only a few hundred milliseconds. Short-term storage traces may last for an infinitely long time, provided nothing interferes with them. The vulnerability to interference is the second characteristic of short-term storage: it has a limited capacity. To make sensory register traces more enduring, an additional process is needed: selective attention. Selective attention allows for a transfer from sensory register to short-term storage, which in turn enables us to name the information or to write it down. This is a first instance of the interaction between selective attention and working memory.

The idea of a transfer from sensory register to short-term storage through selective attention is based on partial report experiments. As discussed in Section 5.3, in such experiments subjects direct attention to a location in space, and items (e.g. letters or digits) at that location are entered into short-term storage. But what actually happens when attention is, or has been, directed to a location in space? It is quite conceivable that an internal representation of the attended location is activated. In other words, a neural activity counterpart of the external location would arise, which may endure in the absence of that external information. This would be a second instance of the interaction between selective attention and short-term memory. In this case, short-term memory subserves selective attention, rather than the other way around.

It has been proposed that short-term storage depends on directing attention. In this context the term working memory is often used, instead of the term short-term memory, to cover the possibility that the information is not just stored or maintained, but may also be manipulated. For example, holding the location of a visual item in working memory after that item has disappeared would depend on shifting attention to that location. This hypothesis is supported by results from behavioural experiments. Awh et al. (1998) had subjects memorize the location of a sample item for several seconds, after which a test stimulus was presented; subjects had to indicate whether sample and test stimulus were at the same location (Figure 6.2). During the retention interval, a coloured circle was presented, either small or large, with the small one at a random location; as a second task, subjects had to identify the colour. The assumption was that to identify the colour of the small circle attention had to be shifted to the location of the circle, whereas no such shifts were necessary to identify the colour of the large circle. Memory performance in this matching to sample task was poorer for colours of the small circles than for large ones. This result is consistent with the idea that working memory for locations depends on spatial attention being directed to that location, assuming that such attention was disrupted by the shift of attention to a small circle.

However, based on such results, it is difficult to draw strong conclusions about covert mental processing. First, it is hard to exclude that selective attention depends on working

Figure 6.2

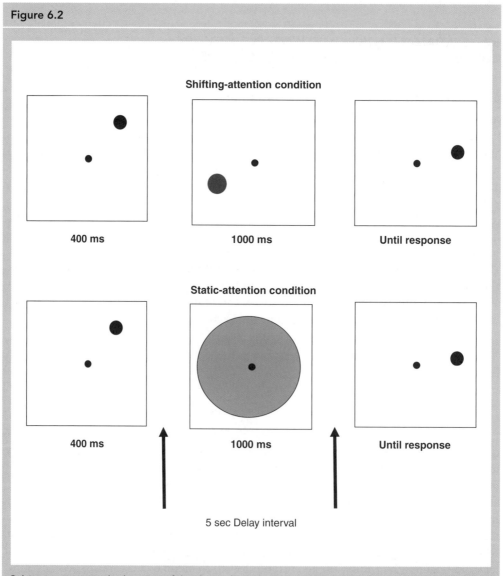

Subjects memorize the location of the dot in the right upper quadrant.
In the static condition, they presumably do not shift attention to the location of the grey circle (middle panel), whereas they presumably do so in the shifting condition.
Source: Based on Awh et al. (1998).

memory and not the other way around. Second, it is still unclear whether one function controls the other, or whether the two functions are, in fact, identical. Some authors have stated that by definition directing and maintaining attention to information implies storing and maintaining it in working memory. Baddely (1995) has proposed that working memory could just as well be termed working attention. Baddely's well-known theory of working memory involves two storage systems (the articulatory or phonological loop and the visual–spatial scratch or sketch pad). These two slave systems are controlled by a central executive system. The central executive system may well be viewed as an attentional control system

Figure 6.3

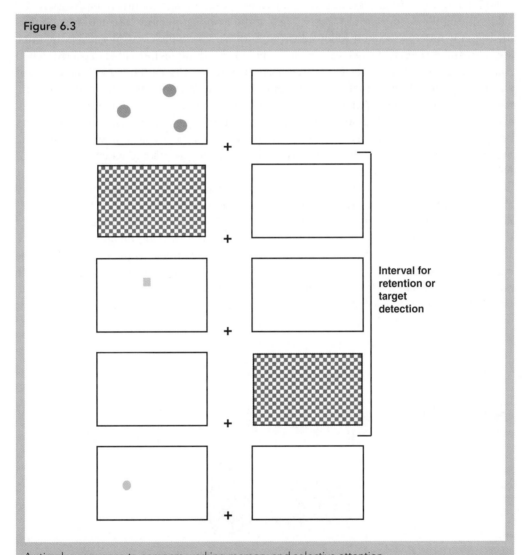

Interval for retention or target detection

A stimulus sequence to compare working memory and selective attention.
In the working memory condition the first stimulus serves as a memory set, and the final one as a memory test stimulus. In the selective attention condition the first stimulus cues the to-be-attended half field, and the third one (in this example) is a to-be-detected target. Checkerboards served as probes to elicit P1s.

(as discussed in Sections 3.3 and 4.1), as it is involved in setting priorities for certain kinds of information, or certain kinds of response tendencies, over others.

To answer questions about what controls what, or whether two functions are identical or not, we can follow our general approach. That is, we can look at brain substrates during conditions in which working memory is supposedly at issue, and compare these conditions to ones in which attention is supposedly at. One interesting attempt was reported in a further study by Awh and colleagues (2000). In this experiment they compared a condition in which subjects were instructed to hold locations in one visual half field in working memory, to a condition in which they were instructed to attend to one visual half field (Figure 6.3). In both conditions task-irrelevant probe stimuli were presented randomly in both visual half fields: during the 8.7 s retention interval (given the working memory instruction), and during the same interval when it followed the attentional cue (which was physically the same as the stimulus that cued the locations to be held in working memory). As expected, when comparing ERPs to the probes when they were presented in the attended half field, versus when that half field was unattended, P1 amplitude was larger to attended probes (Figure 6.4). Recall from Section 3.2 that the P1 effect generally reflects the modulation of stimulus-evoked responses in the secondary visual cortex, at about 100–150 ms post-stimulus. As can be seen in Figure 6.4, probes elicited larger P1s as well when the half field in which they were presented contained the locations held in working memory, relative to when the other half field contained these locations.

To the authors, these results indicated a strong overlap between spatial working memory and spatial attention: both result in very similar modulations of activity in the visual cortex. However, important questions remain. First, in this particular study the genuineness of the working memory aspect can be questioned. Under the working memory instructions, subjects could expect to see the test stimulus in the same half field as the one in which the cued locations were, with 100 per cent certainty. This by itself may have resulted in selective attention to that half field. Second, and more importantly: given that two processes modulate stimulus-related processing in the same way, are the control processes that enable this modulation also identical?

Figure 6.4

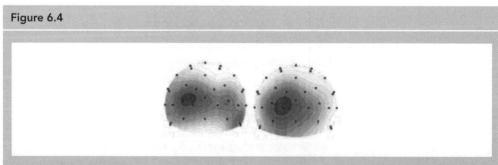

Almost indistinguishable P1 potential distributions over the back of the head for difference ERPs constructed by computing attended minus unattended or held in working memory minus not held in working memory.

Source: Based on Awh et al. (2000).

6.1.2   Working memory and attentional control

A more comprehensive comparison of selective attention and working memory, in terms of brain substrates, has been carried out in a meta-analytic fashion. Corbetta and co-workers (Chelazzi & Corbetta, 1999; Corbetta & Shulman, 2002) surveyed a number of PET and fMRI studies on visual–spatial attention, as well as a group of studies on spatial working memory, and overlayed the results, as shown in Figure 6.5. Right hemisphere cortical areas involved in spatial selective attention are also involved in spatial working memory (intra-parietal sulcus, postcentral and precentral sulcus). The area designated TEO has been marked as the approximate location of the P1 effect discussed in the previous section. In addition, an extended area in the dorsolateral prefrontal cortex is specifically involved in spatial working memory, not in spatial selective attention. Based on this survey, a preliminary conclusion is that spatial attention and working memory overlap in an extensive network of activated brain areas. This network includes not only the secondary visual cortex (P1 effect previously discussed), but also more dorsal areas in the parietal and more anterior cortices. The overlap is not complete however (see prefrontal cortex, PFC, in Figure 6.5.). One could say that working memory needs selective attention, because tasks designed to assess working memory activate all areas known to be activated by spatial selective attention. On the other hand, selective attention does not completely rely on working memory, because selective attention tasks do not activate an area specifically involved in working memory.

We know what the probable functional meaning is of the activity in the occipital–temporal pathway: modulation of stimulus-evoked activity by attention to or working memory of the location of the stimulus. But how about the other overlapping areas in the parietal and

Figure 6.5

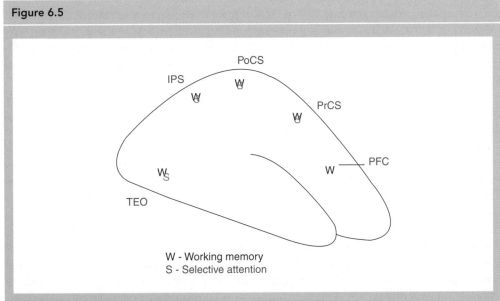

Extent of overlap in activated brain areas between spatial attention and working memory.

IPS = intra-parietal sulcus; PoCS = Postcentral sulcus; PrCS = precentral sulcus; PFC = prefrontal cortex; TEO = occipital–temporal. Pathway: W refers to involved in working memory; S refers to work involved in selective attention.

Source: Adapted from Chelazzi and Corbetta (1999, p. 675).

Figure 6.6

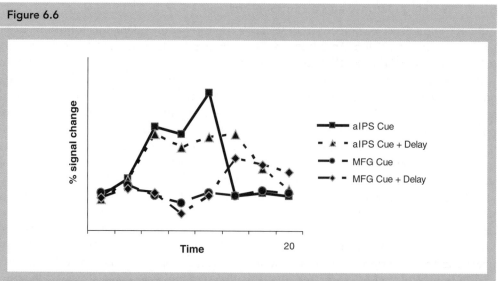

Illustration of fMRI BOLD activations in anterior intra-parietal sulcus (aIPS) and middle frontal gyrus (MFG) to attentional cues.

Both cues and delay elicit activity in IPS. MFG is only activated during the delay. Abscissa: time in seconds. Ordinate: fMRI BOLD response in per cent signal change.

frontal cortices? Could these implement the control processes that enable the modulation of activity in TEO? The data surveyed in Figure 6.5 do not directly answer this question. They are from studies where aggregate PET or fMRI signals were acquired in conditions in which subjects entered locations in working memory or directed attention to them, and then subsequently responded to test stimuli or targets. These data then, reflect both brain activity patterns associated with control processes, and those associated with the ensuing modulation of activity elicited by target or test stimuli.

In recent years, event-related fMRI techniques have been applied to disentangle these two components. As described in Sections 3.3. and 4.1, these techniques reveal activation of brain areas specifically elicited by cue stimuli that indicate which part of the visual field (or any other feature) must be attended to. Figure 6.6 shows the results of an application of these methods and principles. It shows event-related fMRI BOLD curves elicited by arrow location cues, that were followed within a few seconds by either a target or a stimulus signalling the end of the trial, or nothing (delay). As can be seen, both the attention–direction cues, as well as the beginning of the delay period elicited activity in the intra-parietal sulcus (IPS) (Corbetta et al., 2002). The same held for the other areas in Figure 6.5. This includes the area designated TEO, which is the site of modulation by attention or working memory of target-elicited activity. Remember from Section 3.3 that such activation that precedes target presentation is thought to reflect a baseline shift, or a bias, in these areas for one kind of information over others.

However, with regard to Figure 6.6 the qualification should be made that activity in the middle frontal gyrus (the dorsolateral part of the prefrontal cortex) was observed only during the delay period, not in response to the attention-directing cue. So, when we look specifically at attentional control, the idea is confirmed that working memory needs selective attention, because areas activated by the cue were also activated during the delay; on the other hand, selective attention does not completely rely on working memory, because there is at least one area activated during the delay that is not activated directly by the cues.

One could also say that, when the situation demands it, working memory (or the area in which it is implemented, like the dorsolateral prefrontal cortex) may supplement selective attention. This is exactly what happened during the delay period in the Corbetta et al. (2002) study. The experiment by Hopfinger and colleagues, discussed in Section 3.3, (Figure 3.16) revealed not only biasing activity in the visual cortex, but also dorsolateral prefrontal activation by the attentional cues (Hopfinger et al., 2000). One obvious interpretation of such results is that they indicate that a working memory mechanism was invoked in that particular selective attention task. This is consistent with the relatively long interval (8 s) between cue and target in the Hopfinger study.

The special role of the dorsolateral prefrontal cortex in working memory and attentional control is consistent with theories that specifically elaborate on the neural basis of working memory. Figure 6.7 illustrates the model from Smith et al. (1998). These data were acquired in a, so-called, N-back task. In such a task, subjects are presented with a sequence of items, such as letters. For each subsequent letter, the subject has to decide whether it matches the letter presented N letters ago. In some conditions N equals 1, 2, or 3; in others N is 0. Figure 6.7 shows the result of a subtraction of the N=0 condition from an N=3 condition. Areas that are more activated in the N=3 condition are assumed to be instrumental in storing and maintaining the letter in working memory. Following this logic, activity in both parietal and dorsolateral prefrontal, as well as in some other areas, subserves these functions. Furthermore, additional evidence has resulted in the idea that parietal activity is only involved in storage.

Figure 6.7

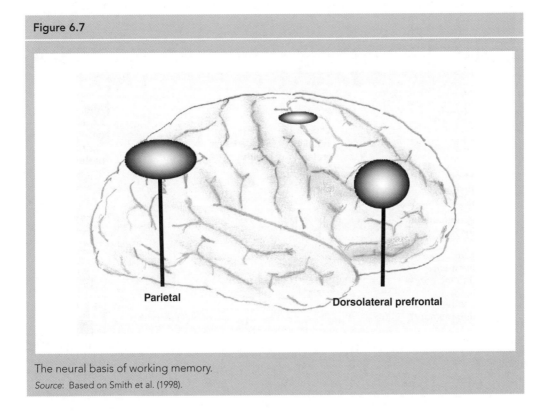

Parietal   Dorsolateral prefrontal

The neural basis of working memory.
Source: Based on Smith et al. (1998).

On the other hand dorsolateral prefrontal activation is increasingly observed as more information has to be manipulated. In N=3 and N=2 versions, items not only have to be stored, but also need a tag that codes how many items back they had been presented. As Smith et al. suggest, another way to increase dorsolateral prefrontal activity is to lengthen the maintenance interval, because that will increase the chance for people to apply elaborate maintenance strategies, like manipulating the information.

6.2   WORKING MEMORY DRIVES ATTENTION, BUT HOW MUCH?

6.2.1   Biased competition

The conclusion from the previous section seems straightforward: selective attention and working memory share common parietal, occipito–temporal, and frontal (not prefrontal) mechanisms; only when working memory is taxed beyond a certain level (long maintenance or manipulation), do dorsolateral prefrontal areas come into play. How far can this conclusion be generalized? The question is important, because in the previous section we limited ourselves to rather specific conditions. We only addressed selective attention to and working memory for locations in space; attention, however, can also be directed to other features in the visual and other modalities. Furthermore, many of the studies discussed thus far involved expectation rather than selective attention. That is, cues told subjects to expect a target stimulus at a certain location, and then the target would appear at that location most of the time, without anything else happening. One could argue that in such a situation selective attention is not really taxed, because there is no distracting information to compete with the target for limited information processing resources. When such competition is not

Figure 6.8

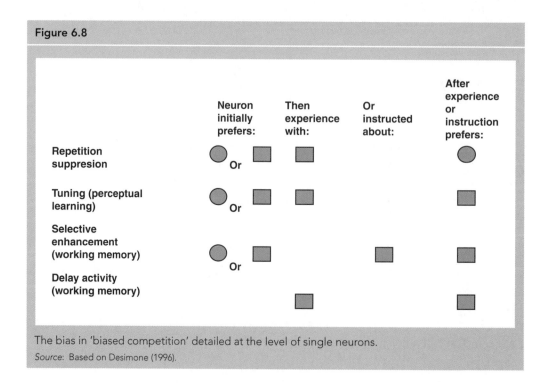

The bias in 'biased competition' detailed at the level of single neurons.
Source: Based on Desimone (1996).

anticipated, cues may not be used to bring about an *a priori* bias in this competition. It could be that the initiation of such a bias is based on additional prefrontal mechanisms. One fMRI study previously discussed (Hopfinger et al., 2000; see Figure 3.16) did use distracters and did find attention-related activity in the dorsolateral prefrontal cortex. However, as mentioned in the previous section, this activity could also reflect working memory demands associated with the long interval between cue and target.

The bias in 'biased competition' has been detailed at the level of single neurons. In particular, research in monkeys by Desimone and colleagues revealed neurons with intriguing properties in posterior visual and prefrontal cortices (Desimone, 1996). We have seen (Section 5.1) how some visual cells respond only to sensory aspects of a stimulus, while others are additionally sensitive to whether the stimulus had been presented before (repetition suppression). In this section we extend this scheme with three additional classes of cells (see Figure 6.8). In two classes (selective enhancement/working memory and tuning, see Figure 5.4) the cells respond more vigorously to a stimulus when that stimulus matches one presented before to indicate a behaviourally relevant target. The activation of these cells by an adequate stimulus can be viewed as being modulated by a preceding instruction or cue. This modulation is the microscopic equivalent of the macroscopic attentional modulation of target-elicited activity as observed with neuroimaging in humans (e.g. the P1 effect). How about the baseline shifts, or bias, that precede the modulation? There appears to be a third class of cells (delay activity/ working memory) that give a sustained response in the interval between the signal indicating which stimulus is behaviourally relevant and the target stimulus itself. Such 'maintained or delay activity…may provide a representation of whatever object is expected or behaviourally important…' (Desimone, 1996, pp. 13, 497; see also Luck et al., 1997). This then is the microscopic equivalent of the baseline shift or bias.

These different classes of cells were identified in the inferior temporal visual cortex (see Figure 6.9). Like area TEO, the inferior temporal cortex is considered a part of the ventral visual pathway. The maintenance/delay cells in the inferior temporal cortex have a further, peculiar property: whenever another visual stimulus was presented during the maintenance interval, the maintenance was greatly interrupted. Yet, the monkey kept responding adequately to the target stimulus that succeeded the interruption. Therefore, the representation of what was relevant and what was not must have been maintained in another way. Indeed, Desimone and colleagues also found maintenance/delay cells in the prefrontal cortex (see Figure 6.9, VL). These cells did NOT show interruption of maintenance activity by an intervening stimulus. To Desimone, this suggested that prefrontal neurons control the development and the maintenance of the bias in the inferior temporal cortex, by realizing a more permanent and interference-proof form of working memory.

The present discussion focusses on ventral posterior and ventral anterior (prefrontal) areas. This is not surprising given the stimulus features concerned: the monkeys attend or memorize specific forms of objects, rather than locations. In fact, Desimone (1996) also surveys evidence from monkey research supporting the idea of a parallel dorsal frontal parietal network subserving selective attention to and working memory for locations. Thus, there would be two frontal-posterior networks: a dorsal one implicated in spatial attention and working memory, and a ventral one involved in attention to and working memory for non-spatial features, like shape or colour.

How does this relate to the conclusion outlined at the beginning of this section: selective attention and working memory share common parietal, occipito–temporal, and frontal (not prefrontal) mechanisms; and that only when working memory is taxed beyond a certain

Figure 6.9

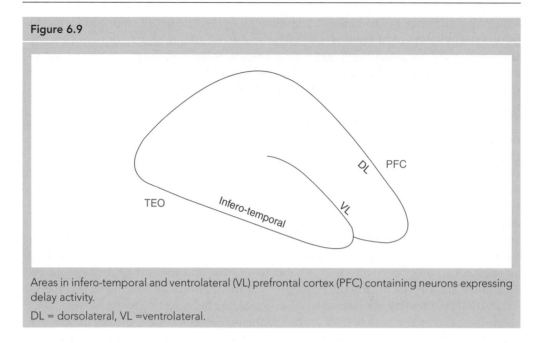

Areas in infero-temporal and ventrolateral (VL) prefrontal cortex (PFC) containing neurons expressing delay activity.

DL = dorsolateral, VL = ventrolateral.

Figure 6.10

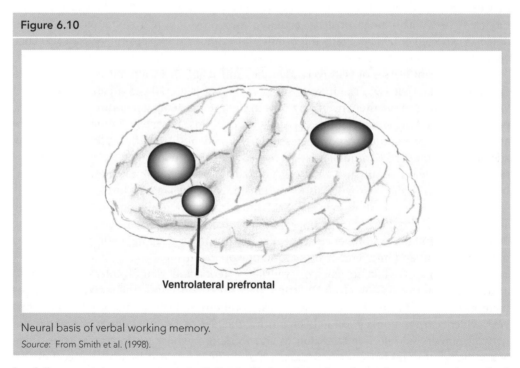

Neural basis of verbal working memory.

Source: From Smith et al. (1998).

level (long maintenance or manipulation), do dorsolateral prefrontal areas come into play? There are several points to consider. First, we are dealing with monkeys, not humans. Indeed, it has been suggested that monkeys need more prefrontal activity to perform spatial selective attention or working memory tasks than humans do (Corbetta et al., 2000; Corbetta & Shulman, 2002). Second, the Desimone model referred to non-spatial features (although a parallel mechanism for spatial features was suggested). It could be that humans also need more prefrontal activity in the case of non-spatial features. Figure 6.10 shows an extension of Figure 6.7, the data from the N-back task that illustrated the Smith et al. model of working memory. Here, activations in the left hemisphere, related to working memory for letters, are shown. In addition to the dorsolateral prefrontal and parietal activations, we see a ventrolateral prefrontal activation. Could this be a sign of a ventral frontal parietal network involved in working memory for non-spatial features (letters)? As already alluded to, based on a review of numerous working memory studies, Smith et al. propose a different scheme. They suggest that the parietal activity subserves mere storage, while the dorsolateral prefrontal activity is related to more elaborate processing. In addition, they propose that ventrolateral prefrontal activity is involved in something between storage and elaborate processing, viz. rehearsal. Furthermore, when going from non-spatial letters to spatial information in such working memory tasks, the major difference in results is not in ventral versus dorsal, but in left (non-spatial) versus right (spatial) prefrontal cortices.

6.2.2   Working memory, prefrontal cortex and conflict

In the preceding section the possibility was raised that, when real competition, or distracters, to the target can be anticipated, this would somehow result in the greater involvement of prefrontal areas. Some authors have proposed that working memory based on prefrontal activity is necessary in conditions in which targets are accompanied by distracters, especially when the latter are associated with inadequate, competing response tendencies (as in conflict paradigms, see Plate XIII; think of the Stroop and flanker letter paradigms discussed in previous chapters). To test this hypothesis, an experiment was devised (De Fockert et al., 2001) in which subjects had to classify written names as referring to either a pop star or a politician. The names were presented against the background of a photograph, which could be congruent with the name in terms of the classification, or incongruent (as in Plate XIII, lower panel). As expected, subjects' classification responses were slower for incongruent photographs (interference effect). Then the researchers applied another manipulation: during the classification task, subjects had to keep digits in their working memory. The reasoning was that this would additionally tax working memory. Therefore, less working memory capacity would be available to control selective attention ('maintain prioritization of relevant information' (names over faces), as the authors put it). This in turn would result in greater interference and, indeed, this was found.

What were the brain substrates of working memory and working memory capacity, and its effect on selective attention? For the latter, the answer seems straightforward. Previous research indicated that certain areas in the ventral visual cortex, especially in the right fusiform gyrus, are specifically activated by pictures of faces. In the De Fockert study, these face-specific areas were activated significantly more when less working memory could be presumed to be available for the control of selective attention (Figure 6.11). In this condition, 'prioritization of relevant information' was less successful, and processing of irrelevant face information was relatively enhanced, as reflected in both increased interference scores and increased activation of face-specific areas in the visual cortex.

For working memory capacity things are less clear. Figure 6.12 shows the areas with higher activation for high working memory load (with less capacity available for attention) than for low-load. These areas include the left ventrolateral prefrontal cortex, extending into the left precentral gyrus. This could be expected, given that subjects rehearsed the digit information

Figure 6.11

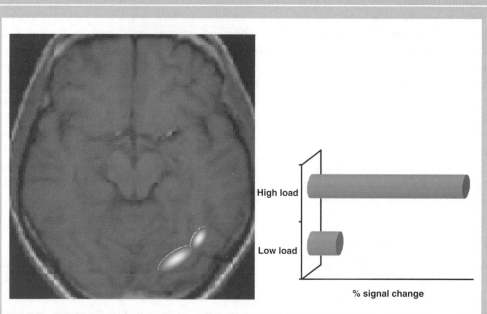

Ventral slice (MNI z = −12) of posterior (bottom) and anterior (top) parts of the brain.
There is more extensive activity (specific to face stimuli, relative to no-face stimuli, white spots in the right posterior hemisphere) with high working memory load.

Figure 6.12

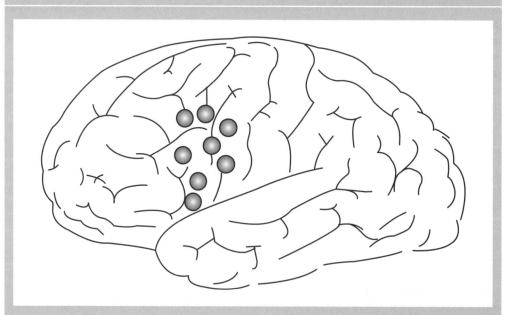

An indication of the areas activated more when digits had to be retained in working memory than when not.

(see Figure 6.10 and corresponding discussion in the text). Conspicuously, there was no activation related to high memory load in the dorsolateral prefrontal cortex. It is possible, that in the condition without imposed working memory load, the resulting spare dorsolateral frontal capacity was in fact deployed in the control of selective attention. Comparing these conditions, as in Figure 6.12, does not reveal any difference in this prefrontal area.

A study that does support the involvement of the dorsolateral prefrontal cortex in the control of selective attention in conflict situations, was reported by MacDonald et al. (2000), and is also discussed in Section 4.3.1. The strength of this study was that event-related fMRI was used to separate cue-related activations from those elicited by subsequent targets. The latter consisted of Stroop stimuli (Plate XIII, upper panel); the cues indicated whether the colour should be named or the word read. It was assumed that suppression of word information was more difficult than that of colour information; therefore, more attentional control would be needed in the colour naming condition. Indeed, the left dorsolateral prefrontal cortex was activated more strongly by cues instructing colour naming than by cues instructing word reading. However, this event-related design used long intervals between cue and target (12.5 s). Therefore, it cannot be excluded that the dorsolateral prefrontal activity mainly reflects the maintenance of prioritization over an extended interval, and that it would not have been observed with much shorter intervals (e.g. less than a second).

In conclusion, to the extent that working memory is implemented in dorsolateral–prefrontal activation, it may be required in the control of selective attention, especially when interference and/or conflict from irrelevant information can be anticipated. However, it is still possible that this working memory function is merely instrumental in maintaining a given prioritization over an extended period of time, and not so much in setting it up.

6.2.3   Working selective attention: Pathology and pharmacology

How is working selective attention implemented biochemically in the prefrontal cortex? Some clues come from research on patients with schizophrenia, who are thought to have impaired dopaminergic transmission in this brain region. One study observed prefrontal activation in both a working memory task and a selective attention task, and both were shown to be reduced in schizophrenic patients, concomitant with performance reductions in both tasks (Perlstein et al., 2003). Another study in a sample of schizophrenic patients found that availability of the D1 dopamine receptor positively predicted performance in the N-back task; increases in D1 levels were interpreted as a compensatory reaction to reduced dopaminergic transmission, which in turn would impair working memory (Abi-Dargham et al., 2002). Older, somewhat isolated studies, suggest dopaminergic effects on typical measures of selective attention, such as spatial cue validity effects (Clark et al., 1986, 1989), and Stroop interference (De Sonneville et al., 1994), in a direction consistent with enhanced selectivity with dopaminergic agonism. However, robust effects of dopaminergic effects on human working memory (e.g. N-back) have turned out to be notoriously hard to find (Bartholomeusz et al., 2003; Mehta & Riedel, 2006). An intriguing theory on how dopamine affects prefrontal selective attention was proposed by Braver and Cohen (Braver & Cohen, 1999): the efficacy of attentional control might depend on a rapid and transient response (80–160 ms after the cue) in one or more subcortical structures. This response involves a massive, rather diffuse, and short-lived release of dopamine in the cortex. Adequate processing of the attentional control cue by the cortex depends on this dopamine boost and the ensuing stimulation of cortical neurons through subcortical–cortical connections. The more activated the cortex is by the subcortical input, the better the cortical processing of the attentional–control cue and the more efficacious is attentional control. Note that this scenario overlaps with the principle of ascending arousal systems as discussed in Section 5.5 and illustrated in Figure 5.16 (the dopamine division).

Recently, interest has turned to the influence of the GABAergic system on working memory in schizophrenia. A study by Menzies and colleagues found that, compared with healthy controls, schizophrenic patients exhibit a disproportional deterioration of N-back performance as N goes stepwise from 1 to 4, suggesting a specific working memory deficit in the patients (Menzies et al., 2007). In healthy controls, areas in parietal and dorsal-medial as well as lateral prefrontal cortices (see Figure 6.7) showed increased activity with increasing N; this N-dependent activity was reduced in the patients, consistent with the idea that underactivation of these regions plays a role in impaired working memory. Then the patients were given flumazenil, a drug that antagonizes GABAergic transmission. This greatly reduced their disproportional decline in performance with increasing N, suggesting it specifically augmented working memory. However, it did not normalize the N-dependent increase in prefrontal/parietal activation at all. From the perspective of brain activity correlates then, flumazenil does not affect the core problem, but augments some compensatory mechanism that in turn produces improvements in the behavioural correlate of working memory. The nature of this compensatory mechanism still remains to be resolved.

6.3   ATTENTION AND WORKING MEMORY MODULATE LONG-TERM EPISODIC MEMORY

6.3.1   Attention predicts long-term episodic memory

It is easy to imagine that the better we attend to something, the better we will remember it later. But does it really work that way? And if so, how?

Results from behavioural studies support the relationship between attention and memory. In levels of processing experiments (Toichi & Kamio, 2002) subjects monitor streams of information (e.g. a sequence of visually presented words). The number of items in these streams should clearly exceed the short-term memory span. In the shallow-level condition subjects have to detect the occurrence of a simple physical feature, such as a letter with a curve. In the deep-level condition they have to select a semantic property, for instance whether the word refers to something animate or inanimate. After these tasks explicit memory tests (see Box 6.1) are administered, in which the subjects have to recall or recognize as many as possible of the previously presented words. The generally obtained result is that memory is better after the deep condition (Figure 6.13). An obvious interpretation is that deep processing comes with attention to the words, and that more attention results in better later memory.

Perhaps an even simpler illustration of the relationship between attention and subsequent memory is directed forgetting (Paller, 1990). In such a set-up subjects view a sequence of items that vary in a simple physical feature. For example, half the items are coloured blue, the other half red. Subjects are instructed to remember the blue items and forget the red ones. Not surprisingly, subsequent memory for the blue items is better. Logically, the instruction of directed forgetting is equivalent to the one used in attention experiments, in which subjects have to attend to stimuli with one feature and ignore those with another (see Section 3.2).

Figure 6.13

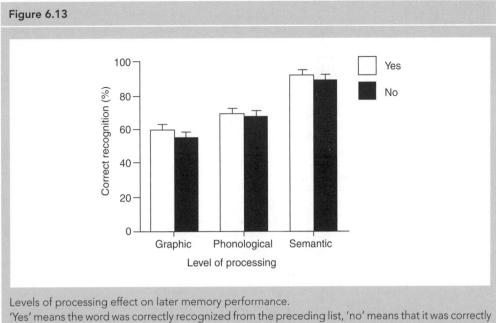

Levels of processing effect on later memory performance.
'Yes' means the word was correctly recognized from the preceding list, 'no' means that it was correctly identified as not present in that list.
Source: Reprinted from Toichi and Kamio (2002), with permission from Elsevier.

Results from levels of processing and directed forgetting experiments have prompted an extension of the model relating attention to memory that was discussed in Sections 5.3 and 6.1.1. According to the extended model (Figure 6.14), attention also affects the transfer of information to long-term storage. But what does it mean when we state that 'attention affects the transfer to ...'? Is it the same attention process affecting transfer to long-term and to short-term storage? To answer these questions we must turn to what happens at a neuro-physiological level.

During the 1980s, Donchin and co-workers started looking at the brain substrate of an attention-related process that was predictive of later memory (Fabiani et al., 1986). They were particularly interested in the functional meaning of the P3 or P300 responses. The P300 is a deflection in the ERP (see Chapter 1) that is elicited by events that are surprising or relevant, and preferably both (Plate XIV). The events may be surprising because they consist of an infrequent deviation from a monotonous background, and they may be relevant because of the subject's task. For example, a sequence of words contains an occasional word that differs in letter size, and this oddball target has to be detected. Relative to the non-targets, the targets typically elicit a large P300 response. Such a P300 is generally considered to be a cortical correlate of attention being attracted to a salient event.

But can the process that is manifest in P300 be described in more specific functional terms? Donchin and colleagues hypothesized that this process concerned context updating: based on salient, often novel information, certain memory traces were modified. In other words, an attention-related process would influence a memory-related process. To test this hypothesis, they applied an incidental learning paradigm, more specifically the Von Restorff effect, named after Hedwig von Restorff who first described this effect in the 1930s.

Figure 6.14

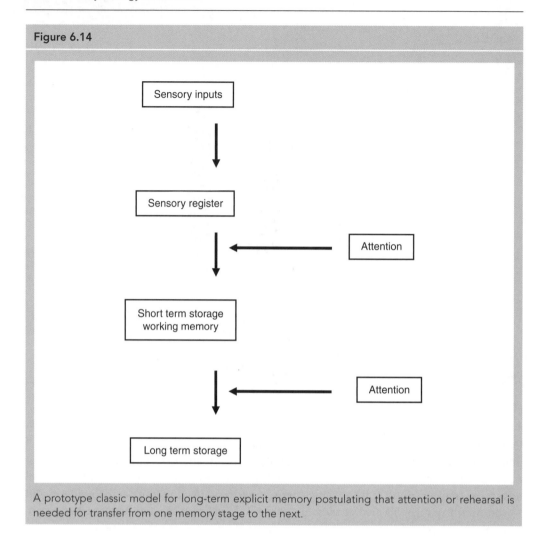

A prototype classic model for long-term explicit memory postulating that attention or rehearsal is needed for transfer from one memory stage to the next.

This effect (illustrated in Figure 6.15) is yet another instance in which attentional modulation of subsequent memory may be suspected. Oddball stimuli are later recalled better than non-oddball stimuli in identical positions in the sequence. The obvious interpretation is that unexpected, or novel, or otherwise salient items attract special attention, which in turn promotes later memory of them.

Given this interpretation, and the antecedent conditions that promote large P300 responses, the Von Restorff paradigm seemed optimal to investigate the relationship between P300 and subsequent memory. Indeed, Donchin and colleagues found that items that were recalled later, on average elicited larger P300 responses than those not recalled (Figure 6.16). So, a cortical response elicited by stimuli upon their first presentation predicted later memory for these stimuli. Similar findings have been reported by other researchers (Wagner et al., 1999). These further results indicate that the relation between P300 or related positive ERP deflections and subsequent memory holds in general, and is not limited to the context of incidental learning

Figure 6.15

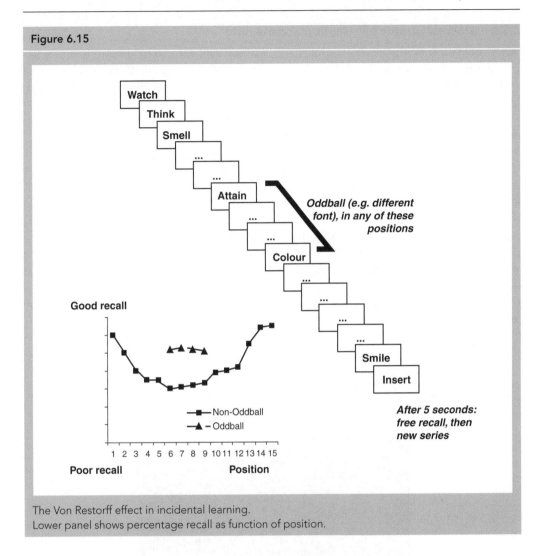

The Von Restorff effect in incidental learning.
Lower panel shows percentage recall as function of position.

Figure 6.16

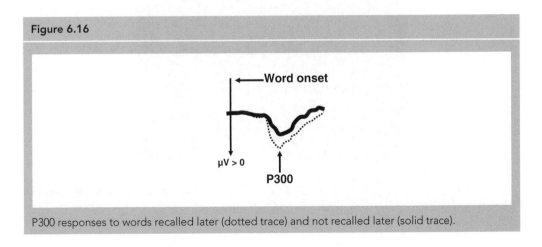

P300 responses to words recalled later (dotted trace) and not recalled later (solid trace).

6.3.2 Brain substrates of attention and memory

What could underlie these behavioural effects, and the P300 effects, in terms of neural activity? Attempts to source localization (see Chapter 1) of P300 have generally been complicated by the fact that P300 probably reflects activity in multiple cortical areas. However, experiments using fMRI (see Chapter 1) have started to reveal these areas.

Wagner and co-workers (Wagner et al., 1998) compared the whole brain fMRI signal in conditions of non-semantic (shallow) versus semantic (deep) processing of sequences of words. They found three areas which were more activated during semantic processing: The inferior frontal gyrus, the parahippocampal gyrus, and the fusiform gyrus, all in the left hemisphere (Figure 6.17). In a subsequent experiment they used event-related fMRI, following the logic of the earlier P300 studies. Again, subjects viewed a sequence of words and were subsequently tested on memory for these words. Average event-related fMRI BOLD responses, as elicited during the initial presentation of the words, were computed both for those words that were later recalled and for those that were not. Stronger activation for words later recalled was found in three areas: the inferior frontal gyrus, the parahippocampal gyrus, and the fusiform gyrus, all in the left hemisphere (Figure 6.18). Indeed, these areas overlapped substantially with those found to be active during semantic processing, relative to non-semantic processing.

Figure 6.17

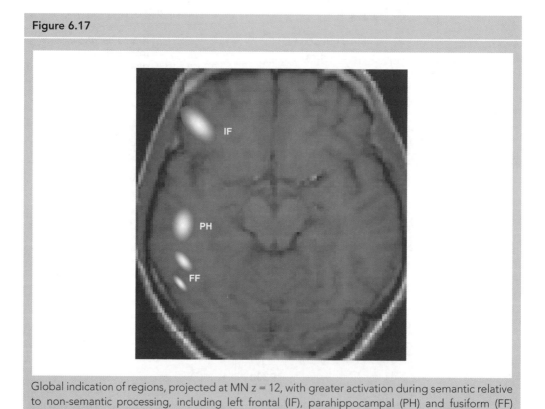

Global indication of regions, projected at MN z = 12, with greater activation during semantic relative to non-semantic processing, including left frontal (IF), parahippocampal (PH) and fusiform (FF) cortices.

Figure 6.18

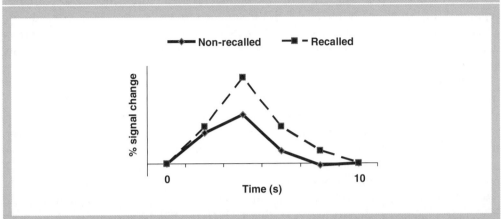

Illustration of the approximate activation of the cortical regions indicated in Figure 6.17 during the encoding of words later recalled versus those not recalled.
This difference was noted in the left inferior frontal gyrus bordering the precentral gyrus (BA 44/6 and 45/47), a region that encompassed the parahippocampal gyrus (BA 36/37/35) and the more medial extent of the fusiform gyrus (BA37), and a region that encompassed the lateral extent of the fusiform gyrus and portions of the inferior temporal gyrus (BA 37).

This overlap suggests that the instruction of semantic processing is one way to activate the frontal–parahippocampal–fusiform network, perhaps just like directed remembering or occasional oddballs. Apparently however, the extent of activation of the network may also vary due to factors beyond experimental control. But even this uncontrolled variation is predictive of subsequent memory.

Now that we have identified a cortical network related to subsequent memory performance, we must ask what functions are served by individual nodes in the network. For example, which nodes are related to attention, and how? To what extent does uncontrolled variation in the network's activation reflect spontaneous fluctuations in attention? Following our general approach, we can ask whether these nodes are known to be activated in experiments directed at attention, rather than memory. Remember that in Section 3.2 we discussed how areas in the visual cortex involved in the perception of shape were specifically activated by instructions to attend to that shape.

These areas are shown again in Figure 6.19. Selective attention to shape activates a number of areas, including the left fusiform gyrus. This prompts the scenario of an analysis of shape invoked when reading words (in fact, claims have been made that a left visual cortex area is dedicated to word perception, but this is not undisputed, see Price et al., 2003). Selective attention to shape augments activity in the areas involved in shape analysis (e.g. left fusiform gyrus). Fluctuations in the extent of activation of this area implement fluctuations in attention to word stimuli. These same fluctuations are predictive of subsequent memory performance. In a similar vein, we can look at another node of the network. The left inferior frontal gyrus has been found to be increasingly activated when subjects have to keep increasing numbers of items in their working memory (Figure 6.10; see Section 6.2.1). It is highly conceivable that these working memory operations promote long-term memory (see the model in Figure 6.14), especially given that the left inferior frontal gyrus (L IFG) has been associated with the rehearsal component of working memory (Smith et al., 1998). A study by Köhler and colleagues, using transcranial magnetic stimulation (TMS), strongly supported the causal involvement of L IFG in long-term memory. Items for which during encoding the L IFG was stimulated by TMS were recognized significantly better later than items for which the TMS pulse during encoding was directed to another brain area (Kohler et al., 2004).

The third component, the parahippocampal gyrus, may be thought of as a kind of gateway to the hippocampus (see Figure 6.1). It may be specific to the aspect of long-term episodic storage, although the parahippocampal activation associated with episodic storage may well depend on input from attention- and working memory-related areas. As an aside, given that patients like H.M. and C.W. had severe hippocampal damage and were no longer able to form new episodic memories, why didn't the hippocampus show up in the studies on a posterior prediction of subsequent memory? One possibility is that it is more involved in (especially short-term) consolidation than in initial storage. This would explain the mild retrograde amnesia in patients like H.M. that adds to the full-blown anterograde amnesia (see Box 6.1).

In sum, there appears to be a network that, when activated in response to information, promotes later, explicit, long-term memory for that information. Individual nodes of the network are activated in tasks that address attention or working memory, rather than long-term memory. Many questions remain to be answered. Some concern the precise conditions under which this particular network is activated. For example, the Von Restorff, as well the as P300 effect, are known to disappear when subjects use strategies to store the word items, rather than just rote learning. Other questions concern the way the nodes in the network interact: which node activates or controls which node, and what neurotransmitters are involved?

As for neurotransmitters, varying amounts of attention devoted to discrete stimuli could typically reflect varying activation of the cholinergic system. Especially in the case of unexpected, deviant stimuli, as in the Von Restorff situation, a special dedicated mechanism for

Figure 6.19

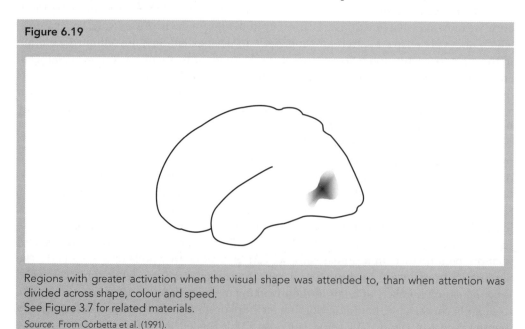

Regions with greater activation when the visual shape was attended to, than when attention was divided across shape, colour and speed.
See Figure 3.7 for related materials.
Source: From Corbetta et al. (1991).

dealing with such events seems to exist (the circuit breaker, see Section 3.4; Corbetta & Shulman, 2002). As discussed, there are strong indications that this mechanism predominantly depends on cholinergic transmission. The idea that the prioritized processing of unexpected, salient stimuli depends on acetylcholine *and* is predictive of later memory fits well with the well-known effects of cholinergic antagonists, like scopolamine, on measures of long-term memory (Riedel et al., 1995).

6.4 CONCLUDING REMARKS

Attention and memory are heavily intertwined. Representing information in short-term working memory and selectively directing attention to it have been shown to affect processing in the visual cortex of that information in similar ways. Is there overlap with respect to the mechanisms that direct selective attention, and those that load working memory? In both cases a network of dorsal parietal and frontal cortical areas has been implicated. Lateral prefrontal areas come into play when the information about what should be attended to must be maintained over long stretches of time, or attention must be preserved in the face of conflicting distracting information. In these cases both working memory and selective attention performance depends on dopaminergic function.

There are also close links between selective attention, working memory, and long-term memory. Stimulus elicited activation in the sensory cortex, as well as in lateral prefrontal and medial temporal regions, is systematically correlated with the long-term retention of these stimuli. The involvement of the lateral prefrontal cortex in long-term memory depends on processing demands during encoding and also concerns retrieval processes. The latter will be discussed in Chapter 10.

A final note concerns the role of diffuse cortical innervation from regional subcortical structures. This was discussed in Section 5.5. as being important for perceptual learning. In the present chapter, diffuse dopaminergic input to the cortex was implicated in the adequate processing of cues for setting attentional control and anticipating distracting events.

Questions

1. See Section 6.1.2, in relation to Figure 6.7. What would an N=0 N-back task look like? What kind of memory process would be crucial in an N=0 condition?

2. At the end of Section 6.2.2, it is stated that 'to the extent that working memory is implemented in dorsolateral–prefrontal activation, it may be required in the control of selective attention, especially when interference and/or conflict from irrelevant information can be anticipated'. However, it is still possible that this working memory function is merely instrumental in maintaining a given prioritization over an extended period of time, rather than setting it up. Can you devise an experiment that would settle this issue, given the experimental work that has been done thus far?

3. In Section 6.2.3 a theory is discussed in which working selective attention depends on a massive, rather diffuse, and short-lived release of dopamine in the cortex. This scenario overlaps with the principle of ascending arousal systems as discussed in Section 5.5 and illustrated in Figure 5.16 (the dopamine division). Specify this overlap, as well as the differences between the application to working selective attention and that to perceptual learning.

4. See Section 6.3.2. A study by Köhler and colleagues, using TMS, strongly supported the causal involvement of L IFG in long-term memory. Items for which during encoding the L IFG was stimulated by TMS were recognized significantly better later than items for which the TMS pulse during

encoding was directed to another brain area. Apparently applying TMS may enhance certain functions. Discuss what could underlie this enhancing effect by TMS.

5. See Section 6.3.2. The Von Restorff, as well as the P300, subsequent memory effects are known to disappear when subjects use strategies to store the word items, rather than just rote learning. What kind of strategies are they using in that case, and which brain network would then modulate subsequent memory?

7 ACTION AND MEMORY

Key Points

- Brain activity as a form of prospective memory predicts action decisions seconds before the subjective timing of the conscious decision.
- The cerebellum is a powerful computing system for continuously adjusting action to incoming sensory information. The incoming signals are modulated by signals from the medulla that represent discrepancies between action goals and effector position. These modulations can take the form of long-term depression, and are sensitive to noradrenergic inputs.
- Implicit learning of continuous serial reactions (sequence learning) may involve combining of several motor acts into one chunk and both sequence learning and chunking are disturbed by damage to the basal ganglia.
- Sequence learning involves shifts from cognitive frontal–striatal loops to motor frontal–striatal loops and is promoted to a certain extent by dopamine. In parallel, it involves a shift from premotor cortex dominance, implicated in externally guided action, to supplementary motor cortex dominance, implicated in internally guided learning.
- Signals from both primary and motor cortices embody memories for specific actions. These signals can be used to control devices that support human action and communication when severe damage in other parts of the nervous system has rendered normal action and communication impossible.

7.0 INTRODUCTION

In the 1950s, H.M. underwent neurosurgery. To relieve his unbearable fits of epilepsy, large portions of both the left and the right temporal lobe, including almost all of the hippocampi, were removed. The consequences of this for his cognitive functioning were not foreseen, and it soon turned out that this might be a case of a treatment being worse than the ailment. Events and experiences happening to H.M. after the surgery no longer left any explicit memory. Someone would enter the room and talk to him, then leave the room and return, when H.M. would act as if he had not seen him for years. However, in 1962, Brenda Milner observed that H.M. performed perfectly normally in a memory task that was of a more implicit kind. This task involved learning mirror drawing of a pattern: tracing the outline of a pattern while viewing it, and the drawing hand, through a mirror, as partly illustrated in Figure 7.1 (see Squire, 2009)

Figure 7.1

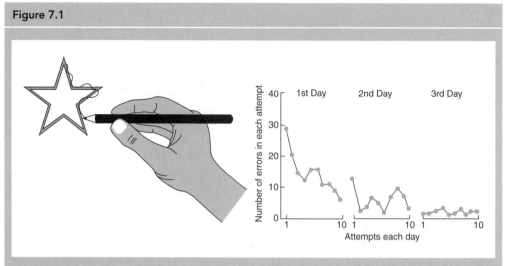

H.M. had bilateral hippocampus damage and was not able to form new episodic memories. However, he learned to trace a pattern with a pencil, while his hand was visible only in a mirror, within a day. The next day however, he had no explicit recall for the previous training session whatsoever. Figure from http://pages.slc.edu/~ebj/iminds09/amnesia-slides/hm-mirror-drawing.htm.

The right panel in Figure 7.1 illustrates a pattern of improvement across attempts on the first day that is very much akin to that of an average healthy individual. On the third day, performance is bordering on perfection. Yet, at the same time, H.M. could not explicitly recall anything about the attempts on the preceding training days. This single dissociation later turned out to be consistent with the distinction between explicit, declarative and episodic memory, depending on the hippocampus, on the one hand, and implicit, procedural memory involving trained skills on the other. As will be discussed later in Section 7.4, the latter kind of memory learning depends strongly on intact functioning of the basal ganglia, to the extent that patients with damage there perform worse during such procedural learning tasks.

Procedural learning, much like instrumental or operant conditioning, explicitly refers to training and actions of various kinds. Thus, such phenomena readily come to mind when one thinks of learning of or memory for action patterns. Indeed, the larger part of this chapter will be devoted to issues of procedural learning, although Sections 7.1 and 7.6 deal with action and memory from a more explicit memory perspective, addressing issues such as consciously imagining a motor act, or how brief memory traces in the motor cortex guide our decisions.

As noted in previous chapters, memory involves the strengthening of existing connections between neural representations, or a change in the relative strengths of these connections. These changes in strength are manifest as a short- or long-lasting changes in the pattern of neural activity or responsivity, which can be detected at a later stage. Action refers to almost anything that has to do with the production of behaviour. In the brain, we can constrain the action system to certain regions, including the primary and secondary (supplementary and pre-) motor cortex, the basal ganglia, and the cerebellum. Therefore, memory in the action system could consist of changes in connection strength within these regions, or between them.

7.1   SHORT-TERM MOTOR PLASTICITY IN MOTOR AND OTHER PARTS OF THE CORTEX

As noted previously (Section 4.1), intentions to act can be traced as enhanced activity in the primary and secondary motor cortex, long before the actual motor act is executed (usually in response to a further dedicated go signal). Just as humans can expect a stimulus in the immediate future to arrive at a certain location, or with a certain appearance (e.g. blue), they can expect to perform a specific act. In either case, attentional or intentional control is implemented by enhanced activity in stimulus-specific or motor effector-specific neurons. Especially for motor-specific neurons, we can think of this activity as a form of prospective memory. Prospective memory usually refers to remembering an action planned in the future. Formally however, an activation of the motor cortex in relation to an intended action involves a change in the pattern of neural activity in that motor cortex; and, however short-lasting it may be, it is therefore an instance of memory. Because it is aimed at realizing the overt act in the near or further future, it can be considered prospective memory.

Such short-term prospective memories in the motor system may actually last for a surprisingly long time. In one particular experiment, participants were asked to press a button at will, either with a left or a right-hand finger, once approximately every 20 seconds (Soon et al., 2008). fMRI scans of the whole brain were taken every 2 seconds. Afterwards, all voxels in each scan were analysed for the extent to which their signal strengths were related to whether the button press to follow was from the right or the left hand. This yielded a set of voxels (in frontal-polar and in posterior-cingulate cortices, see Figure 7.2) that was systematically followed by a right-hand response, and another set that systematically preceded left-hand responses. The astonishing fact was that this hand-selective voxel activity was already visible 8 seconds before the actual response was made. Keeping in mind the sluggish nature of the BOLD response in relation to real neural activity, the relevant neural activity had probably taken place seconds earlier. Referring to the concept of memory, or working memory, this is quite a long delay period to maintain information. You could compare it to the delay period discussed in Section 6.1.2 (Figure 6.6) that was necessary to elicit activity in lateral frontal areas during anticipation of a possible target stimulus at a certain location in the visual field.

Another result worth mentioning from the Soon et al. experiment concerns the subjective timing of the actual decision on the part of the subject to make a left- or right-hand response. As illustrated in Figure 7.3, subjects simultaneously watched a single letter that changed identity every 500 ms. After each left- or right-hand button press, upon presentation of the final four character screen in Figure 7.3, they indicated which letter was showing when they actually *decided* which finger to move. This was intended to provide an estimate of the time point at which a subject was conscious of the decision to use either the left or right finger. By far the most frequent estimates referred either to the letter that was on at the moment the response was issued (Q in Figure 7.3), or the one before. The fascinating thing was that conscious decisions appeared to take place no more than one second prior to the overt response, whereas the (presumably unconscious) decision in the frontal-polar and posterior-cingulate neurons occurred some nine seconds earlier.

Figure 7.2

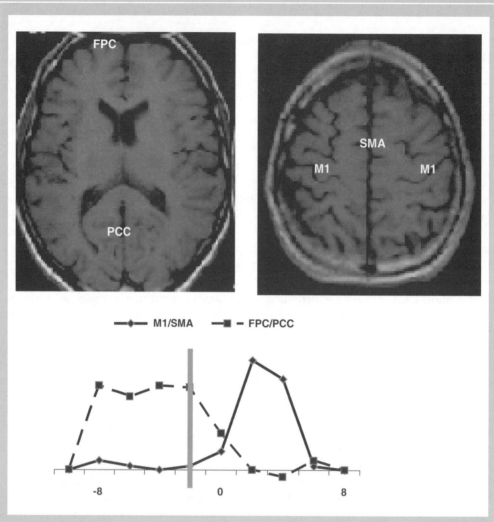

Idealized BOLD traces relative to the actual movement of the left or right hand at timepoint 0. Activity in secondary (pre-SMA) and primary motor cortex (M1) correlates with left versus right mainly after the movement had been made. Activity in the frontal-polar cortex (FPC) and the posterior-cingulate cortex (PCC) correlates with left versus right mainly *before* the movement was made. Grey vertical line denotes subjective timing of decision (see text). Abscissa denotes time in approximate seconds. Ordinate represents a measure of correlation between BOLD signal strength and left-versus right-hand response.

This result is generally viewed as a strong argument for the idea that our brains make all kinds of decisions for us without us being aware of these decisions for quite some time. Already in the 1990s this notion was strongly advocated by authors like Daniel Dennett (Dennett, 1991). One major inspiration was a classic experiment by Benjamin Libet. Libet used the principle of intentional bias in the motor cortex (Libet et al., 1983). In Section 4.1.1

Figure 7.3

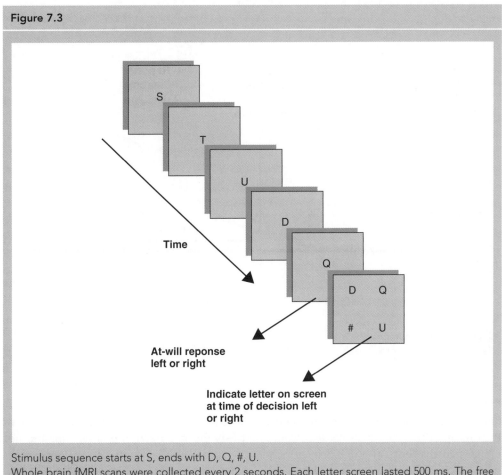

Stimulus sequence starts at S, ends with D, Q, #, U.
Whole brain fMRI scans were collected every 2 seconds. Each letter screen lasted 500 ms. The free left- or right-hand button press response was issued at will, and was always followed by the four character screen that prompted an indication of the letter that was showing at the moment of the conscious decision to choose left or right.

we saw that lateralized readiness potentials (LRPs) could be induced by a stimulus that cued the most likely response hand some half second before a go stimulus appeared that prompted the explicit behavioural response. Libet and colleagues used the non-lateralized readiness potential. They found that it became visible more than half a second before the subject made an overt hand movement. While freely planning the next hand movement subjects also watched a clock. After each hand movement they reported the position of the hand of the clock, again as an estimate of the time point at which they had consciously decided to make the movement. This 'wanting time', on average, followed the onset of the readiness potential by about 350 ms. Figure 7.4 illustrates these findings. Again, conscious decisions seemed to appear after the fact: the decision was visible in the motor cortex way before it was consciously experienced, although in this case the delay was only a fraction of a second.

The fact that the delay between motor cortex activity and estimated consciousness decision time was only a fraction of a second, constituted a major source of criticism. At a certain time point the subject knows that he is going to make another movement. Then he realizes

Figure 7.4

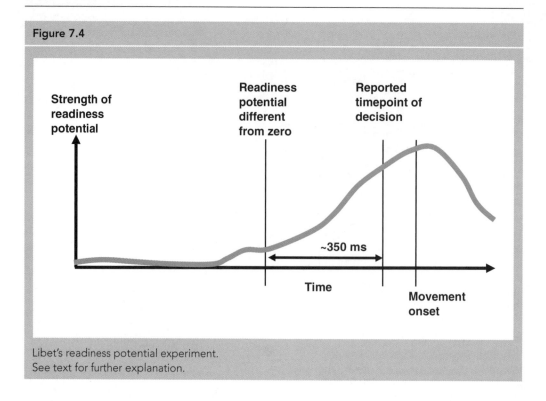

Libet's readiness potential experiment.
See text for further explanation.

that he should keep in mind the position of the clock hand. But how long does that realization take, and when does he actually know that he knows? In other words, the estimate of the timing of the subjective decision could be easily off by a fraction of a second, and not unlikely in the sense of a delay. In principle, the same criticism applies to the Soon et al. study discussed above. However, with a delay of almost ten seconds, people feel more comfortable in accepting the conclusion that the brain decision does precede, in time, the conscious experience of having decided.

7.2   CONDITIONAL MOTOR PROCESSES: THE ROLE OF THE CEREBELLUM

The preceding discussion of self-initiated movements contains a somewhat artificial element of memory: preparation of a movement was viewed as involving the creation of a kind of memory trace in motor areas as well as other parts of the cortex; an intentional memory trace very much like the attentional memory trace or bias as discussed in Sections 3.3 and 6.2.1. Being essentially like other animals, humans react to circumstances and relevant signals, the meaning of which depends on the circumstances. This is also the situation in which we really learn. The discussion in Section 5.1.1 of the work of Kandel and colleagues illustrates this in a fairly primitive neurophysiological system, that of the sea snail or *Aplysia*. Aplysia learns to appreciate the innocuousness of a repeated mild stimulation of its siphon, as evident from the habituation of its gill withdrawal response. In motor terms, the act of withdrawing the gill is adjusted according to a changing appreciation of the siphon stimulation. Box 7.1 details how the Aplysia motor system can also be directed in the opposite direction (i.e. facilitation) if the innocuous stimulus becomes associated with an aversive event.

Box 7.1   Aversive learning in Aplysia

What was also evident from detailed neurophysiological observations in Aplysia, is that the learning (habituation) is not in the motor neurons, but in the neurons producing the input to the motor neurons (sensory neurons and inter-neurons). It is also this output from Aplysia's non-motor neurons that is amenable to other forms of learning. What happens is, if the innocuous siphon stimulus is repeatedly followed, after a few seconds, by a nasty electric shock to the tail (a whole different part of the Aplysia body), habituation of the gill withdrawal reflex is counteracted and perhaps even annihilated. Even though the gill withdrawal cannot relieve the painful effect of the shock, it continues to be elicited specifically by the siphon stimulus that predicts delivery of the shock (but not by a second innocuous stimulus that is not associated with the shock). A specific conditional stimulus then, elicits a general state of withdrawal, in which also motor responses that are not instrumental in avoiding the painful stimulus are facilitated. This could be conceived as a typical motor facilitation component of an emotion (in this case something like the fearful apprehension of yet another shock). However, as indicated, the motor facilitation is actually the indirect consequence of the facilitation of the output from the non-motor neurons. Such learning due to affective reinforcements will be more generally discussed in Chapter 10 (Emotion and memory).

Although learning due to affective reinforcements (see Box 7.1) is more the topic of Chapter 10, several experimental results are relevant to the motor system and are discussed here. One focus region for motor learning in response to aversive feedback in mammals is the cerebellum (see Figure 7.6). Classic studies by Thompson and colleagues revealed that the nucleus interpositus in the cerebellum is crucial in rabbits for learning a well-timed eye blink. Briefly, the rabbit learns to avoid a puff of air hitting its cornea by closing its eyelid in response to a tone that reliably precedes each puff of air. Using reversible cooling procedures, the researchers showed that if the cerebellar interpositus was disabled no eye blink learning occurred, and normal learning proceeded only after the interpositus was switched on again, by stopping the cooling (Thompson & Steinmetz, 2009). In contrast, a structure in the brain stem known to control movements of the eye lid, the red nucleus, appeared to have a different role. If the red nucleus was disabled no sign of learning was visible; but, after it had been switched on again, the rabbit blinked to the tone as if the nothing had ever been deactivated. Thus, when (and only when) the cerebellum is operational does motor learning occur, even when the result of that learning cannot be immediately expressed. The result also shows that mammals do not have to act in the environment to learn about it.

The role of the cerebellum in eye blink learning specifically has also been confirmed in humans with cerebellar lesions. In one study a comparison was made between healthy controls, patients with unilateral damage in the superior cerebellum (including the interpositus), and patients with inferior cerebellum damage. Representative results are shown in Figure 7.5. Healthy controls and patients with inferior damage readily learned to anticipate a puff of air delivered to their eyes. After ten trials or so, during which the puff of air was systematically preceded by a tone at half-second intervals, the eye blink shifted from occurring right after the puff to just before it. However, patients with superior cerebellar damage never learned to do it (Gerwig et al., 2003).

It is worthwhile taking a closer look at how connections run from, to, and between the cerebellar cortex and deep nuclei such as the interpositus to implement such learning phenomena. Dozens of studies, especially in cats and monkeys, utilizing single cell recording or local field potentials, have yielded a comprehensive picture of neural connectivity with and within the cerebellum (Apps & Garwicz, 2005; Dean et al., 2010). The cerebellum embodies

Figure 7.5

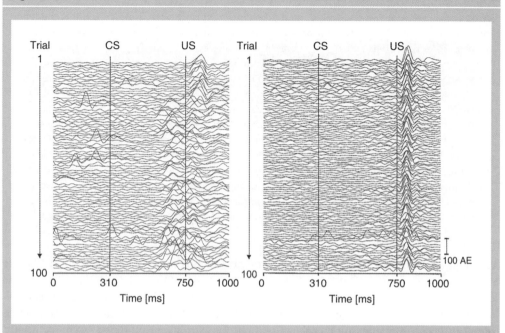

Left: a 66-year old healthy individual learns to use the information from a tone presented at 310 ms (CS) to close the eyelid before presentation of a puff of air to the eye at 750 ms (US).
Successive learning trials range from 1 to 100. Each trace represents an electromyogram (EMG) as recorded from the orbicularis oculi muscle, the muscle that pulls down the eyelid. The EMG signals have been rectified and integrated (for a graphical illustration of eye blink EEG recording as well as the signal-transformation procedure, see Plate XVI). Right: same traces for a patient with superior cerebellar damage. The peak in the EMG that corresponds to the blink never shifts to anticipate the puff of air. Reprinted from Gerwig et al., 2003, by permission of Oxford University Press.

an impressive example of nervous system connectivity, not in the least because it contains about 80 per cent of the central nervous system's 85 billion neurons. Millions of mossy fibres and granule cells convey sensory information from all parts of the body to the cerebellar cortex. This information originates in the skin and the spinal cord, as well as from the visual and auditory cortices. From these regions it is transferred to the brain stem pons, and from there to the cerebellum. Huge numbers of synaptic contacts are realized between the parallel fibres from the granule cells and the Purkinje cells, the cells with the most highly arborized dendrites in the brain (see Figure 7.6).

This huge number of glutamatergic synapses allows for a tremendously fine-grained tuning of Purkinje activations, and therefore of the inhibitory modulation of the Purkinje output targets, the cerebellar nuclei, such as the dentate and the interpositus. Neurons in these nuclei directly modulate the output of the motor cortex and of brain stem structures connected to the motor cortex, to the spinal cord. In this way the 70 billion cerebellar cell machinery contributes to the adjustment of movement to continuously delivered fresh sensory information.

There is still more to it. A rather unbelievable set of connections centres on the inferior olive in the medulla, where information from the motor cortex is integrated with information about the position of the limbs. From the inferior olive, so-called climbing fibres reach into the cerebellum as depicted in Figure 7.6. They convey error signals reflecting the discrepancy between the representation in the motor cortex of the intended action and the position of the relevant limbs. This error signal then quenches the strength of the connections with the parallel fibres in one Purkinje cell. Similarly to what happens in the Aplysia during sensitization, sustained and/or repeated climbing fibre signals may yield prolonged (for a day or longer) inhibition of the targeted parallel fibre–Purkinje cell (PF–PC) connections (Thach et al., 2000). This is termed long-term depression and is thought to involve (sometimes genetically mediated) structural changes in the activation of enzymes and the synthesis of proteins that modulate signal transduction within a neuron.

As if this is not yet enough, the modulating effect of the climbing fibre can be modulated itself. This is realized by a variety of pre-synaptic, indirectly coupled receptors at the climbing axon. These include the cannabinoid receptor and the adenosine receptor, which also act to modulate the PF–PC connection directly. Very specifically however, alpha-2 mediated

Figure 7.6

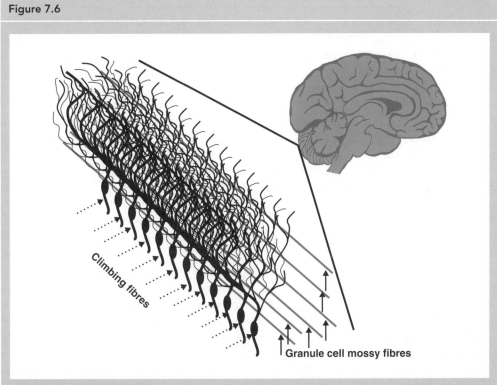

The input through the granule cell mossy fibres conveys, for example, information on the position of a moving visual target.

Through the parallel fibres (grey parallel lines) each granule cell can deliver a signal to a multitude of highly arborized Purkinje cells. The connections between parallel fibres and Purkinje cells are excitatory (glutamate). The climbing fibres originate from the inferior olive in the medulla, where they integrate information from the motor cortex and the position of the limbs to produce an error signal, which then quenches the strength of all parallel fibre–Purkinje connections for one Purkinje cell.

norepinephrine (NE), and possibly dopamine as well, reduce the effect that climbing fibre signals can have on PF–PC connection strength (Carey & Wade, 2009). One idea is that diffuse projections from the locus cereleus end up in these locations in the cerebellum, to deliver NE at the appropriate receptors. Intuitively, high NE levels would seem to make cerebellum-based movement corrections for new sensory input less sensitive to information about movement execution errors.

This wealth of connectivity within and surrounding the cerebellum supports diverse learning mechanisms. One is the learning of associations as described above, which involves the timing of certain motor processes. It is now generally believed that the cerebellum is also essential for learning temporal relations between events outside the domain of motor learning. Another characteristic of learning mediated by the cerebellum is that it relies on sensory output or external guidance, even though the input may be proprioceptive as well as exteroceptive. Obviously, also other forms of learning address the temporal relationship between successive motor acts and external events. Such learning is addressed in the next section, which is about acquiring skills and learning how to act appropriately in a given context.

7.3   INSTRUMENTAL CONDITIONING AND PROCEDURAL LEARNING

Learning to anticipate the occurrence of a certain event and adjust actions to that anticipation is one thing. It is another thing to learn by trial and error the appropriate response to a certain stimulus. This has traditionally been captured in instrumental, or operant, conditioning procedures. Rats learn to find their way in an intricate maze towards a rewarding piece of food if they happen to travel the appropriate route a couple of times and get rewarded on each occasion. Similarly, humans facing a situation that involves uncertainty as to the appropriate action, learn from explicit feedback whether the finally chosen action was appropriate or not. One obvious mechanism in such operant learning in humans is the error signal in the anterior cingulate cortex (ACC), as discussed in Section 4.3.

Consider human subjects in a condition in which the four fingers of one hand each map on one specific stimulus (e.g. car, van, bus, airplane). On half the trials a feedback signal is generated by the computer to inform the subject whether the response was correct or not. Initially, it is by chance which finger subjects use in response to which vehicle. During the course of about 150 trials they manage to reduce their errors to a rate significantly above the level of chance. While this happens at the level of performance, the conflict signal from the ACC in response to the feedback signal also gradually diminishes (Mars et al., 2005). At the same time, the conflict signal from the ACC on trials with incorrect answers but without informative feedback gradually increases. Specifically, after some 90 trials the point is reached where the self-generated error signal becomes larger than the feedback elicited error signal. It is as if the subjects' brains learn to recognize an error more and more independently of the feedback signal, and finally end up in a state in which the error signal is completely internally generated. As noted in Section 4.3, the consequence of this error signal may be that communication within certain perception–action pathways is amplified, while in others it is relatively attenuated.

A more elaborate form of learning involves the recognition of patterns in the environment that, over the course of learning, are increasingly used to predict external events as well as the appropriate response; the net effect then is a steady increase in the speed and accuracy of performance. The idea is that regularities in external information become gradually translated into increasingly organized response patterns; this is perhaps one of the essential aspects of what is often termed procedural learning. A widely used experimental model to investigate such processes uses sequence learning, and one popular variety of the sequence learning paradigm is the Continuous Serial Reaction Time (CSRT) task. Figure 7.7 presents part of a typical example. The complete sequence consists of 24 green light offsets in six possible positions, which correspond to the left-hand ring (1), middle (2) and index (3) fingers, and the right hand (4) index, (5) middle and ring (6) fingers. The upper panel of Figure 7.8 presents two prototypical sequences of 24 digits. One of these is marked by a run in each subsequent triplet (e.g. 123, 321). The other contains no runs, but is identical in terms of hand switches, reversals and repetitions, each of which has its own modulating effect on reaction time.

These modulating effects are visible in the left data panel in Figure 7.8, which shows the average reaction times across 24 repetitions of the runs as well as the no-runs sequence. More importantly, these average RTs are substantially shorter for the runs than for the no-runs

Figure 7.7

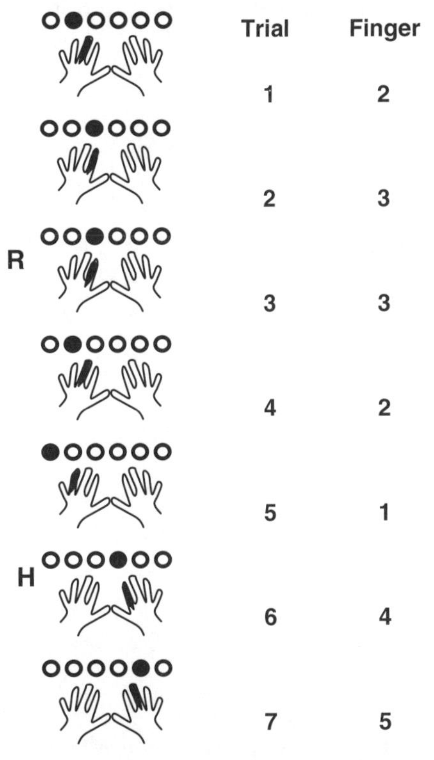

Typical CSRT set-up.
On each trial one of the (green) lights dims. This determines the finger on either the left or the right hand with which to respond. The R signifies a *repetition* of one finger movement. The H signifies a *hand switch*. Trials 3 (R) to 5 constitute a monotonous *run* (in this case from right-to-left)
Source: Jiménez (2008).

sequence. The right data panel shows the RTs averaged across all 192 triplets. The difference in RT in the runs conditions is the typical signature of chunking (Kirsch et al., 2010). This is actually thought to be motor chunking, referring to the idea that over the course of the repeated sequence, the response to the initial digit in a triplet triggers the next two responses in an increasingly efficient manner, hence the difference between RTs in position 1 versus positions 2 and 3.

Chunking is an inferred phenomenon that is familiar to other cognitive domains. Many first year psychology students have noticed that more letters will be recalled from the string CIALTSKGBWMFBISTS if it is recombined, or chunked, into CIA LTS KGB WM FBI STS. This is known as chunking in working or short-term memory. Without chunking, an individual would not be able to repeat the string of 17 letters without errors or omissions. But after reduction to six chunks, the first letter of each chunk can trigger the other parts of the chunk, thus effectively increasing the letter span.

The next questions are: what can be chunked, and what are the limits of chunking? Figure 7.8 also reveals that the chunking signature is much less pronounced in the no-runs conditions. Thus, the presence of regular left-to-right, or right-to-left, triplets seems to promote chunking as well as the speed of response in general. No doubt this is connected to the relative abundance of slackening transitions in the no-runs sequence due to reversals within triplets (e.g. 546) and finger skipping within (from 4 to 6 in 546) and between runs (from

Figure 7.8

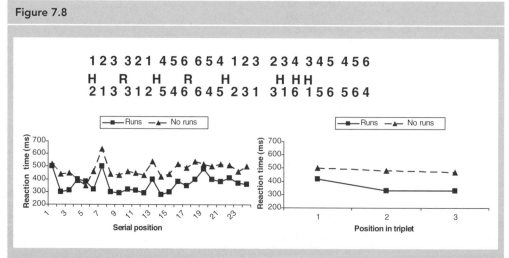

Typical sequences for sequence learning and data.

Upper panel: the upper sequence of 24 letters consists of runs: triplets of digits that dictate regular right-to-left or left-to-right movement across fingers. In addition, part of the runs are initiated by hand switches (H, see Figure 7.7) or repetitions (R), as well as reversals in some cases (e.g. from 123 back to the 2 of the subsequent 234). The lower sequence is identical in terms of hand switches, repetitions, and some of the reversals, but contains no runs. Left lower panel: average reaction times across 24 repetitions of either the runs sequence or the no-runs sequence as a function of position within the sequence. Right lower panel: average reaction times across 192 (24 x 8) triplets for runs and no-runs sequences. The difference in RT in the runs conditions is the typical signature of chunking.
Source: Kirsch et al. (2010).

231 to 316). Thus, a certain degree of regularity is needed for chunking to occur. This is not confined to triplets. It has been shown that a response sequence for one hand consisting of index–ring–middle–index–middle–ring results in a chunking signature across all six elements; in contrast, the sequence ring–middle–index–ring–index–middle was clearly chunked into two triplets (Verwey & Eikelboom, 2003).

In elucidating all these details of the CSRT task and chunking we almost lose track of the original perspective of sequence *learning*. So, where is the learning? A common view is that the average speed in CSRT tasks is elevated by motor chunking. Moreover, the shortening of RTs over the course of sequence learning is thought to be mediated by enhancements in chunking (Kirsch et al., 2010). This implies that the chunking signature should become more pronounced as the amount of practice increases, in other words the position effect (Figure 7.8, right lower panel) should increase with continuing practice. However, from the learning curves for the data depicted in Figure 7.8, this is not readily apparent (Jiménez, 2008; Kirsch et al., 2010). In fact the chunking signature was present across the first eight repetitions as well as across the middle and the last eight repetitions. If anything, a development towards more pronounced chunking signatures was apparent for the no-runs condition, but the final signature for the last eight repetitions was considerably less pronounced than the average signature in the runs condition. It seems that when chunking is easy, it is there from the outset and does not contribute much to learning, as manifest in the evolving increase in response speed; and when it is not so easy, some development with practice may be observed, but the end result is quite limited.

Another question is, is it really motor learning? This holds for both the general reduction of RT in structured sequences as well as for the chunking signature. A study by Grafton et al. (1998) revealed that after 118 repetitions of a sequence of six key presses (in response to six sequential stimuli) involving four fingers of one hand, average reaction times had significantly shortened. In a second phase, the same stimulus sequence was presented, but now a different four responses had to be used, arm movements rather than finger flexions. Nevertheless, in this condition these subjects produced significantly shorter RTs than a group of control subjects who, in the initial phase, had received a completely random sequence of 708 (118 x 6) of the same stimuli (with the same response mapping). This indicates that sequence learning generalized over different effectors and was at least partly independent of the specific part of the motor system being trained.

However, there is still the question of what exactly was transferred from the first to the second phase of the experiment; for example, this could be a memory for the stimulus sequence, or some abstract memory for the maps between the stimulus and the relative positions of response keys. Perhaps a look at the brain structures involved will answer this.

7.4 BRAIN CIRCUITS FOR PROCEDURAL LEARNING: LOOPS FOR THE BASAL GANGLIA

A study of patients with lesions in the basal ganglia (not further specified) revealed an interesting dissociation. These patients were exposed to a twelve stimulus response sequence task similar to the one used in the Grafton et al. experiment. Healthy controls displayed the expected gradual decrease in reaction times, while the basal ganglia patients did so to a lesser extent (Boyd et al., 2009). In addition, measuring the chunking revealed that this was severely reduced in the patients. However, the measure of spontaneous chunking for each group was based on average (across participants or patients) reaction times for each single trial. From this analysis, reaction-time trial-to-trial patterns indicative of chunking were detected only when sufficiently robust across the individuals in a group; individual-specific patterns may have easily gone unnoticed. Chunking patterns in the patient group may therefore have been more variable across individuals, rather than less pronounced in individual patients.

For what it is worth, it may be concluded that deficient basal ganglia prevent a systematic chunking strategy that is observed in an arbitrary group of healthy controls. A fascinating aspect of this study was that the basal ganglia patients did not differ from the controls in the extent of their explicit memory for the structure of the sequence, as tested afterwards (admittedly, the patients were again much more variable in this respect). This could then point to an interesting double dissociation with another group of patients, those with lesions in the hippocampus. For example, as explained at the beginning of Chapter 6, H.M. could learn procedural tasks (like mirror drawing) as skilfully as the average healthy person after a number of daily training sessions; yet he was completely unable to relate anything about the previous sessions. In contrast, the basal ganglia patients display intact episodic memory, but impaired procedural memory.

So, is it motor learning? The authors of the report on basal ganglia patients surmise that the lack of a general increase in speed amongst the patients reflects cognitive rather than motor impairment, because there was no difference with the healthy controls in a random sequence repetition condition. But the question remains whether this also holds for the chunking differences. Another relevant perspective is the extent to which the basal ganglia are appropriately conceived of as a motor structure.

One way to evaluate such a qualification is to look at the connections between the basal ganglia and other parts of the brain. The essence of these connections and those within the basal ganglia is depicted in Figure 4.14. As mentioned in Section 4.3, a hyperdirect pathway runs from the cortex to the STN, and then to the internal globus pallidus that inhibits the thalamo–cortical activation. A second pathway is the direct one: cortex to striatum (which includes caudate nucleus and putamen) to internal globus pallidus to thalamus to cortex; activation eventually excites the cortex. The third pathway is called the indirect pathway and runs from cortex to striatum to external globus pallidus to internal globus pallidus; activation of this pathway results in net inhibition of the thalamo–cortical connection. The balance between these pathways determines the net activation of the thalamus and thence of the cortex. Finally, the efferents from the cortex loop back to the striatum.

The part of the cortex that is targeted through these connections includes both primary and secondary motor cortex. So, to that extent the basal ganglia are implicated in motor control. This fits the observed disturbances of sequence learning in patients with Parkinson's disease (Doyon, 2008; Siegert et al., 2006); these patients are marked by movement dysfunction that involves disturbed signals between the basal ganglia and the motor cortex. However, it has been known for quite some time that the loop with the motor cortex is only one of multiple basal–ganglia–cortex loops. Briefly, the other loops include an oculomotor loop (with the frontal eye fields, FEF), a dorsolateral–prefrontal loop, an orbitofrontal loop, and a mutual connection involving the anterior cingulate cortex and the nucleus accumbens (the nucleus accumbens is sometimes termed the ventral striatum) (Alexander et al., 1986). Each of these loops can be surmised to be implicated in a different function, for example eye movement control and cognition for the first two. The orbitofrontal loop, as well as anterior cingulate and nucleus accumbens, will be discussed more extensively in Chapter 9, in the context of emotion and action. Within the basal ganglia each loop has its own specific compartment into which axons project and leave for the next relay station (Middleton & Strick,

2002). For example, axons from the motor loop terminate in the putamen, those from the dorsolateral prefrontal cortex in the dorsolateral (head of the) caudate nucleus, and those from the orbitofrontal cortex in the ventromedial (head of the) caudate nucleus. Similar distinctions can be made for the next basal ganglia node, which involves the globus pallidus, as well as the reticular part of the substantia nigra (not to be confused with the compacta part of the substantia nigra, which is the region that transmits dopamine to the putamen, and where damage causes the symptoms of Parkinson's disease). With respect to the globus pallidus, the exact site of lesions (in humans) has been shown to determine whether observable impairments are more cognitive or motor (Middleton & Strick, 2002). Finally, also within the thalamus, distinct regions are involved in projections to distinct regions of the cortex.

So what happens when we look at procedural sequence learning? In a recent study, improvements in performance during sequence learning were paralleled by a reduction of activation in the caudate nucleus and an increase in activation in the putamen (Steele & Penhune, 2010). If we project this onto the anatomical connections and their functional labels as outlined above, the obvious conclusion is that, during procedural learning, activation shifts from a cognitive dorsolateral loop to the motor loop. Intuitively, this seems to make sense. In the first phase of sequence learning, you need higher level cognition to decide what the appropriate response is to each subsequent stimulus. As the sequence is repeated over and over, reliance on the stimulus declines and a lower level motor program increasingly takes control.

Other findings in the Steel and Penhune (2010) study were that the premotor cortex (see Figure 2.10) decreased its activity over time while performance improved, as did parts of the cerebellum, while other parts of the cerebellum actually increased in activity. The premotor cortex is normally involved in higher-order motor control (control of the activation of neurons in the primary motor cortex). The reduction of premotor activation is consistent with an influential theory about complementary roles during procedural learning for the premotor cortex (PMC) and other parts of the secondary motor cortex located more medially and dorsally: the supplementary motor area (SMA). Specifically, the PMC would be more active during initial learning, when reliance on external signals is relatively high. The SMA, on the other hand, would become more active during the later phase of the task, when internal signals increasingly take over. Data consistent with the mapping of these areas on the external/internal distinction were presented in an ingenious study by Thut and colleagues. Subjects executed either internally or externally guided finger movements, based on instruction stimuli that either did or did not afford external guidance. ERPs to the instruction stimuli were analysed with regard to the difference between the conditions, which were most pronounced around 150 ms latency (larger amplitudes for external guidance) and around 225 ms latency (larger for internal guidance) (Thut et al., 2000). Figure 7.9 summarizes the main results.

The rather intricate interaction between timing, condition, and contribution of medial versus lateral sources, is explained in the caption to Figure 7.9. In summary, these data are consistent with a shorter-latency, laterally dominated, electrocortical response during external guidance, and a longer-latency, medially dominated response when action is internally controlled. In turn this pattern is consistent with a more PMC dominated action control with external cues, and with a more SMA dominated control during internal guidance.

To complete the picture, the external/internal distinction has been worked out in terms of external versus internal motor loops. The former would include the PMC and the cerebellum, as well as part of the parietal cortex. As discussed in Section 2.2, both PMC and parietal cortex are extensively involved in the translation from external information into appropriate

Figure 7.9

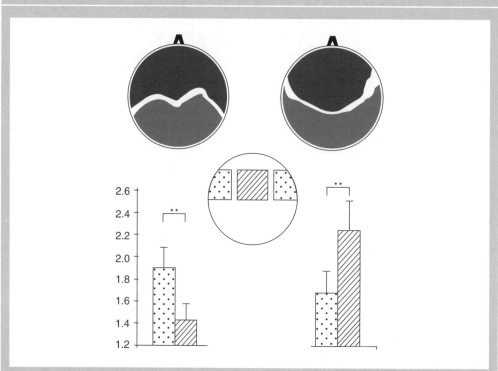

Above: Scalp topographies for ERPs to cues that instruct either internal or external guidance of key presses, at 150 ms (left) and at 225 ms latency (right).
The 150 ms pattern was more pronounced during external guidance, and the 225 ms pattern was more pronounced during internal guidance. Middle: coarse source localization (LORETA) of activity in a more medial (stripes) and more lateral areas (dots) contributing to the scalp topographies. Lower panels: the lateral sources are stronger for the 150 ms pattern, the medial source contributes more to the 225 ms pattern, consistent with a more lateral activation during external guidance and a more medial activation during internal guidance. Note that the differential contributions of lateral versus medial sources can also be deduced from the scalp topographies.
Source: Reprinted from Tuth et al. (2000) with permission from Elsevier.

action parameters (think for example of the visuomotor neurons). As discussed previously in this chapter, circuits in the cerebellum can be viewed as being specialized in modulating action control based on continuous input from several sensory systems (Thach et al., 2000). In contrast, the internal loop is activated when the control of action and action sequences is driven from within, and primarily involves the supplementary motor cortex and the basal ganglia (that is, the motor–basal–ganglia loop). How exactly this relates to the kind of procedural learning discussed so far is still an open question. Procedural learning may involve a shift from external to internal guidance and therefore from the external to the internal loop, but this is certainly not the whole story. As noted, shifts of activation centres within the basal ganglia have also been observed, as have increases in activity in part of the cerebellum with learning; it has even been suggested that the cerebellum may hold representations of learned action sequences (Halsband & Lange, 2006; Steele & Penhune, 2010).

7.5   SEQUENCE LEARNING AND DOPAMINE

This section addresses the role of a neurotransmitter. As briefly mentioned, the aberrant mechanism underlying Parkinson's disease is cell death in the substantia nigra pars compacta. These cells normally signal to the putamen, releasing dopamine from their axon terminals. When they die, the result is a shortage of dopamine release and binding in the putamen, and consequently a decline in inhibition. One of the consequences of which is an overactive globus pallidus that excessively inhibits the thalamus and thence the motor cortex. This leads to the primary symptom of Parkinson's disease, an inability to initiate voluntary movements (tremor is a secondary symptom resulting from hypersensitivity of the dopamine receptors as a consequence of their reduced stimulation). It should be clear by now that this dopamine deficiency may affect more than the motor loop. For example, impairments in patients with Parkinson's disease with respect to sequence learning may also involve the cognitive loop. Recall from Section 4.2.1 that cues used to direct attention in space are not as effective in these patients as they are in the controls, and that their effectiveness is also reduced by dopaminergic antagonists. These cues normally activate the dorsal attentional control network, including the FEF, which are part of the basal ganglia oculomotor loop, and therefore may be excessively inhibited in Parkinson's disease as well. Abnormal dopaminergic mechanisms in this disease are also manifest in reduced error-related signals from the ACC (see Section 4.3) (Willemssen et al., 2009).

In healthy volunteers rapid sequence learning has been found to be positively associated with low (baseline) binding potential for dopamine receptors (Karabanov et al., 2010). This is a parameter that is assessed using PET scans after infusion with a radioactive dopamine (D2) ligand (mostly raclopride). If less raclopride binds, then this may indicate that more receptors are already occupied by endogenous dopamine; it is also possible that there are fewer receptors as a whole, which may also be the long-term consequence of higher tonic dopamine levels (that would be desensitization). In another study, similar PET scans were taken both before and during sequence learning. The striatum as a whole (putamen, caudate) displayed a lower binding potential (again, this *may* reflect a rise in dopamine release) during the task, relative to baseline (Garraux et al., 2007); this is illustrated in Figure 7.10.

In addition, dopamine D2 receptor blocking (through administration of raclopride) in capuchin monkeys disrupted the learning of novel short sequence response patterns as well as the extent to which these were executed in a chunking manner (Figure 7.8). This seems to be more straightforward support for the notion that dopamine D2 binding is instrumental in aspects of sequence learning. In patients with Parkinson's disease a comparison has been made between medication on and off conditions (i.e. during treatment with L-dopa, pramipexole, or rotigotine, or untreated). Unexpectedly, medication impaired sequence learning (Kwak et al., 2010). The reasons for this are as yet unclear. One possible factor is the explicit nature of the instruction, in which the sequence was explained rather thoroughly before the start of the task. Another unexpected result in this study, perhaps related to the explicit nature of the task, was that patients OFF medication did not differ at all from healthy controls.

Dopamine then seems to be implicated in promoting procedural learning, although a simple linear relationship is not supported by all the available data. These dopaminergic mechanisms may work in various loops that involve the basal ganglia, including the cognitive, motor and oculomotor loops. With improved performance during learning, shifts from the cognitive to the motor loop may take place, along with a complementary shift from

Figure 7.10

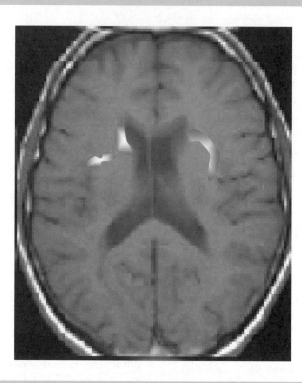

Decrease from baseline during sequence learning, in D2 receptor binding potential as manifest in the striatum (grey–white spots).
Z coordinate = 18. The decrease in binding potential may reflect elevated endogenous dopamine binding.

premotor cortex dominance to supplementary motor cortex dominance. This may be related to an increasing influence of internal control rather than control by external cues over procedural actions as task proficiency progresses.

7.6   RETRIEVAL IN THE MOTOR CORTEX

This last section describes how the motor cortex supports memories and helps imagination; this is analogous to Section 5.4 on retrieval from perceptual cortex In addition, it illustrates how external devices, such as computers, can read information stored or represented in the cortex to control other devices.

A milestone in this line of research was published by Roland and colleagues in 1980 (Roland et al., 1980). These researchers used a primitive PET scan technique, in which a radioactive substance (Xenon) was administered and detectors over the scalp picked up the energy released from decaying particles. This was carried out under different task conditions: resting, producing a simple rhythm with one finger, producing a more complex rhythmic sequence of finger movements, and a third condition in which the human subjects were asked to just rehearse the complex sequence, not execute it. The result of a comparison between the second and third conditions illustrated the relationship between the primary motor cortex (M1) and the secondary supplementary motor area (SMA). With the simple movement, only M1 was activated (as well as the somatosensory cortex (S1), an almost trivial example of how action influences perception). With the more complex pattern however, M1 and S1 were joined by the SMA. The obvious interpretation is that when the movements of single fingers have to be coordinated in a precisely timed pattern, neurons in the SMA send signals to neurons in M1 to control the timing of individual finger movements.

So much for the basic hierarchical relationship between the secondary and primary motor cortices. The central issue for memory and action is what happened in the third condition. There, only the SMA was activated. No finger movements were actually carried out, and (so) no M1 activity was observed. What was observed, was the neural substrate of thinking about, rehearsing, imagining, or retrieving the idea of an arbitrary, self-emitted movement pattern.

The consequences of these insights into the interaction between action and memory at brain level were recently illustrated in a rather dramatic fashion. Researchers Owen and Laureys, along with a number of colleagues, managed to establish communication through brain scans with a coma patient who had not produced any sign of understanding external signals for the last three years.

This endeavour again featured the SMA. As illustrated in Figure 7.11, when a human individual is asked to imagine playing tennis (or soccer, or to produce a complex rhythmic sequence), there will be fMRI BOLD activation in his or her SMA. Alternatively, imagining how to navigate through your own house and visualizing what you encounter will activate the parahippocampal place area (PPA, see Section 3.3 on setting the gains). One step further is to instruct a subject to use these different imagery procedures to provide yes/no answers to specific questions, so that corresponding activations (SMA versus PPA) can be used by someone else to decipher the answer (Figure 7.11).

This same procedure was applied in 54 coma patients. Of these 54, five responded to the imagery instruction (e.g. imaging playing tennis). One of these five was subsequently subjected to the yes/no imagery procedure, with a result that was comparable to that obtained for healthy controls, as illustrated in Figure 7.11 (Monti et al., 2010). This is an astonishing finding when you consider what happens. The patient who has been non-responsive for years is presented with an instruction such as: 'We are going to ask you some questions. If you want to answer yes then think of playing tennis. If you want to answer no then think of the rooms in your house.' Then the first question is posed. Seconds later the signal indicating that the patient's response should be issued is given. This sequence is repeated five times with different questions (see Figure 7.11 for examples). The answers to the questions are objectively verified. For five of the six questions, the patient managed to produce the correct answer.

A further remarkable fact is that not only were five out of six answers correct for the patient, but also for the healthy controls all 48 questions were answered correctly with this procedure. This is remarkable because usually multiple repeated measurements are needed to reliably identify activations that are specific to certain conditions such as yes or no; but in these cases almost each yes or no could be identified from a single BOLD response. To achieve this, the repeated measure principle had been applied in the first phase of the study, when the activations that corresponded to tennis and house were identified as accurately as possible, based on averages of multiple occasions. Templates were then created for each condition (i.e. regions exhibiting condition selective activity), and were subsequently used to determine for each single trial BOLD response during the questioning phase whether the balance tipped more

Figure 7.11

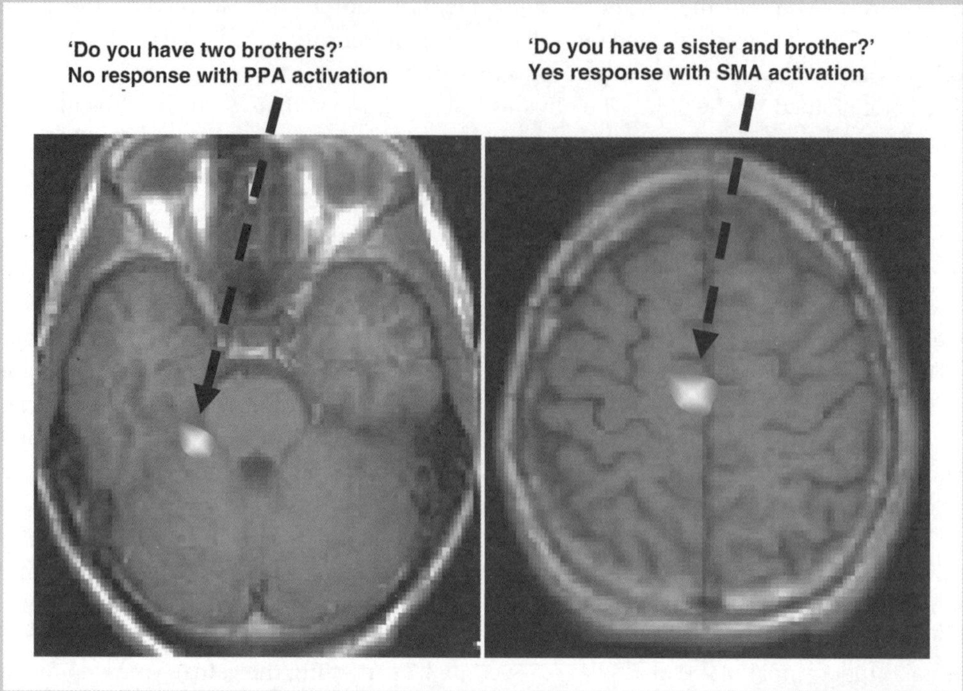

Average healthy individuals manage to produce a 'yes' response by activating the SMA (right panel, z = 60; motor imagery) and a 'no' response by activating the parahippocampal gyrus (PPA in the left panel, z = −30; spatial imagery).
The same was observed in a coma patient.

towards yes than no. For the one question that the patient could not answer, activations in both SMA and PPA were equally low.

A final note concerns the conceptual framework in which the authors (Monti et al.) presented their findings. The title already featured the concept of consciousness. Although this may be understandable from a medical ethical point of view (the findings tell us something about awareness or consciousness in this patient being more substantial than previously thought), from a scientific perspective it is questionable. These results do not reveal a neural substrate of consciousness, but rather, they reveal comprehension: the ability to use information from outside to produce meaningful or sensible responses.

Related procedures have been tested on patients who suffered nerve, muscle or spinal cord damage and therefore were impaired in using their limbs. In one severe case of tetraplegia, an electrode grid was implanted in the primary motor cortex (M1). After quite some time, signals from the M1 could be used to control various devices, such as a cursor on a computer screen, including the ability to click on icons, and opening and closing a prosthetic hand (Hochberg et al., 2006). Again, an astonishing achievement; in this case, a computer algorithm has to learn the language of the primary motor cortex. That is, a series of instructions for motor imagery of various kinds (e.g. imagine that you move the cursor upwards) was given to the patient, and for each imagery condition the pattern of neuronal spike rates across the 100 electrodes (spanning 4 mm by 4 mm) was recorded. Based on this information, a computer program computes a set of software filters that correspond to the various options. After sufficient fine tuning, these filters can be used to translate M1 activity into a specific command for a device to move in a certain way. For each recorded pattern from M1, the filter that yields the strongest output contains the message that the patient intended to convey.

7.7 CONCLUDING REMARKS

We have tried to provide a first glimpse of what it takes in the brain to successfully learn a more or less complex pattern of actions. Circuits in the supercomputer contained in the cerebellum are instrumental in learning appropriately timed actions, as well as other temporal relations. Noradrenergic innervations modulate the extent to which the cerebellum adjusts settings in other parts of the motor system. The cerebellum is a key structure in utilizing sensory information to adjust such settings. This is often a necessary ingredient in, what is termed, procedural learning of more or less complex action patterns. With learning, dependence on external cues in the production of action patterns becomes less, and this is accompanied by shifts from activity in the lateral premotor cortex, certain parts of the cerebellum, and certain regions in the parietal cortex to activation of a more internally oriented system, involving the more medial supplementary motor cortex and the basal ganglia. This last structure complex has loop-wise connections to different parts of the cortex, including a more cognitive loop and a motor loop. With advancing procedural learning, there is also a shift from cognitive to motor loop involvement. In either case, dopamine may be a crucial messenger, and disturbances of the dopamine system often impair cognitive and motor aspects of procedural learning. Finally, signals from the primary and secondary cortices embody memories for a multitude of specific actions. These signals can also be used to control devices that support human action and communication when severe damage in other parts of the nervous system has rendered normal action and communication impossible.

Questions

1. Summarize signals from and to the cerebellum. How do they affect motor processes? What is the role of signals from the inferior olive? And of norepinephrine?
2. Summarize the involvement of implicit and explicit loops in procedural learning. What are the facts, what is as yet speculative? Which cortical and subcortical regions, as well as their mutual connections, have been implicated?
3. In Section 7.6 it is stated that when the movements of single fingers have to be coordinated in a precisely timed pattern, neurons in the SMA send signals to neurons in the primary motor cortex (M1) to control the timing of individual finger movements. How can such putative hierarchical signals be implemented in the activity of individual neurons in the SMA and M1?
4. Consider the fMRI procedure for communication in a coma described in Section 7.6. To apply such a procedure on a larger scale with certain patients (e.g. at the bedside), it would be useful to have a device available that is more manageable, less expensive, and faster in producing a response. Work this out for EEG or MEG or any other method you can think of. How important is accurate functional localization in this context? How would the procedure distinguish between the patient's response options such as yes and no, or any other possibility?

8 PERCEPTION, ATTENTION AND EMOTION

Key Points

- Emotion involves brain controlled activation of the sympathetic nervous system that can be easily recorded in humans.
- The affective content of a stimulus influences perception in various sensory modalities by modulating sensory cortical processing, akin to the modulation caused by 'cognitive attention'. While the latter is controlled by parietal and (sometimes lateral) prefrontal mechanisms, control of affective modulation involves additional or other structures, in particular the amygdala.
- Signals from the amygdala to modulate perceptual processing readily overcome blockades, such as in hemispatial neglect or the attentional blink, but can be suppressed by descending cortical signals, depending on task load.
- There is an interaction between affective appreciation and the direction of attention.
- The interaction between emotion and attention seems to be implemented as mutual signals between subcortical and deep cortical areas on the one hand, and dorsal cortical areas on the other, with a regulating bridge function performed by the rostral anterior cingulate cortex. An imbalance between these ventral and dorsal compartments of the brain can result in affective disorders and constitutes a target for various pharmacological and other kinds of treatments.
- The amygdala response to affective materials may be a specific instance of a general principle, according to which multiple subcortical nuclei, including the locus cereleus, nucleus basalis, and ventral tegmental area, respond to affective or otherwise salient stimuli by producing diffuse cortical activation through their diffuse cortical innervations.

8.0 INTRODUCTION: EMOTION AS A SYMPATHETIC RESPONSE

Figure 8.1 shows a prototypical stimulus for the prototypical emotional response. The dog is probably growling in a particularly ominous way. The crucial thing is that the dog has not, as yet, inflicted pain or damage on the observer. It is the mere threat implied by the attitude, posture and utterance that affects the observer, due to direct prior experience in similar situations, or more indirectly based on acquired general knowledge, or perhaps a genetically determined tendency.

Figure 8.1

An arbitrary dog from the internet.
Source: iStockphoto.

But what exactly happens to the observer when he or she is affected by this stimulus? The observer's response is commonly described as an emotion. It involves a plethora of reactions throughout the brain and the rest of body, notably the motor system and the autonomic nervous system. The latter especially can be viewed as very characteristic of the emotion response, as compared to the systems and mechanisms that we have been discussing in the previous chapters. A brief survey of this autonomic response is suitable at this point.

The autonomic nervous system consist of two subsystems, the sympathetic and the para-sympathetic branches. Together these systems form a front end control for all the activity in the internal organs (heart, lungs, all the different glands, digestive system, etc.). Almost all the internal organs are innervated by both systems, with opposing effects. While the parasympathetic system prepares to build up and conserve energy, the sympathetic branch prepares the body to expend it. This is in line with the notion that the internal bodily component of the emotional response is primarily the activation of the sympathetic nervous system (SNS).

In preparing the body to expend energy, signals from the SNS have various effects in various organs. For example, they increase heartbeat rate and blood flow through the body, and dilate the lungs' bronchioles to expedite and intensify the transport of oxygen to the blood. The SNS signals to the internal organs are conveyed by action potentials over axons that eventually release norepinephrine (NE). To be more precise, most of the connections contain relay stations between the central nervous system (mostly spinal cord, as well some nuclei in the brain) known as the sympathetic ganglia. Axons arriving in the sympathetic ganglia from the spinal cord actually release acetylcholine (ACh) to eventually bind to nicotinic ACh receptors, after which the signals are fed on to the target internal organs.

There are two notable exceptions to the principle of pre-ganglionic ACh and post-ganglionic NE transmission. Both of them happen to be of particular importance to the topic of emotion, and both of them are also exceptional in that there is no additional innervation from the parasympathetic system. These exceptions involve ACh transmission at both pre- and post-ganglionic nerve terminals. One of these exceptions involves connections located at the inner part of the adrenal glands, the adrenal medulla. This connection mediates the release mainly of adrenaline, as well as some NE (also termed nor-adrenaline) to the blood, as if it were a hormone. The (nor-)adrenaline released in this manner essentially copies, and therefore amplifies, the effects of NE, as released from the SNS synaptic terminals, in all the internal organs. Because it has to travel through the blood first, these effects take longer to materialize (in the order of several seconds, rather than in the order of a second or so as is the case for synaptic transmission in internal organs). These hormonal effects are in turn paralleled by an even slower hormonal response system that originates in the brain and finally targets the back of the adrenal gland, the adrenal cortex. This hypothalamus–pituitary–adrenal (HPA) axis eventually results in the release of cortisol from the adrenal cortex, and will be discussed in more detail in Chapter 10.

The second instance of post-ganglionic ACh connections concerns the sweat glands, more abundant in some parts of the body than in others. While the exact functional contribution of this SNS component may be somewhat indirect, or a matter of speculation (temperature regulation, better ability to swing from one branch to another), its use as a readout measure for SNS activation, especially in humans, is unsurpassable. One factor here is that, as mentioned above, it is a specific indicator of SNS activation, not being innervated by the parasympathetic branch. The second factor is that it is very easy to record and has a huge signal-to-noise ratio, enabling convenient analysis at the level of single responses. It should be noted at the outset that it reflects *just* sympathetic activation. It reflects emotion only to the extent that emotion includes sympathetic activation. Furthermore, it does not differentiate between different forms of emotion (such as fear versus positive excitement), to the extent that both emotions involve sympathetic activation. Other responses recordable from the human body are better suited for this (such as startle potentiation, discussed in Chapter 9). In addition, not all forms of sympathetic activation are inexorably viewed as pertaining to the domain of emotion. For example, a defining characteristic of stimulant drugs (such as nicotine, methylphenidate, cocaine) is that they are sympathicomimetic, meaning that they result in a tonic, sometimes enduring, enhancement of SNS activity.

Sympathetic activation results in a change in the properties of sweat gland tissue. Both this change in properties, as well as the release of moisture into the overlying skin, change the electrical properties of this system as a whole. Applying a known electrical potential across two spots on the skin, and recording the resulting electric current, yields an estimate of the electrical conductivity between the two sensors (see Figure 8.2), also known as skin conductance. Transient increases in skin conductance in response to diverse stimuli can be recorded in this way (skin conductance, or galvanic skin, response, SCR), as exemplified in Figure 8.2, and provide a convenient measure of sympathetic activation.

Figure 8.2

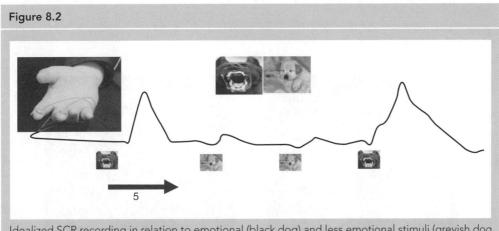

Idealized SCR recording in relation to emotional (black dog) and less emotional stimuli (greyish dog to the right, although this may also be exciting for some individuals). The arrow length represents approximately 5 seconds.

Sympathetic responses of the kind illustrated in Figure 8.2 are in turn triggered by processing such stimuli at brain level, most notably in structures such as the amygdala and the hypothalamus. In turn, sympathetic activation is generally thought to be fed back to the brain, through either direct or indirect projections from the internal organs. This feedback system may contribute to feeling, the subjective component of emotion, as well as to the special status of emotional materials and events in the formation of stable memory traces. In addition, a feedforward relationship exists between sympathetic activation and preparedness of the motor system, to take action in the sense of fighting, fleeing, or freezing. These relations to action and memory form the topics of the next two chapters. This chapter discusses how emotion interacts in the domains of perception and attention: how does it bias perception, and how does it help in attracting or diverting attention, and making it more or less selective? And the other way around, can attention modulate emotional responses?

8.1   AFFECTIVE CONTENT MODULATES SENSORY CORTICAL PROCESSING

As noted in Section 3.3, the insula contains the primary gustatory cortex, and also responds to the mere expectation of a taste stimulus. Here we take this one step further: neurons in the insula are also activated by signs of events known to elicit disgust. Primary examples are depictions of rotten meat, mouldy bread, as well as repellent animals (black beetles), eczema and dirty toilets. In one study BOLD responses were compared between typical disgust referring stimuli and stimuli typically associated with fear. Both stimulus categories elicited larger SCRs than neutral pictures did. However, there was hardly any correlation between judgements of fear and those of disgust. Furthermore, regions of the insula were only activated by disgust associations (see Figure 8.3), and the extent of that activation only correlated with the intensity of the disgust experience (Stark et al., 2007). In another study, the extent of insula activation directly predicted the self-reported sensitivity to disgust (e.g. answers to questions such as 'I never let any part of my body touch the toilet seat in public toilets') (Calder et al., 2007).

Figure 8.3

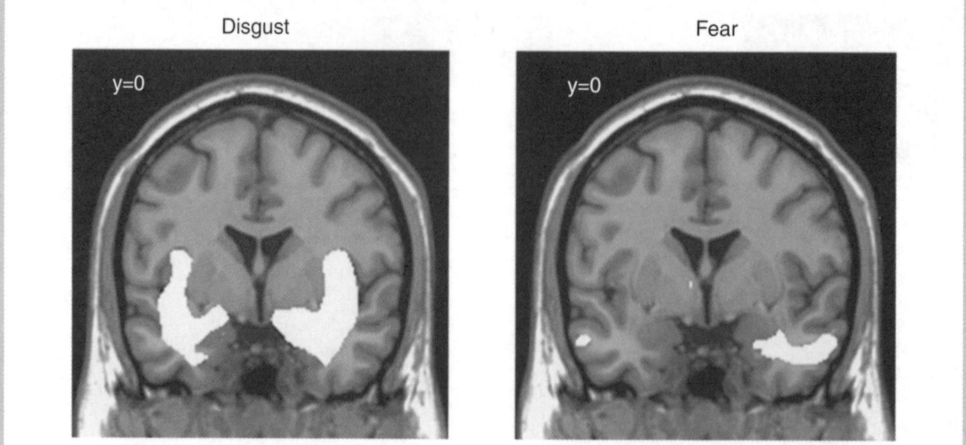

Insulas on both sides, at Talairach y coordinate 0, are activated by disgust-associated pictures, not by fear-related materials.

Source: Reprinted from Stark et al. (2007) with permission from Elsevier.

It should be noted that the centres of gravity of the insula activations in these two studies were quite remote, in the order of a centimetre in the anterior–posterior direction. More generally, it can be asked whether it is really the same neurons that are activated by real physical (bad) taste, and also by signals for physical disgust. This question becomes even more pressing when we think of insula activations to apparently disgusting social events (see Chapter 11).

The affective content of a stimulus influences perception in various sensory modalities, by modulating sensory cortical processing, akin to the modulation caused by 'cognitive attention'. Consider the example described by Eimer and Holmes (2007). Subjects were presented with either neutral or fearful faces (see Plate XV). The difference in electrocortical response to the different face categories was observed at a latency of about 130 ms post-stimulus.

A more direct form of threat can be attributed to inherently neutral stimuli that predict physical inconvenience. In anticipatory anxiety paradigms, participants are instructed that one of two inherently neutral visual stimuli might be followed by a mild, but nevertheless unpleasant, electric shock (for example to the wrist). Such shock predicting stimuli, relative to the ones that signal safety, have been reported to elicit enhanced processing in the visual cortex at a latency as early as 80 ms (Baas et al., 2002b). In a more recent study, Lee and colleagues used an angry face as a predictor for a subsequent electric shock. After a number of sequential face shock presentations (conditioning), masked face stimuli of the same identity with a neutral expression elicited an enhanced negativity (EPN, earlier posterior negativity) over the occipital cortex between 200 ms and 250 ms latency (Lee et al., 2009). This may seem a little late in view of the earlier effects obtained with a more indirect threat, such as that conveyed by fearful faces; the masked nature of the conditional stimuli may have played a role here.

These studies reported on the top–down effect on sensory cortex processing as the result of acquired affective relevance. A similar EPN deflection was reported for unpleasant (mutilations, violence) versus neutral, but also for pleasant pictures (erotica, babies) (Schupp et al., 2003). Instead of conditional stimuli or affective pictures threatening (i.e. angry) faces were used in a study by Eldar and colleagues. These stimuli elicited greater visual evoked responses by 80 ms latency in anxious (healthy students scoring high on a questionnaire for anxiety), compared to non-anxious participants, this difference was not seen for happy or neutral faces (Eldar et al., 2010). In addition, neutral targets presented as dot probes 500 ms after face onset were detected faster at the location of the angry than at that of happy or neutral faces, but only in the anxious subjects (attentional bias).

The Schupp et al. and Eldar et al. studies, just as the Eimer and Holmes (2007) study (Plate XV), represent paradigms in which the inherent affective quality of the stimuli, be it positive or negative, triggers the short latency modulated visual cortical response. The Baas et al. (2002b) and Lee et al. (2009) studies describe modulated responses to inherently neutral stimuli that acquired affective relevance due to conditioning. In both cases, modulations in the visual cortex may occur as early as 80 ms post-stimulus, which is more rapid than in the case of the cognitive attentional modulations described in Section 3.2. Something special seems to be going on.

This becomes even more apparent in light of the results of a study by Tamietto and colleagues (2007). These researchers looked at patients (indeed, no healthy controls) with a

Figure 8.4

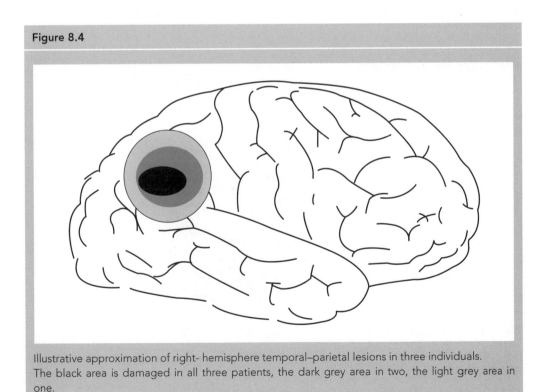

Illustrative approximation of right-hemisphere temporal–parietal lesions in three individuals. The black area is damaged in all three patients, the dark grey area in two, the light grey area in one.

more subtle form of neglect, termed visual extinction. Recall the discussions of hemispatial neglect in Sections 3.0 and 3.4. Those patients lacked the ability to orient attention to locations in extrapersonal space that are contralateral to the lesion. Visual extinction involves the same impairment, but mainly, or only, when there is a competing object ipsilaterally to the lesion. With visual extinction, the core of the impairment seems to be even more concerned with the ability to disengage attention from an object or from a certain location. As also discussed in Section 3.4, neurons in the temporal–parietal junction are crucial to the ability for disengagement or circuit breaking.

This idea is again revived when looking at the lesion pattern of the three neglect patients in the Tamietto et al. study, as shown in Figure 8.4. The crucial finding in this study was that the neglect was significantly reduced when contralesional stimuli (as usual, in the left visual field) were used that contained sufficiently salient, if not to say emotionally tinged materials. Specifically, these stimulus configurations consisted of bilateral displays of whole body expressions of mental states that were either neutral (like combing the hair), elated (a joyful welcoming gesture), or fearful (a repelling, shrinking pose). The three patients simply had to indicate whether these displays contained a figure on either the right side, the left side, or on both sides. With happy and/or neutral stimuli on both sides, the patients missed about 50 per cent to 60 per cent of the left-field stimuli (i.e. responded with 'right' instead of 'both'). With one fearful posture in the right visual field, the percentage of misses of the left visual stimuli increased to about 84 per cent. However, with one fearful pose in the left field, and neutral or happy in the right field, the number of misses was reduced by more than 50 per cent, to 24 per cent (Tamietto et al., 2007).

These results show again that certain stimulus characteristics can induce bottom-up driven processing, in this case evidenced in the awareness of stimulus elements. Apparently, this is

Figure 8.5

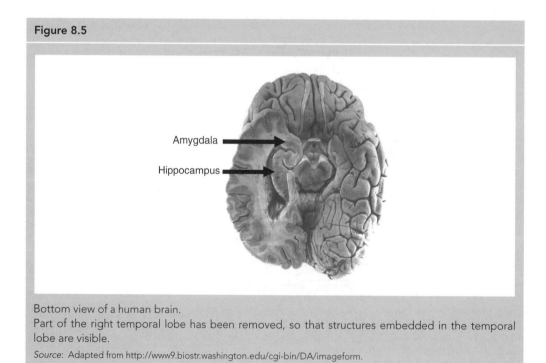

Bottom view of a human brain.
Part of the right temporal lobe has been removed, so that structures embedded in the temporal lobe are visible.
Source: Adapted from http://www9.biostr.washington.edu/cgi-bin/DA/imageform.

also possible with significant damage in (the vicinity of) the temporal–parietal junction (TPJ), which, as discussed earlier, contains neurons that are essential for circuit breaking (Section 3.4). Note that this only works for fearful expressions, not for neutral or happy expressions. Whether other forms of salience (like expressions of vehement action, or explicit motion) can also induce awareness for TPJ contralesional stimuli remains to be seen. For the time being, these data suggest that, at least for certain types of information, there are routes around the TPJ that drive attention and/or awareness.

8.2   SUBCORTICAL STRUCTURES IN THE CONTROL OF ATTENTION

One of the routes around TPJ to drive attention may involve neurons in a subcortical structure named the amygdala. It is depicted in Figure 8.5, and is visible in Figure 6.0. Richard Davidson noted that the amygdala may orchestrate 'cortical arousal and vigilant attention', especially in the face of uncertainty, which is generally thought to be valued as negative, and is also exemplified in bodily expressions of fear ('What's happening, where's the danger?') (Davidson, 2003). Such cortical arousal may rest on diffuse connections between the amygdala and multiple cortical regions, a principle discussed in relation to other subcortical structures (see Section 5.5, Figure 5.16, as well as the final section of this chapter). Vigilant attention is normally viewed as involving the right hemisphere circuit breaker network, but, as outlined in the previous section, with damage in the right hemisphere the contribution of other regions of the brain becomes manifest. Depressed mood and pathological depression have traditionally been associated with excessive right hemisphere dominance, resulting in excessive circuit breaker activity and excessive sensitivity to anything that might possibly be novel, unexpected, or threatening. However, depression has also been associated with an enlarged or hyperactive amygdala, underscoring that such complex disorders must have a multiplicity of causes (Davidson et al., 2002). It is this amygdala driven sensitivity to certain emotion-laden materials that may be instrumental in the case of reduced visual extinction, even in patients with right TPJ lesions who are marked by severe visual extinction for neutral or more positively valued materials.

How exactly does the amygdala modulate cortical processing? One possibility is that it influences activity in the attentional control network described in Section 3.3. However, more direct connections may also be instrumental. At least in primates, the amygdala has efferent connections to almost every level of the visual system (Amaral et al., 1992). These connections may drive the early upstream modulations of visual cortex responses to emotional materials as described above. In humans, pertinent suggestions about the role of the amygdala in the affective modulation of perception, attention, action and memory have been acquired by studying patients in whom the amygdala is partially or completely damaged, especially in its basolateral part. Perhaps the most famous of these patients is S.M., to be fully introduced later in this and subsequent chapters. While S.M. presents with a very selective bilateral lesion of the amygdala, other patients have unilateral damage that is far less selective.

One such group of patients had damage not only in the right or left amygdala, but also in large portions of the surrounding anterior temporal cortex, as well as in the hippocampus (see Figure 8.5). The hippocampus is traditionally associated with episodic memory (Section 6.0), but these unilateral patients mostly score normally in tests of episodic memory. In this group of patients the role of the amygdala in emotional modulation of perception and attention has become very clear using the attentional blink (AB) paradigm, discussed in Section

Figure 8.6

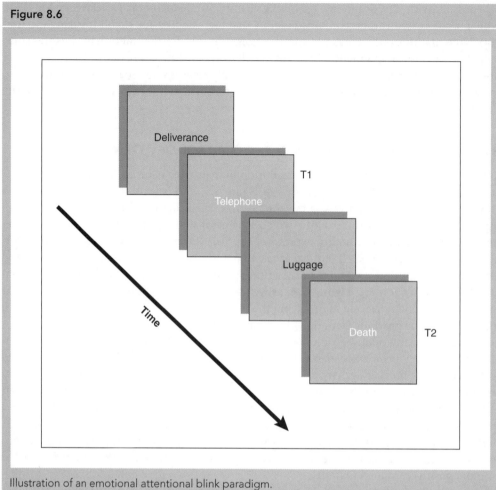

Illustration of an emotional attentional blink paradigm.
Subjects are instructed to report the white words, which can be emotionally laden or not. T1–T2 (target-probe, see Section 3.1) interval is either shorter than about 600 ms (attentional blink expected) or longer (attentional blink not expected).

3.1. Figure 8.6 represents an emotional variety of the AB task, and Figure 8.7 shows typical results for neutral versus emotional words in control subjects, as well as for patients with unilateral amygdala damage, either left or right (Anderson & Phelps, 2001). Healthy controls, like patients with right amygdala damage, show an attentional blink for neutral words at an appropriate T2 ('probe', see 3.1), which is reduced for emotional words at the same T2. Patients with left amygdala damage exhibit attentional blinks for both word categories.

Affective modulation of perception and attention has also become evident in other classic paradigms. Remember the visual spatial cuing (VSC) paradigm extensively discussed in Section 3.3. Inherently neutral visual stimuli are used as cues that indicate the most likely position of a subsequent (also inherently neutral) target stimulus. This yields the validity effect: invalidly cued targets are responded to more slowly then validly cued targets. The VSC set-up has been adjusted to find out whether an emotional quality of the cue would affect the attentional control process that the cue instigates. A cue with one colour would

Figure 8.7

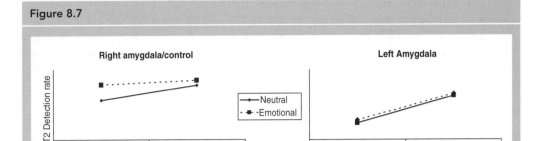

Illustration of emotionally modulated attentional blinks.
T1–T2 interval is either shorter than about 600 ms (attentional blink expected) or longer (attentional blink not expected). Left panel: results representative for healthy controls and patients with right temporal lobe (amygdala) damage; Left: same for patients with left temporal lobe (amygdala) damage.

not only cue the target, but also predict the presentation of an aversive noise stimulus after the target. A cue with another colour would only cue the target. The general result is that the validity effect is enhanced for the cue that predicts the aversive stimulus (Koster et al., 2004). The next question is, which brain regions are instrumental in producing the attentional control and bias as modulated by the emotional quality of the cue? In a somewhat related set-up, Armony and Dolan (2002) found indirect evidence for emotional modulation of the dorsal FEF–IPS attentional control network (as discussed in Section 3.3). Face stimuli that were systematically followed by an aversive noise, relative to face stimuli which were not, elicited strong activation in both the amygdala and the visual fusiform gyrus. When noise predicting and non-predictive face stimuli were presented simultaneously, behavioural responses to subsequent target dot probes were faster when the probes were presented at the location of the noise predicting stimulus. With such simultaneous presentations, relative to separate presentations of the two face stimuli, the dorsal FEF–IPS network was activated more strongly. Note that with the simultaneous presentation, attention could be selectively directed to the location of the noise predicting stimulus, whereas with separate presentations either stimulus was presented at both locations. These results are consistent with a model in which amygdala activation by an affective stimulus concurs and perhaps triggers activity in the dorsal attentional control network, as well as with enhanced activation in the visual cortex, which may reflect the ensuing bias.

An affective variety of another classic paradigm, the Stroop task, has been used to investigate the interaction between emotion and attention to features other than location in space. In this emotional Stroop task, subjects name the colour of monochrome pictures of faces with either emotional or neutral expressions (cf. Plate XV). In the case of fearful faces, colour naming is delayed, relative to colour naming for neutral faces. In one study, this attentional bias was completely reversed after slow, repetitive transcranial magnetic stimulation (TMS) over the right frontal hemisphere (van Honk et al., 2002b). This kind of TMS causes a shift in dominance from the right to the left hemisphere. The result is therefore consistent with the notion that especially the right hemisphere implements the kind of vigilance that is invoked by a fearful expression on the face of a conspecific (left versus right hemisphere involvement in emotion will be discussed more extensively in Chapter 9). However, the TMS effect was only observed for normally viewed face stimuli. When these face stimuli were presented subliminally, there was no effect of TMS on attentional bias, consistent with the notion that the bias was driven by signals from subcortical regions, such as the amygdala. A consistent finding in another study is that the right amygdala was activated by face stimuli that predicted

Figure 8.8

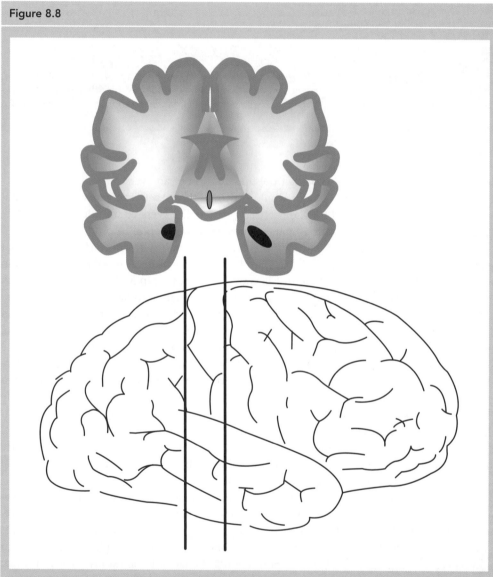

Illustration of amygdala damage with spared hippocampus.
Coronal slice (upper panel, anterior–posterior level indicated by right vertical line in bottom panel) shows bilateral amygdala damage (black dots). The spared hippocampus is located at the level of the left vertical line in the lower panel, just posterior to the amygdala.

an aversive noise, but only when these face stimuli were presented subliminally (Morris et al., 1999).

That the amygdala plays a role in the appreciation, or even recognition, of a fearful expression is also supported by research on one patient, S.M.. S.M. was characterized by selective bilateral damage of the amygdala (see Figure 8.8). When asked to judge the nature of various expressions (including happiness, surprise, anger, disgust, sadness and fear), she performed just like the normal controls, except for the recognition of a fearful expression, which was greatly reduced (Adolphs et al., 1994). A later study revealed that S.M. deviated from the normal controls in the way she looked at faces, independent of the particular emotional expression (Adolphs et al., 2005a). She hardly looked at the eyes, whereas the normal controls fixated on the eyes quite a lot. When specifically instructed to fixate on the eyes, S.M. was able to follow this instruction and subsequently demonstrated normal fear recognition. This can be taken as another example of the amygdala influencing the deployment of attention to emotional materials. Of course, it remains to be seen how much the reported effects generalize when multiple individuals with amygdala damage are taken into account. This is actually a viable option since some hundred individuals living in South Africa, just like S.M., suffer the heritable disorder named after Urbach-Wiethe, characterized by progressively calcified amygdalas.

The amygdala is not the only subcortical structure that has been associated with emotional processing, especially in relation to fear. Remember the dog from Figure 8.1? It has been suggested that the way the brain deals with threat depends on its imminence. When fear is near, for example when a predator comes very close and severe pain is highly likely, an area in the brain called the peri-aqueductal grey (PAG) becomes increasingly active; this is paralleled by a reduction of activity in the ventral medial prefrontal cortex, or more specifically, the subgenual part of the anterior cingulate cortex, also termed Cg25 (Mobbs et al., 2007; see Section 8.4 on the struggle between the dorsal and the ventral). It seems that inhibitory signals from this region to the PAG are inhibited in the face of intense and proximal danger. In turn, signals from neurons in the PAG complement and/or substitute those from neurons in the amygdala and hypothalamus to initiate and control rapid action. Note that the PAG is located quite inferiorly to the amygdala and hypothalamus, in the midbrain, at the level of the substantia nigra, and quite close to the locus cereleus and raphe nuclei. It consists of a lump of grey matter surrounding the canal that connects the ventricles to the central canal in the spinal cord. Its special role when pain is near is not surprising because neurons in the PAG are also instrumental in the regulation of real pain experience.

8.3 ATTENTION DRIVES EMOTION

The experimental results discussed in the previous section show how emotions drive attention in the brain. Can we conceive of the opposite as well? We have seen that affectively mediated activations of the amygdala can even overturn fundamental attentional constraints such as the attentional blink, and occur without conscious awareness. Notwithstanding these apparently immovable effects, signs of the opposite pattern have been reported. These concern effects of cognitive attention on subsequent affective valuation, as well as affect-related activations of the amygdala very much sensitive to cognitive attentional control.

In one study, some faces were designated as targets to respond to, others as distracters to be ignored. In a subsequent test, previous distracter faces were judged as less trustworthy than attended targets (Kiss et al., 2007). In a further experiment these researchers recorded the N2pc (see Section 3.3) to target faces embedded in distracter faces. Distracters subsequently judged as more trustworthy were found to have been presented in the preceding phase during trials on which simultaneous targets had elicited smaller N2pcs. Hence, top–down attentional control resulting in prioritized cortical processing of target stimuli can result in a subsequent devaluation of the distracter stimuli that had been presented simultaneously with the target information. A possible caveat regarding this inference is that reduced suppression of distracter faces during initial presentation (as reflected in relatively small N2pcs) was actually caused by the fact that they were relatively positively valued from the outset (e.g. were considered inherently more trustworthy). The nature of trust evaluation will be discussed in Chapter 11.

In addition to attention modulating the valence of affective appreciation, it can also modulate the impact of emotional materials in various neuronal ensembles, such as the amygdala, as well as visual cortex regions known to be specifically sensitive to these kinds of stimuli. There are both older as well as more recent examples of cognitive attentional modulation of affectively mediated amygdala activity (Morawetz et al., 2010; Pessoa et al., 2002). Such studies can be seen as attempts to invert the null hypothesis. Instead of confirming that

Figure 8.9

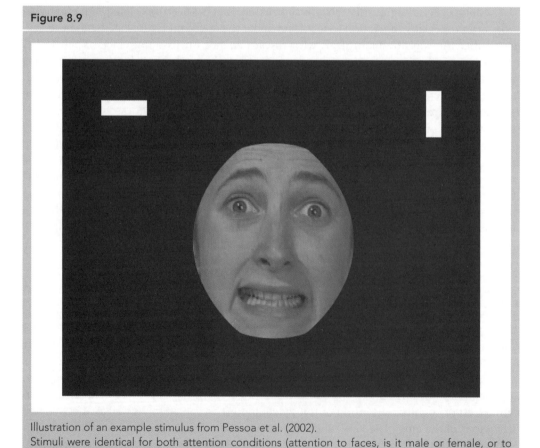

Illustration of an example stimulus from Pessoa et al. (2002).
Stimuli were identical for both attention conditions (attention to faces, is it male or female, or to the bars, are the orientations identical or not?). Faces could either express fear or happiness, or be neutral. For illustrative examples of face stimuli, see Plate XVA.

a certain manipulation (e.g. of selective attention) has a null effect on some variable (e.g. amygdala activation), they seek to drive the manipulation to the limit in an ultimate attempt to show that an effect of the manipulation can in fact be demonstrated. An obvious perspective with respect to ultimate attentional control is Lavie's load theory. As discussed in Section 3.1, this theory implies that leakage of the irrelevant, to-be-ignored stimuli into any form of objective behavioural interference or explicit report, depends on the load that the primary task imposes on the system: high loads constrain the 'breakthrough of the unattended'.

The Pessoa et al. paradigm is illustrated in Figure 8.9. Subjects attended either to the faces presented at fixation (gender discrimination) or to the orientation (equal or not) of the peripherally presented bars. Error rates for orientation judgements were 36 per cent with reaction times of more than a second, attesting to the difficulty of the task and therefore presumably the high load it imposed. Furthermore, orientation reaction time was not dependent on valence of the faces; so no attentional bias of the sort discussed in relation to the emotional Stroop task in the previous section was apparent (admittedly, this is the confirmation of a null hypothesis), and attentional capture by the emotional aspect seemed to be absent.

Figure 8.10 presents the results for amygdala activation. Significant activation, and significant differential activation as a function of emotional valence, was observed only for the attend faces condition, and not at all for the unattend faces/attend bars condition. Moreover, an almost identical pattern of activations was observed for the fusiform face area, a region selected based on its specific sensitivity to face stimuli independent of emotional expression. These combined results are consistent with the idea of amygdala controlled activations in the visual cortex, as expressed in the previous section. In this case however, reduced amygdala control coincided with reduced fusiform–face–area modulation.

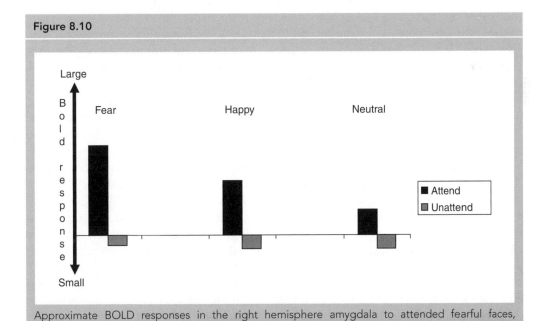

Figure 8.10

Approximate BOLD responses in the right hemisphere amygdala to attended fearful faces, unattended fearful faces, attended happy faces, unattended happy faces, attended neutral faces and unattended neutral faces.
Similar patterns were observed for left amygdala and bilateral fusiform gyrus.

These results suggest that the effects of affectively mediated amygdala control on visual cortex activity can be reduced by descending influences from other parts of the brain, such as the lateral prefrontal cortex or the dorsal attentional control system. Moreover, this reduction of the modulating influence appears to be mediated by a similar reduction of the activation in the amygdala itself. This may be contrasted with situations in which there are no competing signals from attentional control systems that respond to specific, additional task demands; in such situations signals from the amygdala overturn the constraints of the attentional system (as with the attentional blink), or need only minimal subliminal input to become instantiated.

As to the latter case, it has been suggested that there is actually an optimal amount of input that results in maximal activation of the amygdala. If this optimal level is exceeded, as can be the case with supraliminal stimuli, the input not only results in amygdala activation, but also in cortical activation that subsequently suppresses the signals from the amygdala (Morris et al., 1999; Taylor & Fragopanagos, 2005). A similar mechanism has been demonstrated in a realm that is apparently purely cognitive. Recall from Section 3.1 that patterns of moving dots, or other items, activate a specific part of visual cortex, V5, and that this activation is suppressed when a concurrent task (at fixation, with respect to stationary stimuli) imposes a sufficiently high load. In a fascinating experiment by Tsushima and colleagues (2006), subjects were exposed to similar conditions and showed no more distraction, in terms of behavioural interference, from a collection of dots within which 20 per cent moved coherently, as compared to a similar collection with zero coherent movement. V5 showed similar activation in both conditions, although in a separate condition without any concurrent task, 20 per cent coherence resulted in much more V5 activation than 0 per cent coherence did. Apparently, the normally occurring 20 per cent V5 activation was suppressed in the case of the concurrent task. This idea fits nicely with the fact that the prefrontal cortex, during the concurrent task condition, was activated much more for 20 per cent coherence than for zero coherence (when there was no, or far less, bottom-up V5 activation to be suppressed). But, guess what happened with 5 per cent coherence. Without a task, this amount of coherence does not result in a detectable dominant direction of motion, but it activates V5 much more than zero coherence does (remember also Section 5.5 on long-term perceptual plasticity). With the concurrent task, in the 5 per cent condition the prefrontal cortex was as silent as it was with zero coherence; V5 was normally activated, and therefore much more than in the 20 per cent concurrent task condition; and greater interference was noticed with respect to performance for the concurrent task.

Indeed then, bottom-up signals need to exceed a certain level for top–down signals to be able to suppress them. This may have seemed a 'cognitive' example but for many individuals, on the other hand, unexpected motion seen out of the corner of the eyes is a powerful trigger for a state of alarm. Weak emotional or alarming signals may escape top–down control; on the other hand, relatively strong affective stimuli may go unnoticed or are severely suppressed when task demands are sufficiently compulsory. A final illustration of the latter principle was provided by Veldhuijzen and colleagues (2006). In their experiment, task load was manipulated by varying the number of distracters in a visual search task. Concurrently, subjects immersed a hand in water at 2°C and reported how annoying it was. The authors may have expected that pain would disrupt task performance, especially in the high-load condition, but the opposite happened: during a higher task load, the experience of pain was reduced.

Such results point to mutual interactions between more bottom-up driven affective processes, or even direct intense signals from the body, and other processes concerned with top–down signals to these affective mechanisms. The next section addresses in more detail how these interactions are implemented in reciprocal signals between different parts of the brain.

8.4　THE STRUGGLE BETWEEN THE DORSAL AND THE VENTRAL

In Section 3.4 we discussed the interactions between a more dorsally localized, top–down attentional control system and a more ventrally, right hemisphere, localized circuit breaker system that responds to salient stimuli outside the current task focus, and that may break through the current task set. Earlier in this chapter it was noted that the amygdala especially could also be viewed as a system that responds to salient events, either expected or unexpected, especially when these events can be considered affective in nature. A natural question then is whether such salience detectors overlap or interact in their communication with the dorsal top–down system. In one theory, such a functional pathway has indeed been postulated, and the amygdala would signal the ventral circuit breaker that in turn signals to the dorsal top–down system (Taylor & Fragopanagos, 2005). However, in the same model, an additional parallel pathway was also assumed to influence the dorsal system. This pathway originates from the ventromedial prefrontal cortex (VMPFC), an extended region encompassing both the anterior cingulate cortex (ACC) as well as the orbitofrontal cortex (OFC). Both are illustrated in Figure 8.11.

The ACC was extensively discussed in Section 4.3, in relation to situations of conflict between response options (indecisiveness), or between expected and unexpected outcomes, including negative feedback on performance, and self-emitted as well as self-perceived downright errors. Activation of the ACC in such conditions was also discussed in terms of an affective component, specifically interruptions of the flow of dopamine in the reward system, including the nucleus accumbens. In Section 4.3, the caudal region of the ACC was discussed. However, its rostral zone, as depicted in Figure 8.11, has been argued to contain neurons that are responsive to more specifically affective conditions, such as in the previously discussed emotional Stroop task, relative to traditional cognitive Stroop tasks that activate neurons in the caudal region (Bush et al., 2000). The OFC is heavily connected to the rostral ACC and generally assumed to represent the reward value of stimuli and situations, but also the extent of negative valence. It has extensive connections to the basal ganglia, and will be discussed in the next chapter on emotion and action.

For the time being we discuss rostral ACC and medial OFC as one VMPFC system that may provide the bridge between the subcortical affective system (including the amygdala, as well as the nucleus accumbens and septum, and perhaps part of the basal ganglia) on the one hand, and the dorsal top–down attentional control system on the other. As such, this trajectory for the interaction between emotion and attention runs parallel to the one that is mediated by the ventrolateral circuit breaking system. The idea of this trajectory is consistent with the massive connections known to exist between the VMPFC and the lateral and dorsal frontal cortices on the one hand, and between the VMPFC and the subcortical structures on the other. Earlier this chapter we discussed the sensitivity to fearful expressions that helped in overcoming hemispatial neglect in patients with lesions in the right TPJ, an integral component of the ventral circuit breaker system; this also supports the functionality of an independent parallel trajectory for capturing attention for at least certain emotional materials.

The dorsal ventral distinction has in particular been articulated in relation to depression, or the syndrome that encompasses its most severe form, major depressive disorder (MDD).

Figure 8.11

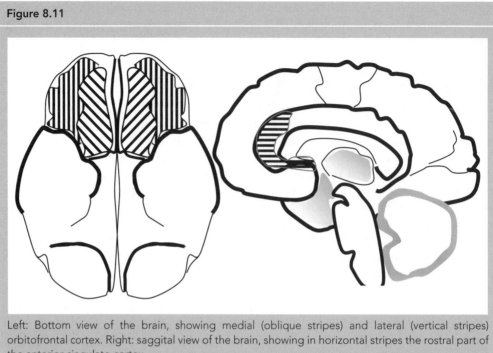

Left: Bottom view of the brain, showing medial (oblique stripes) and lateral (vertical stripes) orbitofrontal cortex. Right: saggital view of the brain, showing in horizontal stripes the rostral part of the anterior cingulate cortex.

Source: see also Davidson et al., (2000).

MDD is marked by enduring feelings of sadness, lack of self-esteem and helplessness, accompanied by indecisiveness, lack of energy and suicidal tendencies. Often, a limited set of these symptoms dominates individual cases and great inter-individual differences exist as to which subset dominates the symptomatology. This is consistent with the notion that abnormalities in several brain circuits may underlie depression or MDD, including reduced prefrontal function, excessive limbic activity, abnormal amygdala–hippocampus interactions, or excessive ventral right hemisphere activity (Davidson et al., 2002). Another perspective emphasizes a disturbed balance between dorsal and ventral (including cortical and subcortical components) compartments of the brain (Mayberg, 1997; Ressler & Mayberg, 2007). The dorsal compartment includes dorsal (lateral) prefrontal cortex and the intra-parietal sulcus, as well as the dorsal (caudal) ACC. The ventral compartment includes the amygdala and hippocampus, the ventral (lateral) frontal cortex and anterior insula, as well as a specific part of the ACC. This ACC region lies ventrally to the anterior part (the knee or genus) of the corpus callosum, and is termed subgenual ACC or Cg25, referring to its Brodmann code, area 25. In Figure 8.11 it can be identified as the inferior part of the horizontally striped ACC section, right underneath the corpus callosum. The remaining part of the rostral ACC, located anteriorly to the corpus callosum in Brodmann area 24 (Cg24), appears to fulfil the function of the bridge proper between the ventral and dorsal compartments, at least as far as can be derived from brain imaging research in MDD patients.

Positron emission tomography (PET) in a sample of depressed patients during a resting state has revealed reduced activity in dorsal areas, and abnormally elevated activity in ventral areas. A similar pattern was observed in healthy volunteers who had been exposed to an acute sadness induction procedure. A six week treatment of depressed patients with selective serotonine reuptake inhibitors (SSRIs) resulted in an elevation of the resting state activity in dorsal areas, in concert with a reduction of ventral activity (Mayberg, 1997). Cg24, the anterior rostral part of the ACC, seemed to play a special role. Resting state activity in Cg24 predicted the response to SSRIs, in that relatively elevated pre-treatment activity in Cg24 was associated with a favourable clinical response to SSRIs, whereas lowered activity characterized non-responders. It appears then that the rostral ACC (Cg24) plays a special role in the course of depression, as if it realizes a kind of compensatory effort to overcome the imbalance between the dorsal and ventral compartments; this effort is supported by pharmacological treatment that, probably through another route, positively modulates the balance between the dorsal and the ventral. Interestingly, Cg24 activity itself, although not sensitive to SSRIs, was boosted by cognitive behavioural therapy, aimed at training depressed patients to suppress the negative affect and cognition that characterize MDD (Ressler & Mayberg, 2007).

The effects of SSRIs in depressed patients are consistent with the documented connections between the major subcortical serotoninergic regions, the raphe nuclei and the ventral compartment. However, depression and MDD are multi-faceted phenomena, and several neurotransmitter systems are involved. This is reflected in the diverse target systems for antidepressant medication, these include serotonine, norepinephrine and dopamine (Candy et al., 2008). In Box 3.6 we noticed that depression was associated with a reduced capacity for disengagement, a function that involves the cholinergic system. This suggests that in addition to the above listed neurotransmitter systems, the cholinergic system may also be implicated and provide a potential, hitherto unexplored, target for treatment of depression.

Complex interactions between the subcortical affective, deep cortex affective, lateral ventral cortex, and top–down dorsal cognitive cortex have been described as implementing the crosstalk between ventral, affective and dorsal cognitive mechanisms. These interactions were discussed in the context of attentional control and perceptual modulation, but may well have implications for the more intentional, action-related components of top–down control (see Section 4.1.2). While the next chapter discusses in more detail the interactions between emotion and action, the final section of this chapter takes us into even deeper areas of the brain and their capacity to modulate what is going on in the superior areas.

8.5   IGNITING THE CORTEX

In Section 5.5 diffuse cortical projections from the ventral tegmental area, the locus cereleus and nucleus basalis were described. These projections mediate a diffuse cortical release of dopamine, norepinephrine and acetylcholine, which can be elicited by any novel, or otherwise potentially relevant, stimulus (Aston-Jones et al., 1999; Redgrave & Gurney, 2006). Such diffuse activation of the cortex may promote learning from the stimulus. Such learning may reveal that it is either harmless or uninteresting, or more subtle aspects such as discriminating it from other stimuli that more or less resemble it, as in typical perceptual learning.

Recently it has been suggested that the amygdala can be added to this orchestra of subcortical innervations that diffusely and profoundly modulate the general level of activity of the cortex (Pessoa, 2010). As with the other ascending influences, the diffuse projections originating from the amygdala promote action readiness as well as learning from the eliciting stimulus. A general term applied to the diffuse cortical activation is arousal; and as we will see in Chapter 10, it is mainly this arousing effect of amygdala activation that promotes learning, in that valence (whether the stimulus has a negative or positive emotional value) is rather inconsequential.

The main route through which the amygdala exerts this function is the connection between neurons in the central part of the amygdala and those in the nucleus basalis (of Meynert), situated in the basal forebrain as part of the more extended substantia innominata (see Figure 5.16). The nucleus basalis also receives massive cholinergic inputs from a specified region (horizontally striped in Figure 8.12) in the midbrain located anteriorly to the noradrenergic locus cereleus. In turn, the nucleus basalis sends diffuse projections throughout the cortex from which acetylcholine is released. Thus, relatively short-range projections from the central amygdala to the nucleus basalis contribute to cortical arousal in all its facets. As for a specific contribution, electrical stimulation of neurons in the central amygdala has been shown to result in desynchronization of the cortical EEG, a prototypical sign of cortical arousal (Pessoa, 2010). More specifically, these cholinergic cortical projections innervate the ventral circuit breaker system, and this could be the mechanism for the amygdala to trigger the cortical response to emotionally salient events via the ventral circuit breaker. It should be noted that modulation of processing in the sensory cortex may follow a different route consisting of direct connections between the basolateral part of the amygdala and the primary and secondary sensory cortices (Amaral et al., 1992).

Figure 8.12

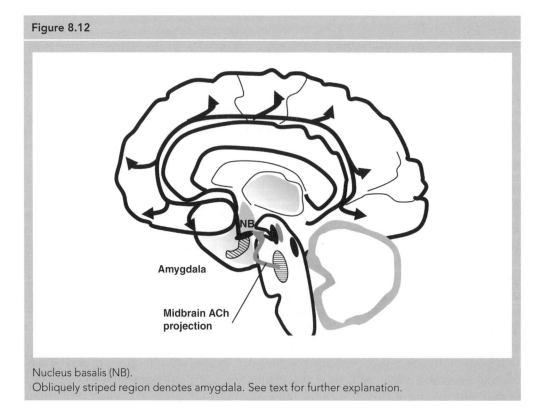

Nucleus basalis (NB).
Obliquely striped region denotes amygdala. See text for further explanation.

All these different diffuse cortical activation systems appear to follow the principle of responsivity to salient stimuli of any kind, be it dopaminergic signals from the ventral tegmental area, noradrenergic signals from the locus cereleus, or cholinergic signals from the nucleus basalis, whether or not instigated by signals from the amygdala. The common denominator seems to be novelty or surprise. While this is a widely accepted view with respect to cholinergic and noradrenergic projections, dopaminergic and amygdala based projections have traditionally been associated with specific motivational or emotional aspects (reward and threat, respectively). However, there is ample evidence that at least the diffuse dopaminergic projections to the cortex (e.g. from the ventral tegmental area) respond to sheer novelty (Redgrave & Gurney, 2006). Perhaps the role of novelty is best illustrated in relation to the response of dopaminergic neurons in the ventral tegmental area (VTA). Such neurons do not just respond to a reward (e.g. a drop of juice delivered to a thirsty monkey); they only respond to *unexpected* reward. As soon as the reward has become predictable, it does not elicit a dopamine response in the VTA. However, an inherently neutral stimulus that systematically precedes, and therefore predicts, the reward, does elicit a VTA dopamine response (Schultz et al., 1997a). One can think of a configuration in which all diffuse subcortical-to-cortical innervation systems respond in concert to stimuli that are interesting, novel, potentially relevant, or threatening. Rapid, trial-by-trial learning processes then determine how enduring these stimulus elicited activations are with repeated presentation of the stimulus (see Section 5.1 on short-term perceptual plasticity). These learning processes involve feedback signals from the cortex, and this may bring some specificity to the subcortical activity, at least with respect to how it evolves with repeated stimulation. For example, feedback from more ventral cholinergically innervated cortical regions may render the subcortical activity novelty dependent, while feedback from more dorsal noradrenergic terminals is related to task relevance of the stimulus, and feedback from more anterior dopaminergic terminals is more action-related. As said, neurons in the amygdala are thought to play their own specific role in this scenario, especially where they have been described as being sensitive to conditions of ambiguity and uncertainty (see review by Pessoa, 2010).

Not only is it the overall activity of these systems, but also their mutual balance, that has a profound influence on what we perceive and how much we attend. This is perhaps best illustrated when we look at different stages during sleep. Rapid eye movement (REM) sleep is a special stage of high cortical arousal, motor inhibition (except for the eye movements) and vivid imagination (termed dreaming). According to the dominant theory (Hobson, 1992), the initiation of REM sleep depends on a shift in the balance between the ponto-mesencephalic ACH system (see Figure 8.12) on the one hand, and the combined locus cereleus NE and raphe serotonin systems on the other. The more the former is active, the more likely the initiation and maintenance of REM sleep is. This example illustrates one further point: the balance, but especially the overall activity level, of these systems does not only respond to discrete stimuli, but also to internal signals, spontaneously as it were. That is, we wake up as the result of vehement activation of the subcortical ACh and NE systems, whether they are activated by a loud stimulus, or by spontaneous internal signals. The next question is: where do these spontaneous signals originate? A possible answer refers to a subcortical structure that is generally considered to be the seat of the biological clock: the nucleus suprachiasmaticus. Neurons in this structure send projections at least to the locus cereleus (Aston-Jones et al., 2001). These neurons have firing rates that vary according to a spontaneous circadian rhythm that is dictated in turn by the circadian fluctuation in the protein expression of certain genes.

8.6   CONCLUDING REMARKS

Emotion involves brain controlled activation of the sympathetic nervous system. This activation feeds into the motor system and back to the brain to influence learning and memory. Emotional responses are also seen at brain level at much shorter latencies. Both direct emotional messages (fearful expression, aversive picture), as well as inherently neutral stimuli that signal, for example, threat, have been reported to elicit enhanced responses from the visual cortex at a latency shorter than 100 ms. Emotional materials even overcome blockades by visual neglect as associated with damage in the temporal–parietal junction. Emotional materials seem to have a privileged status, and the question is, which brain signals convey this priority? Such signals seem to originate in the amygdala, as manifest, for example, in reduced attentional blinks for affective stimuli. These signals may utilize direct connections between the amygdala and the visual cortex, but may also hijack the dorsal attentional control system. As compulsory as the amygdala signals may seem, they can, in fact, be suppressed by descending signals from cortical attentional control regions, provided that the engagement of observers in a task performed concurrently with the presence of 'irrelevant' emotional materials is sufficiently strong. Such suppressing signals may also result in a subsequent affective devaluation of the items that were explicitly ignored during the task. The interaction between emotion and attention seems to be implemented according to a general principle of mutual signals between subcortical and deep cortical areas on the one hand, and dorsal cortical areas on the other, with a regulating bridge function performed by a specific part of the anterior cingulate cortex (its rostral zone). An imbalance between these ventral and dorsal compartments of the brain can result in affective disorders and constitutes a target for various pharmacological and other types of treatments. Within the set of subcortical components the amygdala joins the concerted modulation of general cortical arousal as controlled by numerous subcortical nuclei such as the locus cereleus, the nucleus basalis and the ventral tegmental area.

Questions

1. See Section 8.1: It can be asked whether the same neurons really are activated by real physical (bad) taste, as well as by signals for physical disgust. How can we address this question with the procedure outlined in Box 5.1, using an ERP or a BOLD response? And how about a procedure analogous to the one discussed in Section 6.2.2, in relation to Figures 6.10 and 6.11 and Plate XIII?

2. Sections 8.1 and 8.2 only address affective modulation of visual processing. How would this work for other modalities (for example, audition)? See, for example, Anders et al. (2008), *Social Cognitive and Affective Neuroscience, 3,* 233–243.

3. Refer to Section 8.3. Faces that are ignored as the result of selective attention may be devaluated afterwards. What would be the role of the amygdala here, and the signals to and from it? What would happen if, during affective evaluation, the faces were presented subliminally?

4. Refer to Section 8.5. Draw schematically (with boxes) the major diffuse subcortical–cortical connections, including the origins, as well as target regions, for these projections. Do this for the cholinergic, dopaminergic, noradrenergic and serotoninergic systems. Specify the two-step projection in the cholinergic system, as well as how the amygdala is connected to these systems.

9 EMOTION AND ACTION

Key Points

- Emotional facial expressions induce implicit and subliminal activity in corresponding facial muscles, and emotional bodily expressions induce activity in the motor cortex and a number of other brain regions.
- Emotional modulation can be viewed as a changing balance between approach and avoidance tendencies. Withdrawal reflexes such as the startle are potentiated during avoidance, and this potentiation depends on signals from the amygdala, which may be modulated by GABAergic treatment.
- Other reflections of approach versus avoidance, such as attentional bias for fearful or angry faces, depend on the relative dominance of left versus right hemisphere frontal cortices, along with medial versus lateral orbitofrontal cortices (OFC), and subtle shifts in the connections between OFC, amygdala, and nucleus accumbens.
- Signals between OFC and basal ganglia are instrumental in instigating or maintaining compulsive behaviour as manifest in obsessive–compulsive disorder, and being sensitive to serotoninergic manipulation.
- There are dissociations between affective appreciation and affect driven action, such as in the urge to take a drug without really liking it.

9.0 INTRODUCTION

'For many years, S.M. has repeatedly told us that she "hates" snakes and spiders and "tries to avoid them". To test her real-life behaviour, we took her to an exotic pet store and focussed on probing for external manifestations of fear with a particular eye toward any signs of avoidance behaviour. Upon entering the store, S.M. was spontaneously drawn to the snake terrariums and appeared visually captivated by the large collection of snakes. A store employee asked S.M. whether she would like to hold a snake, and she agreed (Figure 9.1). S.M. held the snake for over 3 minutes while displaying a wide range of exploratory behaviours: she rubbed its leathery scales, touched its flicking tongue, and closely watched its movements as it slithered through her hands. Her verbal behaviour revealed a comparable degree of fascination and inquisitiveness: she repeatedly commented, "This is so cool!" and asked the store employee numerous questions (e.g. "When they look at you, what do they see?"). ... She also attempted to touch a tarantula but had to be stopped because of the high risk of being bitten. When asked why she would want to touch something that she knows is dangerous and that she claims to hate, S.M. replied that she was overcome with "curiosity". The disconnection between S.M.'s verbally stated aversion to snakes and spiders and her actual real-life behaviour was striking. She did not display

Figure 9.1

S.M., a patient with bilateral amygdal damage, handling a dangerous snake without restraint or hesitation.

Source: Reprinted from Feinstein et al. (2011) with permission from Elsevier.

any signs of avoidance, but instead exhibited an excessive degree of approach.' (Feinstein et al., 2011).

S.M. is the most researched person with amygdala damage in both hemispheres (see Figure 9.2). Perhaps the most fascinating thing in the above rendering of S.M.'s behaviour is the dissociation between what she relates about her general feelings for snakes and spiders, and the way she acts out when faced with them. However, on closer examination, her subjectively reported attitude towards the specific situation related above, as well as more generally during a diversity of lifetime episodes, does in fact reflect an expression of fear towards average fear evoking events that is certainly below average, paralleling her above average tendency to approach dangerous animals. Furthermore, as detailed further in Chapter 10, S.M. does not show a significant sympathetic response to an inherently neutral stimulus that she has learned predicts an aversive event, whereas average healthy controls do acquire this conditioned response (Bechara et al., 1995). However, in contrast, she did show awareness of the contingency between the conditional and the unconditional stimulus.

Importantly for this chapter, the case of S.M. illustrates dissociations between certain forms of subjective report on the one hand, and direction (approach versus avoidance) and intensity of action tendencies on the other, where the latter constitutes a component of the emotion

Figure 9.2

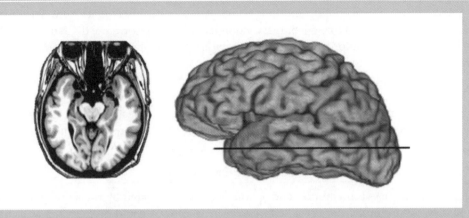

S.M.'s bilateral amygdala
The black holes in the medial anterior part of the temporal lobe, and (right) the axial level in the temporal lobe at which the slice on the left was taken.
Source: Reprinted from Feinstein et al. (2011) with permission from Elsevier.

Figure 9.3

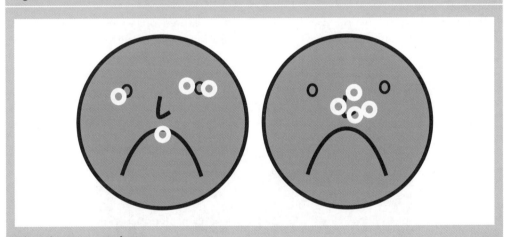

White dots represent fixations.
Left: pattern for typical healthy controls. Right: pattern for typical amygdala damage.

with potentially far-reaching implications. It should be mentioned that such abnormal emotional responses were specific for fear, and that nothing abnormal was noted with respect to other emotions. Again, it remains to be seen how much the reported effects generalize when multiple individuals with amygdala damage are taken into account. There is another study which strongly suggests that deviating responses, which are presumably typical for amygdala damage, can be found systematically across multiple patients with such damage, even when only unilaterally (Buchanan et al., 2004). These findings will be discussed further in Section 9.2 on reflex potentiation. Another striking feature of S.M. has already been mentioned in

Chapter 8: her inability to spontaneously inspect parts of pictured faces, like the eyes, that were relevant for detecting fearful or other expressions (see Figure 9.3).

According to Frijda (1988), emotions primarily reflect the discrepancy between actual and desired states, and therefore encompass action readiness to resolve the discrepancy. A closely related term is motivation, or motivated behaviour. This has been defined as actions taken in response to stimuli to achieve a goal involving two alternative sets, approach or avoidance (including no action, or withdrawal) (Ernst & Fudge, 2009). This dichotomy will lead the way throughout much of the remainder of this chapter. First, however, we will dwell a little on one of the primary reactions to emotion-laden materials, especially in the case of physical inconvenience: facial expressions as realized through contractions of specific muscles.

9.1   THE MUSCULAR EXPRESSION OF EMOTION

The close link between emotion and action is clearly illustrated by the activity of the facial muscles. For example, the fearful expression in Figure 9.4 could be expected as a primary reaction to the experience of the dog as depicted in Figure 8.1. One hallmark of the expression of fear, and one that was probably missed by S.M. unless she was instructed to look at it, is the raising of the eyebrows, as realized by a contraction of the frontalis muscles localized in slightly lateral regions of the middle forehead. In contrast, the expression of disgust is marked by an absence, or even reduction of frontalis contraction, and instead features a contraction of the corrugator muscles much closer to the nose, that pull the eyebrows towards the nose (frowning).

How fast is this primary response? In one study, facial expressions were elicited in response to stimuli also depicting facial expressions. Figure 9.5 shows some of the results. Such reactive

Figure 9.4

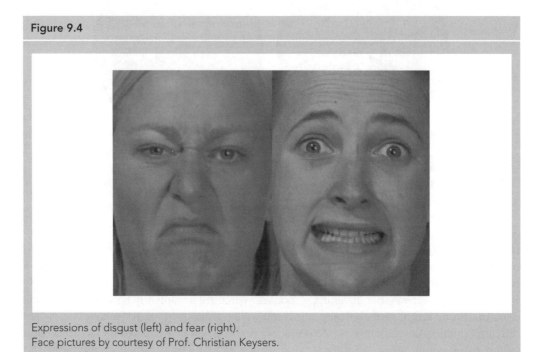

Expressions of disgust (left) and fear (right).
Face pictures by courtesy of Prof. Christian Keysers.

Figure 9.5

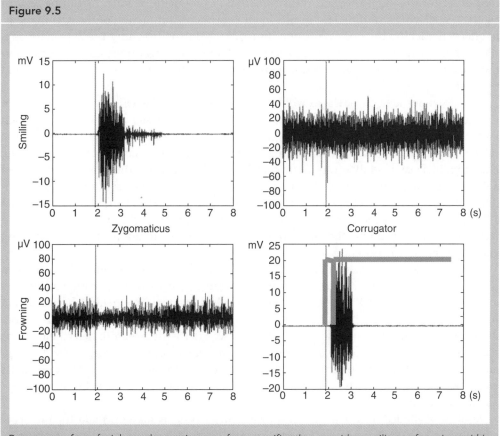

Responses of two facial muscles to pictures of conspecifics that are either smiling or frowning, within less than half a second (distance between two grey vertical bars).
Note differences in scaling between epochs with clear responses and with no response or even decrement.

Source: Adapted from Lee et al. (2008), by permission of Oxford University Press.

muscle contractions emerge within a couple of hundreds of milliseconds (Lee et al., 2008). This is (obviously) a little slow compared to the sensory cortex responses that are specific for emotional stimuli (as discussed in Section 8.1); but is much faster than the bodily responses (e.g. the sympathetic response as discussed in Section 8.0).

What could be the use of such a rapid peripheral response to emotion-laden events? One obvious possibility is that it used to have survival value: the expression of fear would serve as a warning signal for a conspecific who happened to notice the expression that danger was imminent. Something similar is apparent from the phenomenon of gaze cuing. In terms of the visual spatial cuing logic discussed in Chapters 3.3 and 8.3, a gazing conspecific is a powerful cue for directing attention in the direction of the perceived gaze, with significant validity effects ensuing.

But how do we recognize the state of fear from a particular configuration of facial muscular contractions? One factor, but certainly not the main source, is actually visible in Figure 9.5. As mentioned, these muscular responses occur when observing similar muscular activity in someone else's face. Contraction of the zygomaticus muscles pulls up the corners of the mouth, which is instrumental in producing a smile. As can be seen in Figure 9.5, viewing a smiling face results in an equivalent contraction of the zygomaticus, in effect mimicking the observed smile. In contrast, during frowning the zygomaticus is silent or even suppressed. This pattern is reversed for the corrugator muscle: it contracts in response to an observed frown, resulting in mimicry of the frown, and does not respond to a smile.

Such reactions are best observed when elicited implicitly, i.e. when the observers are not instructed to copy the facial expressions they view. The next step is to realize that such muscle contractions result in feedback signals to the brain, which probably implement the subjective experience of the corresponding emotion (e.g. happiness in the case of zygomatic mimicry). In a classic study it was found that forcing the corners of the mouth upwards had a significant impact on the appreciation of supposedly funny materials: in the upwards condition these materials were rated much funnier than in the control condition (Strack et al., 1988). The upwards condition was created by having subjects hold a pencil between their teeth. Apparently, manipulations that primarily target the condition of the muscles influence the subjective experience.

A further question is, which brain mechanisms control the muscle mimicry in the first place? One possibility is a kind of mirror neuron system, as discussed in Chapter 2. Viewing a specific pattern of facial muscle contractions could activate mirror neurons that respond to both the observation of an action as well as in preparation for self-emitting this action. A conspicuous aspect of spontaneous facial mimicry is that it is hardly detectable to the naked eye. This fits the presumed properties of mirror neurons, in that their activity fluctuates around the threshold for actually producing action. In this scenario, the mirror neurons would have to send signals to the brain stem nuclei of the cranial nerves that in turn innervate the facial muscles.

As already alluded to in Chapter 2, mirror neuron systems may thus add to conveying empathy, and seem to be disturbed in certain populations, such as autistic patients. Consistent findings have been reported with respect to reduced facial mimicry in autistic patients, and even healthy individuals scoring high on autistiform characteristics. Furthermore, certain hormones influence spontaneous facial mimicry, either positively (oxytocin) or negatively (testosterone). We will return to this in Chapter 11.

Other studies have looked at the response to pictures of whole bodily expressions, as a function of the emotional quality of the expression. In one fMRI study, stills of implied motion were used, as briefly introduced in Box 5.1 (Chapter 5; see Figure 9.6). Such stimuli were also used to demonstrate that fearful expressions could help to overcome mild spatial neglect, as discussed in Section 8.1. Perhaps more than faces, fearful poses, relative to neutral ones, activate a wealth of brain regions: striate and extrastriate visual cortices, subcortical regions in the thalamus and superior colliculi, and well-known emotion areas such as the amygdala, orbitofrontal cortex and the anterior insula (de Gelder et al., 2004). Just as in the case of the neglect study, this only works for fearful, not happy, poses.

Moreover, activations to fearful bodily expressions were also reported for a set of cortical regions conventionally associated with various forms of motor control. These included the supplementary motor area, with spillover to the primary motor cortex. It would have been interesting to find out whether subjects actually had enhanced muscle contraction in the fearful condition, but this was not reported. In general, muscle contraction data in relation to observed bodily expressions, analogous to facial muscle/facial expression studies, are hard to find. It is documented however, that viewing movies of movements that are

Figure 9.6

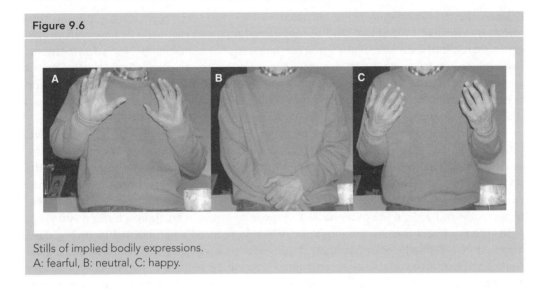

Stills of implied bodily expressions.
A: fearful, B: neutral, C: happy.

incongruent with simultaneous self-emitted movements results in interference with the latter (e.g. Bouquet et al., 2011).

Other motor-related activations were in bilateral inferior frontal gyri (IFG) (BAs 44, 45, 47; de Gelder et al., 2004). While such IFG activations might reflect the activity of the mirror neuron system (see Section 2.2), an alternative possibility is that it is a manifestation of inhibitory control signals (as discussed in Section 4.4) that prevent the actual body movement, even though the primary motor cortex is activated. A more exact comparison between the localization of mirror neuron-related activity, inhibitory control-related activity, and that of the IFG response to bodily expression is necessary to resolve this issue. A final group of activations was observed in the basal ganglia (caudate and putamen), which may also bear on the control of action, either with respect to its compulsory nature (see Section 9.5 on liking versus wanting) or to the need for inhibition.

In sum, affective stimuli, including conspecific facial as well as bodily expressions, elicit muscle contraction or, at least, activation of motor control areas in the brain. In the next section we review more subtle but also more general interactions between emotion and the motor system, which relate to the global motivational state that can be induced by affective events and conditions.

9.2 EMOTION POTENTIATES REFLEXES

At the end of Section 9.0 we briefly mentioned motivation and motivated behaviour defined as actions taken in response to stimuli to achieve a goal, involving two alternative sets, approach or avoidance. Although the most useful response to the dog in Figure 8.1 would probably be to freeze, in many other situations it is better to fight, flee, repel, or perhaps even approach. In all these cases a general readiness for action would be useful, not only at the level of the brain, but also in terms of enhanced excitability in the spinal cord and enhanced contractibility of the muscles. One further point is that the enhancement in excitability is selective, in that certain foreseen actions are facilitated (e.g. protective withdrawal) while others (e.g. approach) are not. Such preparatory states may become manifest by eliciting reflexes, the rapid, semi-automatic muscular responses to sufficiently intense stimuli, controlled by circuits in the spinal cord or midbrain. Enhanced excitability of a circuit should generally result in a stronger reflex when it is based in that same circuit. Non-selective motor readiness results in stronger non-specific reflexes such as the tendon reflex. Selective motor readiness potentiates one reflex and may even inhibit another. Conversely, some reflexes may be facilitated during one kind of motor readiness (or motivation), and may be inhibited during another kind.

One of the best known and most researched reflexes is the startle reflex. This is a defensive, protective action (with elements of wincing, doubling up and detaching from the environment) in response to intense stimulation, with the most likely function of protecting the body from physical damage. The startle reflex is therefore a typical withdrawal or avoidance reaction, and it should be congruent with motivational states marked by avoidance and tendencies to withdraw. On the other hand, it is incongruent with an approach motivation (e.g. fight or enjoy), and therefore it should be relatively reduced when elicited in such a state. Stated more informally: scared animals startle more strongly. This logic has inspired a great deal of research into whether the startle reflex can indeed be used as an objective index for the approach withdrawal state, and what such an objective index can tell us about motivation when the question is how motivation is affected by certain manipulations.

Another reason for the popularity of the startle reflex paradigm is that it works for various kinds of animals, including rats, as well as for humans. While in rats the startle is usually recorded as a response from the whole body, human research has capitalized on a specific component that is very robust in being elicited and relatively simple to record: the eye blink. (You may have never noticed that a sudden loud sound makes you blink your eye, but from now on you will no longer fail to notice it.) The preferred way of assessing the human eye blink is by electromyography of the orbicularis oculi muscle, as shown in Plate XVI.

The signal traces in Plate XVI illustrate that the eye blink startle reflex has a very rapid onset, within 50 ms after the presentation of the startle stimulus, usually an abrupt burst of loud noise. These traces also illustrate that the reflex may be stronger in one case than in another. This exemplifies the logic of the startle reflex paradigm: the more intense reflex in the left panel is more likely to be evoked (by the loud sound) during a withdrawal state, the weaker one on the right during a state of approach. Often the approach withdrawal terminology is exchanged for one referring to valence, the quality of motivation or rather emotion as being positive (joy) or negative (fear, sadness, disgust). Although these two distinctions at first sight seem to be equivalent, they are not completely so, as becomes apparent when thinking of anger or aggression, which can be conceived as a state of negative approach. But whether one refers to valence or to motivation, there is an important difference between the somatic startle reflex and measures of sympathetic activation such as the SCR (discussed in Section 8.0). While enhanced SCRs are associated with both positive approach and negative avoidance, the startle reflex is potentiated in the latter case, but relatively suppressed in the former.

The real scientific value of the paradigm is that it can be transformed into a startle modulation paradigm. Startle modulation as a proof of concept has resulted from two basic lines of research. One line originated in the work of Peter J. Lang and colleagues (Lang et al., 1990, 1998). In their set-up, a series of pictures from the International Affective Picture System (IAPS) is shown, each for a couple of seconds, including varieties of negative (like the dog in Figure 8.1, and also mutilations, violent scenes etc.), positive (certain foods, sports figures, erotica) and neutral (a table) materials. As can be expected, there is a more or less linear decline of the startle reflex to auditory probes when these are presented during negative, versus neutral, versus positive materials. The other startle modulation procedure places more emphasis on a situation of explicit physical inconvenience. In this anticipatory anxiety, or instructed fear set-up, subjects are told that one inherently neutral stimulus (e.g. a yellow square) can be followed by a mild, but nevertheless unpleasant, electrical shock (usually to the wrist); in contrast, they are told that a second neutral stimulus (e.g. a blue square) will never be followed by a shock (Grillon & Baas, 2003). As can be expected, startle probes presented while the yellow square is on evoke stronger eye blink startles than those presented during the blue square. This happens even when subjects actually experience the shock just once or twice, or not at all.

Startle potentiation has revealed a rather precise role for the amygdala in emotion modulated action. In rats, lesions of the amygdala do not affect the startle reflex as such, but completely disrupt the startle potentiation. This makes sense if one considers the anatomical pathways involved. Auditory evoked startles result from inputs to a subcortical auditory nucleus (the cochlear root), which results in signals to a region in the pons, the nucleus reticularis pontis caudalis, and from this region signals are sent to various cranial nerves and sites in the spinal cord that control muscle contraction. Signals in this pathway can be modulated through descending connections from the amygdala to the nucleus reticularis pontis caudalis, and this is what happens in conditions of varying emotional or motivational states.

Consistent results were obtained in a group of twelve patients with unilateral damage to the medial temporal lobe, including the amygdala and the hippocampus. Within the IAPS procedure, healthy controls showed a neat linear pattern of increasing startle reflexes to pleasant, neutral, fearful and disgusting pictures. Unilateral patients however, failed to show a clear potentiation for fearful and disgusting pictures, relative to neutral and pleasant (Buchanan et al., 2004). Hence, although the amygdala damage was not selective, it could be the major cause for the lack of startle potentiation. Conspicuously, the disruption of startle modulation was confined to negative materials, while the positive pictures were rated as equally arousing. As discussed above, amygdala and motor system activation in response to observed bodily expressions were also confined to defensive (versus approaching) poses. It could be then, that in relation to action preparation, the amygdala is relatively selective for withdrawal tendencies. This may be contrasted with its influence on later memory, which seems to be much more valence independent (further discussed in Chapter 10). Finally, the lack of startle potentiation is also consistent with the excessive approach towards real-life snakes and spiders as exhibited by S.M. and discussed at the beginning of this chapter.

Hence, startle potentiation seems to be a valid, objective measure for motivational states, including its sensitivity to amygdala mechanisms. It has therefore also been widely applied as a model for excessive avoidance, in particular in relation to anxiety disorders. In line with its translational nature, this model has been implemented in both rats and human healthy volunteers (for references see below). As for anxiety disorder patients, potentiation is not always evident. For example, patients with post-traumatic stress disorder (PTSD, see Box 10.1 in Chapter 10) startle more intensely in response to loud sounds in general, but exhibit startle potentiation similar to that in healthy controls (Grillon & Morgan III, 1999).

A first step towards a proof of concept as a model for excessive anxiety would be to test the effect on startle potentiation of a well-known anxiety-reducing drug. In many anxiety disorder cases, the preferred treatment consists of a repeated administration of benzodiazepines (e.g. oxazepam, alprazolam, diazepam). Benzodiazepines promote the inhibitory effects of $GABA_A$ receptor stimulation. These inhibitory effects are widespread in the brain and may work in the amygdala to reduce anxiety or fear, but also throughout the cortex and other structures, contributing to side effects such as impaired selective attention and amnesia. Unfortunately, in the instructed fear paradigm, benzodiazepines do not always reduce startle potentiation in humans (Baas et al., 2002a). This contrasts with the effects of benzodiazepines in rats, which seem to be rather robust. It turns out that benzodiazepines did affect the, so-called, contextual potentiation in humans. During such contextual potentiation, shocks are delivered as often as in the typical predictable situation, but they are not predicted by the cues. Contextual potentiation is assessed by comparing the startle magnitude during an unpredictable shock context with startle magnitude during a no-shock context, and this contextual potentiation is reduced by the benzodiazepine alprazolam, whereas cue specific potentiation was not (Grillon et al., 2006).

We will return to these pharmacological issues in relation to emotional memory in Chapter 10. For the time being, it is concluded that contextual anxiety and cue specific fear can be dissociated in healthy human beings. In rats, on the other hand, things seem to work differently.

Box 9.1   More about fear potentiated startle and pharmacology

In the instructed fear paradigm, benzodiazepines do not always reduce startle potentiation. One clue is that clinically, benzodiazepines are more efficacious against excessive non-specific, generalized anxiety (with respect to anything) than they are against specific fears (such as for spiders). This inspired a variation on the instructed fear paradigm, in which subjects were exposed to a context in which shocks were not predicted by a discrete cue stimulus. Contextual potentiation is assessed by comparing the startle magnitude during an unpredictable shock context with startle magnitude during a no-shock context. This contextual potentiation was reduced by the benzodiazepine alprazolam, whereas cue specific potentiation was not (Grillon et al., 2006). In contrast, a metabotropic glumatergic antagonist reduced cue specific potentiation, but not contextual potentiation (Grillon et al., 2003).

Another substance that reduces cue specific startle potentiation is the hormone testosterone (Hermans et al., 2006a). As we will see in Chapter 11, testosterones also reduce facial mimicry. Thus, testosterone affects several emotional modulated actions, including facial mimicry, as well as withdrawal-related reflex potentiation.

9.3   THE STRUGGLE BETWEEN LEFT AND RIGHT

In Chapter 8 (Section 8.2) differential contributions from the two hemispheres to emotional responses and mood were discussed. For example, depressed mood was related to excessive right hemisphere dominance, resulting in excessive circuit breaker activity and excessive sensitivity to anything that might possibly be novel, unexpected, or threatening. So, depression may involve an over-dominant right hemisphere, in addition to imbalances between ventral and dorsal brain areas, and/or dysfunction of the limbic system. As another example, an attentional bias to fearful faces was reduced by TMS-induced (transcranial magnetic stimulation) shifting of the inter-hemispheric dominance to the left.

Such experimental results have contributed to a left–right hemispheric balance perspective on emotion and motivation. This view is based mainly on the reported effects of manipulation of left–right hemispheric balance using TMS, and the reported associations between EEG measures of left–right balance and measures of approach avoidance tendencies. Even more specifically, the theory asserts it is mainly the balance between left and right frontal cortex activations that is crucial (Harmon-Jones et al., 2010). Finally, the frontal asymmetry perspective explicitly addresses the approach avoidance distinction, rather than the positive–negative valence distinction (these two classifications have already been briefly compared in the preceding section). That is, excessive right hemisphere dominance is associated with fear, depression, inhibition and withdrawal; shifting the balance to the left induces more positive affect and approach tendencies; but excessive left hemisphere dominance is associated with anger and aggression, or excessive approach.

As an example, consider the application of TMS aimed at modulating right–left balance. Remember from Section 8.2 that in an emotional Stroop task, subjects name the colour of monochrome pictures of faces with either emotional or neutral expressions. In the case of fearful faces, colour naming is delayed, relative to colour naming for neutral faces. This attentional bias was reversed after TMS-induced suppression of the right frontal cortex (van Honk et al., 2002b). In contrast, this TMS-induced suppression of the right frontal cortex enhanced attentional bias for angry-looking faces (van Honk et al., 2002a). From an approach avoidance perspective this indicates that left frontal cortex dominance induces an enhanced approach tendency towards social threat as expressed by conspecifics. Consistently, left-over-right hemisphere dominance as an individual characteristic has been reported to be associated with attentional bias for angry faces (Hofman & Schutter, 2009).

How do these associations between frontal asymmetry and approach avoidance tendencies match with withdrawal reflex potentiation (as discussed in the previous section)? This is a complex story, not backed up by abundant experimental results. One study found that exposure to angry faces potentiates startle reflexes relative to happy faces (as well as fearful faces) (Springer et al., 2007). This would indicate that, on average, exposure to angry faces induces an avoidance tendency associated with right hemisphere dominance. But, as discussed, the balance between approaching and avoiding angry conspecifics depends on right–left frontal balance. In another study, EEG measures were used to assess frontal asymmetry. Here, left frontal dominance was associated with a stronger reduction of startle potentiation upon termination of presentation of aversive IAPS pictures (Jackson et al., 2003). This could be taken as being consistent with a direct relationship between left hemisphere dominance and reduced avoidance-related startle potentiation. However, note that this relationship was manifest *in the absence* of a threatening event (i.e. after its disappearance), not during the threat. It could still be then, that the subcortical control of approach avoidance tendencies, as manifest in withdrawal reflex potentiation, functions independently of the control mechanism that involves the left–right cortical balance. This is also attested to by the, previously discussed, reducing effect of testosterone on startle potentiation, whereas no relationship between testosterone and frontal asymmetry has been uncovered thus far (van Honk et al., 2010).

An obvious perspective on approach tendencies is that they are aimed at objects that are generally valued positively. Gable and Harmon-Jones (2010b) examined P300-like ERPs (late positive potential or LPP) to appetitive pictures (desserts), relative to neutral ones (rocks). The appetitive pictures elicited larger LPPs over parietal and central midline areas, especially over the left, but not the right, frontal cortex. Again, this is consistent with the idea of a link between approach and the left frontal cortex. In another study such left hemisphere bias appears to depend on whether the body is in an approach congruent posture, or in an approach incongruent position (supine). Specifically, the left lateralized response disappeared when subjects were put in a supine position (Harmon-Jones & Peterson, 2009). It should be noted that this last result was obtained in relation to anger invoking stimuli, but it may also hold for positive approach situations.

Figure 9.7

Angry or determined?
Source: Fotolia.

Another interesting tendency concerns determination (see Figure 9.7), presumed to be a high-approach motivated positive affect. Facial expressions of determination were easily confused with those of anger (presumed to be a high-approach motivated negative affect). Intensity of perceived determination and perceived anger were positively correlated, but both intensities were negatively correlated with that of happiness (presumed to be a low-approach motivated positive affect) (Harmon-Jones et al., 2011). Also at this level of processing (which may involve mirror neurons since it concerns the judgement of facial expressions), the approach avoidance dimension seems to be of more importance than valence (positive versus negative). It is possible that mirror neurons are instrumental in judging and confusing these emotional expressions. If so, they must be governed by the functional direction (approach versus avoidance) associated with the emotion, rather than its valence.

A recent model for aggression has emphasized imbalances between the subcortex and the cortex as well as between the two hemispheres, but it also noted the role of serotonin (van Honk et al., 2010). Specifically, excessive approach tendencies have been related to low levels of serotonin. It has been noted that the prefrontal cortex (PFC) is rich in 5HT-2 receptors, and that various regions in the PFC, including the orbitofrontal cortex and anterior cingulate, as well as dorsal and ventral lateral areas, are activated in response to an acute elevation of serotonin (by application of fenfluramine). Most notably, these activations were blunted or absent in individuals with an aggressive impulsive personality disorder (Davidson et al., 2000). As noted before, other evidence strongly suggests inhibitory signals from these areas to the amygdala.

Orthogonal to the left–right distinction a, so-called, triadic neural systems model of approach and avoidance motivation was presented by Ernst and Fudge (2009; Figure 9.8).

The model postulates three anatomical nodes: the ventral striatum (referring to the ventral caudate and putamen), implementing approach; the amygdala (central and basolateral), implementing avoidance; and the prefrontal cortex, most notably the OFC, that modulates and balances the activation of the other two nodes. Furthermore, within each node, this triadic schedule repeats itself, and the model becomes fractal. For example, within the PFC, the medial OFC leans more towards approach and the lateral OFC more towards avoidance (Kringelbach, 2005; see Figure 9.9; Kringelbach & Rolls, 2004); the anterior ventral striatum is more activated in relation to reward, but the posterior part more in relation to loss. These local topographical specificities correspond to specificities in connections. For example, the medial OFC is more connected to the striatum, while the lateral OFC is more connected to the amygdala. Within the ventral striatum, posterior regions receive more input from the amygdala, and anterior regions more input from the nucleus accumbens.

Such a model might be able to accommodate many of the intricate findings with respect to affective approach and the role of the OFC, striatum, and amygdala, as well as their interactions. For example, in a study by Seymour et al. (2007) it was found that the anterior striatum is indeed more activated when people experience unexpected rewards, and the posterior part when they experience unexpected losses. In Section 9.5 on liking versus wanting we will see

Figure 9.8

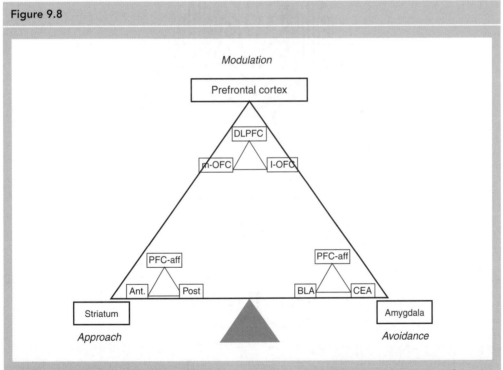

Fractal, triadic model for approach, avoidance, and their modulation by afferent signals from the prefrontal cortex (PFC-aff).
m – medial, l – lateral. Ant. – anterior, Post – posterior. BLA – basolateral amygdale, CEA – central amygdala.
Source: From Ernst and Fudge (2009). Reprinted with permission by Elsevier.

how yet another transition, from nucleus accumbens to dorsal striatum, is involved in yet another aspect of approach behaviour.

This model connects the subcortical influence discussed in previous sections with cortical ones. Specifically, it postulates more connections between approach-related medial OFC and the anterior striatum, as well as the nucleus accumbens, and more between avoidance-related lateral OFC and the amygdala. It also allows for differentiation within each of these structures with respect to the association of approach and avoidance with different subregions (for example, even within the amygdala, neurons in one region drive more towards avoidance, but neurons in another may actually promote approach). Questions remain with respect to whether this integrated cortical–subcortical system interacts with, or functions independently from, the left–right frontal cortical system in determining the balance between approach and avoidance.

Figure 9.9

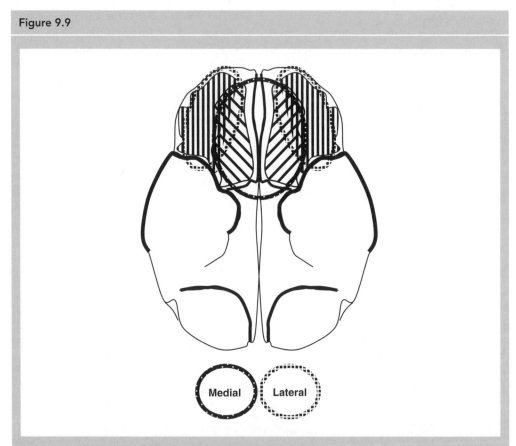

Functional subdivision in the orbitofrontal cortex: a survey of human neuroimaging studies.
Ventral view of the brain, the temporal lobes are at the lower left and right. The medial ring encloses the locations, as observed in numerous studies, of activations during approach or reward experience. The lateral rings enclose the locations, as observed in numerous studies, of activations during withdrawal or punishment necessitating behavioural change. The rings have been superposed over the medial and lateral orbitofrontal areas as distinguished in Chapter 8, specifically Figure 8.11.

9.4 COMPULSIONS: ORBITOFRONTAL CORTEX, BASAL GANGLIA AND SEROTONIN

As noted in Chapter 7, five loops between the basal ganglia and various frontal cortical regions have been described (Alexander et al., 1986). One of them is especially relevant to the present topic. This is the OFC striatal loop, which involves a circuit from orbitofrontal cortex to ventral caudate nucleus, to globus pallidus, to thalamus and back to OFC. At the level of the caudate, this circuit also receives input from the anterior cingulate cortex (ACC).

It turns out that this loop is important in relation to a disorder that is prototypical of emotionally modulated action: obsessive–compulsive disorder (OCD). The compulsive behaviour may include obsessive hand washing, endless checking and double checking, or hoarding. It can be so extreme that it is completely incapacitating with respect to personal and professional functioning. One special example is thrichotillomania. This behavioural disorder is characterized by excessive pulling of one's own hair. Thrichotillomaniacs feel tension before, and relief and pleasure after, hair has been pulled. There may be a prevalence of this behaviour of up to 2 per cent, with more than three times as many women than men suffering from it. The hair is even eaten, resulting in thrichobezoars, hairballs that can obstruct the gastrointestinal pathway. There is no successful medication for it, but behavioural therapy (including stress management training) may significantly alleviate the symptoms (van Minnen et al., 2003).

OCD patients are marked by excessive error monitoring as assessed in the typical flanker task (see Chapter 4). Both ERN and P_e have been shown to be enhanced, and the site of the major difference between patients and healthy controls is the rostral ACC (Cg24, a major regulating area in depression, as discussed in Chapter 8; Endrass et al., 2008; Fitzgerald et al., 2005). Is it perhaps over-regulating in OCD? This could take the form of excessive input to the OFC striatal loop. Indeed, OCD patients are also characterized by excessive activation of the basal ganglia (Maia et al., 2008), as well as increased volume of grey matter in that region (Pujol et al., 2004). This is often seen in combination with abnormal OFC activation and structure. Another study revealed hyperactivity during resting conditions especially in the left OFC (Whiteside et al., 2004), indicative of excessive spontaneous approach tendencies. On the other hand, task dependent activation in the lateral OFC has been reported to be reduced (Chamberlain et al., 2008).

This reduced activity was observed in the context of reversal learning. In reversal learning subjects learn, over the course of a sequence of trials, that certain choices are rewarded and others are not. At arbitrary moments, the reward contingencies are switched, and for a while subjects are in limbo as to what is the most beneficial choice. The hypo-activation of lateral OFC during reversal learning may reflect a relative incapacity to redefine the potential reward that is associated with certain stimulus conditions (especially unfavourable conditions, see Figure 9.9). We will return to this hypothesis in Chapter 10, where we discuss impaired learning in patients with OFC damage during the Iowa gambling task. In the Iowa gambling task subjects have to learn that picking from one deck of cards occasionally yields a high win but in the longer term results in net financial loss. Relative to healthy controls, OCD patients persist in choosing from the risky desks even though this results in monetary loss (Cavedini et al., 2002), and this seems to be consistent with abnormal activation during reversal learning, as well as with similar Iowa gambling performance in patients with OFC damage (Chapter 10).

Figure 9.10

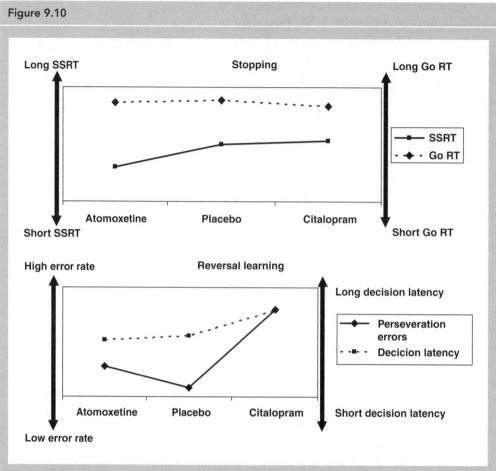

Schematized acute effects of the SSRI citalopram and the selective norepinephrine-reuptake inhibitor atomoxetine, relative to a placebo, on stopping performance and reversal learning.
Upper left: atomoxetine reduces SSRT, but not Go RT; citalopram affects neither. Citalopram increases perseveration errors after reversal of the reward contingencies and lengthens decision times during reversal; atomoxetine affects neither.

The kind of compulsivity as assessed with reversal learning has been contrasted with the lack of inhibitory control or impulsivity that we encountered in Section 4.4. Remember that impulsivity was assessed using the stop task, and that the medications typically applied to reduce impulsive behaviour, methylphenidate and atomoxetine, improve stopping perform-ance (at least in patients with ADHD), as well as restore the function of a cortical circuit that could be instrumental in inhibitory control. This has been contrasted with the effects of selective serotonin reuptake inhibitors (SSRIs), that elevate serotonin levels throughout the brain. Compulsive behaviour is often, and successfully, treated with SSRIs. SSRIs such as citalopram and paroxetine, do not affect or improve stopping (Chamberlain et al., 2006; Overtoom et al., 2009). Citalopram however, does affect reversal learning performance, as illustrated in Figure 9.10, while atomoxetine does not (see Box 9.2 for more details). To the extent that reversal learning really depends on the interaction between the basal ganglia and the OFC, it can be concluded that this circuit depends on serotoninergic, and not on nore-pinephrinergic mechanisms.

In all, these combined findings of structural and functional, as well as behavioural abnormalities, are consistent with an integrated circuit, in which the OFC represents the characteristics of the rewards and reward-predicting stimuli. Through its connections with the basal ganglia it regulates behavioural decisions in light of the current reward contingencies. At the level of the caudate nucleus the OFC circuit receives input from the ACC and, possibly indirectly, from the nucleus accumbens, which may also contribute to reward-related processing. Abnormal activation of the OFC, paralleled by excessive caudate and ACC activity, may play a role in compulsive, as well as risky behaviour. This seems an important factor, at least in the compulsory aspect of disorders like OCD. It may be noted that in such disorders other emotion action mechanisms may also operate: at least one study has reported exaggerated startle reflexes in OCD patients (Kumari et al., 2001).

Box 9.2   Reversal learning and acute versus chronic effects of SSRIs

A conspicuous aspect of Figure 9.10 is that the number of perseveration errors (i.e. continuing to obey to a reward contingency that is no longer valid) actually increases under citalopram (while stop signal reaction times, SSRTs, get shorter under atomoxetine). Remember that the idea was that enhanced serotoninergic function reduces compulsivity and therefore should reduce the number of perseveration errors. A point in case is that this study looked at the acute effect of an SSRI of one single dose within a couple of hours. In contrast, the desired clinical effects of SSRIs often take weeks to evolve. It has been argued that SSRIs stimulate both pre-synaptic autoreceptors and postsynaptic receptors, and that the former dominates after initial, acute administration (Cools et al., 2008). The acute effect would be to reduce serotoninergic transmission, which would in turn explain the increase in perseveration errors under citalopram. Subsequent chronic administration would result in differential desensitization of pre- and postsynaptic receptors, upon which the postsynaptic receptors would eventually dominate the effect and serotoninergic transmission is enhanced.

9.5   LIKING VERSUS WANTING: FROM VENTRAL TO DORSAL STRIATUM

A special case of compulsory behaviour is that of substance abuse. Substance abuse seems to present an explicit dissociation between the subjective valence and the action component of emotion. In the context of substance abuse, valence has been coupled to 'liking', and excessive approach tendencies to 'wanting'. Liking refers to the subjective hedonic appreciation of a drug that often wanes after chronic use. One mechanism for reduced liking may be desensitization of receptors that have been chronically and excessively stimulated by the drug. However, drug addiction probably also involves another mechanism: wanting, which refers to the powerful desire to obtain and take the drug (craving), even when liking has noticeably declined (Berridge et al., 2009). Liking may be inferred by, for example, lip smacking, and wanting may be inferred from explicit approach behaviour. Neurons in the rat nucleus accumbens (in particular its shell), when stimulated, are associated with liking but not with wanting. In contrast, neurons in the basal ganglia (putamen) have been associated with wanting, in the absence of a liking response (Berridge et al., 2009).

In humans a comparable functional anatomical dissociation has been reported (Vollstädt-Klein et al., 2010). The likers in this study were light consumers of alcohol (less than one unit per day). The wanters consisted of heavy drinkers: more than five alcoholic consumptions a day. During fMRI scanning, either alcohol-related pictures (e.g. a tray filled with glasses full of beer) or neutral IAPS pictures were presented. In the likers, BOLD responses to alcohol cues, relative to neutral ones, were observed in the ventral striatum (they liked it), as well as in the prefrontal cortex (this could be an inhibitory signal). In the wanters, the pattern was quite different: no nucleus accumbens (no liking), no prefrontal cortex (no inhibition), but a strong basal ganglia response (a reminder of excessive striatal activity as associated with compulsory behaviour, as discussed in the preceding section). Of note, the medial activations shown in the left part of Plate XVIIA (y=14) only partially overlap with the average location of the nucleus accumbens and perhaps to a larger extent with the ventral part of, especially, the putamen.

9.5.1   The case for nicotine

The Vollstädt-Klein et al. study suggests a hyperresponsive role for the basal ganglia in substance abuse. However, other brain circuits play a role as well, including the amygdala and the insula. Consider smoking as an example. Quitting smoking is hard, just look at a recent evaluation of attempts to do so. Two hundred smokers were each offered a 6-month program consisting of telephone calls, newsletters, e-mail alerts, and so on, all aimed at modifying their smoking behaviour. After 12 months less than 7 per cent had actually quit, no more than in a control group who, over the same period, had only received some general information on health (Glasgow et al., 2009). One additional factor that makes matters more difficult may be amygdala activation, as has been observed in rats that were first addicted to nicotine and then had to abstain (Marcinkiewcz et al., 2009). It is possible that this mechanism contributes to an acute state of fear upon nicotine abstinence. Perhaps, at least in some cases, anxiety-reducing substances, such as the benzodiazepines or SSRIs, may be helpful in quitting. But there are other factors as well. The actylcholine receptor specific for nicotine as a ligand becomes hypersensitive in the course of chronic nicotine use, and this hypersensitivity increases after a limited period of withdrawal (Stahl, 2008). That is why smoking one cigarette after a brief period of abstinence is likely to cause a relapse, and why it is difficult just to smoke 'a little less'. This is a kind of hyperresponsivity similar to that encountered for the basal ganglia. Moreover, dopamine receptors in the nucleus accumbens present the opposite pattern: they are relatively insensitive after sustained nicotine administration, making it harder to experience the rewarding effects of healthy pleasures (Epping-Jordan et al., 1998). This is the symptom of anhedonia, which is also characteristic in many cases of depression, as noted before. Only nicotine can compensate for this anhedonia in smokers. In addition, smokers have abnormal error-related responses in the ACC (Chiu et al., 2008).

Treatment with substances that target these neurotransmitter systems can be helpful in quitting, with or without combined behaviour modification procedures (Eisenberg et al., 2008). Varenicline blocks the nicotinic receptor while partially mimicking the effects of nicotine. Bupropion is sometimes prescribed as an anti-depressant and can help compensate for the hyposensitivity of the dopamine system. Both treatments result in significantly more successful quitters than do placebos, and also work better than nicotine gum or transdermal patches. Varenicline leads to slightly better results than bupropion. But which is better? Of 2,180 smokers treated with varenicline, only 26 per cent were still not smoking after twelve months, compared to 15 per cent treated with a placebo. Perhaps more drastic measures should be taken. One study found that smokers who acquired damage to either the right or left insula spontaneously quit smoking, without ever showing the classic addiction symptoms like craving (Naqvi et al., 2007). One possibility then, is that disgust is a decisive factor.

9.6 CONCLUDING REMARKS

One view on emotion is that it reflects a discrepancy between actual and desired states and therefore promotes action. These actions are also said to reflect motivation, and the two major motivational drives that have been presented as a framework for this chapter are the ones that result in tendencies to approach or to avoid (or withdraw). Following up on Chapter 8, observation of patients with damage in the amygdala shows that there is a relationship between amygdala function and emotion driven action, such as excessive approaches to dangerous animate objects and sensory orientation to affectively relevant information (e.g. eye movements to conspecific eyes). Events conventionally considered to be affective (e.g. the dog in Figure 8.1) not only rapidly tax perceptual cortical mechanisms (Chapter 8), but also, and only a fraction of a second later, muscles in the face. They massively recruit the brain and body motor system, including primary and secondary motor cortices, basal ganglia, and, in the case of affective materials consisting of conspecific emotional expressions, possibly also the mirror neuron system.

An explicit role for the amygdala in modulating the state of the motor system has been established in relation to potentiation of reflexes. This potentiation can be specific to the direction of the action tendency. As a prime example, the startle reflex is a typical withdrawal response, and is potentiated by avoidance inducing cues or contexts, but is inhibited when approach tendencies are provoked. Startle reflexes are augmented in individuals suffering from post-traumatic stress disorder or obsessive–compulsive disorder. Startle potentiation in withdrawal provoking conditions has been used extensively as a model for anxiety and fear, especially for elucidating the relevant neurochemical mechanisms. The latter involve GABAergic and glutamatergic components, but the exact contribution of these systems depends on subtle aspects of the way in which anxiety or fear are induced.

Quite a different angle to approach versus avoidance refers to the left frontal cortex promoting approach, whereas right frontal cortex dominance is associated with avoidance. The approach system concerns both generally positively valued tendencies as well as generally more negatively valued ones, such as aggressive behaviour. A further dichotomy that has been mapped on approach avoidance is the medial versus lateral orbitofrontal cortex. It has been suggested that this functional specificity rests on connections with the amygdala (lateral OFC) and striatum and nucleus accumbens (medial OFC). However, as also illustrated by the model of Ernst and Fudge (Figure 9.8), things are more complicated. For example, aberrant function of the avoidance-related lateral OFC is associated with excessive basal ganglia activation and compulsory behaviour (as characteristic for OCD). Serotonin plays an important regulating role in compulsive behaviour (more serotonin, less compulsion; something similar holds for aggression). Finally, hypersensitive basal ganglia also seem to be a hallmark of another form of compulsive approach, substance abuse; this specifically concerns the aspect of craving or wanting without liking.

Questions

1. Section 9.2 describes how, in the human instructed fear paradigm, benzodiazepines do not always reduce startle potentiation, whereas in rats this seems to be a robust effect. How would you instruct fear to a rat? What could be the differences in brain mechanisms between humans and rodents underlying startle reflex potentiation and its pharmacological modulation? When would a rodent model for anxiety or fear nevertheless be useful?

2. Section 9.3 reviews how left lateralized P300-like responses disappeared when subjects were put in a supine position. Summarize the relationship with approach avoidance tendencies, and consider what this means for the interpretation of fMRI BOLD response effects.

3. Consider the extent of expressions of fear by patient S.M. who had bilateral amygdala damage (Section 9.0). How does this relate to S.M.'s action tendencies with respect to, for example, snakes? Was there a dissociation and how does this relate to the dissociations between affective appreciation and affect driven action, as in the case of taking a drug without really liking it (Section 9.5)?

10 EMOTION AND MEMORY

Key Points

- Signals from the amygdala to the hippocampus promote the formation of explicit long-term memory for emotional materials. This depends mainly on the arousing quality of the information and pertains to the essence of the information rather than additional details.
- Non-arousing materials can be encoded for better later retrieval through signals from the inferior prefrontal cortex to the hippocampus.
- The amygdala–hippocampus interaction is modulated by noradrenergic and cortisolergic mechanisms, albeit in quite intricate ways.
- More implicit forms of learning, such as in conditioning, are more specifically dependent on amygdala activation, as well as on orbitofrontal or ventral medial prefrontal cortex mechanisms in the case of reinforcement learning.
- Implicitly acquired fear or anxiety responses can be deconsolidated or extinguished by applying noradrenergic antagonists or NMDA/glutamate agonists.
- Explicit retrieval involves interactions between prefrontal cortex and hippocampus, and amygdala in the case of emotional materials.

10.0 INTRODUCTION

'When I first heard about the explosion I was sitting in my freshman dorm with my roommate and we were watching TV. It came on a news flash and we were both totally shocked. I was really upset and I went upstairs to talk to a friend of mine and then I called my parents.'

The Challenger space shuttle exploded right after take-off on January 28, 1986. The above account is from a student about 2½ years after the disaster. It seems to be a very vivid and detailed memory of the circumstances in which she first learned about the news. In that sense it qualifies as a, so-called, flashbulb memory. A flashbulb memory is a recollection of an arousing or emotion-eliciting event, especially characterized by an accurate rendering not only of the event but also of the context and the circumstances that accompanied the event (but are not in themselves inherently arousing). It is as if the emotional quality of the event ignited a flashbulb that shed light on all the details in its immediate spatial or temporal vicinity. But do such flashbulb memories really exist? Let's hear the account of the same event from the same person just 24 hours after the disaster (Neisser & Harsch, 1992):

I was in my religion class and some people walked in and started talking about (it). I didn't know any details except that it had exploded and the schoolteacher's students had all been watching, which I thought was so sad. Then after class I went to my room and watched the TV program talking about it and I got all the details from that.

This suggests that the flashbulb memory 2½ years later was, in fact, completely unreliable. It is unreliable because the same procedure (an answer to, 'What did you do when...?'), when repeated, did not replicate the initial result at all. This strongly suggests that flashbulb memories as a separate category do not exist.

The lack of reliability, or consistency, across repeated measurements, has since been addressed systematically in numerous studies. In one study the event was the 9/11 attack on the Twin Towers. Tens of accounts taken just after the day were compared to accounts from the same individuals collected one, six or 32 weeks later. Similar comparisons were made for individual everyday memories of events just preceding 9/11 that were neither particularly arousing nor emotion evoking. The conclusions were straightforward: flashbulb memories were not more consistent over time than everyday memories, and therefore they are not flashbulb memories (Talarico & Rubin, 2003). What was much more characteristic for the disaster memories than for the everyday memories, was each individual's belief that the memory was accurate, as well as its vividness and the sense of re-experiencing the context in which the subjects had initially become aware of the event.

Although a telling example of the failure of human explicit memory, this exposure of the flashbulb memory should not be taken as indicating that there is no effect of emotion on memory. Modulations by emotion of typical human explicit episodic memory have been amply documented, as the next section will illustrate. But they do not work like a flashbulb. On the contrary, emotions, especially negative ones, appear to draw the focus away from surrounding irrelevant details, and instead result in tunnel memory, or weapon focus (on the gun pointing at you). Classic studies by Christianson and Loftus (1991) revealed that emotional materials are remembered differently from neutral or unusual materials. With emotional pictures (a woman injured near a bicycle) central details were later recalled more than peripheral details. For neutral materials (riding a bike) this pattern was reversed, and for unusual events (carrying the bike) recollections of both central and peripheral details were worse. A more recent example addressed analogous links for positive valence. Anticipating a monetary reward enhanced memory for centrally presented information. In contrast, after the monetary reward had been obtained, memory for peripherally presented information was enhanced. Presumably, the anticipation of the reward entailed a stronger approach tendency, and this was associated with a more centrally focussed encoding in relation to later retention (Gable & Harmon-Jones, 2010a).

Centrally focussed memory for both negative and positive valence suggests that it is neither valence nor approach/avoidance tendency that determines the emphasis in memory. This is in line with the well-supported notion that enhanced explicit memory for emotional materials is independent of valence or approach versus avoidance, especially when the amygdala plays a mediating role (LaBar & Cabeza, 2006). For example, in individuals with damage in the amygdala the pattern of memory preference for central details is disrupted (Adolphs et al., 2005b). This sets the stage for a more detailed analysis of how emotions influence long-term episodic memory through specific connections in the human brain.

10.1 LONG-TERM EPISODIC MEMORY IS MODULATED BY AFFECTIVE CONTENT THROUGH SIGNALS IN THE BRAIN

The emotional content of information boosts the behavioural manifestation of explicit, episodic long-term memory (Hamann, 2001; LaBar & Cabeza, 2006). Such modulation of subsequent retrieval performance is often seen with relatively short-term retention intervals (e.g. 10 minutes), but the effects may become even stronger with longer intervals (over one hour), suggestive of a mechanism that works on consolidation, perhaps the pre-eminent function of the human hippocampus. This suggests that signals to the hippocampus from other regions in the brain play a decisive role. Hamann and colleagues (1999) examined amygdala activation during confrontations with pictures that were either pleasant (for example appetitive food, appealing animals), aversive (mutilations) or interesting (an exotic parade). Pleasant, aversive and interesting pictures were all recognized or recalled better than neutral pictures, not only ten minutes after initial presentation, but also four weeks later. However, significant across-subject correlations, between later retention (relative to neutral) and activation of the amygdala during initial encoding, were only observed for pleasant and aversive pictures. A similar pattern was observed for hippocampal activation, which also correlated positively with later retention of interesting pictures. These data are consistent with (although by no means proof of) the role of amygdala to hippocampus signals during encoding being instrumental in better explicit memory, specifically for emotional materials. As for the interesting pictures, it is worth asking whether signals to the hippocampus from other parts of the brain could modulate the quality of memory. This issue is addressed in Section 10.1.2.

These correlative data are corroborated by reports about bilateral amygdala damage. For example, in two such patients memory for emotional pictures after 24 hours was clearly impaired (Adolphs et al., 1997), whereas this was much less the case for neutral materials. The relationship between amygdala and hippocampus activation concerns both pleasant and aversive materials, this again suggests that memory modulation does not depend on valence but on something less specific, such as arousal, referring to the general capacity of emotional materials to diffusively activate both the cortex and the sympathetic nervous system. Furthermore, research on patients with damage in the amygdala (including patient S.M., extensively discussed in Sections 8.2 and 9.0) has revealed a specific characteristic of amygdala modulated memory. In normal controls, in an emotional context (e.g. parents travelling towards the site of an accident in which their children were involved), memory after 24 hours is better for the conceptual aspects (or the gist) of pictures (the people on the picture were grown-up) than for details (a couple of trees in the background). However, for patients with unilateral amygdala damage this gist advantage is not present, it can even be reversed (Adolphs et al., 2005b). These results support an amygdala implemented mechanism for an enhanced explicit memory focus on central, relevant information (relative to peripheral details) under emotion arousing conditions.

Can we be more precise as to how amygdala neurons signal to other regions to augment certain types of memory? Although correlations between amygdalar and hippocampal activation, and subsequent explicit memory, have been described above, it is hard to prove that direct connections between the amygdala and the hippocampus are instrumental in this association, at least in humans. In rats, by contrast, direct effects have been reported, in the sense of evoked synaptic potentials in the dentate gyrus of the hippocampus following electrical stimulation in the basolateral part of the amygdala (Abe, 2001). However, it is hard to determine how this relates to the specifically human competence of declarative, explicit memory, and how likely direct connections between amygdala and hippocampus contribute to emotional memory.

A useful perspective is to look at how the amygdala and the hippocampus are connected through nerve fibres. As visible in Figure 6.1, the amygdala is closely located to the head of the hippocampus, almost touching it. Figure 10.1 shows another view of their relative positions.

Figure 10.1

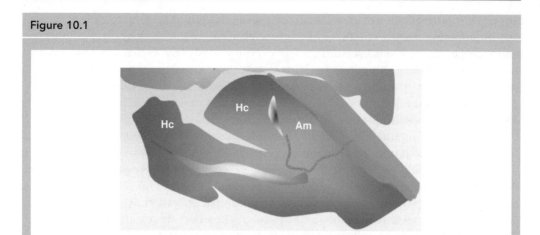

Sagittal view at the level of the border between the amygdala and the hippocampus. Amygdala and hippocampus are separated by cerebral-spinal fluid (the dark slit), as well as (perhaps, in a number of individuals) some white matter, presumably the stria terminalis. Right anterior, left posterior.

Based on detailed studies in rats, cats and non-human primates direct bi-directional axonal connections between amygdala and hippocampus have been established, which circumvent the region where amygdala and hippocampus almost touch. Hence, the direct connection appears to exist, at least in non-human species. This connection may be instrumental in effectuating emotional memory, in concert with hormonal influences. Interestingly, functional coupling between amygdala and hippocampus follows their anatomical relationship. In another study on amygdalar–hippocampal activation and subsequent memory, both positive and negative arousing stimuli (pictures) were again remembered better than neutral ones (Dolcos et al., 2004b). Activations in the amygdala and hippocampus predicted subsequent memory, especially for the emotional pictures, and the subsequent memory dependent activations in both structures correlated significantly across subjects. Hippocampal activity related to subsequent memory for emotional pictures was found primarily in the head of the hippocampus, in the part closest to the amygdala. In contrast, hippocampal activity related to subsequent memory for neutral pictures was primarily found in the posterior part of the hippocampus. Similar functional–anatomical relations were found for the parahippocampal gyrus, the part of the cortex that winds along the inferior side of the hippocampus. Thus, emotion–memory interactions prefer parts of the hippocampus and surrounding structures that are localized relatively closely to the amygdala. It remains to be seen however, whether this is the only route emotions can take to modulate long-term explicit memory.

10.1.1 Some pharmacology and endocrinology

Unravelling the pathway for amygdalar modulations of explicit memory is even more complicated by the existence of peripheral feedback systems (see Section 8.0). Amygdalar–hypothalamic activations of the sympathetic nervous system eventually result in adrenaline release from the adrenal medulla. Substances that antagonize (nor)adrenergic transmission by

blocking beta-noradrenergic receptors also impair subsequent explicit memory after administration during encoding. In one study explicit memory for emotional materials one week
later was better than for neutral materials, but the advantage for emotional materials disappeared after prior administration of propranolol, a beta-adrenergic antagonist (Cahill et al.,
1994). Because the same task was used as in the Adolphs et al. (1997) study described above,
it could be established that the patterns of emotional memory (relative to neutral memory) were comparable between amygdala damage and propranolol administration (LaBar &
Cabeza, 2006). Consistently, the administration of propranolol during encoding disrupts the
predictive power of amygdala activation on subsequent explicit memory (Strange & Dolan,
2004).

The exact primary locus of the noradrenergic effects is hard to determine. One possibility is a direct effect on the beta receptors in the amygdala. An alternative, much slower
route, is through stimulation of the beta-adrenergic receptors in the body (e.g. in the heart).
Adrenaline stimulates vagal afferents (see Section 8.0), which in turn indirectly activate neurons in the basolateral part of the amygdala. A possible way to resolve this issue is to contrast
a beta-antagonist that crosses the blood–brain barrier with one that does not. If the latter
does not augment emotional memory, then a direct central effect of noradrenaline is more
likely to be decisive. One study found that propranolol, known to act centrally as well as peripherally, did disrupt subsequent memory (one week later), whereas nandolol, known to act
mainly peripherally, did not (van Stegeren et al., 1998). However, another study used basically the same design, including identical dosages of propranolol and nandolol (40 mg), as
well as the same combination of slides and narrative for emotional stimulus materials; again,
subsequent memory was tested one week later, but this time no drug effect was observed
(O'Carroll et al., 1999). The discrepancy between the two studies remains a puzzle. What can
be concluded is, that if noradrenergic modulation of emotional memory occurs, at least it
does so with centrally acting beta-receptor antagonists.

Emotional materials may also result in enhanced cortisol responses through the
hypothalamus–pituitary–adrenal axis (HPA axis, see Section 8.0), and these elevated levels of
cortisol may feed back directly and result in increased stimulation of glucocorticoid receptors
in the amygdala and the hippocampus. For example, Buchanan and Lovallo (2001) administered 20 mg cortisol prior to initial encoding of pleasant, neutral and negative items from the
International Affective Picture System (IAPS, discussed in Section in 9.2) (Lang et al., 1998).
One week later memory was better after cortisol, more so for the arousing (positive and
negative) pictures. However, this held for only one of their three memory tests (cued recall).
Furthermore, the results from other studies obviate a simple conclusion about the effects of
cortisol. Another study used a slightly higher dose and the standard task (slide show plus
narrative) to assess the impact of emotional materials on subsequent memory. Again, one
week later, memory after cortisol was better, but only for the neutral materials (the emotional
material advantage after placebo actually reversed after cortisol) (Rimmele et al., 2003). In
this study, resulting peak cortisol levels as sampled from saliva were much higher than in the
Buchanan and Lovallo study. Indeed, yet another study demonstrated that 20 mg cortisol,
resulting in low saliva concentrations similar to those in the Buchanan and Lovallo study,
improved memory for IAPS materials two days later; this improvement was substantially
less when 40 mg was used instead (resulting in correspondingly higher saliva peak values
of two or more times), suggestive of an inverted U-curve relationship between cortisol dose
during encoding and later memory (Abercrombie et al., 2003). To complicate matters further,
this study found no differences with respect to cortisol effects between negative and neutral

materials. Thus, the effects of cortisol in relation to emotion are not simple. Furthermore, cortisol may bind to receptors in both the amygdala and the hippocampus. In fact, the dominant view seems to be that memory modulation due to cortisol during encoding is driven by amygdala glucocorticoid receptors, rather than those in the hippocampus (e.g. Wolf, 2009). Finally, cortisol may also play a delicate role in the vulnerability to the syndrome of post-traumatic stress disorder (PTSD, see Box 10.1). It turns out that individuals exposed to traumatizing events (as in soldiers during a war) are more likely to develop PTSD after trauma when they have low basic cortisol levels and also, perhaps, a low cortisol response to the traumatizing event.

Box 10.1   Post-traumatic stress disorder (PTSD)

Post-traumatic stress disorder (PTSD) is marked by repeatedly re-experiencing a traumatic event, such as battle incidents in war veterans, or assaults in victims of physical maltreatment or sexual abuse. Especially problematic are the intensely negative, mostly fearful emotions that accompany the re-experience. It is mostly this excessive fear or anxiety that renders the individual incapable of pursuing a normal life, hence the use of the word disorder in PTSD. About 5 per cent to 10 per cent of individuals who have been exposed to substantial trauma develop PTSD. In addition to the excessive emotions during re-experiencing, PTSD patients present with hypersensitivity to unexpected and intense stimulation. For example, PTSD patients are characterized by excessive mismatch negativity during simple oddball paradigms (Morgan III & Grillon, 1999; see Section 5.1.4). They also startle much more intensely in response to loud sounds, although they fail to develop startle potentiation specifically to threat signals (Grillon & Morgan III, 1999; see Section 9.2); it is as if they are just overly sensitive to any unexpected or intense event.

PTSD patients appear to be marked by low basic cortisol levels as well as reduced hippocampal volumes. However, these characteristics appear to be already present before or at the time of the traumatic event, and therefore may represent a vulnerability rather than a disease-contingent characteristic (Wolf, 2009; Zohar et al., 2008). In addition, low cortisol may provide a handle for preventing undesirable retrieval processes. Treating these patients with cortisol and with other memory-modulating substances, such as beta-adrenergic antagonists, might be a useful option, and an alternative to conventional treatment with selective serotonin reuptake inhibitors (SSRIs). This may especially hold to the extent that cortisol or beta antagonists not only interfere with retrieval, but also with the quality of the memory trace after the initial retrieval operation, as will be elaborated upon in Section 10.4 on reconsolidation and deconsolidation of emotion.

Following up briefly on other aspects of cortisol and memory, retrieval mechanisms are generally impaired after cortisol. For example, Kuhlmann and colleagues (2005) had subjects study 15 negative and 15 neutral words. Four hours later they applied either none or 30 mg cortisol. One additional hour later subjects were tested for recall of the words studied five hours before. Under placebo, retrieval was better for negative than for positive words. Under cortisol there was no such difference, and retrieval performance for both emotional categories was at the level of placebo neutral. Such negative effects of cortisol on relatively pure measures of retrieval (as opposed to encoding), especially for negative materials, may be relevant to conditions in which it is actually desirable to suppress memories (such as in PTSD, see Box 10.1 and Section 10.4 on reconsolidation and deconsolidation of emotion). One factor here may be the negative effect of acute cortisol on working memory function. A study by Lupien and co-workers (1999) suggests that with increasing working memory load, acute cortisol (600 µg/kg) increasingly lengthens search time. (It should be noted that this study did not use a maximally pure measure of working memory.) As will also be discussed in Section 10.4, such impairing effects on working memory may also have consequences for retrieval processes.

Long-term effects of elevated cortisol levels should also be mentioned here briefly. In one study, cortisol levels were positively associated with impaired delayed recall in standard explicit memory tests, as well as with reduced hippocampal volume (Lupien et al., 1998). Blood samples in senescent individuals (70+) were taken and revealed tonic cortisol levels ranging between 6 μg/dl and 16 μg/dl. Both the measure of current cortisol, as well its development over 5–6 years, correlated significantly and negatively with hippocampal volume, and hippocampal volume in turn correlated positively with delayed explicit memory. An important factor in rising and elevated cortisol level is the endurance of stress, the sympathetic and HPA-driven response of the brain and body to aversive conditions. Individuals with increasing and elevated final levels of cortisol also report enhanced stress levels (Lupien et al., 1998).

10.1.2   Other routes for emotion to the hippocampus

In Section 6.3.2 we saw that neuronal activations in a number of cortical areas during initial encoding predict subsequent explicit memory. These activations were manifest in regions in fusiform, inferior frontal and parahippocampal cortices. Activations in the former two regions especially were related to attentional and working memory mechanisms contributing to long-term memory. Could it be possible that emotional stimuli, by virtue of their emotional nature, capture attention and occupy working memory more than neutral materials, and that this may contribute to better long-term memory for these emotional stimuli?

Behavioural results already hint in this direction. In one study, memory for both negative/high-arousal (death) words as well as for negative/low-arousal (sorrow) words were compared to that for neutral words. It turned out that subsequent memory was equally accurate for both negative categories, and much better than for neutral words (Kensinger & Corkin, 2004). Given the notion expressed earlier that amygdala mediated memory modulation is only observed for highly arousing stimuli, this behavioural result indicates that other pathways are instrumental in producing the better memory for non-arousing negative stimuli.

From fMRI scans taken in the same study during the initial encoding phase, the hippocampus was found to be more activated by stimuli that were remembered later than by those forgotten later. Notably, this was the case in each of the three conditions: negative arousing, negative non-arousing, and neutral (Kensinger & Corkin, 2004). Activation in two regions however, suggests that routes to subsequent memory are different for the three conditions. Amygdala activation was also stronger for subsequently recognized versus non-recognized words, but only for the arousing stimuli, consistent with previously discussed results. In contrast, in the left inferior frontal gyrus (L IFG) activation was also stronger for subsequently recognized versus non-recognized words, but only for the non-arousing words (negative or neutral; see Box 10.2 for more details). In addition, the higher memory scores for negative/non-arousing versus neutral disappeared when a demanding task was performed simultaneously with initial encoding, suggesting that the L IFG contribution to later long-term memory indeed reflects a limited capacity, attention control/working memory mechanism. In contrast, the memory advantage for highly arousing words was not sensitive to the concomitant task demands, consistent with the idea that this memory modulation is mediated by a different pathway, including, for example, the amygdala.

Box 10.2   Comparing the coordinates (2)

Is the L IFG activation in the Kensinger study (2004) reflecting activity of the same neurons as the L IFG activation discussed in relation to subsequent memory in Chapter 6? As a first approximation, let's compare the Talairach coordinates from the Kensinger study to those from Wagner et al. (1998) and Köhler et al. (2004). If we take one L IFG local maximum from each study in such way that the mutual distances are minimized, then we obtain (−51, 36, 15), (−50, 25, 12) and (−52, 28, 6), which cover regions in BAs 45, 46 and 47. The distance between the Kensinger study location especially and the locations from the other studies exceeds 1 cm. However, determination of the exact centre of gravity may differ between the studies (in Kensinger & Corkin they were determined from the contrast between any word presented and only fixation). More importantly, the Kensinger study actually included a condition of neutral words in which subsequent memory effects at (−51, 36, 15) were found, as with negative words (sorrow) at that same location. From a functional point of view then, the neurons in that L IFG region can be equated with those in the regions as specified in the other two studies.

Neurons in the L IFG could therefore be instrumental in facilitating memory for emotionally laden materials, even when these are not subjectively arousing. One can ask whether such non-arousing stimuli can be considered truly emotional; after all, they do not elicit sympathetic activations. In another study, left inferior frontal neurons in a similar region (Talairach $xyz = −49, 29, −1$) contributed to subsequent memory under conditions of high arousal, with either negative or positive pictures, much more than with low arousal neutral pictures (Dolcos et al., 2004a). However, in this study no emotionally laden low arousal stimuli were used, so it cannot be excluded that these would also have allowed for large L IFG activity effects on subsequent memory.

10.2   EMOTION AND IMPLICIT MEMORY

As before, we have to distinguish between explicit, episodic, declarative learning on the one hand, and implicit learning of various kinds on the other (see Box 6.1). Procedural learning is intimately tied to action, and therefore was the topic of Chapter 7. In a way, human procedural learning can be compared to operant conditioning. Just as the behaviour of a rat or a pigeon is gradually shaped by appropriate reinforcement schedules, sequence learning in humans also depends on feedback schemes that reinforce the desired pattern of responses. Although, as discussed in Chapter 7.3, procedural memory is often preceded by deliberate, explicitly controlled actions (as in learning to ride a bike or play the piano), in other cases, such as sequence learning, the learning procedure is implicit: the learner cannot explicitly relate the elements of the learned procedure, but is also not aware of the learning process itself while it proceeds. Think of a hippocampal patient like H.M. (check Section 6.0). He was very well able to master a mirror drawing task just like any average healthy individual, but at any given training session he had no explicit memory of ever having attended a previous training session.

Box 10.3   Mutual interactions between memory, attention and emotion: Classical conditioning

Classical conditioning procedures reveal a delicate interplay between memory, attention and emotion. Pavlov's dog learned to salivate (a parasympathetic response) in response to an inherently neutral stimulus after repeated sequential presentation of this neutral stimulus and the subsequent meaningful food stimulus. Aplysia's gill withdrawal response (see Section 5.1.1) to an innocuous tap to its siphon does not habituate when the tap is systematically followed by an electric shock to its tail (note that the logic of this procedure is quite different from that of Pavlov's with respect to the initial timing of the unconditional response (UR, salivation or withdrawal). Similarly to aplysia, human skin conductance responses (SCRs, Section 8.0) to an inherently neutral conditional stimulus (CS) remain elevated as long as the CS is systematically followed by an electric shock (the unconditional stimulus or US). This also applies, both in humans and in aplysia, when the CS becomes a CS+ and is randomly alternating with a CS− that is never followed by a shock (e.g. CS+ is a blue square or a mild stimulation of the siphon, and CS− is a yellow square or a mild stimulation of the mantle): CS+ elicits a stronger SCR or gill withdrawal than the CS−. In this kind of conditioning, the CS gradually comes to elicit the emotional response, as the result of a learning process. Stated more accurately, upon first presentation the CS already elicits the unconditional response, and keeps doing so when it turns out be the CS+, as compared to when it becomes the CS− (in that case it habituates more quickly, see Figure 10.2). It is generally believed that the UR to the initial CS is mandatory for conditioning to develop. Especially in the human case, the initial UR is conceived as a kind of attentional orienting, even though it is a sympathetic response that is also characteristic of the emotional response (Section 8.0). The necessity of this attentional response for conditioning to occur is stressed by the phenomenon of latent inhibition: thorough habituation of the UR to non-reinforced presentations of the CS prevents subsequent conditioning in response to repeated CS–US pairings from occurring. Furthermore, as also discussed in relation to Figure 10.2, individuals with weak attentional URs to initial CS presentation show a marked reduction of conditioning. It seems then, that an attentional response that shares a crucial characteristic with an emotional response, is necessary for a memory process to occur that results in the CS attaining emotional significance.

Also, in quite a different context, selective attention through a learning process influences the affective value of stimuli. In the Kiss et al. study (2007), discussed in Chapter 8, directing attention away from a distracter face reduced the subsequent affective appreciation of that face (how trustworthy it looked). It seems that the negative priming (as a result of attention to a simultaneous target face) of the distracter lingers for a second and a half or so (a memory trace), to result in turn in an affective devaluation of the distracter face (but not in a higher valuation of the target face). Moreover, electrocortical indices (N2pc) of the selectivity of attention during the cognitive phase of the task, correlated positively with the extent of devaluation during the affective phase of the task.

A typical experimental model for emotional learning is classical condition (for a recapitulation of the essential principles, see Box 10.3). For classical conditioning we can ask to what extent it involves implicit or explicit learning. A case in point are the results of the Kiss et al. study, discussed in Box 10.3 as well as in Section 8.3. Based on prior exposure to certain stimuli, in combination with an instruction that these stimuli should be ignored and treated as (perhaps even annoying) distracters, people explicitly value these stimuli as less positive. A related phenomenon is evaluative conditioning (De Houwer et al., 2001): as a result of typical classical conditioning (such as being paired with and predicting an aversive event), subjects afterwards evaluate a stimulus as relatively negative. But these declarative expressions are the result of a learning process that, in itself, may have proceeded implicitly, in the sense of without conscious awareness of the relationship between conditional and unconditional stimuli. A simple way to shed more light on this awareness is to subject people to a classical conditioning procedure and afterwards ask them whether they noticed any contingency between the various (conditional and unconditional) stimuli. Given an on-line readout measure for the dynamics of the emotional response (e.g. sympathetic activation) across the conditioning procedure, it can be inferred whether an explicit memory for what actually happened, in terms of the stimulus configuration, is associated with the extent of emotional learning.

Figure 10.2

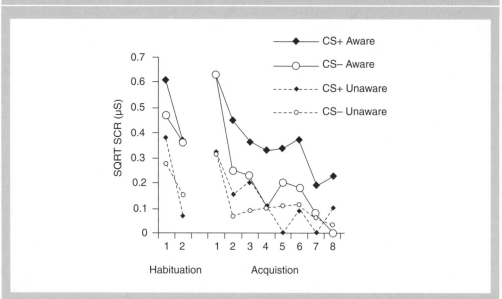

Acquisition of a conditional sympathetic response to the CS (for explanation of the terminology see Box 10.3), when the CS+ is systematically followed by electric shock and the CS− never, in subjects who afterwards reported an awareness of the contingency between CS+ and shock, and subjects who had not become aware.
Skin conductance responses (SCR) in microSiemens reflect sympathetic activation and have been transformed to their square roots. Acquisition is preceded by a habituation phase without any shock

Source: From Baas (2001); see also Grillon (2002).

Consider the example in Figure 10.2. The conditioning procedure proper is captured in the acquisition phase. The readout measure for sympathetic activation is the skin conductance response (SCR). During acquisition, an unpredictable sequence of two alternative repeated stimuli (e.g. blue and yellow rectangles) is presented, one of which, the CS+, is mostly followed by an aversive unconditional stimulus (e.g. electric shock), and another one, the CS−, is never followed by such a stimulus. Even during the acquisition phase there is a considerable amount of habituation, but the pace of decline is clearly different for the CS+ and CS−: habituation already appears to be delayed after the second CS+ presentation. Thus, a rather quick learning process yields enhanced SCRs to CS+, relative to the CS−. However, this pattern is only observed for subjects who afterwards reported being aware of the temporal relationship between CS+, CS− and the unconditional stimulus. In other words, conscious awareness of what was going on and emotional learning observed as it proceeds go hand in hand.

As an aside, note that aware subjects also have more pronounced SCRs to the very first CSs, when shocks have not yet been received, as well in the preceding habituation phase. This is not the emotional response as it is learned from the systematic pairing with the unconditional stimulus; it is rather conceived of as an attentional (orienting) response of the kind discussed in Section 5.1.2 and Box 10.3, and suggests that the amount of attention drives the extent of emotional learning.

The next question then is, what drives what? Is sympathetic conditioning a prerequisite for explicit learning, or do subjects first become aware and then start exhibiting (rather quickly) sympathetic conditioning? In Section 10.3 we will discuss a situation in which SCRs and explicit behaviour are both recorded on-line, and learning at SCR level appears to lead learning of explicit behaviour.

A relevant clue might be derived from research on patients with selective brain damage such that either emotional learning or contingency awareness is selectively compromised. Consider the study reported by Bechara and colleagues (1995). In addition to four control participants, three patients with bilateral brain damage were included. Again, one of them was S.M., the person with selective amygdala damage discussed in Sections 8.2, 9.0 and 10.1. The others were W.C., with severe hippocampal damage but intact amygdala, and R.H. with severely damaged hippocampi as well as amygdala. In a conditioning procedure quite similar to the ones described above, amygdala damage was associated with a complete lack of SCR

Figure 10.3

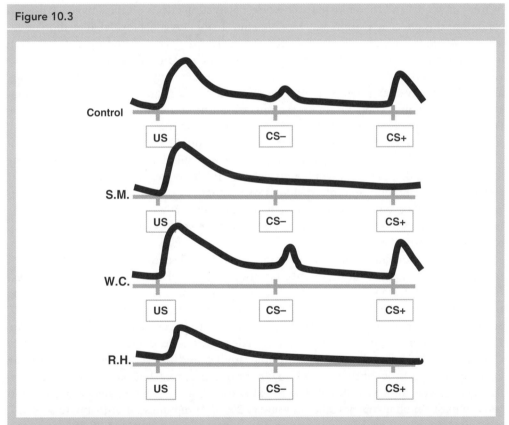

Idealized polygraph output of the SCRs to an unconditional aversive noise stimulus (US), as well as to an unpaired neutral control stimulus (CS–) and to a paired conditional neutral stimulus (CS+). Control subjects have no damage; S.M. has specific amygdala damage; W.C. has specific hippocampal damage; and R.H. has damage in both structures (Bechara et al., 1995). Note that although S.M. is responsive to the aversive stimulus (US) itself, she does not respond to the proper emotional stimulus (the conditional stimulus, CS). Abscissa: time across tens of seconds. Ordinate: skin conductance level.

level learning in S.M. and R.H. (see Figure 10.3). However, S.M., but not R.H., was perfectly able to describe afterwards the temporal relation between conditional and unconditional stimuli (as were the controls in this experiment). In contrast, hippocampal damage, as in W.C. and R.H., was associated with normal SCR conditioning but a complete lack of awareness of the stimulus contingencies.

These results constitute a perfect double dissociation (as in Box 2.1) between amygdala and hippocampus on the one hand, and explicit awareness versus sympathetic conditioning on the other. Everything would be fine if it weren't for the fact that healthy individuals do show an association between awareness and sympathetic conditioning, and explicit memory modulations by emotional aspects have been amply described, even to the extent that they are absent in S.M. (Section 10.1). Based on the reported relationships between the amygdala and explicit memory, one would expect that selective amygdala damage would interfere with the explicit recollection of the stimulus contingencies. This apparent discrepancy may be due to differences in experimental context. The emotional materials that result in better long-term memory are normally presented just once, and are inherently emotional (e.g. negative pictures or words) and therefore may have direct activating effects on the amygdala; in such conditions this direct activation may be a prerequisite for amygdala mediated memory modulation, which is therefore absent when the amygdala is damaged or destroyed. In contrast, inherently neutral conditional stimuli may not activate the amygdala directly, and moreover are presented multiple times. The former may preclude amygdala modulated learning, and the latter may strengthen hippocampus mediated learning and this stronger hippocampal contribution may compensate for the missing contribution from a damaged amygdala. Furthermore, hippocampus and amygdala modulate the strength of different connections, such as those between memory nodes in the neocortex and the prefrontal cortex (implement explicit report), and those between memory nodes and subcortical structures (controlling SCRs). This would explain the double dissociation in the patients between explicit report and SCR. On the other hand, in individuals without damage, neurons in the hippocampus and the amygdala exchange signals, thereby mutually strengthening the modulation in the two pathways, and producing the kind of association between explicit report and emotional response as described above.

Connections from amygdala to hippocampus may be indispensable for enhanced explicit memory. However, anatomical evidence (as discussed in 10.1) suggests that these connections are reciprocal. How then are signals from the hippocampus instrumental in modulating the emotional learning that is supposed to be primarily under the control of the amygdala? Such influence is revealed in rather subtle extensions of the classical conditioning paradigm. First, the paradigm often involves a third, so-called, extinction phase. With extinction, the CSs are presented a number of times without any US and the conditioned responses are extinguished. It is thought that extinction is not just unlearning, but actually learning something new about the CSs and that, due to extinction, two, possibly incompatible, memories may exist simultaneously (LaBar & Cabeza, 2006). Sometimes a fourth phase is added, reinstatement, which involves one or two presentations of the US alone. If, after reinstatement, the CS is presented again, reinstatement induced recovery (RIR) of the original CR can be observed. However, RIR depends on two factors. First, the context for the reinstatement and the recovery CS need to be identical. For example, resorting to a different testing room for the reinstatement procedure and then returning to the original testing room to assess recovery to the CS, will prevent RIR from occurring. Second, you need an intact hippocampus for RIR to take place (LaBar & Phelps, 2005). Conspicuously, hippocampal damage did not affect the rate of extinction. So, to the extent that extinction involves new learning, a different brain region may be crucial, perhaps one in the prefrontal cortex. But for RIR, the contribution of the hippocampus appears to be decisive. Reinstatement of sympathetic conditioning depends on hippocampal signals, which may or may not run via the amygdala. More specifically, the role of the amygdala in, and the effect of amygdala damage on, RIR are, to the best of the authors' knowledge, still open to investigation. A further question is, what exactly is learned during the reinstatement (the mere presentation of the US)? It must have something to do with a strengthening of the representation of the US, as it is influenced by a representation of the context (e.g. the testing room). This strengthening then translates to a recovered reaction to the original CS when it is encountered in the same context.

The differential roles of context and specific conditioning cues are also strongly suggested by neuroimaging work in healthy human subjects. These paradigms indicate that during classical conditioning (or rather classical conditioning-like paradigms adapted for fMRI), the amygdala is only activated during the first part of the sequence of CS and US. This is consistent with a specific role for amygdala neurons in creating or learning the association between CS and US (e.g. Büchel et al., 1998). Activation in other areas is much more stable across the conditioning sequence and therefore may primarily represent what has been learned through conditioning. These regions are found in the anterior insular cortex and the anterior cingulate cortex (ACC) (see Sections 8.1 and 4.3). The same dissociation was observed in a recent study: transient activations in the amygdala, but stable activations across the conditioning procedure in anterior insula and ACC (Marschner et al., 2008). A comparison was also made in this study between a typical (although fMRI-adapted) CS+/CS− paradigm, and as similar as possible a paradigm, but this time without systematic temporal contingency between CS and US. Specifically, the US would occur as much, but completely unpredictably, and only in one context (testing environment), not in another. Similar stable activations in the anterior insula and ACC were observed in the context conditioning condition. However, instead of transient activation in the amygdala, the researchers reported transient activation in...? Right, the hippocampus (Marschner et al., 2008).

10.2.1   The psychopharmacology of fear and anxiety

The paradigms described above have inspired several studies aimed at increasing insight into the mechanisms of fear and anxiety, especially in the light of disorders marked by excessive fear or anxiety. These include phobia (for relatively specific cues or circumstances, such as certain animals or height), generalized anxiety disorder (anxiety induced by relatively global contexts, such as anything in the outside world), and PTSD (see Box 10.1). One important insight from such studies is that, while excessive cue conditionability may play a role in phobia, it has an inverse relation to context conditionability: relatively weak conditioning to a discrete cue is associated with relatively strong conditioning to the context in which the CS was presented, and this enhanced sensitivity to context may actually present greater problems in everyday life than enhanced sensitivity to a specific cue. For example, think of the possibility that generalized anxiety disorder can be much more invalidating, and more difficult to treat, than a simple phobia.

Indeed, such studies have revealed that after cue conditioning in a first session, healthy volunteers are less anxious upon returning to the same context for a second session, relative to when there was no conditioning in the first session, either because of it did not work for some volunteers or because the USi were delivered in equal amounts but were not predicted by the CS (Grillon, 2008). In fact, subjects that were not conditioned in the first session failed to show up for the second session more often than those who were conditioned in the first session.

An obvious next step is to apply these paradigms in psychopharmacological research, in search of neurotransmitter systems and substances that affect either cue or context conditioning. Mainly for practical reasons, in these endeavours the typical classical conditioning paradigm has often been adjusted to, what has been termed, anticipatory anxiety or instructed fear. This procedure capitalizes on the possibility that human volunteers or patients can simply be instructed about the contingency between a discrete CS or context on the one hand, and an aversive US on the other. Such studies have revealed that benzodiazepines do not reduce cue conditioning, but they do reduce context conditioning (Baas et al., 2002a; Grillon, 2008), although this dissociation is slightly less clear in other studies (Riba et al., 2001). The dissociation would fit the clinical experience that benzodiazepines are more suitable for the treatment of generalized anxiety disorder, than they are for specific phobias. Furthermore, the context conditioning reducing effects of benzodiazepines (specifically, alprazolam) cannot be attributed to general sedation. Another substance, a histaminergic antagonist with sedating properties similar to the effective dose of alprazolam, did not affect context conditioning. Finally, one can ask if there are substances that specifically affect cue conditioning and not context conditioning. One lead in this respect was the finding that cue specific startle potentiation, but not startle potentiation that was driven by the context (darkness versus light), was reduced after application of a metabotropic glumatergic antagonist (Grillon et al., 2003).

We will return to glutamatergic mechanisms (specifically the NMDA receptor) in Section 10.4 on de- and reconsolidation. First, we turn to a further elaboration of the principles of classical conditioning and entertain the possibility that emotional learning may guide rational decision making.

10.3   EMOTIONAL LEARNING AND RATIONAL DECISION MAKING

It has been proposed that emotional factors may be especially relevant for learning optimal decision making. In the Iowa gambling task, subjects draw sequentially at will from two piles of cards. One pile initially yields substantial monetary wins, but after a while even bigger *losses* start to be incurred. The other pile yields the same pattern but with substantially lower wins and correspondingly lower losses. In effect (from the way the cards have been sorted at the outset), drawing from the second set is more advantageous. The question is, will the average individual learn to apply this decision strategy, and if so, what are the underlying mechanisms? Figure 10.4 depicts some typical behavioural results. Indeed, average healthy controls learn to reduce the number of disadvantageous selections. However, patients with certain lesions do not (Bechara et al., 1997). In Figure 10.4 this applies to patients with lesions in the orbitofrontal cortex (OFC), or in the wider ventromedial (VM) prefrontal cortex region. In contrast, patients with control lesions in the occipital–temporal cortex show a normal learning curve.

As to the mechanisms, one clue was derived from looking at sympathetic activation, both in response to, as well as in anticipation of, negative feedback (a substantial loss card). As can be seen in Figure 10.4, healthy controls emit enhanced SCRs preceding their choice of the bad deck, relative to choosing the good deck. This is reminiscent of conditioning: it is the sight of, or attention to, the bad deck, or the thought of picking from it, or the preparation at the level of the motor cortex (see Section 2.1 and 4.1) that may trigger the sympathetic response. This could be viewed as a kind of classical conditioning, although the operant component is also quite explicit, in the sense that non-OFC damaged individuals eventually learn to avoid the bad deck. The kind of learning in this task has been dubbed reinforcement learning, a form of operant conditioning (Fellows, 2007). Whatever it is, OFC patients do not exhibit it either (Figure 10.4), and this is not because they are not able to emit SCRs: they do show pronounced SCRs in response to the punishment embodied in the card that signals a sizable loss.

Something else must then be going on. Remember that S.M., the patient with selective amygdala damage, did not respond to a classical SCR conditioning procedure. How would amygdala patients do in the Iowa gambling tasks, and how would VM patients respond to a classical conditioning procedure? In a comparative analysis including five amygdala patients and five VM patients, as well as 13 controls, both group of patients performed the same way in the Iowa gambling task as the VM group discussed above (Bechara et al., 1999). Moreover, they did not show anticipatory SCRs either. In the same study, a typical classical conditioning procedure was also administered (aversive loud sounds predicted by neutral visual stimuli). Here the patient groups clearly differed. As for S.M. (see discussion above), the amygdala

Figure 10.4

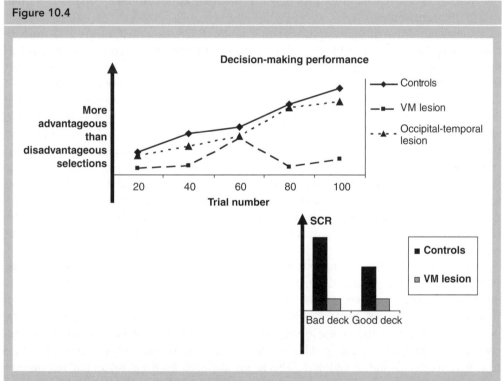

Overview of the data from Bechara (2004).
Upper panel: Number of advantageous, relative to the number of disadvantageous, cards as drawn in each of five twenty-card blocks in the Iowa gambling task, in a group of healthy controls, control patients with damage in the occipital–temporal cortex, and patients with damage in the ventromedial (VM, including orbito-) frontal cortex. Lower panel: SCRs in anticipation of drawing a card from either the advantageous (good) or the disadvantageous (bad) decks.

patients failed to show any sign of conditioning, although their response to the US was quite normal. In contrast, the VM patients did not differ from the controls in any respect within the conditioning procedure.

The results point to a hierarchical relation between the amygdala and the VM frontal cortex (including OFC). The amygdala is necessary for relatively simple conditioning, as well as for the more complex reinforcement learning in Iowa gambling. VM/OFC only kicks in in the latter case. So what is this more complex aspect? Abnormally reduced VMFC/OFC has been associated with problems with reversal learning, the task discussed in Chapter 9.4, in which reward or punishment contingencies are learned and then suddenly reverse. The original version of the Iowa gambling task contains an initial uninterrupted series of win cards from the bad deck, that were then followed by the first substantial losses. Indeed, shuffling the decks in such a way that large losses occurred much more from the outset, annihilated the difference between VM patients and healthy controls (Fellows, 2007). In Section 9.3 it was concluded that cells in the VMFC/OFC region represent or code reward value or punishment, depending on the exact region (Figure 9.9). Perhaps a better description of the role of these neurons is in terms of shifting between reward and punishment representations, in relation to the choice between alternative actions that are afforded by the context. A comparable shift may take place with the transition from liking to wanting (see Section 9.5); wanting is marked by excessive striatal activation, which in turn may be contingent upon suboptimal VMFC/OFC functioning.

A somewhat different view capitalizes on a subtle difference noted in Box 10.2. In contrast to what happened to Pavlov's dog, straightforward human SCR conditioning involves the strengthening of a response (the SCR) that is elicited anyway by the CS, also without the association with the US. However, in the gambling task SCRs grow in anticipation of drawing from the bad deck after the first negative consequences of drawing from the bad deck have been encountered. It is conceivable that for such a CR to develop in a situation when it is initially not emitted, some brain circuit additional to the amygdala is needed, and this could run via the VMFC/OC. A comparable example was encountered in Section 7.2, in relation to the conditioning of the eye blink in anticipation of an air puff to the eye, while the CS initially did not elicit any eye blink. In that case, neurons in the cerebellum appear to be essential. In the case of the gambling task, a putative role for VMFC/OFC in the gradual development of the sympathetic response to the CS would also be consistent with the observation that VMFC/OFC is only influential when initial draws from the bad deck are all rewarded.

In parallel to establishing the special role of the VMFC/OFC in decision learning tasks, such as Iowa gambling, an explicit theory has been proposed for the function of the gradually developing, anticipatory sympathetic activation. This concerns the notion of the, so-called, somatic marker (Bechara, 2004). To some extent, this notion rephrases the assertions in the preceding paragraphs. After a few losses, the mere idea of the bad deck, or of drawing from the bad deck, instigates a replay of a brain–body process that was initially emitted in response to a loss incurred from the bad deck. This replay depends on the sympathetic response to losses, presumably mediated by the amygdala, on the resulting feedback from the body to the brain, and on the function of VMFC/OFC to register this feedback. It has been proposed that this registration gradually translates into a representation (the marker in VMFC/OFC), and that subsequently there are two possibilities: either VMFC/OFC triggers the full-blown anticipatory sympathetic response; or a kind of equivalent activation ensues in a specific brain circuit, involving the amygdala and other regions sensitive to peripheral feedback, such as the insula (Bechara, 2004). As a further extension of this notion, Bechara proposes that the body–loop replay, rather than the equivalent brain–circuit replay, is invoked in the case of ambiguous situations, such as Iowa gambling, where the bad deck always encompasses the promise of a substantial win, especially when such wins materialized in the initial phase of the gambling game.

One question that remains is whether the body–loop or the internal brain–circuit replay mechanism lead the way to the change in behaviour, or the adjustment of the decision strategy. From the original report by Bechara and colleagues (Bechara et al., 1997) it is not clear whether the development of the anticipatory SCR precedes the adjustment in choice behaviour (bad versus good deck). In effect, on-line monitoring of somatic markers in parallel to monitoring behavioural adjustments has not revealed the expected lead–lag relationship between somatic marker and behavioural adjustment.

An alternative link to other functional anatomical brain–body systems is worthwhile mentioning. In Section 4.3, the brain circuit that implements conflict monitoring, especially error monitoring, was discussed. An important node in this monitoring system, and the likely generator of the reflection in fMRI and EEG signals, is the ACC. Neurons in the ACC are known to be involved in triggering sympathetic responses (Critchley et al., 2003). Consistently, conditions that elicit conflict, or error-related, brain potentials also elicit SCRs, and there is a significant correlation between these cortical components and the strength of the SCR (Bechara, 2004; Hajcak et al., 2003). Together with signals from VMFC/OFC and the amygdala, this mechanism may implement somatic markers and provide a gut feeling in situations in which the odds are ambiguous and suboptimal decision making lurks.

10.4   RECONSOLIDATING AND DECONSOLIDATING THE EMOTION

Emotion during encoding modulates later memory, but what is the role of retrieval processes in producing this effect? A more specific version of this question is whether manipulation of retrieval can modulate the emotional modulation of the memory. This may have important consequences in real-life situations. Patients with post-traumatic stress disorder (PTSD) present with various symptoms, including unbearably painful memories of the traumatizing event. Vulnerability to PTSD may have its main impact on encoding during the traumatic experience, but most of the time the problems of the disorder only become manifest years later. Is it conceivable that retrieval processes can be modulated in such way that PTSD symptoms can be alleviated or even prevented? A couple of leads from the previous section may be followed. One has to do with reinstatement induced recovery (RIR); perhaps this process can be reversed? Another lead is that (nor)adrenaline and cortisol during encoding strengthen subsequent memories, but cortisol impairs retrieval as well as working memory.

Another idea is the reconsolidation hypothesis. This notion holds that retrieval can be seen as taking a copy of an item in the long-term memory store (thought to be distributed across the neocortex). This working memory copy is malleable, AND it is put back in the position of the original in the long-term store, overwriting the original from which the copy was taken. This opens up the possibility not only of strengthening existing associations (reconsolidation), but also of modifying them, even to the extent that they are weakened or erased (deconsolidation).

These ideas have been applied in the context of classical conditioning procedures and reinstatement. In a study by Kindt and colleagues (Kindt et al., 2009), spiders from IAPS were used for differential classical conditioning (one spider predicted electric shock, the other predicted absence of shock). A potentiated startle reflex during the CS+, relative to the CS–, was readily established. The next day, a reconsolidation phase consisted of exactly one presentation of the CS+. On the third day, extinction was achieved within six to ten CS+ presentations without US. Then three USi were presented for reinstatement, which in return resulted in significant RIR (again a potentiated startle for CS+ versus CS–). This is what happened under a placebo. In a second condition, on day two subjects received 40 mg propranolol 1½ hours before the single reconsolidation CS+. This manipulation profoundly changed what happened on the third day. First, extinction was immediately present, from the very first CS+, as if the association with the US had been completely wiped out. Second, reinstatement had no effect whatsoever, again consistent with a complete loss of the CS+–US association. Two other findings shed further light on what was going on. First, continuous shock expectancy ratings closely followed the startle potentiation pattern under placebo; this held for both ratings under placebo and ratings after propranolol. Second, applying 40 mg propranolol did not have any effect when the single reconsolidation CS+ was left out.

The dominant interpretation for these results is that reconsolidation of an emotional memory depends on signals from neurons in the amygdala. If these neurons are interfered with, as in the propranolol condition, reconsolidation turns into deconsolidation. This can be noticed during extinction and even after hippocampus driven reinstatement: the memory for the association has simply been wiped out. That is, its emotional aspect has been; its declarative aspect was still completely intact. Thus, we do not lose the memory of the painful event, but only the re-experience of pain that normally accompanies it. It remains to be seen how well this principle applies when the memory goes back for many years. As will be discussed below (explicit retrieval), some of these principles may work across a period of days as well as years.

Another pharmacological lead concerns D-cycloserine (DCS), a partial agonist at the glycine unit of the NMDA receptor complex. Several clinical trials have confirmed that DCS promotes the beneficial effects of Exposure-Based Therapy (EBT). EBT relies on the principle that repeated exposure to a feared stimulus (say, a door handle) results in a loss of the association between the stimulus and the potential consequence of interacting with it (like contamination). The stimulating effects of DCS during EBT have been reported for fear of heights (Ressler et al., 2004), social phobia (Hofmann et al., 2006), and obsessive–compulsive disorder (OCD; see Section 9.4) (Kushner et al., 2007). As with the preceding example, this points to the possibility of applying pharmacological treatment as a means to cure a disorder, rather than just alleviate symptoms. However, it has turned out to be difficult to establish similar effects of DCS on extinction in laboratory-type classical conditioning procedures (Grillon, 2009), which in turn hampers the understanding of the mechanisms on which the DCS effects are based. One possibility is that DCS, through its agonistic effect on the NMDA receptor, promotes learning in other senses as well, which may, at least in humans, mask the effects on simple extinction (e.g. both hippocampus and amygdala based learning is affected, possibly in opposite ways).

In the preceding sections we noted that cortisol has negative effects on retrieval as well as on working memory. The mechanisms underlying these more explicit retrieval processes, in relation to emotion, are the topic of the next section. Cortisol has been applied in the context of PTSD as well as of specific phobias. The initial reports on its ability to reduce subjective fear and anxiety seem promising (de Quervain & Margraf, 2008). This holds both for more long-term low daily dosages (10 mg) and for single acute higher dosages. Moreover, in both cases the beneficial effects appeared to last for a couple of days or even a month, again suggestive of a mechanism of enhanced deconsolidation underlying the effect.

10.5   EXPLICIT RETRIEVAL

The ideas of reconsolidation and deconsolidation have also been entertained in the realm of explicit memory. Specifically, retrieval would involve the transfer of information from long-term to working memory, and malfunctioning working memory impedes the retrieval response. One step further, working memory not only takes a copy from long-term memory, but it also puts the copy back at the location of the original. With bad working memory, the copy that is transferred back to long-term memory is also bound to be bad. This would also be the mechanism through which cortisol, and possibly (nor)adrenergic antagonists, could affect both acute retrieval as well as the quality of memories after a longer period. One additional perspective is that the prefrontal cortex contains a significant number of gluco-corticoid receptors. These receptors may mediate the cortisol effect of weakening prefrontal function and therefore working memory.

What exactly happens during retrieval, especially in the hippocampus and amygdala? Retrieval processes are often associated with simultaneous activations in both structures. For

Figure 10.5

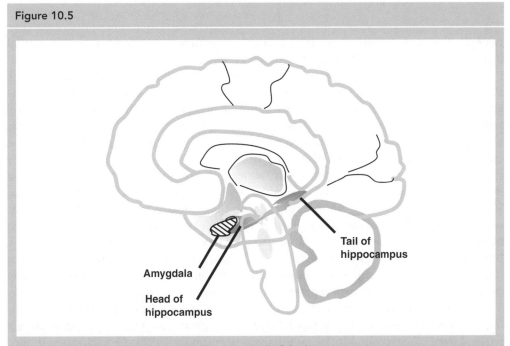

Schematic rendering of amygdala, and head and tail of the hippocampus.
In each of these three regions activations were stronger for successful relative to failed recognition, and enhanced for emotional relative to neutral pictures. This also held for entorhinal cortex bordering the hippocampus inferiorly (not shown). The reported differences in activation (Dolcos et al., 2005) were localized at MNI y coordinates −4 to −38. Amygdala and hippocampus are situated laterally relative to more medial structures in the background (see Figure 8.8 for a view of the approximate medial lateral locations).

Figure 10.6

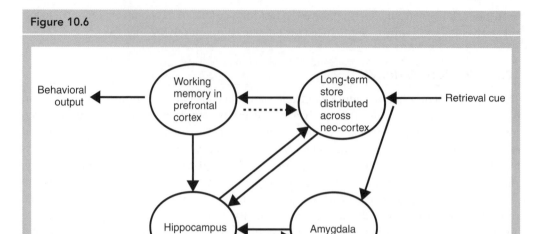

Interactions within cortex and subcortex, as well as between cortex and subcortex, during retrieval operations.
See text for further explanation.

example, Dolcos and co-workers (2005) looked at recognition of affective as well as neutral pictures in nine subjects one year after initial encoding. Recollection was better for emotional (either positive or negative) pictures than for neutral ones. This is consistent with the effects of enhanced amygdala and hippocampus activation, as well as perhaps noradrenergic and cortisolergic contributions during encoding, the effects of which linger on for a long time. fMRI scans during retrieval revealed that both the amygdala and the hippocampus were more activated in response to successfully retrieved items than for failed retrieval, and especially so for emotional materials (Figure 10.5).

These activation results cannot be taken as direct proof for the idea that the amygdala and the hippocampus are instrumental in superior retrieval, especially for emotional materials. Such a notion would be difficult to reconcile with the evidence from hippocampal patients who have no problems with pure explicit retrieval operations pertaining to episodes that occurred years before the hippocampal damage (see Box 6.1). An alternative view is that the hippocampal and amygdalar activations are correlated with the behavioural phenomena of superior retrieval for specific materials. This allows for an interpretation in terms of parallel streams in cortical and subcortical pathways, as outlined in Figure 10.6.

In this model a retrieval cue, such as a picture, activates long-term representations resulting from prior exposure to that picture (this idea is very much akin to what happens during retrieval from the perceptual cortex, as discussed in Section 5.4). This first activation in turn results in a working memory representation in the prefrontal cortex (PFC) that can be used for behavioural output (via connections to the motor cortex). In other situations, such as a free recall condition, perhaps PFC takes the lead, as represented by the dotted arrow from the PFC to the long-term storage. By definition, the long-term storage/PFC pathway is activated more strongly by items that are successfully retrieved, relative to those that are not retrieved; and more strongly by the average emotional item than by neutral ones. This is the first, cortical, stream. Parallel to the cortical stream, subcortical interactions take place. These are initiated by descending signals from the cortex. A first descending signal travels from long-term storage to the hippocampus and back, embodying the classic pathway for hippocampus mediated encoding and consolidation of whatever event. This in turn leads to hippocampal signals to the amygdala and back (Section 10.1), associated with amplification of representations of emotional materials (cf. Dolcos et al., 2005; Nieuwenhuys et al., 1988). The amygdala may also receive signals independently of the hippocampus, especially when the retrieval cue is emotional (conditionally or unconditionally), either cortically mediated or through a low route. Finally, the PFC signals to the hippocampus. This symbolizes the starting point of this section: working memory representations of past events as derived from the long-term store result in new versions of the corresponding long-term store representation, which can be either accurate (reconsolidation) or less accurate (deconsolidation). Thus, the combined amygdala–hippocampus activations are not instrumental in producing acutely enhanced retrieval, but may affect later retrieval of the same items.

A similar mechanism may operate in the fascinating studies of Anderson and co-workers. Subjects learned arbitrary relationships between words (such as ordeal and roach). They then participated in an fMRI experiment where they were asked to either respond to each first word of a pair (ordeal) with the learned associate (roach), or to completely suppress the learned associate and block it out of consciousness as much as possible ('to think or not to think', which should work for at least the few seconds duration of a trial). After that, subjects were again tested on the paired associates, with the first words of the pairs again as recall cues. It turned out that associates that had been suppressed during scanning were recalled much less than in the case of cues that had been responded to normally during scanning (Anderson et al., 2004), which seems to be another case of deconsolidation. This deconsolidation was apparently mediated by suppression during scanning, and this suppression, relative to normal responding, was marked by enhanced prefrontal activation and pronounced hippocampal deactivation.

The relationship between emotion and retrieval process may not be mediated only by the amygdala; signals from other subcortical structures may also be involved. In one study, neutral faces were remembered better when previously presented in an emotional, relative to a neutral, context. During successful retrieval, not only the amygdala, but also the locus cereleus was activated more strongly, and this effect was augmented when the remembered materials had initially been presented in an emotional context (Sterpenich et al., 2006). Following the logic of Figure 10.6, the diffuse noradrenergic projections from the locus cereleus to widespread areas of the neocortex may be instrumental in producing this enhanced retrieval (see Figure 10.7, as well as 5.16, right upper panel; the noradrenergic diffuse innervation of the cortex is called the cingulum). As a spin-off from the cingulum, noradrenergic fibres also project to the hippocampus; in addition there are more direct connections from the locus cereleus to the amygdala (Nieuwenhuys et al., 1988).

What could be the benefit of the PFC–hippocampus–neocortex pathway activation, if not for acute, one time retrieval? It turns out that the ensuing reconsolidation can be very effective in augmenting learning over time. In one American study, students learned the English translation of Swahili words. During the learning phase they followed one of four trajectories: classic, repeated (four cycles) studying and testing of the complete list of words; no repeated studying but maintaining repeated testing of the complete list; repeated studying without repeated testing; and neither repeated studying nor repeated testing. In a final test one week later, students who had practised in one of the first two conditions were able

Figure 10.7

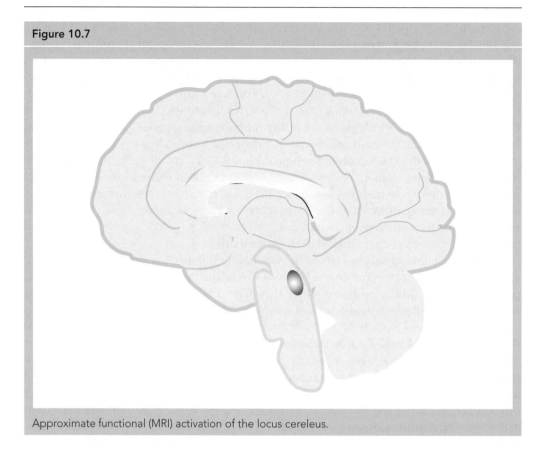

Approximate functional (MRI) activation of the locus cereleus.

to translate about 80 per cent of the Swahili words. However, when trained in the second two conditions, they only achieved about 35 per cent correct answers (Karpicke & Roediger, 2008). This happened even though the learning rates during the practising phase were indistinguishable across conditions, and the predictions of the students as to how they would perform on a final test one week later were also equal across the four practice conditions (about 50 per cent).

Thus, study practices that include repeated testing, which presumably draw pre-eminently on repeated retrieval operations, are superior to methods that do not include repeated testing, even though they did include repeated studying. It is possible that the PFC–hippocampus–neocortex pathway is activated throughout each of the repeated retrieval operations and therefore is instrumental in continuously improving the accuracy and availability of neocortex based long-term memories. We can take this a bit further.

As said, if retrieval implies reconsolidation, through the PFC–hippocampus–neocortex trajectory, it may also imply deconsolidation, which in many cases is actually undesirable. This happens, for example, when the representation in the PFC is not so accurate, especially when the result is a downright error. This may in turn result in erroneous consolidation in the long-term store. This idea is reminiscent of the rationale that is often expressed for a procedure termed errorless learning. Briefly, errorless learning entails a strategy of testing in which the production of an error is highly unlikely, most of the time because test questions are framed in such a way that the tested individual is carefully guided towards the correct answer. One common rationale for errorless learning is that the production of errors actually rubs in the erroneous representation even more firmly in the long-term store. This may be a particular problem in individuals with memory problems, and errorless learning has proved superior in terms of final memory performance over errorful learning in diverse memory patients (Wilson et al., 1994). Consider, for example, someone with long-term memory retrieval problems due to damage or impaired function of the prefrontal cortex. Not only will this person perform badly during initial retrieval, but deconsolidation due to initial retrieval errors will additionally make things worse in the future.

Interestingly, unwanted effects of errorful learning have also been related to an emotional aspect. When errors are followed by negative feedback, the ensuing negative emotional reaction to the feedback can be additionally instrumental in rubbing in the incorrect representation through deconsolidation. This is conceivably realized by means of the subcortical interactions as indicated in Figure 10.6. Another contributing factor may be the activation of the circuit discussed in Section 4.3, the conflict, or error, monitoring network, involving connections between the nucleus accumbens, hippocampus and ACC. Briefly, one can think of a balance between two effects of typical error-related activity in this network (thought to rely on disinhibition of the hippocampus–ACC connection, which produces the typical error-related activity recordable with human EEG or fMRI). One is the postulated signal from ACC to PFC (also discussed in Section 4.3), thought to result in augmented attentional, or inhibitory, control and a lower probability of similar errors in the (near) future. The second effect capitalizes on reduced nucleus accumbens activation, reduced available dopamine, and negative valence, perhaps activating the amygdala to strengthen the consolidation of the incorrect representation, perhaps in concert with ACC-controlled sympathetic responses (Critchley et al., 2003). It is conceivable that in certain individuals the balance is shifted towards the second effect, especially with prefrontal damage, which by itself distorts the representation in working memory. In these cases errorless learning can be particularly helpful.

Indeed, conflict monitoring, as manifest in the error-related negativity (ERN), seems to be reduced in the context of errorless learning, relative to errorful learning. In one paradigm,

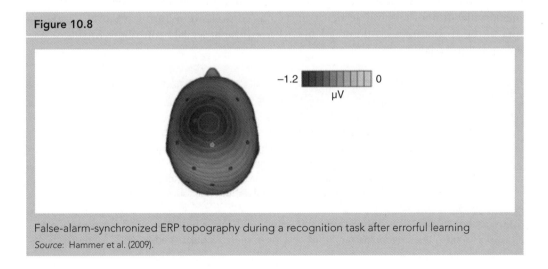

Figure 10.8

False-alarm-synchronized ERP topography during a recognition task after errorful learning
Source: Hammer et al. (2009).

errorful learning entailed the production of multiple potential target words during the initial study phase, with only one of them being identified immediately afterwards as the correct one. In contrast, during errorless learning the correct target word was identified instantaneously (by the experimenter). During subsequent recognition, larger response-locked, centrally distributed ERP negativities were elicited after errorful than after errorless learning (Hammer et al., 2009). Based on its scalp topography, this negativity was identified as an ERN (see Figure 10.8, compare with Figure 4.12). However, this paradigm is rather complicated, and not nearly all its aspects are well understood, as evident from the fact that the smaller ERNs for errorless learning are not very consistent across studies, even when they are from the same research group (see Heldmann et al., 2008; Rodriguez-Fornells et al., 2004).

10.6 CONCLUDING REMARKS

For explicit memory, during encoding, interactions between the amygdala and the prefrontal cortex on the one hand, and the hippocampus on the other, implement the subsequent memory modulation by emotion. The amygdala–hippocampus interaction especially is sensitive to (nor)adrenaline and cortisol, the renowned stress hormones. The prefrontal cortex–hippocampus interaction is instrumental in promoting explicit memory for non-arousing, but nevertheless interesting, information.

Double dissociations have been demonstrated between hippocampal and amygdalar contributions to emotional memory. More implicit measures of fear conditioning are affected by amygdala, not by hippocampus, damage; for explicit awareness of contingencies between conditional and aversive stimuli, it is the other way around. The more implicit aspects of extinction, and other retrieval-related phenomena such as reconsolidation, are negatively affected by adrenergic antagonists, and are also sensitive to other neurotransmitter systems such as that of NMDA/glutamate.

Selective reinforcement of choice behaviour is instrumental in developing behavioural strategies that yield maximum reward in the near future. This is thought to depend on a somatic marker, a representation of the emotional response in the orbitofrontal cortex that also depends on amygdalar function, as revealed in patient studies.

With explicit retrieval, parallel cortical and subcortical streams interact to produce either deconsolidation or reconsolidation. Specifically, prefrontal cortex implemented working memory determines retrieval accuracy, as well as consolidation during retrieval, by signalling to the hippocampus. Additional signals from the amygdala contribute in the case of emotional materials.

Questions

1. In relation to Section 10.1.1 and 10.1.2, as well as Section 6.3, survey explicit memory modulation by attention, working memory and emotion. Do this in terms of signals to the hippocampus from various other structures, and the associated biochemistry (neurotransmitters).

2. In the movie *Memento*, Harry Jankis could apparently not form any new explicit memories, but he also did not respond to avoidance conditioning (that is, he did not learn to refrain from touching an electrified object). In terms of the pattern of results shown in Figure 10.3, what could have been wrong with his brain?

3. In Section 10.2 it is mentioned that stable activations during a classical conditioning sequence were found in the anterior insular cortex and the anterior cingulate cortex (ACC). Anterior insula

was also discussed in Sections 3.3 and 8.1, and ACC in 4.3. Do the functions discussed in these sections really involve the same neurons as those referred in Section 10.2? Answer in terms of coordinates and/or experimental logic.

4. See Section 10.4. What would happen if D-cycloserine is given prior to the reconsolidation stimulus in the Kindt et al. procedure, and propranolol prior to exposure therapy?

11 SOCIAL COGNITION AND COMMUNICATION

Key Points

- Watching others may induce subtle muscle adjustments that are probably driven by the amygdala and the mirror neuron system. The latter may also be involved in the production of cortical motor potentials corresponding to observed actions of other agents. If these actions are judged as inappropriate, observers emit a conflict-monitoring signal in the anterior cingulate cortex.
- The substance oxytocin appears to increase trust or reduce betrayal aversion, and reduces ACC error signals and amygdala responses to the emotional expressions of others.
- Neurons in the anterior insula represent disgust as well as unfairness and may hamper rational decision making. The insula is part of an extended social neural network that may work in a manner complementary to the mirror neuron system, dependent on the amount of social interaction.
- Social coordination in the brain is visible in the EEG phi complex, possibly reflecting the tuning of parietal mirror neurons to observed actions of another person.
- Language in the brain involves the activation of widespread cortical areas during reading or the production of words (e.g. the premotor cortex in relation to action verbs).
- Typical language regions, such as Broca's and Wernicke's areas, may be part of general purpose brain networks involved in procedural and declarative learning, and working memory.

11.0 INTRODUCTION

This book ends with a chapter on how humans interact and how their brains can, or don't, become more or less synchronized. This chapter provides a snapshot of recent attempts to reveal and understand how individual human behaviour and brain function relates to that of other individuals. To that end we'll discuss a number of issues and paradigms in the field of social neuroscience and, furthermore, we will not evade the function that makes humans look even more human than does the possession of a huge prefrontal cortex: language. Fitting the general perspective of this book, the overview illustrates that social cognition and communication are firmly rooted in the functions we discussed in previous chapters: perception, action, attention, memory and emotion. In a manner of speaking, it's all just one big interface; as if some hidden evolutionary plan prescribes how human social behaviour and communication emerge from these other, more basic faculties.

Also in relation to social cognition, the question of what really goes on in the brain(s) pops up continuously. Consider the following example: as a professor you have managed to obtain an external grant so you can hire a postdoc. In contrast, your fellow professor in the office next door has not been successful in that respect for quite a while. However, he happens to be the one who has to take care of personnel matters and annual progress evaluations. After a year or so, the progress report on your newly acquired postdoc is created and the conclusion is that his work is excellent, so far. However, the report gets lost in the department's proverbial red tape. Your colleague notices the absence of the mandatory progress report and sends your postdoc a letter notifying him that he has been dismissed.

In such matters it is often hard to say what the colleague's motives were (envy, annoyance?), or whether there were actual motives and he had just been sloppy or indifferent. Of course, when asked, your colleague would claim the latter; but why would you believe him, even when he himself was convinced that this was a fair and true representation of his own (lack of) motives? Perhaps the only way to gain more certainty is to look in his brain when he retrieves the situation and see what is activated: the signature of anger, or envy , or some kind of default resting mode that is characteristic for lack of engagement? This approach may not be practically feasible in everyday life, but at least in the lab it can teach us a lot about what is actually going on. One possibility is that we get more enlightened about the subjective feeling that we often have, namely that there seems to be no difference at all between acting out of sloppiness or indifference and when the action is driven by malevolence.

11.1 WATCHING OTHERS: MUSCLES, MOTOR SYSTEM, AND CONFLICT DETECTION

In Chapter 9 we noted that events conventionally considered to be affective not only rapidly tax perceptual cortical mechanisms, but also recruit the brain and body motor system, including primary and secondary motor cortices, basal ganglia, and possibly the mirror neuron system. This was especially apparent when subjects were exposed to depictions of others' behavioural expressions that signalled motivational states such as joy or fear. These activations at brain level easily leak into subtle adjustments in muscle contraction, which may not even be noticeable with the naked eye or even by a camera, but can be revealed by sensitive recording of the electrical discharges that underlie muscle contraction.

As another example, consider the movie clips illustrated in Figure 11.1. When average college students view such clips, within half a second, and unbeknownst to themselves, they contract their muscles in accordance with the dynamically evolving expression they are watching (for details of the muscle and the procedure, refer to Chapter 9). In the study from which this example was taken, an acute dosage of the hormone testosterone significantly reduced muscle contraction patterns that were congruent with the observed expression (mimicry) (Hermans et al., 2006b). Remember from Section 9.2 that testosterone also reduces fear potentiated startle, a finding consistent with the quenching effects of testosterone on neural activation in the amygdala. Another interesting lead is that the strength of mimicry is positively-related to self-reported measures of empathy, the ability to sense, experience, or feel what others are sensing or feeling or experiencing (Sonnby–Borgström, 2002).

As Hermans and colleagues note, mimicry phenomena are consistent with interaction between limbic regions (amygdala, possibly also the insula) on the one hand, and the mirror

Figure 11.1

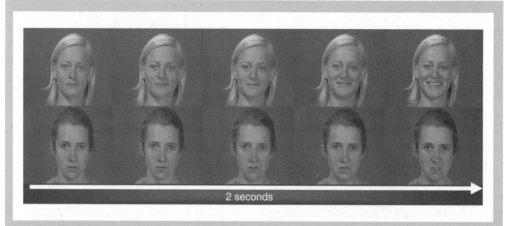

2 seconds

Within 2 seconds an initially neutral expression changes into one of happiness or anger or other emotion.
Illustrative face pictures by courtesy of Prof. Christian Keysers.

neuron system (MNS) on the other. The question is *how* amygdala and MNS interact to modulate the ability to sense what others experience. The distribution of testosterone receptors may provide a clue: at least in rats they are present in the amygdala hippocampus circuits (see Section 10.1), including surrounding regions of the neocortex (Sarkey et al., 2008). Also, we noted in Section 9.3 that direct links between testosterone and left–right cortical balance have not been established thus far. Together, these pieces of knowledge fit a model in which facial mimicry is instigated by the MNS, which in turn is driven by the amygdala (note that the reverse scenario would not predict mimicry effects of testosterone, assuming that there are no direct effects of testosterone on the MNS). This scenario would also allow for the amygdala to mediate certain affective aspects of empathy (e.g. sympathetic arousal), while feedback from the muscles to the brain may be instrumental in completing the full inter-subjective experience.

Watching others can also be associated with brain mechanisms that, at first, seem a little more prosaic. Observing others perform a task that is sufficiently difficult to induce both cortical signatures of covert incorrect decisions as well as overt performance errors, activates brain mechanisms that greatly overlap with those activated when the observer would have performed the task himself. One such task is the standard Eriksen flanker task (see Figures 2.7 and 4.11, and related text): average subjects produce a substantial number of errors in this task, which are accompanied by pronounced error signals from the anterior- and posterior-cingulate cortices (as explained in Section 4.1). Even on correct performance trials, lateralized readiness potentials (LRPs) from the motor cortex indicate that the wrong response was initially prepared at the level of the motor cortex, even when it converts to correct preparation in time to prevent an overt error. It turns out that people who watch other people making errors in a flanker task activate basically the same cortical mechanisms. Confronted with the other's erroneous response they develop LRPs themselves (just as they develop LRPs congruent with the correct response when that is observed). Moreover, they also emit a pronounced error signal, albeit only from the anterior, not from the posterior, cingulate

Figure 11.2

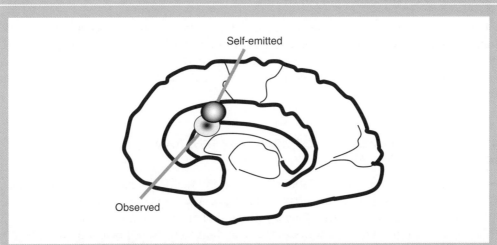

Schematic overview of equivalent dipoles as estimated with the BESA procedure for cortical activation associated with self-emitted and observed errors.
Slight displacement of the OBSERVED dipole illustrates misalignment between subjects' head space and that of the MNI template on to which the localization estimates where projected; however, this does not affect the relative positions of the two dipoles.

cortex (van Schie et al., 2004). Figure 11.2 shows the equivalent dipoles for the error-related negativity, as estimated for observed errors as well as self-emitted errors. Of note, the LRPs in the observers were not paralleled by any overt actions, or even sub-threshold muscle contractions, as recorded through EMG. It appears then that watching others make errors activates a dopamine governed response from the ACC; and, as discussed in Section 4.1, this ACC mechanism is supposed to signal to other structures, such as in the prefrontal cortex, the need to adjust the strength of connections in specific perception action pathways. What we see here is a mechanism for vicarious learning in the human brain.

Section 2.2 discussed how desynchronization of the mu rhythm, even in very young children, could be used as a reflection of MNS signals to the motor cortex. It is possible that a similar mechanism is also operating throughout in the above LRP study. This form of motor contagion is paralleled by error signals that may be instrumental in conveying a sense of disappointment about the unsuccessful actions of a conspecific. Independently of the subjective experience of the observer, the dopaminergic error mechanism may promote learning by observation of the actions of others. Other subcortical–cortical interactions, involving signals between the amygdala and the MNS, are instrumental in sensing another's experience by monitoring the other's expression of his experience.

A slightly different perspective on the role of the MNS in social cognition is based on Friston's unified brain theory (UBT) (from Bahrami et al., 2010). Briefly, UBT postulates that:

1. the brain continuously strives to optimize expectation and reduce surprise; surprising events are considered to be aversive and of negative value; therefore, value (experienced reward or punishment) is the inverse of surprise;

2. the brain does so by continuously adjusting either internal perceptual expectations or external perceptual data (through action).

From this perspective, the MNS represents action intentions from conspecifics that can be transformed into signals to the motor system. These in turn may represent preparation to go along with the observed actions, or to adjust in a more complementary manner to the expected action of the other (for instance, so as to result in the successful repulsion of an expected blow on the head).

11.2 TRUSTING OTHERS: A HORMONE FOR TRUST AND REDUCED BETRAYAL AVERSION?

In Section 8.3 and Box 10.2, a relationship between attentional suppression and subjective trustworthiness was described (Kiss et al., 2007). A first question is, how could typical attentional control mechanisms influence this kind of affective appreciation? One possibility refers to a comprehensive network in the brain termed the social neural network (SNN). The SNN comprises a plethora of cortical and subcortical regions, to be specified further in Section 11.3, that are activated by a diversity of social signals. It may be the mutual signals between these cortical areas and the amygdala especially that implement the association between attentional suppression of the representation of a face stimulus and the devaluation of that same face with respect to trustworthiness.

Following up on the previous section, testosterone has recently been shown to reduce trustworthiness ratings in relation to diverse photographs of faces (Bos et al., 2011). This begs the question whether there would be a role for the MNS, and perhaps even the facial muscle system, in trust. For example, trust judgement could rest on feedback from amygdala/MNS-driven muscle contractions during mimicry. Reduced mimicry under testosterone would reduce internal feedback signals that convey information about the state of mind of the other. In a manner of speaking, empathy is reduced, therefore also sympathy, as well as trust. These ideas are, as yet, speculative. The facts are however, that MNS-related emotional action, amygdala-related reflex potentiation and amygdala activation, as well as trust, are all reduced by testosterone. The positive side to this is that there is also a hormone that does almost exactly the opposite. This hormone goes under the name of oxytocin. It is often termed the trust hormone, and it has received a lot of scientific and popular attention over the last decade or so.

Although oxytocin travels through the body as a hormone, its workings in the brain rely on its release from axons in the hypothalamus so that it can bind to specific receptors in the amygdala (Insel et al., 1997), and possibly in structures such as the nucleus accumbens, something that may be suspected given certain experimental findings detailed below. The most celebrated case for oxytocin concerns its effect in versions of a trust experiment. Subjects were told that they could invest an amount of money in a business project that was governed by another subject (the trustee). The investment had a maximum profit of three times the original bid, but the true payback was completely dependent on the willingness of the trustee to share a fair part of the profit with the subject. In a first version of the experiment subjects decided on investments a number of times, without ever knowing what the yield had been. In this version the amounts of invested money were higher under oxytocin than under a placebo (Kosfeld et al., 2005).

Could this result be explained by an increased tendency for risky decisions caused by oxytocin? Another group of subjects was confronted with an identical payback schedule.

Figure 11.3

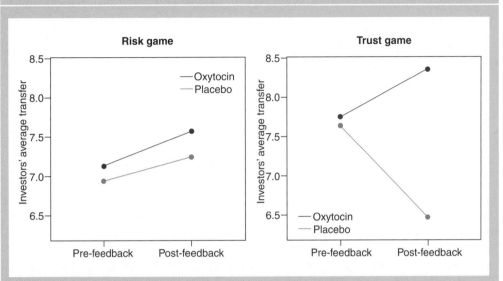

In the lottery (left), subjects only slightly increase their investments after having received somewhat discouraging feedback about what their previous investments had yielded. When these yields had been framed as the consequence of a trustee's decision in the trust game (right), subjects under placebo displayed a sharp decline in their investments, whereas subjects under oxytocin did not.

Source: Reprinted from Baumgartner et al. (2008) with permission from Elsevier.

However, in this case, they were told that the eventual profit was purely dependent on a random process (the lottery); there was no trustee, but the odds and risks were identical to those in the first experiment. In this version oxytocin made no difference with respect to the size of investments. Apparently, it is the tendency to share with others that is strengthened by oxytocin. Another perspective is that oxytocin reduces the aversion against, or the extent of anticipation of cheating by the trustee, or betrayal, as it was termed by these researchers.

In a third study subjects were told, after they had invested a number of times, that the trustees had refunded for only half the transactions. After being given this information the subjects had to make a new series of investment decisions. Subjects who had been administered a placebo substantially reduced their subsequent investments, whereas subjects under oxytocin did not reduce them at all (Figure 11.3) (Baumgartner et al., 2008). In contrast, in the lottery version, neither group reduced its investments after having been informed that only half their investments had yielded a payback (as was determined by a random algorithm). The deviant condition then is the placebo/trust condition: this is where people make decisions that are consistent with betrayal aversion. In the lottery version (Figure 11.3, left), in which there is no hint of a social transaction, betrayal aversion does not seem to be an influence; and neither does it in either oxytocin condition.

There is an alternative to the betrayal aversion theory. Subjects in the lottery version may think of that procedure being a true random process; therefore a negative result is not considered to be a reason for an investment reduction. In contrast, bad paybacks due to a fellow human being are considered predictive for future paybacks on subsequent investments, and this results in reduced investment. It is this short-term learning process due to negative feedback that leads to an adjustment of investment decisions. However, the impact of this mechanism is reduced by oxytocin, or perhaps we should say that oxytocin actually impairs this mechanism.

Inevitably we are wondering at this point whether oxytocin reduces brain response to the feedback in a manner that is directly visible. Indeed, BOLD responses associated with the feedback were substantially reduced under oxytocin, relative to feedback. Consistently with previous discussions of this error, or conflict, signal, this BOLD response was prominent in a part of the ACC that seems to be slightly anterior to the ones depicted in Figure 11.2. Hence, oxytocin appears to interfere with the transient dip in dopamine release somewhere in the chain between subcortical structures like the nucleus accumbens and the ACC.

A study outside the field of trust experiments yielded another telling result. Whereas in normal circumstances angry faces resulted in amygdala activation and happy faces did not, administration of oxytocin suppressed the amygdala response to fearful faces, but also turned the zero response to happy faces into a significant deactivation (Domes et al., 2007). Is seems that oxytocin reduces sensitivity to what others have in mind, and the capacity to learn from negative information about the intentions of others. From this viewpoint it is questionable whether oxytocin induces the kind of trust that is favourable for either the individual that takes it, or for others in that individual's environment.

11.3   LOATHING OTHERS: THE INSULA AND THE SOCIAL NEURAL NETWORK

Reconsider the example given in the introduction to this chapter: your colleague who instigates the dismissal of your postdoc because of a procedural slip. Whereas formerly you may have trusted this colleague, your attitude towards him after this incident might easily convert into quite the opposite. One possibility is that from now on, even the faintest thought about this colleague brings you to a mental state that is perhaps best represented by the facial expression depicted in Figure 9.4 (left panel).

The insular cortex, especially the anterior part of it, has featured in several sections of this book. It has been described as a kind of gustatory cortex that also responds to more symbolic instances of bad states: a variety of events, objects, or graphics, generally considered negative or downright aversive. As a mechanism that is not only somewhat complementary to that implemented in the amygdala but also greatly overlaps in terms of antecedent conditions for its activation, neurons in the insula represent primarily what is commonly referred to as disgust. The anterior insula is also consistently considered a major projection zone for signals from the majority of internal organs in the body, not in the least for those signals that convey the sense of nausea, however slight.

While at times this may be adaptive in the sense described in Section 10.3, it seems that in other contexts insula activation actually costs us, promoting irrational behaviour that is unfavourable to achieving obvious goals. A pertinent illustration of this principle has been offered in the context of the experiment paradigm referred to as the ultimatum game. The ultimatum game can be viewed as a convincing model for social disgust and is illustrated in Figure 11.4. Your partner, Keith, is represented by a photograph on a computer screen. At one time he makes you an offer to split evenly the ten dollars he has just received: he gets five, you get five. The majority of subjects accept this offer in the majority of cases. At other times Keith gets ten dollars but offers you two and keeps eight for himself. A substantial number of subjects now refuse this offer in a substantial number of cases (Sanfey et al., 2003). Although

Figure 11.4

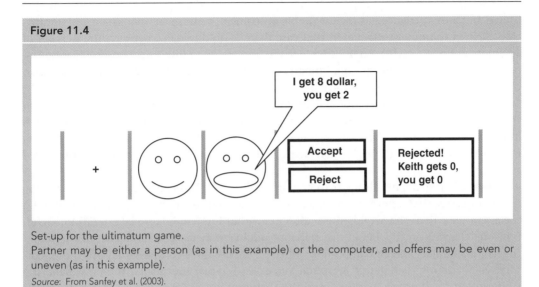

Set-up for the ultimatum game.
Partner may be either a person (as in this example) or the computer, and offers may be even or uneven (as in this example).
Source: From Sanfey et al. (2003).

Figure 11.5

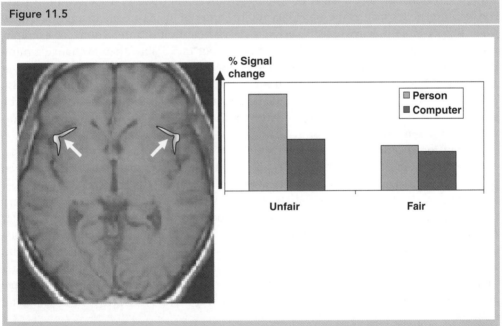

Approximate BOLD responses in the right insula to financial offers by either a person or a computer that might be considered either fair or unfair.
See Figure 3.22 for indication of the location of the insula along the ventral dorsal dimension.

it should be noted that rejecting the offer also results in a zero yield for Keith, these subjects are, in effect, repeatedly throwing away two dollars.

What is behind this, apparently self-defeating, strategy? Two things actually. First, the seemingly unfair offers are not often rejected when they are not associated with a human source, but are experienced as the inevitable outcome of running an inanimate and immovable piece of computer software; in that case there is no difference between the number of acceptances for fair versus unfair offers. Second, in parallel to resulting in a significant number of rejections, unfair offers from human conspecifics activate the insula, much more than computer offers do (see Figure 11.4).

Although certainly not a proof of causality, these findings are consistent with the notion that activation of the insula keeps us from making cold-blooded, rational decisions, such as just to take the money and run, whatever the context. This is especially apparent when the context involves another human being acting in a manner that might be considered unfair.

The insula is generally thought to be part of the SNN. If social cognition refers to cognitive processes that determine how we perceive, attend to, act within, and learn about a social context, then the SNN is the brain circuit that implements social cognition. Given previous chapters in this book, this network might easily cover a large part of the brain. Indeed, a summary of the components of the SNN includes ventromedial prefrontal cortex (see Section 8.4), superior temporal sulcus and gyrus, the insula, the amygdala, the fusiform gyrus (Chapters 3 and 8), and the temporal poles (Santos et al., 2010). Contexts for activating the SNN involve a certain degree of animatedness, which humans normally attribute to moving objects (such as when the movement appears to be self-propelled). Furthermore, nodes such as the amygdala and the anterior insula are increasingly activated when two or more moving objects spread a clear suggestion of interaction; for example, two spheres may move towards each other slowly but inexorably, then exchange a number of bumps, after which they stick together tightly and remain motionless (Santos et al., 2010). While this kind of interaction may seem disgusting to some individuals, it also underscores the point that has been made before, namely, that the idea of neurons in the amygdala and in the insula as being only responsive to negatively valued events or information is too limited.

As mentioned earlier this chapter, SNN and MNS may both, and in an interactive way, contribute to understanding the actions and mental states of others. The SNN has been postulated as crucial especially for fathoming the emotional aspect of others (Gallese et al., 2004). In the context of animatedness and interactiveness, a more complementary relationship has been described. While the SNN nodes, as discussed above, increased their activation with increases in animation and interaction, the putative MNS regions in the inferior frontal gyrus and the parietal cortex decreased their activation (Santos et al., 2010). Hence, it could be that when social cognition bears on more than just sensing what another individual is experiencing (and instead pertains to social interactions between multiple others), the mirror neuron system is actually giving way to the more extended social neural network.

11.4 WORKING WITH OTHERS: SOCIAL OSCILLATIONS

Social cognition refers to the processing of information pertaining to the behaviour and presumed mental experience of one or more conspecifics. In recent years researchers have increasingly focussed on aspects of social cognition and social behaviour that are relatively automatic, implicit, involuntary, and perhaps even unconscious. These phenomena are rooted in basic perceptual, action and attention mechanisms, such as reaching a consensus in psychophysical detection tasks, spontaneously coordinating each other's actions, or

Figure 11.6

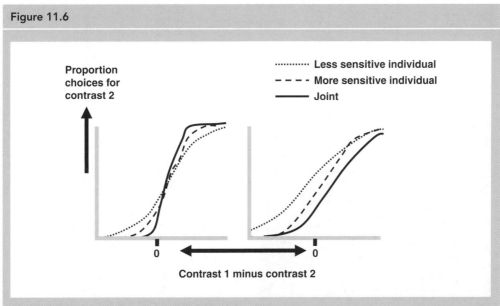

Representative individual decision functions for the more (striped) and less (dotted) sensitive participant in a dyad, as well as the pattern for the joint decision (solid trace).

Decisions are plotted as a function of the pop-out contrast difference between the second and the first interval display. Maximum sensitivity would be reflected in a step function with a transition from 0 to 1 at contrast difference zero.

automatically joining your attention to the direction in which a conspecific is focussed (e.g. based on a gaze cue).

Figure 11.6 presents an example of social psychophysics with respect to consensus (Bahrami et al., 2010). Participants are organized in dyads and must decide which of two successive displays contained a contrast pop-out. Within each dyad, individual decisions are made first, and then a joint decision. In Figure 11.6 decisions are plotted as a function of the pop-out contrast difference between the second and the first interval display. Maximum sensitivity would be reflected in a step function with a transition from zero choices for the second display to the maximum choices for the second display at contrast difference zero. On average, joint decisions (solid curves) are better (steeper function) than individual ones (the dotted and the striped traces), as they are in the dyad in the left panel. However, in some dyads one of the observers performed relatively weakly (dotted line in the right panel); in this particular case the collective decision pattern more or less resembles the pattern of the more sensitive observer.

These findings show that social processes can be tracked in the context of basic perception psychology and psychophysics. But consensus, coordination and commonality (the three Cs) as to what is deemed relevant should also be visible at a neurophysiological level. This would involve brain processes that underlie the three Cs and can also be assessed in contexts where there is no observable behaviour but questions of consensus or coordination are nevertheless crucial (just think of the necessary invisible coordination between a

Figure 11.7

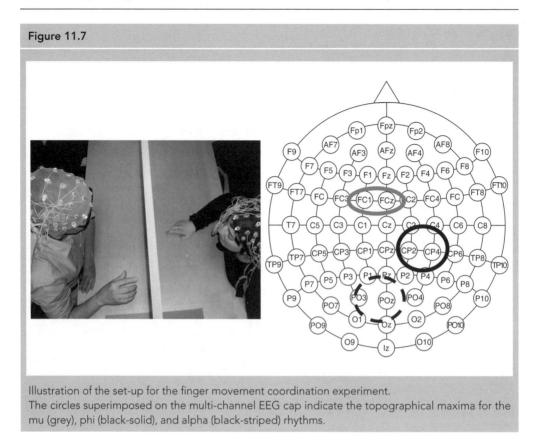

Illustration of the set-up for the finger movement coordination experiment.
The circles superimposed on the multi-channel EEG cap indicate the topographical maxima for the
mu (grey), phi (black-solid), and alpha (black-striped) rhythms.

midfielder intending a forward pass and the striker who needs to time his forward movements exactly so that he will get to the ball before the defenders and at the same time evades off-side). These brain processes would also be a valuable asset in situations or groups where consensus or coordination is severely lacking, and an objective diagnostic of possible causes is needed.

Consensus and coordination may often rely on benevolence or submissiveness in a part of the group. For example, if two persons have to cooperate, this may be realized by one of them in that he or she just follows the other (who is then, by definition, the leader). This feature was exploited in an as yet isolated study into the possible brain correlates of social coordination (Tognoli et al., 2007). These researchers capitalized on the idea that when social coordination emerges between two individuals, at least one of them should display behaviour that is critical for coordination to occur. Eight pairs of people each engaged in self-paced finger flexion–extension alternations. In a vision on condition they viewed each other's moving fingers, while in a vision off condition this was not possible. In five of the eight pairs vision on led to spontaneous synchronization of the movement, that is, the same frequency of flexion–extension alternations was adopted by both participants.

Concurrent EEG recordings revealed mu and alpha rhythms that waxed with vision off and waned with vision on (Figure 11.7; see also the discussion of the mu rhythm in Section 2.2). However, the more interesting rhythms were those that co-varied specifically during vision on with the extent of spontaneous synchronization. Figure 11.8 shows the extent of dominance over the right hemisphere within frequency bands in the 8 Hz to 13 Hz range. Alpha and mu have maxima at midline sites and therefore cancel out in the left minus right subtraction. However, two other spectral peaks are marked by a clear right hemisphere dominance, especially over central parietal regions. These were termed by the authors phi1 and phi2, together making up the phi complex. Both were pronounced only during the vision on condition. Phi1 was especially pronounced when finger movements were not synchronized, whereas phi2 was especially pronounced during synchronized movements (Tognoli et al., 2007). The right panel of Figure 11.8 illustrates how phi2 emerged only during vision on (20 s to 40 s), and specifically only during synchronized movement; it disappears when there is no coordination (at timepoint 3).

The authors speculate that the right lateralized central parietal signature of the phi components is consistent with generators in the parietal premotor/mirror neuron region. Specifically, phi2 would reflect the tuning of parietal mirror neurons to the observed finger movements of the partner, while phi1 may reflect the inhibition of these same mirror neurons, driven by signals from another part of the brain, and therefore adopting a slightly different oscillating frequency. This phi complex can serve as an index of individual tendencies to contribute to social coordination. This is especially useful in situations where such tendencies are not visible in overt behaviour, such as in the preparatory stages of a process that must eventually lead to a joint decision. More generally, it is simply fascinating to see how this kind of social psychology works in the human brain. Knowledge about these mechanisms in average healthy brains also provides clues for deficient mechanisms underlying a profound lack of coordination in social behaviour.

Figure 11.8

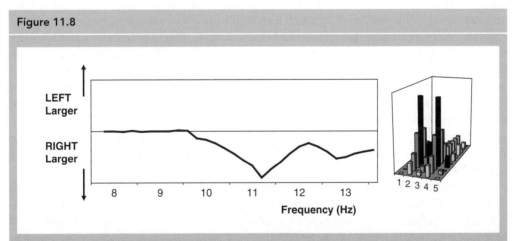

Left: the difference in signal strength or power (during vision on) between left (e.g. CP3) and right (e.g. CP4) hemisphere is plotted for the phi region in Figure 11.7, revealing two right-lateralized spectral components, phi1 and phi2.

Right: Simplified time-frequency spectrum. Values 1 to 5 represent arbitrary time units (e.g. ten seconds each). Vision off during 1st and 5th period; vision on in periods 2–4. The bars represent the time-varying signal-power values, with black corresponding to 12–13 Hz, and the lighter shades to correspondingly lower or higher frequency bands. At time point 3 there was a momentary interruption of synchronized movement, with a parallel suppression of phi2.

11.5   UNDERSTANDING OTHERS: LANGUAGE PROCESSING IN THE BRAIN

Plate XVIII shows how the human cortex deals with nouns and verbs, either during understanding, as in semantic categorization, or during production, as in picture naming (Crepaldi et al., 2011). As can be seen, these mechanisms are all over the brain. This probably, at least partly, reflects that semantic processing, the processing of the meaning of information (especially linguistic information), refers to representations that are activated in widely varying contexts. For example, not only does watching somebody else perform a specific act activate our own motor cortex (Section 11.1), but so does hearing or reading words like throw, hit or jump (see below).

This is a quite a different perspective from older models that mainly featured Broca's and Wernicke's area, and their interconnections, as the seat of language. Specifically, the older idea was that the posterior third frontal convolution (Broca, BA44), and the posterior superior temporal gyrus, anterior to the angular gyrus (Wernicke) in the left hemisphere implemented language production and language comprehension respectively. Then it turned out that brain damage in Broca's area also affected comprehension, especially of syntax and grammar, and that damage in Wernicke's area rendered speech formally correct but void of meaning and content (see Box 11.1). Furthermore, other brain areas also appeared to be involved in semantic processing. In Section 3.1 we encountered the N400 event-related potential, which reflects the brain's effort to integrate verbal information into the current semantic context. Intracranial recordings in humans strongly suggest that N400 is generated deep in the inferior temporal cortex, rather than in the superior temporal gyrus (Nobre et al., 1994; see Section 11.6 for further details).

In Section 4.3 we looked at activation of the ACC during the production of novel verbs in response to semantically related nouns. Plate XIX reveals the complete set of activations in that particular condition. PET contrasts between generating novel, but semantically adequate, verbs and just repeating the same verb, revealed activations not only in the ACC, but also at coordinates that overlapped with those of Wernicke's and Broca's areas. If we accept that it is indeed the activation of Broca's area which is revealed in the novel minus repeated contrast, then this may have several, partially mutually exclusive, implications. A first implication additionally addresses the fact that in the original study (Petersen et al., 1989) Broca was not activated merely by reading the nouns aloud (relative to passive viewing); so, since Broca was activated only by a semantically tinged language-production operation, this was an indication that not only is Broca's area involved in certain aspects of language comprehension (in addition to production), but also that it is involved in semantic aspects in particular (in Section 11.6 some evidence is discussed for Broca's involvement in semantic comprehension as well).

A second possible implication refers to the general involvement of the right *and* left inferior frontal convolutions, including Broca's area, in mechanisms of inhibition (see Section 4.4.5). That is, finding a suitable verb for a newly encountered noun involves rejecting and therefore suppressing numerous different options, a situation rich in conflict which may be instrumental in activating the ACC. A third implication is that Broca's area may be instrumental in maintaining a working memory representation of, in this case, the noun for which a suitable verb has to be found (note that this quite the opposite of a working memory representation of what has to be suppressed, as discussed in 4.4.5). This working memory representation is especially suggested by the event-related potential data depicted in Plate XIX: a quick (250 ms latency) activation of Broca, and a much later activation (650 ms) of Wernicke's area. This is compatible with the idea that the noun is represented in working memory for matching purposes during the search for the suitable verb. Similar working memory functions of Broca's area are discussed in Section 11.6.

This section has so far discussed distinct linguistic operations, such as syntactic and semantic processing. What can we say about the materials, the operandi, that these operations take as arguments? The discussion of Plate XVIII already hints at the possibility that there is no separate local box that contains all these representations, but rather that these representations reside in widespread areas of the brain, especially the cortex. Let's consider some dedicated studies. One looked at brain activity patterns during reading and separated the data according to what was read. For example, interactions with objects versus changes in goals, versus movement in space on the part of the main character were separated. The resulting activity patterns were informally compared to what is known in the literature about the corresponding activity patterns when individuals move or interact with objects or set goals themselves, or watch others doing it. There was a good global correspondence between reading about something on the one hand and doing it or viewing it on the other (Speer et al., 2009). For example, reading about navigating in space activated the frontal eye fields (BA6; Chapters 2 and 3); reading about object interaction activated the premotor and somatosensory hand areas; and setting goals activated area 46 of the dorsolateral prefrontal cortex (as well as Broca's area). As the authors put it, such embodiment for language comprehension 'may reflect a more general neural mechanism for grounding cognition in real-world experiences' (p. 998).

Something special during this, so-called, mental simulating as invoked when reading, has to do with individual personal history. Viewing a left hand movement will elicit right hemisphere motor cortex activity in almost anyone. However, when reading the words throw or kick, there is often no reference to a specific site of the body. It turns out that whichever hemisphere is predominantly activated depends on the relative strengths of contralateral connections between the motor cortices and the body. That is, reading such words activates the left hemisphere premotor cortex in right-handed individuals, but the right hemisphere premotor cortex in left-handed ones (Willems et al., 2010). Remember that in Sections 7.1 and 7.5 we discussed the phenomenon that imaging the performance of certain motor acts recruits the supplementary motor area (SMA), or even primary motor cortex (M1). In this particular reading case, M1 was not activated; in contrast, during explicit imagery in response to the same verbs, both the premotor cortex and M1 were activated (Willems et al., 2010). Thus, subtle differences between more implicit referrals to motor acts, such as during reading, and more explicit operations of imagery or retrieval may determine exactly how the motor system is involved in interactions with differences in individual development.

11.6   TALKING TO OTHERS: LANGUAGE AND MEMORY IN THE BRAIN

Intuitively, producing meaningful language can be conceived of as involving a mixture of applying learned procedures (as in Section 7.3) and retrieving information from (perhaps explicit) long-term memory. From this framework interesting observations have been made. These pertain especially to the well-studied domain of past tense verb inflection. As in many languages, English features regular past tense forms such as walked or cooked, as well as irregular past tense forms, such as thought or kept. Test subjects can be asked to detail past tense forms given either regular or irregular verb stems.

In such tests, non-fluent aphasics have a relative deficit for producing the regular past tense: they have a high incidence of saying looking or just look instead of looked. Their impairment in producing irregular past tenses is much less pronounced. Conversely, fluent aphasics have a relative (and relative it is) deficit in producing irregular past tenses: they have a high incidence of saying digged rather than dug (Ullman et al., 2005). A similar double dissociation was reported for patients with Alzheimer's disease versus patients with Parkinson's disease (Ullman et al., 1997), although the regular deficit was rather subtle in the Parkinson group especially.

Box 11.1   Aphasia

Aphasia stems from the ancient Greek *a phasic*, meaning without speech. The term is used to denote language impairments due to damage in typical (left hemisphere) language regions such as Broca's area and Wernicke's area (as described in Section 11.5), or in their mutual connections (sometimes referred to as conduction aphasia). Broca's original patient, Tan, was heavily impaired in producing linguistic utterances and led to the supposition that, so-called, Broca's aphasia entailed a specific speech production deficit. This idea was further reinforced when Wernicke described a patient with damage in the posterior superior temporal lobe, who presented with a profound deficit in language comprehension with apparently spared language production. However, closer examination of such patients revealed that Broca's aphasia was also marked by deficits in understanding relatively complex sentences, and a more general impairment in formal aspects of language production *and* comprehension has since been assumed. In parallel, damage in Wernicke's area also turned out to result in deficiencies in finding content words (anomia), and since then Wernicke's aphasia is seen as being characterized by more general problems in lexical, semantic and phonological aspects of language comprehension *and* production. Because of the relative fluency of the formal production aspects, Wernicke's is also termed fluent aphasia. In contrast, Broca's aphasia is often referred to as non-fluent aphasia.

These double dissociations have been taken as evidence for a dual process organization of past tense formation. Inflection of regular verbs can be accomplished by applying a specific rule, namely add suffix -ed. Inflection of irregular verbs cannot be accomplished in such a way and necessitates a search in the long-term memory store. Disturbed rule based inflection has been associated with non-fluent aphasia, and disturbed memory search inflection with fluent aphasia. Figure 11.9 shows typical damage associated with non-fluent and fluent aphasia. Non-fluent aphasia can be seen to be associated with an anterior region in the left inferior prefrontal cortex, including Broca's area (BA 44). In contrast, fluent aphasia involves damage in a left posterior, temporal parietal area, including Wernicke's area. Hence, rule based inflection is associated with an anterior system and memory search based inflection with a posterior system.

Of course this not the complete story. A double dissociation for rule based versus memory search based inflection was also observed for Parkinson's disease versus Alzheimer's disease. The latter is generally associated with primary damage to the temporal cortex, partially overlapping the smooth area in Figure 11.9. Parkinson's disease however, primarily involves damage in the basal ganglia (see Section 7.4), not the prefrontal cortex. It is possible to reconcile these differences in functional localization with respect to verb inflection by referring to the extensive loops between the frontal cortex regions and the basal ganglia, also described in Section 7.4. If signals to the frontal cortex from the basal ganglia are not adequate, then frontal cortex function must also be compromised. If anything, this goes to show that brain mechanisms underlying rule based inflection involve more than just signals within the prefrontal cortex.

Figure 11.9

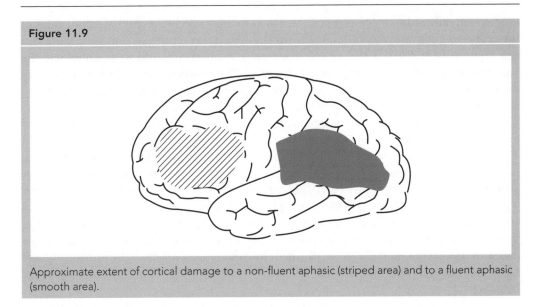

Approximate extent of cortical damage to a non-fluent aphasic (striped area) and to a fluent aphasic (smooth area).

In healthy individuals it may be different again. Plate XX shows estimated (LORETA) cortical generators for ERPs elicited by verb stems during a past tense production task (Lavric et al., 2001a, 2001b). Such source localization procedures provide an estimation of the approximate cortical regions, as well as of the strength of the signal across time, for each cortical generator. At a latency of around 300 ms, one cortical region was more active for regular verbs, and another one was more active for irregular verbs. As can be seen in Plate XX, irregular past tense production is associated with a region in the vicinity of Wernicke's area. However, regular past tense production goes with activation in a prefrontal region that is much more dorsal and anterior than the inferior frontal gyrus, and is even in the right hemisphere. Again then, for rule based procedures the relevant brain mechanisms may involve more than just Broca's area and its immediate surroundings. Nevertheless, all these data are consistent with a more anteriorly based rule based inflection system, and a more posteriorly based memory search based inflection system.

The preceding discussion focussed on a dual process account for the specific domain of past tense verb inflection, but this account has been applied to a much wider sphere, including most of the typical aspects of language (Ullman, 2001). First, it not only claims to account for issues of past tense verb production, but also for issues of comprehension. Second, the dual process account has also been applied outside the domain of verb inflection, for example to plural inflection and to article selection. In fact, the general version of this theory holds that language as a whole is based on two distinct systems. One is based in anterior brain regions and deals with everything that can be conceived of as being governed by a fixed and limited set of rules: the *procedural* aspect of language. The second system is based in posterior regions and is invoked whenever a long-term memory search is needed: to search for an irregular verb inflection, or a single word, or a typical way of phrasing. This second system is involved in the *declarative* aspect of language. The procedural system overlaps anatomically with the frontal cortex–basal ganglia network, extensively discussed in Section 7.4, and supports typical procedural aspects of language such as syntax and grammar.

People with difficulties in competences such as verb inflection often also have difficulties in the expression of learned procedures. The declarative system centres around Wernicke's area and supports typical declarative aspects of language, such as semantics and phonology. The border between semantics and syntax is not always clear however, as should be evident from the example of irregular verb inflection, which can be considered a grammatical operation that draws on the declarative system. Indeed, individuals who are weak in past tense inflection of irregular verbs, also have relative difficulties in working with semantic associations between non-verbal items (for example, visually represented events).

It is interesting to note the relationship between this procedural/declarative model and the original Broca/Wernicke theorems. While the latter originally postulated that language comprehension was posteriorly based and language production anteriorly, this soon gave way to a more nuanced model in which the posterior system supported lexical, phonological and semantic aspects, and the anterior aspects of syntax and grammar. This was also a better fit with the post-Broca/Wernicke observations that Wernicke's aphasia was also marked by a deficit in production (anomia, an impairment in coming up with the right words), whereas Broca's aphasia was also marked by a deficit in comprehending complex formal aspects of language.

This more subtle distinction has also received support from ERP studies on comprehension in healthy volunteers. The, so-called, semantic violation paradigm has already been mentioned in Section 3.1 (in relation to the attentional blink). Discrete word items that are at odds with the semantic context elicit an N400 (as in 'she ate pizza with *glue*', relative to 'she ate pizza with cheese'). Intracranial recordings in epilepsy patients have revealed a pronounced reflection of N400-like potentials in the anterior, temporal cortex part of the fusiform gyrus (Nobre et al., 1994). On the other hand, violations of the syntactic context ('I witnessed several *event*') do not elicit an N400, but rather a lateral anterior negativity (LAN), with a scalp distribution that is quite consistent with generators in the lateral prefrontal cortex. For example, Newman and colleagues reported that LAN was observed in response to incorrect regular past tense inflections (Newman et al., 2007). As may be expected from the foregoing discussion, LAN was not observed in response to incorrect irregular past tense inflections.

The procedural/declarative language theory takes the distinction between anterior and posterior language systems one step further. It implies that these dual language systems are integrated in more general purpose systems implemented in the same brain networks that support episodic long-term memory (see Sections 6.0 and 6.3.1), and procedural learning (see Sections 7.3 and 7.4). From this viewpoint, neurotransmitter systems that carry the signals within the general purpose networks could also be relevant to the two major subdomains of language processing. That is, dopaminergic mechanisms could be important for procedural language as far as regions like the inferior frontal gyrus and the basal ganglia are involved. For example, language deficits associated with the malfunctioning of anterior brain areas might benefit from treatment stimulants such as methylphenidate (as discussed in Section 4.4.4) or dopaminergic enhancers such as L-dopa (Section 7.4). On the other hand, cholinergic mechanisms could be relevant to declarative language to the extent that temporal lobe and temporal parietal regions are involved. Thus, cholinergic agonists, such as nicotine, may be an interesting possibility for language deficits based on compromised posterior cortex function (as already hinted at in Section 6.3.2). It is important to note that such considerations must be taken extremely carefully. It has been suggested that there is a balance between dopaminergic and cholinergic activity, and that this balance is implemented by a direct, mutually inhibitory interaction between the two systems (Vakalopoulos, 2006). Thus, giving one substance to boost a specific system could have the undesired side effect of hampering the other.

Another reason for reluctance with respect to these pharmacological applications is that there are some unresolved issues surrounding the dual procedural/declarative model. The evidence discussed thus far is mainly correlative in nature, and we cannot be at all sure that an overlap in global functional anatomy reflects an overlap in local neural micro-circuits. To that end, techniques such as fMRI or ERP adaptation (Box 5.1), or mutual capacity reduction such as discussed in Section 6.2.2 (in relation to working memory and selective attention), should be applied more systematically. Furthermore, the global picture is neither watertight nor completely understood. First, deficits in irregular participle formation have been reported in aphasics with anterior damage that have more of the signature of a disturbance in the declarative system (Penke et al., 1999). Second, semantic processing in healthy volunteers has been associated with anterior cortical areas, even in the vicinity of Broca's area. As discussed in Section 4.4.5, inferior frontal regions, ventrally and anteriorly to Broca's area, have been implicated in semantic processing (Hagoort, 2005; Poldrack et al., 1999). Third, and perhaps most importantly, declarative aspects of language mostly involve retrieval operations (or, in the terminology used above, memory search). As outlined in Section 10.5, although medial temporal structures, including the hippocampus, are activated in association with retrieval operations, the dominant idea about retrieval operations is that they are primarily implemented as interactions between the prefrontal cortex and other widespread cortical areas (see Plate XVIII), including the visual (Section 5.4), motor (Section 7.5) and temporal cortices, as well as the ventral visual pathway (Chapter 2). Thus, prefrontal mechanisms would be important for many of the putative declarative processes described above.

The involvement of prefrontal mechanisms in long-term episodic memory retrieval may be well be related to the building of a working memory representation of the retrieved information. On the other hand, a working memory mechanism that has recently been proposed as being a central characteristic of Broca's area, is instrumental in maintaining a representation of new information that has to be retained for a relatively short time (Rogalsky & Hickok, 2011). In sentence comprehension, this mechanism would be indispensable in dealing with instances of syntactic movement. In the famous example, 'John loved the woman that David pinched', syntactic movement refers to the fact that 'pinched' must be integrated with a relatively remote victim, namely the woman. Specifically, something called articulatory rehearsal would be implemented in at least part of Broca's area, and this kind of subvocal, articulatory-loop-like repetition would be essential for maintaining 'the woman' over the time it takes to perceive and process 'pinched'. In conclusion, it seems that at least in language comprehension, neurons in Broca's area implement a rule based syntactic mechanism that is necessary for intact semantic processing.

11.7 CONCLUDING REMARKS

Social cognition is rooted in brain circuits known to be involved in perception, (mirroring) action, attention, and especially in various kinds of affective processing and behaviour. This chapter presented examples of how a social context by itself can activate brain circuits that are also involved in information processing in isolated individuals. Such examples included motor system activation from merely watching others act, error monitoring system activation when watching others err, and disgust system activation associated with unfair offers specifically when made by another human being. Even the SNN consists mainly of components that were also manifest in other domains as listed above. The main job for social neuroscience then, is to decipher how old nodes wire up to form new circuits that may be specifically dedicated to social cognition; in other words, how social psychology is implemented in the brain. Something similar may hold for our understanding of language comprehension and production. The sections on language in the brain highlighted the activation of widespread cortical areas during reading or the production of words (e.g. the premotor cortex in relation to action verbs) and the possibility that typical language areas are part of more general purpose brain networks involved in procedural and declarative learning and working memory.

Questions

1. See Section 11.1 where interactions between the amygdala and the mirror neuron system are discussed. How would distinct characteristics of the left versus right hemisphere fit in here, and which additional cortical or subcortical regions would contribute? Refer to Section 9.3.
2. See Section 11.2. What would testosterone do to the insula and the social neural network?
3. Think of the social oscillations in Section 11.4. How could social interaction be modulated by signals from procedural learning systems (7.3, 7.4), especially when these are involved in compulsive behaviour (Section 9.4)?
4. See Section 11.6. It is stated that inflection of regular verbs can be accomplished by applying a specific rule, as in add suffix -ed, and that inflection of irregular verbs cannot be accomplished in such a way and necessitates searching in a long-term memory store. But how do our brains know that the verb is regular or irregular in the first place? Try to make up a scenario for the brain to solve this problem.
5. Think of patient H.M. (Section 6.0). How would he fare in tasks contrasting the more procedural versus the more declarative language systems?

References

Abdullaev, Y. G., & Posner, M. I. (1998). Event-related brain potential imaging of semantic encoding during processing single words. *NeuroImage, 7*(1), 1.

Abe, K. (2001). Modulation of hippocampal long-term potentiation by the amygdala: A synaptic mechanism linking emotion and memory. *The Japanese Journal of Pharmacology, 86*(1), 18–22.

Abercrombie, H. C., Kalin, N. H., Thurow, M. E., Rosenkranz, M. A., & Davidson, R. J. (2003). Cortisol variation in humans affects memory for emotionally laden and neutral information. *Behavioral Neuroscience, 117*(3), 505–516.

Abi-Dargham, A., Mawlawi, O., Lombardo, I., Gil, R., Martinez, D., Huang, Y., *et al.* (2002). Prefrontal dopamine D1 receptors and working memory in Schizophrenia. *The Journal of Neuroscience, 22*(9), 3708–3719.

Adolphs, R., Cahill, L., Schul, R., & Babinsky, R. (1997). Impaired declarative memory for emotional material following bilateral amygdala damage in humans. *Learning & Memory, 4*(3), 291–300.

Adolphs, R., Gosselin, F., Buchanan, T. W., Tranel, D., Schyns, P., & Damasio, A. R. (2005a). A mechanism for impaired fear recognition after amygdala damage. *Nature, 433*(7021), 68–72.

Adolphs, R., Tranel, D., & Buchanan, T. W. (2005b). Amygdala damage impairs emotional memory for gist but not details of complex stimuli. *Nature Neuroscience, 8*(4), 512–518.

Adolphs, R., Tranel, D., Damasio, H., & Damasio, A. (1994). Impaired recognition of emotion in facial expressions following bilateral damage to the human amygdala. *Nature, 372*(6507), 669–672.

Alexander, G. E., DeLong, M. R., & Strick, P. L. (1986). Parallel organization of functionally segregated circuits linking basal ganglia and cortex. *Annual Review of Neuroscience, 9*(1), 357–381.

Allport, D. A. (1989). Visual attention. In M. I. Posner (Ed.), *Foundations of Cognitive Science*, 631–682. Cambridge, MA: MIT Press.

Amaral, D. G., Price, J. L., Pitkänen, A., & Carmichael, S. T. (1992). Anatomical organization of the primate amygdaloid complex. In J. Aggleton (Ed.), *The Amygdala*, 1–66. New York: Wiley-Liss.

Anderson, A. K., & Phelps, E. A. (2001). Lesions of the human amygdala impair enhanced perception of emotionally salient events. *Nature, 411*(6835), 305–309.

Anderson, M. C., Ochsner, K. N., Kuhl, B., Cooper, J., Robertson, E., Gabrieli, S. W., *et al.* (2004). Neural systems underlying the suppression of unwanted memories. *Science, 303*(5655), 232–235.

Apps, R., & Garwicz, M. (2005). Anatomical and physiological foundations of cerebellar information processing. *Nature Reviews Neuroscience, 6*(4), 297–311.

Armony, J. L., & Dolan, R. J. (2002). Modulation of spatial attention by fear-conditioned stimuli: An event-related fMRI study. *Neuropsychologia, 40*(7), 817–826.

Aron, A. R., Behrens, T. E., Smith, S., Frank, M. J., & Poldrack, R. A. (2007). Triangulating a cognitive control network using diffusion-weighted magnetic resonance imaging (MRI) and functional MRI. *The Journal of Neuroscience, 27*(14), 3743–3752.

Aron, A. R., Dowson, J. H., Sahakian, B. J., & Robbins, T. W. (2003a). Methylphenidate improves response inhibition in adults with attention-deficit/hyperactivity disorder. *Biological Psychiatry, 54*(12), 1465–1468.

Aron, A. R., Fletcher, P. C., Bullmore, E. T., Sahakian, B. J., & Robbins, T. W. (2003b). Stop-signal inhibition disrupted by damage to right inferior frontal gyrus in humans. *Nature Neuroscience, 6*(2), 115–116.

Aron, A. R., & Poldrack, R. A. (2006). Cortical and subcortical contributions to stop signal response inhibition: Role of the subthalamic nucleus. *The Journal of Neuroscience, 26*(9), 2424–2433.

Aston-Jones, G., Chen, S., Zhu, Y., & Oshinsky, M. L. (2001). A neural circuit for circadian regulation of arousal. *Nature Neuroscience, 4*(7), 732–738.

Aston-Jones, G., Rajkowski, J., & Cohen, J. (1999). Role of locus coeruleus in attention and behavioral flexibility. *Biological Psychiatry, 46*(9), 1309–1320.

Attwell, D., Buchan, A., Charpak, S., Lauritzen, M., Macvicar, B., & Newman, E. (2010). Glial and neuronal control of brain blood flow. *Nature, 468*, 232–243.

Attwell, D., & Iadecola, C. (2002). The neural basis of functional brain imaging signals. *Trends in Neurosciences, 25*, 621–625.

Awh, E., Anllo-Vento, L., & Hillyard, S. A. (2000). The role of spatial selective attention in working memory for locations: Evidence from event-related potentials. *Journal of Cognitive Neuroscience* 12, 840–847.

Awh, E., Jonides, J., & Reuter-Lorenz, P. A. (1998). Rehearsal in spatial working memory. *Journal of Experimental Psychology: HPP* 24, 780–790.

Baas, J., Grillon, C., Böcker, K., Brack, A., Morgan, C., Kenemans, L., *et al.* (2002a). Benzodiazepines have no effect on fear-potentiated startle in humans. *Psychopharmacology, 161*(3), 233–247.

Baas, J. M. P. (2001). Startles, drugs, and brain waves: A human model for fear and anxiety. *Thesis, Utrecht University*.

Baas, J. M. P., Kenemans, J. L., Böcker, K. B. E., & Verbaten, M. N. (2002b). Threat-induced cortical processing and startle potentiation. *NeuroReport, 13*, 133–137.

Baddeley, A.E. (1995). Working memory or working attention? In Baddeley, A.E, and Lawrence Weiskrantz (Eds), *Attention: Selection, Awareness and Control. A Tribute to Donald Broadbent,* 152–170. Oxford University Press.

Bahrami, B., Olsen, K., Latham, P. E., Roepstorff, A., Rees, G., & Frith, C. D. (2010). Optimally interacting minds. *Science, 329*(5995), 1081–1085.

Band, G. P. H., van der Molen, M. W., & Logan, G. D. (2003). Horse-race model simulations of the stop-signal procedure. *Acta Psychologica, 112*(2), 105.

Bao, S., Chan, V. T., & Merzenich, M. M. (2001). Cortical remodelling induced by activity of ventral tegmental dopamine neurons. *Nature, 412*(6842), 79.

Bartholomeusz, C. F., Box, G., van Rooy, C., & Nathan, P. J. (2003). The modulatory effects of dopamine D1 and D2 receptor function on object working memory in humans 10.1177/0269881103017001688. *Journal of Psychopharmacology, 17*(1), 9–15.

Baumgartner, T., Heinrichs, M., Vonlanthen, A., Fischbacher, U., & Fehr, E. (2008). Oxytocin shapes the neural circuitry of trust and trust adaptation in humans. *Neuron, 58*(4), 639–650.

Bechara, A. (2004). The role of emotion in decision-making: Evidence from neurological patients with orbitofrontal damage. *Brain and Cognition, 55*(1), 30–40.

Bechara, A., Damasio, A. R., Damasio, H., & Anderson, S. W. (1994). Insensitivity to future consequences following damage to human prefrontal cortex. *Cognition, 50*(1–3), 7–15.

Bechara, A., Damasio, H., Damasio, A. R., & Lee, G. P. (1999). Different contributions of the human amygdala and ventromedial prefrontal cortex to decision-making. *The Journal of Neuroscience, 19*(13), 5473–5481.

Bechara, A., Damasio, H., Tranel, D., & Damasio, A. R. (1997). Deciding advantageously before knowing the advantageous strategy. *Science, 275*(5304), 1293–1295.

Bechara, A., Tranel, D., Damasio, H., Adolphs, R., Rockland, C., & Damasio, A. R. (1995). Double dissociation of conditioning and declarative knowledge relative to the amygdala and hippocampus in humans. *Science, 269*(5227), 1115–1118.

Bedard, A.-C., Ickowicz, A., Logan, G. D., Hogg-Johnson, S., Schachar, R., & Tannock, R. (2003). Selective inhibition in children with attention-deficit hyperactivity disorder off and on stimulant medication. *Journal of Abnormal Child Psychology, 31*(3), 315–327.

Bekker, E. M., Kenemans, J. L., Hoeksma, M. R., Talsma, D., & Verbaten, M. N. (2005a). The pure electrophysiology of stopping. *International Journal of Psychophysiology, 55*(2), 191–198.

Bekker, E. M., Overtoom, C. C. E., Kooij, J. J. S., Buitelaar, J. K., Verbaten, M. N., & Kenemans, J. L. (2005b). Disentangling deficits in adults with attention-deficit/hyperactivity disorder. *Archives of General Psychiatry, 62*(10), 1129–1136.

Bekkering, H., & Neggers, S. F. W. (2002). Visual search is modulated by action intentions. *Psychological Science, 13*(4), 370–374.

Berger, H. (1929). Uber das elektroenkephalogramm des menschen. *Archiv fur Psychiatrie Nervenkrankheiten, 87*, 527–570.

Berridge, K. C., Robinson, T. E., & Aldridge, J. W. (2009). Dissecting components of reward: 'liking', 'wanting', and learning. *Current Opinion in Pharmacology, 9*(1), 65–73.

Bisiach, E., & Luzzatti, C. (1978). Unilateral neglect of representational space. *Cortex, 14*, 129–133.

Boas, D., Dale, A., & Franceschin, M. (2004). Diffuse optical imaging of brain activation: Approaches to optimizing image sensitivity, resolution, and accuracy. *Neuroimage, 231*(Suppl.), S275–288.

Bos, P. A., Terburg, D., & van Honk, J. (2011). Testosterone decreases trust in socially naive humans. *Proceedings of the National Academy of Sciences, 107*(22), 9991–9995.

Botvinick, M., Nystrom, L. E., Fissell, K., Carter, C. S., & Cohen, J. D. (1999). Conflict monitoring versus selection-for-action in anterior cingulate cortex. *Nature, 402*(6758), 179–181.

Bouquet, C. A., Shipley, T. F., Capa, R. L., & Marshall, P. J. (2011). Motor contagion: Goal-directed actions are more contagious than non-goal-directed actions. *Experimental Psychology, 58*(1), 71–78.

Boyd, L. A., Edwards, J. D., Siengsukon, C. S., Vidoni, E. D., Wessel, B. D., & Linsdell, M. A. (2009). Motor sequence chunking is impaired by basal ganglia stroke. *Neurobiology of Learning and Memory, 92*(1), 35–44.

Braver, T. S., & Cohen, J. D. (1999). Dopamine, cognitive control, and schizophrenia: The gating model. *Progress in Brain Research, 121*, 327–349.

Broadbent, D. E. (1958). *Perception and communication*: Pergamon.

Brown, J. W., & Braver, T. S. (2005). Learned predictions of error likelihood in the anterior cingulate cortex. *Science, 307*(5712), 1118–1121.

Buchanan, T. W., & Lovallo, W. R. (2001). Enhanced memory for emotional material following stress-level cortisol treatment in humans. *Psychoneuroendocrinology, 26*(3), 307–317.

Buchanan, T. W., Tranel, D., & Adolphs, R. (2004). Anteromedial temporal lobe damage blocks startle modulation by fear and disgust. *Behavioral Neuroscience, 118*(2), 429–437.

Büchel, C., Morris, J., Dolan, R. J., & Friston, K. J. (1998). Brain systems mediating aversive conditioning: An event-related fMRI study. *Neuron, 20*(5), 947–957.

Bullmore, E., & Sporns, O. M. (2009). Complex brain networks: Graph theoretical analysis of structural and functional systems. *Nature Reviews Neuroscience, 10*(3), 186–198.

Bush, G., Luu, P., & Posner, M. I. (2000). Cognitive and emotional influences in anterior cingulate cortex. *Trends in Cognitive Sciences, 4*(6), 215–222.

Buzsaki, G. (2006). *Rhythms of the brain*: Oxford Press.

Bymaster, F. P., Katner, J. S., Nelson, D. L., Hemrick-Luecke, S. K., Threlkeld, P. G., Heiligenstein, J. H., et al. (2002). Atomoxetine increases extracellular levels of norepinephrine and dopamine in prefrontal cortex of rat: A potential mechanism for efficacy in attention deficit/hyperactivity disorder. *Neuropsychopharmacology, 27*, 699–711.

Cahill, L., Prins, B., Weber, M., & McGaugh, J. L. (1994). [beta]-adrenergic activation and memory for emotional events. *Nature, 371*(6499), 702–704.

Calder, A. J., Beaver, J. D., Davis, M. H., Van Ditzhuijzen, J., Keane, J., & Lawrence, A. D. (2007). Disgust sensitivity predicts the insula and pallidal response to pictures of disgusting foods. *European Journal of Neuroscience, 25*(11), 3422–3428.

Candy, B., Jones, L., Williams, R., Tookman, A., & King, M. (2008). Psychostimulants for depression. *Cochrane Database of Systematic Reviews, 2009* (Apr 16).

Carey, M. R., & Wade, G. R. (2009). Noradrenergic control of associative synaptic plasticity by selective modulation of instructive signals. *Neuron, 62*, 112–122.

Carter, C. S., Braver, T. S., Barch, D. M., Botvinick, M. M., Noll, D., & Cohen, J. D. (1998). Anterior cingulate cortex, error detection, and the online monitoring of performance. *Science, 280*(5364), 747–749.

Carter, C. S., Macdonald, A. M., Botvinick, M., Ross, L. L., Stenger, V. A., Noll, D., *et al.* (2000). Parsing executive processes: Strategic vs. Evaluative functions of the anterior cingulate cortex. *Proceedings of the National Academy of Sciences USA, 97*(4), 1944–1948.

Cavedini, P., Riboldi, G., D'Annucci, A., Belotti, P., Cisima, M., & Bellodi, L. (2002). Decision-making heterogeneity in obsessive-compulsive disorder: Ventromedial prefrontal cortex function predicts different treatment outcomes. *Neuropsychologia, 40*(2), 205–211.

Chamberlain, S. R., del Campo, N., Dowson, J., Müller, U., Clark, L., Robbins, T. W., *et al.* (2007). Atomoxetine improved response inhibition in adults with attention deficit/hyperactivity disorder. *Biological Psychiatry, 62*(9), 977–984.

Chamberlain, S. R., Hampshire, A., Müller, U., Rubia, K., Campo, N. d., Craig, K., *et al.* (2009). Atomoxetine modulates right inferior frontal activation during inhibitory control: A pharmacological functional magnetic resonance imaging study. *Biological Psychiatry, 65*(7), 550–555.

Chamberlain, S. R., Menzies, L., Hampshire, A., Suckling, J., Fineberg, N. A., del Campo, N., *et al.* (2008). Orbitofrontal dysfunction in patients with obsessive-compulsive disorder and their unaffected relatives. *Science, 321*(5887), 421–422.

Chamberlain, S. R., Muller, U., Blackwell, A. D., Clark, L., Robbins, T. W., & Sahakian, B. J. (2006). Neurochemical modulation of response inhibition and probabilistic learning in humans 10.1126/science.1121218. *Science, 311*(5762), 861–863.

Chaudhuri, A. (1990). Modulation of the motion aftereffect by selective attention. *Nature*, 60–62.

Chelazzi, L., & Corbetta, M. (1999). Cortical mechanisms of visuospatial attention in the primate brain. In M. Gazzaniga (Ed.), *The New Cognitive Neurosciences*, 667–686 Cambridge, MIT.

Cherry, E. C. (1953). Some experiments on the recognition of speech, with one and with two ears. *Journal of the Acoustical Society of America, 25*, 975–979.

Cherry, S., & Phelps, M. (2002). Imaging brain function with positron emission tomography. In A. Toga & J. Mazziotta (Eds.), *Brain mapping: The methods*. Academic Press: Waltham, Massachusetts.

Chiu, P. H., Lohrenz, T. M., & Montague, P. R. (2008). Smokers' brains compute, but ignore, a fictive error signal in a sequential investment task. *Nature Neuroscience, 11*(4), 514–520.

Christianson, S.-Ã. k., & Loftus, E. F. (1991). Remembering emotional events: The fate of detailed information. *Cognition & Emotion, 5*(2), 81–108.

Chun, M. M., & Potter, M. C. (1995). A two-stage model for multiple target detection in rapid serial visual presentation. *Journal of Experimental Psychology: Human Perception and Performance, 21*(1), 109.

Clark, C. R., Geffen, G. M., & Geffen, L. B. (1989). Catecholamines and the covert orientation of attention in humans. *Neuropsychologia, 27*(2), 131–139.

Clark, C. R., Geffen, G. M., & Geffen, L. B. (1986). Role of monoamine pathways in the control of attention: Effects of droperidol and methylphenidate in normal adult humans. *Psychopharmacology, 90*(1), 28–34.

Clark, L., Blackwell, A. D., Aron, A. R., Turner, D. C., Dowson, J., Robbins, T. W., *et al.* (2007). Association between response inhibition and working memory in adult ADHD: A link to right frontal cortex pathology? *Biological Psychiatry, 61*(12), 1395.

Clark, V. P., & Hillyard, S. A. (1996). Spatial selective attention affects early extrastriate but not striate components of the visual evoked potential. *Journal of Cognitive Neuroscience, 8*, 387–402.

Cohen, D., & Cuffin, B. (1991). EEG versus MEG localization accuracy: Theory and experiment. Winter. *Brain Topography, 4*, 95–103.

Cohen, J. D., Romero, R. D., Servan-Schreiber, D., & Farah, M. J. (1994). Mechanisms of spatial attention: The relation of macrostructure to microstructure in parietal neglect. *Journal of Cognitive Neuroscience, 6*(4), 377–387.

Compton, R. J. (2000). Ability to disengage attention predicts negative affect. *Cognition and Emotion, 14*(3), 401–415.

Cools, R., Roberts, A. C., & Robbins, T. W. (2008). Serotoninergic regulation of emotional and behavioural control processes. *Trends in Cognitive Sciences, 12*(1), 31–40.

Cools, R., Sheridan, M., Jacobs, E., & D'Esposito, M. (2007). Impulsive personality predicts dopamine-dependent changes in frontostriatal activity during component processes of working memory. *The Journal of Neuroscience, 27*(20), 5506–5514.

Corbetta, M., Kincade, M., & Shulman, G.L. (2002). Neural systems for visual orienting and their relationships to spatial working memory. *Journal of Cognitive Neuroscience, 14*(3), 508–523.

Corbetta, M., Kincade, J. M., Ollinger, J. M., McAvoy, M. P., & Shulman, G. L. (2000). Voluntary orienting is dissociated from target detection in human posterior parietal cortex. *Nature Neuroscience, 3*(3), 292–297.

Corbetta, M., Miezin, F. M., Dobmeyer, S., Shulman, G. L., & Petersen, S. E. (1991). Selective and divided attention during visual discriminations of shape, color, and speed: Functional anatomy by positron emission tomography. *Journal of Neuroscience, 11*(8), 2383–2402.

Corbetta, M., & Shulman, G. L. (2002). Control of goal-directed and stimulus-driven attention in the brain. *Nature Reviews Neuroscience, 3*, 201–214.

Coull, J. T., Nobre, A. C., & Frith, C. D. (2001). The noradrenergic alpha2 agonist clonidine modulates behavioural and neuroanatomical correlates of human attentional orienting and alerting. *Cerebral Cortex, 11*(1), 73–84.

Cowan, N. (1995). *Attention and memory: An integrated framework.* Oxford: Oxford University Press.

Crepaldi, D., Berlingeri, M., Paulesu, E., & Luzzatti, C. (2011). A place for nouns and a place for verbs? A critical review of neurocognitive data on grammatical-class effects. *Brain and Language, 116*(1), 33–49.

Critchley, H. D., Mathias, C. J., Josephs, O., O'Doherty, J., Zanini, S., Dewar, B.-K., *et al.* (2003). Human cingulate cortex and autonomic control: Converging neuroimaging and clinical evidence. *Brain, 126*(10), 2139–2152.

Culham, J., Danckert, S., Souza, J. X. D., Gati, J., Menon, R., & Goodale, M. (2003). Visually guided grasping produces fMRI activation in dorsal but not ventral stream brain areas. *Experimental Brain Research, V153*(2), 180–189.

Curio, G. N., Jussi Numminen, Veikko Jousmäki, & Riitta Hari (2000). Speaking modifies voice-evoked activity in the human auditory cortex. *Human Brain Mapping, 9*(4), 183–191.

Czigler, I., Balazs, L., & Winkler, I. (2002). Memory-based detection of task-irrelevant visual changes. *Psychophysiology, 39*(6), 869–873.

Czigler, I., Weisz, J., & Winkler, I. (2006a). ERPS and deviance detection: Visual mismatch negativity to repeated visual stimuli. *Neuroscience Letters, 401*(1–2), 178–182.

Czigler, I., Winkler, I., Pato, L., Varnagy, A., Weisz, J., & Balazs, L. (2006b). Visual temporal window of integration as revealed by the visual mismatch negativity event-related potential to stimulus omissions. *Brain Research, 1104*(1), 129–140.

D'Esposito, M., Aguirre, G. K., Zarahn, E., Ballard, D., Shin, R. K., & Lease, J. (1998). Functional MRI studies of spatial and nonspatial working memory. *Cognitive Brain Research, 7*(1), 1.

Dalley, J. W., McGaughy, J., O'Connell, M. T., Cardinal, R. N., Levita, L., & Robbins, T. W. (2001). Distinct changes in cortical acetylcholine and noradrenaline efflux during contingent and noncontingent performance of a visual attentional task. *Journal of Neuroscience, 21*(13), 4908–4914.

Damoiseaux, J., & Greicius, M. (2009). Greater than the sum of its parts: A review of studies combining structural connectivity and resting-state functional connectivity. *Brain Structure and Function, 213*(6), 525–533.

Dapretto, M., Davies, M. S., Pfeifer, J. H., Scott, A. A., Sigman, M., Bookheimer, S. Y., *et al.* (2006). Understanding emotions in others: Mirror neuron dysfunction in children with autism spectrum disorders. *Nature Neuroscience, 9*(1), 28–30.

Darby, D. G., Nobre, A. C., Thangaraj, V., Edelman, R., Mesulam, M. M., & Warach, S. (1996). Cortical activation in the human brain during lateral saccades using epistar functional magnetic resonance imaging. *NeuroImage, 3*(1), 53.

Davidson, R. J. (2003). Affective neuroscience and psychophysiology: Toward a synthesis. *Psychophysiology, 40*(5), 655–665.

Davidson, R. J., Pizzagalli, D., Nitschke, J. B., & Putnam, K. (2002). Depression: Perspectives from affective neuroscience. *Annual Review of Psychology, 53*(1), 545–574.

Davidson, R. J., Putnam, K. M., & Larson, C. L. (2000). Dysfunction in the neural circuitry of emotion regulation – a possible prelude to violence. *Science, 289*, 591–594.

De Bruijn, E. R. A., Hulstijn, W., Verkes, R. J., Ruigt, G. S. F., & Sabbe, B. G. C. (2004). Drug-induced stimulation and suppression of action monitoring in healthy volunteers. *Psychopharmacology, 177*(1), 151–160.

De Bruijn, E. R. A., Sabbe, B. G. C., Hulstijn, W., Ruigt, G. S. F., & Verkes, R. J. (2006). Effects of antipsychotic and antidepressant drugs on action monitoring in healthy volunteers. *Brain Research, 1105*(1), 122–129.

De Fockert, J.W., Rees. G., Frith, C.D., & Lavie, N. (2001). The role of working memory in selective attention. *Science, 291*, 1803–1806,

de Gelder, B., Snyder, J., Greve, D., Gerard, G., & Hadjikhani, N. (2004). Fear fosters flight: A mechanism for fear contagion when perceiving emotion expressed by a whole body. *Proceedings of the National Academy of Sciences USA, 101*(47), 16701–16706.

De Houwer, J., Thomas, S., & Baeyens, F. (2001). Associative learning of likes and dislikes: A review of 25 years of research on human evaluative conditioning. *Psychological Bulletin, 127*(6), 853–869.

De Jong, R., Coles, M. G., Logan, G. D., & Gratton, G. (1990). In search of the point of no return: The control of response processes. *Journal of Experimental Psychology: Human Perception and Performance, 16*(1), 164–182.

De Jong, R., Coles, M. G. H., & Logan, G. D. (1995). Strategies and mechanisms in nonselective and selective inhibitory motor control. *Journal of Experimental Psychology: Human Perception and Performance, 21*(3), 498–511.

De Jong, R., Wierda, M., Mulder, G., & Mulder, L. J. M. (1988). Use of partial stimulus information in response processing. *Journal of Experimental Psychology: Human Perception and Performance, 14*(4), 682–692.

de Quervain, D. J. F., & Margraf, J. (2008). Glucocorticoids for the treatment of post-traumatic stress disorder and phobias: A novel therapeutic approach. *European Journal of Pharmacology, 583*(2–3), 365–371.

De Sanctis, P., Molholm, S., Shpaner, M., Ritter, W., & Foxe, J. J. (2009). Right hemispheric contributions to fine auditory temporal discriminations: High-density electrical mapping of the duration mismatch negativity (MMN). *Frontiers in Integrative Neuroscience, 3*, 5.

De Sonneville, L.M.J., Njiokiktjien, C., & Bos, H. (1994) Methylphenidate and information processing. *Journal of Clinical and Experimental Neuropsychology, 16*, 877–897.

Dean, P., Porrill, J., Ekerot, C.-F., & Jorntell, H. (2010). The cerebellar microcircuit as an adaptive filter: Experimental and computational evidence. *Nature Reviews Neuroscience, 11*(1), 30–43.

Dehaene, S., Posner, M. I., & Tucker, D. M. (1994). Localization of a neural system for error detection and compensation. *Psychological Science, 5*(5), 303–305.

Dennett, D. C. (1991). *Consciousness explained.* Little, Brown and Co.

Desimone, R. (1996). Neural mechanisms for visual memory and their role in attention. *Proceedings of the National Academy of Sciences USA, 93*(24), 13494–13499.

Deubel, H., & Schneider, W. X. (1996). Saccade target selection and object recognition: Evidence for a common attentional mechanism. *Vision Research, 36*(12), 1827–1837.

Deutsch, J. A., & Deutsch, D. (1963). Attention: Some theoretical considerations. *Psychological Review, 70*(1), 80–90.

Di Lollo, V., Kawahara, J.-i., Shahab Ghorashi, S. M., & Enns, J. T. (2005). The attentional blink: Resource depletion or temporary loss of control? *Psychological Research, 69*(3), 191.

di Michele, F., Prichep, L., John, E. R., & Chabot, R. J. (2005). The neurophysiology of attention-deficit/hyperactivity disorder. *International Journal of Psychophysiology Electrophysiology in Attention-Deficit/Hyperactivity Disorder, 58*(1), 81–93.

Di Pellegrino, G., Fadigo, L., Fogassi, L., Gallese, V., & Rizolatti, G. (1992). Understanding motor events: A neurophysiological study. *Experimental Brain Research, 91,* 176–180.

Dinse, H. R., Ragert, P., Pleger, B., Schwenkreis, P., & Tegenthoff, M. (2003). Pharmacological modulation of perceptual learning and associated cortical reorganization. *Science, 301*(5629), 91.

Dolcos, F., LaBar, K. S., & Cabeza, R. (2004a). Dissociable effects of arousal and valence on prefrontal activity indexing emotional evaluation and subsequent memory: An event-related fMRI study. *NeuroImage, 23*(1), 64–74.

Dolcos, F., LaBar, K. S., & Cabeza, R. (2004b). Interaction between the amygdala and the medial temporal lobe memory system predicts better memory for emotional events. *Neuron, 42*(5), 855–863.

Dolcos, F., LaBar, K. S., & Cabeza, R. (2005). Remembering one year later: Role of the amygdala and the medial temporal lobe memory system in retrieving emotional memories. *Proceedings of the National Academy of Sciences USA, 102*(7), 2626–2631.

Domes, G., Heinrichs, M., Gläscher, J., Büchel, C., Braus, D. F., & Herpertz, S. C. (2007). Oxytocin attenuates amygdala responses to emotional faces regardless of valence. *Biological Psychiatry, 62*(10), 1187–1190.

Doyon, J. (2008). Motor sequence learning and movement disorders. *Current Opinion in Neurology, 2,* 478–483.

Driver, J., & Frith, C. (2000). Shifting baselines in attention research. *Nature Reviews Neuroscience, 1*(2), 147–148.

Driver, J., & Mattingley, J. B. (1998). Parietal neglect and visual awareness. *Nature Reviews Neuroscience, 1*(1), 17.

Duhamel, J. R., Colby, C., & Goldberg, M. (1992). The updating of the representation of visual space in parietal cortex by intended eye movements. *Science, 255*(5040), 90–92.

Duncan, J. (2001). An adaptive coding model of neural function in prefrontal cortex. *Nature Reviews Neuroscience, 2*(11), 820.

Eimer, M., & Holmes, A. (2007). Event-related brain potential correlates of emotional face processing. *Neuropsychologia, 45*(1), 15–31.

Eisenberg, M. J., Filion, K. B., Yavin, D., Belisle, P., Mottillo, S., Joseph, L., *et al.* (2008). Pharmacotherapies for smoking cessation: A meta-analysis of randomized controlled trials. *Canadian Medical Association Journal, 179*(2), 135–144.

Eldar, S., Yankelevitch, R., Lamy, D., & Bar-Haim, Y. (2010). Enhanced neural reactivity and selective attention to threat in anxiety. *Biological Psychology, 85*(2), 252–257.

Endrass, T., Klawohn, J., Schuster, F., & Kathmann, N. (2008). Overactive performance monitoring in obsessive-compulsive disorder: ERP evidence from correct and erroneous reactions. *Neuropsychologia, 46*(7), 1877–1887.

Enticott, P. G., Ogloff, J. R. P., & Bradshaw, J. L. (2008). Response inhibition and impulsivity in schizophrenia. *Psychiatry Research, 157*(1–3), 251–254.

Epping-Jordan, M. P., Watkins, S. S., Koob, G. F., & Markou, A. (1998). Dramatic decreases in brain reward function during nicotine withdrawal. *Nature, 393*(6680), 76–79.

Epstein, R., & Kanwisher, N. (1998). A cortical representation of the local visual environment. *Nature, 392*(6676), 598–601.

Ernst, M., & Fudge, J. L. (2009). A developmental neurobiological model of motivated behavior: Anatomy, connectivity and ontogeny of the triadic nodes. *Neuroscience & Biobehavioral Reviews, 33*(3), 367–382.

Fabiani, M., Karis, D., & Donchin, E. (1986). P300 and recall in an incidental memory paradigm. *Psychophysiology, 23*(3), 298–308.

Falkenstein, M., Hohnsbein, J., Hoormann, J., & Blanke, L. (1991). Effects of crossmodal divided attention on late ERP components. II. Error processing in choice reaction tasks. *Electroencephalography and Clinical Neurophysiology, 78*(6), 447–455.

Farah, M. J. (1989). The neural basis of mental imagery. *Trends in Neurosciences, 12*(10), 395–399.

Feinstein, J. S., Adolphs, R., Damasio, A., & Tranel, D. (2011). The human amygdala and the induction and experience of fear. *Current Biology, 21*, 34–38.

Fellows, L. K. (2007). The role of orbitofrontal cortex in decision making. *Annals of the New York Academy of Sciences, 1121*(1), 421–430.

Fellows, L. K., & Farah, M. J. (2005). Is anterior cingulate cortex necessary for cognitive control? *Brain, 128*(4), 788–796.

Fisher, S. E., Francks, C., McCracken, J. T., McGough, J. J., Marlow, A. J., MacPhie, I. L., *et al.* (2002). A genomewide scan for loci involved in attention-deficit/hyperactivity disorder. *American Journal of Human Genetics, 70*(5), 1183–1196.

Fitzgerald, K. D., Welsh, R. C., Gehring, W. J., Abelson, J. L., Himle, J. A., Liberzon, I., *et al.* (2005). Error-related hyperactivity of the anterior cingulate cortex in obsessive-compulsive disorder. *Biological Psychiatry, 57*(3), 287–294.

Floden, D., & Stuss, D. T. (2006). Inhibitory control is slowed in patients with right superior medial frontal damage. *Journal of Cognitive Neuroscience, 18*(11), 1843–1849.

Ford, J. M., & Mathalon, D. H. (2005). Corollary discharge dysfunction in schizophrenia: Can it explain auditory hallucinations? *International Journal of Psychophysiology, 58*(2–3), 179–189.

Ford, J. M., Mathalon, D. H., Kalba, S., Whitfield, S., Faustman, W. O., & Roth, W. T. (2001). Cortical responsiveness during talking and listening in schizophrenia: an event-related brain potential study. *Biological Psychiatry, 50*(7), 540–549.

Ford, J. M., Mathalon, D. H., Whitfield, S., Faustman, W. O., & Roth, W. T. (2002). Reduced communication between frontal and temporal lobes during talking in schizophrenia. *Biological Psychiatry, 51*(6), 485–492.

Fox, P., Mintun, M., Raichle, M., & Herscovitch, P. (1984). A noninvasive approach to quantitative functional brain mapping with H2 (15)o and positron emission tomography. *Journal of Cerebral Blood Flow and Metabolics, 4*, 329–333.

Frijda, N. H. (1988). The laws of emotion. *American Psychologist, 43*(5), 349–358.

Furey, M. L., Pietrini, P., & Haxby, J. V. (2000). Cholinergic enhancement and increased selectivity of perceptual processing during working memory. *Science, 290*(5500), 2315–2319.

Fuster, J. M., Bauer, R. H., & Jervey, J. P. (1985). Functional interactions between inferotemporal and prefrontal cortex in a cognitive task. *Brain Research, 330*(2), 299–307.

Gable, P. A., & Harmon-Jones, E. (2010a). The effect of low versus high approach-motivated positive affect on memory for peripherally versus centrally presented information. *Emotion, 10*(4), 599–603.

Gable, P. A., & Harmon-Jones, E. (2010b). Late positive potential to appetitive stimuli and local attentional bias. *Emotion, 10*(3), 441–446.

Gallese, V., Fadiga, L., Fogassi, L., & Rizzolatti, G. (1996). Action recognition in the premotor cortex. *Brain, 119*(2), 593–609.

Gallese, V., Keysers, C., & Rizzolatti, G. (2004). A unifying view of the basis of social cognition. *Trends in Cognitive Sciences, 8*(9), 396–403.

Gallinat, J., Kunz, D., Senkowski, D., Kienast, T., Seifert, F., Schubert, F., *et al.* (2006). Hippocampal glutamate concentration predicts cerebral theta oscillations during cognitive processing. *Psychopharmacology, 187*(1), 103–111.

Garraux, G., Peigneux, P., Carson, R. E., & Hallett, M. (2007). Task-related interaction between basal ganglia and cortical dopamine release. *The Journal of Neuroscience, 27*(52), 14434–14441.

Garrido, M. I., Kilner, J. M., Stephan, K. E., & Friston, K. J. (2009). The mismatch negativity: A review of underlying mechanisms. *Clinical Neurophysiology, 120*(3), 453.

Gauggel, S., Rieger, M., & Feghoff, T. A. (2004). Inhibition of ongoing responses in patients with Parkinson's disease. *Journal of Neurology, Neurosurgery & Psychiatry, 75*(4), 539–544.

Gazzaniga, M., S., Ivry, R. B., & Mangun, G. R. (1998). *Cognitive Neuroscience: The Biology of Mind* (1st ed.). New York: W.W. Norton.

Gazzaniga, M., S., Ivry, R. B., & Mangun, G. R. (2002). *Cognitive Neuroscience: The Biology of Mind* (2nd ed.). New York: W.W. Norton.

Gazzaniga, M. S., Ivry, R. B., & Mangun, G. R. (2008). *Cognitive Neuroscience: The Biology of Mind* (3rd ed.). New York: W.W. Norton.

Gehring, W. J., Goss, B., Coles, M. G. H., Meyer, D. E., & Donchin, E. (1993). A neural system for error detection and compensation. *Psychological Science, 4*(6), 385–390.

Gerwig, M., Dimitrova, A., Kolb, F. P., Maschke, M., Brol, B., Kunnel, A., *et al.* (2003). Comparison of eyeblink conditioning in patients with superior and posterior inferior cerebellar lesions. *Brain, 126*(1), 71–94.

Gevins, A., Leong, H., Smith, M., Le, J., & Du, R. (1995). Mapping cognitive brain function with modern high-resolution electroencephalography. *Trends in Neurosciences, 18*(10), 429–436.

Giesbrecht, B., Woldorff, M. G., Song, A. W., & Mangun, G. R. (2003). Neural mechanisms of top-down control during spatial and feature attention. *Neuroimage, 19*(3), 496–512.

Gilbert, C. D., Sigman, M., & Crist, R. E. (2001). The neural basis of perceptual learning. *Neuron, 31*(5), 681–697.

Glasgow, R., Gaglio, B., Estabrooks, P., Marcus, A., Ritzwoller, D., Smith, T., *et al.* (2009). Long-term results of a smoking reduction program. *Medical Care, 47*, 115–120.

Glimcher, P. W. (2003). *Decisions, Uncertainty and the Brain: The Science of Neuroeconomics.* Cambridge, MA: MIT Press.

Goodale, M. A., & Milner, A. D. (1992). Separate visual pathways for perception and action. *Trends in Neurosciences, 15*(1), 20–25.

Goodale, M. A., Milner, A. D., Jakobson, L. S., & Carey, D. P. (1991). A neurological dissociation between perceiving objects and grasping them. *Nature, 349*(6305), 154–156.

Gordon, B., Allen, E. E., & Trombley, P. Q. (1988). The role of norepinephrine in plasticity of visual cortex. *Progress in Neurobiology, 30*(2–3), 171–191.

Grafton, S. T., Hazeltine, E., & Ivry, R. B. (1998). Abstract and effector-specific representations of motor sequences identified with PET. *The Journal of Neuroscience, 18*(22), 9420–9428.

Grent-'t-Jong, T., & Woldorff, M. G. (2007). Timing and sequence of brain activity in top-down control of visual-spatial attention. *PLoS Biology, 5*(1), e12.

Grillon, C. (2002). Startle reactivity and anxiety disorders: Aversive conditioning, context, and neurobiology. *Biological Psychiatry, 52*(10), 958–975.

Grillon, C. (2008). Models and mechanisms of anxiety: Evidence from startle studies. *Psychopharmacology, 199*, 421–437.

Grillon, C. (2009). D-cycloserine facilitation of fear extinction and exposure-based therapy might rely on lower-level, automatic mechanisms. *Biological Psychiatry, 66*(7), 636–641.

Grillon, C., & Baas, J. (2003). A review of the modulation of the startle reflex by affective states and its application in psychiatry. *Clinical Neurophysiology, 114*(9), 1557–1579.

Grillon, C., Baas, J. M. P., Pine, D. S., Lissek, S., Lawley, M., Ellis, V., *et al.* (2006). The benzodiazepine alprazolam dissociates contextual fear from cued fear in humans as assessed by fear-potentiated startle. *Biological Psychiatry, 60*(7), 760–766.

Grillon, C., Cordova, J., Levine, L. R., & Morgan, I., Charles A. (2003). Anxiolytic effects of a novel group ii metabotropic glutamate receptor agonist (ly354740) in the fear-potentiated startle paradigm in humans. *Psychopharmacology, 168*(4), 446–454.

Grillon, C., & Morgan III, C. A. (1999). Fear-potentiated startle conditioning to explicit and contextual cues in gulf war veterans with posttraumatic stress disorder. *Journal of Abnormal Psychology, 108*(1), 134–142.

Grilly, D. M. (2006). *Drugs and human behavior.* Boston: Pearson.

Groves, P. M., & Thompson, R. F. (1970). Habituation: A dual-process theory. *Psychological Review, 77*(5), 419.

Hagoort, P. (2005). On Broca, brain, and binding: A new framework. *Trends in Cognitive Sciences, 9*, 416–423.

Hajcak, G., McDonald, N., & Simons, R. F. (2003). To err is autonomic: Error-related brain potentials, ANS activity, and post-error compensatory behavior. *Psychophysiology, 40*(6), 895–903.

Halsband, U., & Lange, R. K. (2006). Motor learning in man: A review of functional and clinical studies. *Journal of Physiology-Paris, 99*(4–6), 414–424.

Hamann, S. (2001). Cognitive and neural mechanisms of emotional memory. *Trends in Cognitive Sciences, 5*(9), 394–400.

Hamann, S. B., Ely, T. D., Grafton, S. T., & Kilts, C. D. (1999). Amygdala activity related to enhanced memory for pleasant and aversive stimuli. *Nature Neuroscience, 2*(3), 289–293.

Hammer, A., Kordon, A., Heldmann, M., Zurowski, B., & Münte, T. F. (2009). Brain potentials of conflict and error-likelihood following errorful and errorless learning in obsessive-compulsive disorder. *PLoS ONE, 4*(8), e6553.

Handy, T. C., Grafton, S. T., Shroff, N. M., Ketay, S., & Gazzaniga, M. S. (2003). Graspable objects grab attention when the potential for action is recognized. *Nature Neuroscience, 6*(4), 421–427.

Hari, R., Forss, N., Avikainen, S., Kirveskari, E., Salenius, S., & Rizzolatti, G. (1998). Activation of human primary motor cortex during action observation: A neuromagnetic study. *Proceedings of the National Academy of Sciences, 95*(25), 15061–15065.

Harmon-Jones, C., Schmeichel, B. J., Mennitt, E., & Harmon-Jones, E. (2011). The expression of determination: Similarities between anger and approach-related positive affect. *Journal of Personality and Social Psychology, 100*(1), 172–181.

Harmon-Jones, E., Gable, P. A., & Peterson, C. K. (2010). The role of asymmetric frontal cortical activity in emotion-related phenomena: A review and update. *Biological Psychology, 84*(3), 451–462.

Harmon-Jones, E., & Peterson, C. K. (2009). Supine body position reduces neural response to anger evocation. *Psychological Science (Wiley-Blackwell), 20*(10), 1209–1210.

Harter, M. R., & Aine, C. J. (1984). Brain mechanisms of visual selective attention. In R. Parasuraman, & D. R. Davies (Eds), *Varieties of Attention*, 293–321. London: Academic Press.

Harter, M. R., & Anllo-Vento, L. (1991). Visual-spatial attention: Preparation and selection in children and adults. *Electroencephalography and Clinical Neurophysiology Supplement, 42*, 183–194.

Harter, M. R., Miller, S. L., Price, N. J., LaLonde, M. E., & Keyes, A. L. (1989). Neural processes involved in directing attention. *Journal of Cognitive Neuroscience, 1*, 223–237.

Heiser, M., Iacoboni, M., Maeda, F., Marcus, J., & Mazziotta, J. C. (2003). The essential role of Broca's area in imitation. *European Journal of Neuroscience, 17*(5), 1123–1128.

Heinze, H. J., Mangun, G. R., Burchert, W., Hinrichs, H., Scholz, M., Munte, T. F., *et al.* (1994). Combined spatial and temporal imaging of brain activity during visual selective attention in humans. *Nature, 372*(6506), 543–546.

Heldmann, M., Markgraf, U., Rodríguez-Fornells, A., & Münte, T. F. (2008). Brain potentials reveal the role of conflict in human errorful and errorless learning. *Neuroscience Letters, 444*(1), 64–68.

Hermans, E. J., Putman, P., Baas, J. M., Koppeschaar, H. P., & van Honk, J. (2006a). A single administration of testosterone reduces fear-potentiated startle in humans. *Biological Psychiatry, 59*(9), 872–874.

Hermans, E. J., Putman, P., & van Honk, J. (2006b). Testosterone administration reduces empathetic behavior: A facial mimicry study. *Psychoneuroendocrinology, 31*(7), 859–866.

Hillebrand, A., Singh, K., Holliday, I., Furlong, P., & Barnes, G. (2005). A new approach to neuroimaging with magnetoencephalography. *Human Brain Mapping, 25*, 199–211.

Hillyard, S. A., Hink, R. F., Schwent, V. L., & Picton, T. W. (1973). Electrical signs of selective attention in the human brain. *Science, 182*(108), 177–180.

Hillyard, S. A., Vogel, E. K., & Luck, S. J. (1998). Sensory gain control (amplification) as a mechanism of selective attention: Electrophysiological and neuroimaging evidence. *Philosophical Transactions of the Royal Society: Biological Sciences, 353*(1373), 1257–1270.

Hobson, J. A. (1992). Sleep and dreaming: Induction and mediation of REM sleep by cholinergic mechanisms. *Current Opinion in Neurobiology, 2*(6), 759–763.

Hochberg, L. R., Serruya, M. D., Friehs, G. M., Mukand, J. A., Saleh, M., Caplan, A. H., *et al.* (2006). Neuronal ensemble control of prosthetic devices by a human with tetraplegia. *Nature, 442*(7099), 164–171.

Hodgkin, A., & Huxley, A. (1952). A quantitative description of membrane current and its application to conduction and excitation in nerve. *Journal of Physiology, 117*, 500–544.

Hofman, D., & Schutter, D. J. L. G. (2009). Inside the wire: Aggression and functional interhemispheric connectivity in the human brain. *Psychophysiology, 46*(5), 1054–1058.

Hofmann, S. G., Meuret, A. E., Smits, J. A. J., Simon, N. M., Pollack, M. H., Eisenmenger, K., *et al.* (2006). Augmentation of exposure therapy with D-cycloserine for social anxiety disorder. *Archives of General Psychiatry, 63*(3), 298–304.

Holroyd, C. B., & Coles, M. G. H. (2002). The neural basis of human error processing: Reinforcement learning, dopamine, and the error-related negativity. *Psychological Review, 109*(4), 679–709.

Hommel, B., Kessler, K., Schmitz, F., Gross, J., Akyürek, E., Shapiro, K., *et al.* (2006). How the brain blinks: Towards a neurocognitive model of the attentional blink. *Psychological Research, 70*(6), 425.

Hopf, J. M., & Mangun, G. R. (2000). Shifting visual attention in space: An electrophysiological analysis using high spatial resolution mapping. *Clinical Neurophysiology, 111*(7), 1241–1257.

Hopfinger, J. B., Buonocore, M. H., & Mangun, G. R. (2000). The neural mechanisms of top–down attentional control. *Nature Neuroscience, 3*(3), 284–291.

Hopfinger, J. B., & Mangun, G. R. (1998). Reflexive attention modulates processing of visual stimuli in human extrastriate cortex. *Psychological Science, 9*, 441–447.

Huang-Pollock, C. L., & Nigg, J. T. (2003). Searching for the attention deficit in attention deficit hyperactivity disorder: The case of visuospatial orienting. *Clinical Psychology Review, 23*(6), 801–830.

Hyder, F., Patel, A., Gjedde, A., Rothman, D., Behar, K., & Shulman, R. (2006). Neuronal–glial glucose oxidation and glutamatergic–gabaergic function. *Journal of Cerebral Blood Flow and Metabolism, 26*, 865–877.

Iacoboni, M., & Dapretto, M. (2006). The mirror neuron system and the consequences of its dysfunction. *Nature Reviews Neuroscience 7*(12), 942–951.

Iacoboni, M., Woods, R. P., Brass, M., Bekkering, H., Mazziotta, J. C., & Rizzolatti, G. (1999). Cortical Mechanisms of Human Imitation. *Science, 286*(5449), 2526–2528.

Insel, T. R., Young, L., & Wang, Z. (1997). Central oxytocin and reproductive behaviours. *Reviews of Reproduction, 2*, 28–37.

Jackson, D. C., Mueller, C. J., Dolski, I., Dalton, K. M., Nitschke, J. B., Urry, H. L., *et al.* (2003). Now you feel it, now you don't: Frontal brain electrical asymmetry and individual differences in emotion regulation. *Psychological Science (Wiley-Blackwell), 14*(6), 612–617.

Jiang, Y., & Kanwisher, N. (2003a). Common neural mechanisms for response selection and perceptual processing. *Journal of Cognitive Neuroscience, 15*(8), 1095–1110.

Jiang, Y., & Kanwisher, N. (2003b). Common neural substrates for response selection across modalities and mapping paradigms. *Journal of Cognitive Neuroscience, 15*(8), 1080–1094.

Jiménez, L. (2008). Taking patterns for chunks: Is there any evidence of chunk learning in continuous serial reaction-time tasks? *Psychological Research, 72*(4), 387–396.

Jongen, E. M. M., Smulders, F. T. Y., Ranson, S. M. G., Arts, B. M. G., & Krabbendam, L. (2007). Attentional bias and general orienting processes in bipolar disorder. *Journal of Behavior Therapy and Experimental Psychiatry, 38*(2), 168.

Jonkman, L. M., van Melis, J. J. M., Kemner, C., & Markus, C. R. (2007). Methylphenidate improves deficient error evaluation in children with ADHD: An event-related brain potential study. *Biological Psychology, 76*(3), 217–229.

Kahneman, D., & Treisman, A. (1984). Changing views of attention and automaticity. In R. Parasuraman, D. R. Davies, & J. Beatty (Eds), *Varieties of Attention*, 29–61. New York: Academic Press.

Kandel, E. R., Schwarz, J. H., & Jessel, T. M. (1991). *Principles of Neural Science*. New York: Elsevier.

Kanwisher, N., McDermott, J., & Chun, M. M. (1997). The fusiform face area: A module in human extrastriate cortex specialized for face perception. *The Journal of Neuroscience, 17*(11), 4302–4311.

Karabanov, A., Cervenka, S., de Manzano, Ö., Forssberg, H., Farde, L., & Ullén, F. (2010). Dopamine D2 receptor density in the limbic striatum is related to implicit but not explicit movement sequence learning. *Proceedings of the National Academy of Sciences, 107*(16), 7574–7579.

Karnath, H.-O., Ferber, S., & Himmelbach, M. (2001). Spatial awareness is a function of the temporal not the posterior parietal lobe. *Nature, 411*(6840), 950.

Karpicke, J. D., & Roediger, H. L. (2008). The critical importance of retrieval for learning. *Science, 319*(5865), 966–968.

Kenemans, J. L., Baas, J. M. P., Mangun, G. R., Lijffijt, M., & Verbaten, M. N. (2000). On the processing of spatial frequencies as revealed by evoked-potential source modeling. *Clinical Neurophysiology, 111*(6), 1113–1123.

Kenemans, J. L., Bekker, E. M., Lijffijt, M., Overtoom, C. C. E., Jonkman, L. M., & Verbaten, M. N. (2005). Attention deficit and impulsivity: Selecting, shifting, and stopping. *International Journal of Psychophysiology, 58*(1), 59–70.

Kenemans, J. L., Grent-'t-Jong, T., & Verbaten, M. N. (2003). Detection of visual change: Mismatch or rareness? *NeuroReport., 14*, 1239–1243.

Kenemans, J. L., Hebly, W., van den Heuvel, E., & Grent-'t-Jong, T. (2010). Moderate alcohol disrupts a mechanism for detection of rare events in human visual cortex. *Journal of Psychopharmacology, 24*(6), 839–845.

Kenemans, J. L., Lijffijt, M., Camfferman, G., & Verbaten, M. N. (2002). Split-second sequential selective activation in human secondary visual cortex. *Journal of Cognitive Neuroscience, 14*(1), 48–61.

Kenemans, J. L., Smulders, F. T. Y., & Kok, A. (1995). Selective processing of two-dimensional visual stimuli in young and old subjects: electrophysiological analysis. *Psychophysiology, 32*, 108–120.

Kensinger, E. A., & Corkin, S. (2004). Two routes to emotional memory: Distinct neural processes for valence and arousal. *Proceedings of the National Academy of Sciences USA, 101*(9), 3310–3315.

Kerns, J. G., Cohen, J. D., MacDonald, A. W., 3rd, Cho, R. Y., Stenger, V. A., & Carter, C. S. (2004). Anterior cingulate conflict monitoring and adjustments in control. *Science, 303*(5660), 1023–1026.

Kilgard, M. P., & Merzenich, M. M. (1998). Cortical map reorganization enabled by nucleus basalis activity. *Science, 279*(5357), 1714.

Kim, C.-Y., & Blake, R. (2005). Psychophysical magic: Rendering the visible 'invisible'. *Trends in Cognitive Sciences, 9*(8), 381.

Kimura, M., Katayama, J., Ohira, H., & Schröger, E. (2009). Visual mismatch negativity: New evidence from the equiprobable paradigm. *Psychophysiology, 46*(2), 402–409.

Kindt, M., Soeter, M., & Vervliet, B. (2009). Beyond extinction: Erasing human fear responses and preventing the return of fear. *Nature Neuroscience, 12*(3), 256–258.

Kirsch, W., Sebald, A., & Hoffmann, J. (2010). RT patterns and chunks in SRT tasks: A reply to Jiménez (2008). *Psychological Research, 74*(3), 352–358.

Kiss, M., Goolsby, B. A., Raymond, J. E., Shapiro, K. L., Silvert, L., Nobre, A. C., *et al.* (2007). Efficient attentional selection predicts distractor devaluation: Event-related potential evidence for a direct link between attention and emotion. *Journal of Cognitive Neuroscience, 19*(8), 1316–1322.

Klingberg, T., Fernell, E., Olesen, P. J., Johnson, M., Gustafsson, P., Dahlström, K., *et al.* (2005). Computerized training of working memory in children with ADHD – a randomized, controlled trial. *Journal of the American Academy of Child & Adolescent Psychiatry, 44*(2), 177–186.

Kohler, S., Paus, T., Buckner, R. L., & Milner, B. (2004). Effects of left inferior prefrontal stimulation on episodic memory formation: a two-stage fMRI-rTMS study. *Journal of Cognitive Neuroscience, 16*(2), 178–188.

Konishi, S., Nakajima, K., Uchida, I., Kameyama, M., Nakahara, K., Sekihara, K., *et al.* (1998). Transient activation of inferior prefrontal cortex during cognitive set shifting. *Nature Neuroscience, 1*(1), 80–84.

Kosfeld, M., Heinrichs, M., Zak, P. J., Fischbacher, U., & Fehr, E. (2005). Oxytocin increases trust in humans. *Nature, 435*(7042), 673–676.

Koster, E. H. W., Crombez, G., Van Damme, S., Verschuere, B., & De Houwer, J. (2004). Does imminent threat capture and hold attention? *Emotion, 4*(3), 312–317.

Kringelbach, M. L. (2005). The human orbitofrontal cortex: Linking reward to hedonic experience. *Nature Reviews Neuroscience, 6*(9), 691–702.

Kringelbach, M. L., & Rolls, E. T. (2004). The functional neuroanatomy of the human orbitofrontal cortex: Evidence from neuroimaging and neuropsychology. *Progress in Neurobiology, 72*(5), 341–372.

Kuhlmann, S., Kirschbaum, C., & Wolf, O. T. (2005). Effects of oral cortisol treatment in healthy young women on memory retrieval of negative and neutral words. *Neurobiology of Learning and Memory, 83*(2), 158–162.

Kumari, V., Kaviani, H., Raven, P. W., Gray, J. A., & Checkley, S. A. (2001). Enhanced startle reactions to acoustic stimuli in patients with obsessive-compulsive disorder. *American Journal of Psychiatry, 158*(1), 134–136.

Kushner, M. G., Kim, S. W., Donahue, C., Thuras, P., Adson, D., Kotlyar, M., et al. (2007). D-cycloserine augmented exposure therapy for obsessive-compulsive disorder. *Biological Psychiatry, 62*(8), 835–838.

Kwak, Y., Müller, M. L. T. M., Bohnen, N. I., Dayalu, P., & Seidler, R. D. (2010). Effect of dopaminergic medications on the time course of explicit motor sequence learning in Parkinson's disease. *Journal of Neurophysiology, 103*(2), 942–949.

Kwong, H., Belliveau, J., Chesler, D., Goldberg, I., Weiskoff, R., Poncelet, B., et al. (1992). Dynamic magnetic resonance imaging of human brain activity during primary sensory stimulation. *Proceedings of the National Academy of Sciences USA, 89*, 5675–5679.

LaBar, K. S., & Cabeza, R. (2006). Cognitive neuroscience of emotional memory. *Nature Reviews Neuroscience, 7*(1), 54–64.

LaBar, K. S., & Phelps, E. A. (2005). Reinstatement of conditioned fear in humans is context dependent and impaired in amnesia. *Behavioral Neuroscience, 119*(3), 677–686.

Lang, P. J., Bradley, M. M., & Cuthbert, B. N. (1990). Emotion, attention, and the startle reflex. *Psychological Review, 97*(3), 377–395.

Lang, P. J., Bradley, M. M., & Cuthbert, B. N. (1998). *International Affective Picture System (IAPS): Technical Manual and Affective Ratings*. Gainesville: The Center for Research in Psychophysiology, University of Florida.

Lansbergen, M. M., Böcker, K. B. E., Bekker, E. M., & Kenemans, J. L. (2007a). Neural correlates of stopping and self-reported impulsivity. *Clinical Neurophysiology, 118*(9), 2089–2103.

Lansbergen, M. M., Kenemans, J. L., & van Engeland, H. (2007b). Stroop interference and attention-deficit/hyperactivity disorder: A review and meta-analysis. *Neuropsychology, 21*(2), 251–262.

Lansbergen, M. M., van Hell, E., & Kenemans, J. L. (2007c). Impulsivity and conflict in the Stroop task: An ERP study. *Journal of Psychophysiology, 21*(1), 33–50.

Lavie, N. (2005). Distracted and confused? Selective attention under load. *Trends in Cognitive Sciences, 9*(2), 75–82.

Lavric, A., Pizzagalli, D., Forstmeier, S., & Rippon, G. (2001a). A double-dissociation of English past-tense production revealed by event-related potentials and low-resolution electromagnetic tomography (LORETA). *Clinical Neurophysiology, 112*(10), 1833–1849.

Lavric, A., Pizzagalli, D., Forstmeier, S., & Rippon, G. (2001b). Mapping dissociations in verb morphology. *Trends in Cognitive Sciences, 5*(7), 301–308.

Lee, T.-H., Lim, S.-L., Lee, K.-Y., & Choi, J.-S. (2009). Facilitation of visual processing by masked presentation of a conditioned facial stimulus. *Neuroreport, 20*, 750–754.

Lee, T., Dolan, R. J., & Critchley, H. D. (2008). Controlling emotional expression: Behavioral and neural correlates of nonimitative emotional responses. *Cerebral Cortex, 18*, 104–113.

Lepage, J.-F., & Theoret, H. (2006). EEG evidence for the presence of an action observation-execution matching system in children. *European Journal of Neuroscience, 23*(9), 2505–2510.

Libet, B., Gleason, C., Wright, E., & Pearl, D. (1983). Time of conscious intention to act in relation to onset of cerebral activity (readiness-potential). The unconscious initiation of a freely voluntary act. *Brain, 106*, 623–642.

Lieberman, J. A., Javitch, J. A., & Moore, H. (2008). Cholinergic agonists as novel treatments for schizophrenia: The promise of rational drug development for psychiatry. *American Journal of Psychiatry, 165*(8), 931–936.

Light, G., Williams, L., Minow, F., Sprock, J., Rissling, A., Sharp, R., et al. (2010). Electroencephalography (EEG) and event-related potentials (ERPS) with human participants. *Current Protocols in Neuroscience, 52*, 6.25.21–26.25.24.

Lijffijt, M., Kenemans, J. L., ter Wal, A., Quik, E. H., Kemner, C., Westenberg, H., et al. (2006). Dose-related effect of methylphenidate on stopping and changing in children with attention-deficit/hyperactivity disorder. *European Psychiatry, 21*(8), 544–547.

Lijffijt, M., Kenemans, J. L., Verbaten, M. N., & van Engeland, H. (2005). A meta-analytic review of stopping performance in attention-deficit/hyperactivity disorder: Deficient inhibitory motor control? *Journal of Abnormal Psychology, 114*(2), 216–222.

Liotti, M., Woldorff, M. G., Perez, R., & Mayberg, H. S. (2000). An ERP study of the temporal course of the Stroop color-word interference effect. *Neuropsychologia, 38*(5), 701–711.

Logan, G. D. (1994). On the ability to inhibit thought and action: A user's guide to the stop signal. In D. Dagenbach & T. H. Carr (Eds), *Inhibitory Processes in Attention, Memory, and Language,* 189–239. San Diego, CA: Academic Press.

Logan, G. D., & Cowan, W. B. (1984). On the ability to inhibit thought and action: A theory of an act of control. *Psychological Review, 91,* 295–327.

Logothetis, N. (2008). What we can do and what we cannot do with fMRI. *Nature, 453,* 869–878.

Lorteije, J. A. M., Kenemans, J. L., Jellema, T., van der Lubbe, R. H. J., Lommers, M. W., & van Wezel, R. J. A. (2007). Adaptation to real motion reveals direction-selective interactions between real and implied motion processing. *Journal of Cognitive Neuroscience, 19*(8), 1231–1240.

Luck, S. J., & Hillyard, S. A. (1994). Spatial filtering during visual search: Evidence from human electrophysiology. *Journal of Experimental Psychology: Human Perception and Performance, 20*(5), 1000.

Luck, S. J., Vogel, E. K., & Shapiro, K. L. (1996). Word meanings can be accessed but not reported during the attentional blink. *Nature, 383*(6601), 616.

Luck, S. J., Chelazzi, L., Hillyard, S. A., & Desimone, R. (1997). Neural mechanisms of spatial selective attention in areas V1, V2, and V4 of Macaque visual cortex. *Journal of Neurophysiology, 77*(1), 24–42.

Lupien, S., Gillin, C., & Hauger, R. (1999). Working memory is more sensitive than declarative memory to the acute effects of corticosteroids: A dose-response study in humans. *Behavioral Neuroscience, 113,* 420–430.

Lupien, S. J., de Leon, M., de Santi, S., Convit, A., Tarshish, C., Nair, N. P. V., et al. (1998). Cortisol levels during human aging predict hippocampal atrophy and memory deficits. *Nature Neuroscience, 1*(1), 69–73.

MacDonald, A. W., 3rd, Cohen, J. D., Stenger, V. A., & Carter, C. S. (2000). Dissociating the role of the dorsolateral prefrontal and anterior cingulate cortex in cognitive control. *Science, 288*(5472), 1835–1838.

Mack, A., & Rock, I. (1998). *Inattentional Blindness.* Cambridge: The MIT Press.

MacLeod, C. M. (1991). Half a century of research on the Stroop effect: An integrative review. *Psychological Bulletin, 109*(2), 163–203.

Maguire, E. A., Frackowiak, R. S. J., & Frith, C. D. (1997). Recalling routes around London: Activation of the right hippocampus in taxi drivers. *The Journal of Neuroscience, 17*(18), 7103–7110.

Maguire, E. A., Gadian, D. G., Johnsrude, I. S., Good, C. D., Ashburner, J., Frackowiak, R. S. J., et al. (2000). Navigation-related structural change in the hippocampi of taxi drivers. *Proceedings of the National Academy of Sciences USA, 97*(8), 4398.

Maia, T. V., Cooney, R. E., & Peterson, B. S. (2008). The neural bases of obsessive-compulsive disorder in children and adults. *Development and Psychopathology, 20*(Special Issue 04), 1251–1283.

Mangun, G. R. (1995). Neural mechanisms of visual selective attention. *Psychophysiology, 32*(1), 4–18.

Mangun, G. R., & Hillyard, S. A. (1991). Modulations of sensory-evoked brain potentials indicate changes in perceptual processing during visual-spatial priming. *Journal of Experimental Psychology: Human Perception and Performance, 17*(4), 1057–1074.

Mangun, G. R., Hinrichs, H., Scholz, M., Mueller-Gaertner, H. W., Herzog, H., Krause, B. J., et al. (2001). Integrating electrophysiology and neuroimaging of spatial selective attention to simple isolated visual stimuli. *Vision Research, 41*(10–11), 1423–1435.

Marcinkiewcz, C. A., Prado, M. M., Isaac, S. K., Marshall, A., Rylkova, D., & Bruijnzeel, A. W. (2009). Corticotropin-releasing factor within the central nucleus of the amygdala and the nucleus accumbens shell mediates the negative affective state of nicotine withdrawal in rats. *Neuropsychopharmacology, 34*(7), 1743–1752.

Mars, R. B., Coles, M. G. H., Grol, M. J., Holroyd, C. B., Nieuwenhuis, S., Hulstijn, W., *et al.* (2005). Neural dynamics of error processing in medial frontal cortex. *NeuroImage, 28*(4), 1007–1013.

Marschner, A., Kalisch, R., Vervliet, B., Vansteenwegen, D., & Buchel, C. (2008). Dissociable roles for the hippocampus and the amygdala in human cued versus context fear conditioning. *The Journal of Neuroscience, 28*(36), 9030–9036.

Mathews, A., & MacLeod, C. (2005). Cognitive vulnerability to emotional disorders. *Annual Review of Clinical Psychology, 1*(1), 167–195.

Mayberg, H. S. (1997). Limbic-cortical dysregulation: A proposed model of depression. *Journal of Neuropsychiatry, 9,* 471–481.

McRobbie, D., Moore, E., Graves, M., & Prince, M. (2007). *MRI, from Picture to Proton.* Cambridge University Press.

Mehta, M. A., Goodyer, I. M., & Sahakian, B. J. (2004). Methylphenidate improves working memory and set-shifting in AD/HD: Relationships to baseline memory capacity. *Journal of Child Psychology and Psychiatry, 45*(2), 293–305.

Mehta, M. A., & Riedel, W. J. (2006). Dopaminergic enhancement of function. *Current Pharmaceutical Design, 12*(20), 2487–2500.

Menzies, L., Ooi, C., Kamath, S., Suckling, J., McKenna, P., Fletcher, P., *et al.* (2007). Effects of gamma-aminobutyric acid-modulating drugs on working memory and brain function in patients with schizophrenia. *Archives of General Psychiatry, 64*(2), 156–167.

Mesulam, M. M. (1999a). Spatial attention and neglect: Parietal, frontal and cingulate contributions to the mental representation and attentional targeting of salient extrapersonal events. *Philosophical Transactions of the Royal Society of London. Series B: Biological Sciences, 354*(1387), 1325–1346.

Mesulam, M. M. (1999b). Spatial attention and neglect: Parietal, frontal and cingulate contributions to the mental representation and attentional targeting of salient extrapersonal events. *Philosophical Transactions of the Royal Society London Biological Science, 254,* 1325–1346.

Middleton, F. A., & Strick, P. L. (2002). Basal-ganglia 'projections' to the prefrontal cortex of the primate. *Cerebral Cortex, 12*(9), 926–935.

Miller, J. (1982). Discrete versus continuous stage models of human information processing: In search of partial output. *Journal of Experimental Psychology: Human Perception and Performance, 8*(2), 273–296.

Miller, J. (1988). Discrete and continuous models of human information processing: Theoretical distinctions and empirical results. *Acta Psychologica, 67*(3), 191–257.

Miller, J., & Hackley, S. A. (1992). Electrophysiological evidence for temporal overlap among Contingent mental processes. *Journal of Experimental Psychology: General, 121*(2), 195–209.

Miyawaki, Y., Uchida, H., Yamashita, O., Sato, M. A., Morito, Y., Tanabe, H. C., *et al.* (2008). Visual image reconstruction from human brain activity using a combination of multiscale local image decoders. *Neuron, 60*(5), 915–929.

Mobbs, D., Petrovic, P., Marchant, J. L., Hassabis, D., Weiskopf, N., Seymour, B., *et al.* (2007). When fear is near: Threat imminence elicits prefrontal-periaqueductal gray shifts in humans. *Science, 317*(5841), 1079–1083.

Mogg, K., & Bradley, B. P. (2005). Attentional bias in generalized anxiety disorder versus depressive disorder. *Cognitive Therapy and Research, 29*(1), 29–45.

Monti, M. M., Vanhaudenhuyse, A., Coleman, M. R., Boly, M., Pickard, J. D., Tshibanda, L., *et al.* (2010). Willful modulation of brain activity in disorders of consciousness. *New England Journal of Medicine, 362*(7), 579–589.

Moore, T. (1999). Shape representations and visual guidance of Saccadic eye movements. *Science, 285*(5435), 1914–1917.

Moore, T., & Armstrong, K. M. (2003). Selective gating of visual signals by microstimulation of frontal cortex. *Nature, 421*(6921), 370–373.

Moran, J., & Desimone, R. (1985). Selective attention gates visual processing in the extrastriate cortex. *Science, 229*(4715), 782–784.

Morawetz, C., Baudewig, J., Treue, S., & Dechent, P. (2010). Diverting attention suppresses human amygdala responses to faces. *Frontiers in Human Neuroscience, 4, 226.*

Morgan III, C. A., & Grillon, C. (1999). Abnormal mismatch negativity in women with sexual assault-related posttraumatic stress disorder. *Biological Psychiatry, 45*(7), 827–832.

Morris, J. S., Öhman, A., & Dolan, R. J. (1999). A subcortical pathway to the right amygdala mediating "unseen" fear. *Proceedings of the National Academy of Sciences USA, 96*(4), 1680–1685.

Mort, D. J., Malhotra, P., Mannan, S. K., Rorden, C., Pambakian, A., Kennard, C., et al. (2003). The anatomy of visual neglect. *Brain, 126*(9), 1986–1997.

Muller, U., von Cramon, D. Y., & Pollmann, S. (1998). D1- versus D2-receptor modulation of visuospatial working memory in humans. *Journal of Neuroscience, 18*(7), 2720–2728.

Müller-Preuss, P., & Ploog, D. (1981). Inhibition of auditory cortical neurons during phonation. *Brain Research, 215*(1–2), 61–76.

Murakami, S., & Okada, Y. (2006). Contributions of principal neocortical neurons to magnetoencephalography and electroencephalography signals. *Journal of Physiology, 575*(Pt 3), 925–936.

Muthukumaraswamy, S. D., Johnson, B. W., & McNair, N. A. (2004). Mu rhythm modulation during observation of an object-directed grasp. *Cognitive Brain Research, 19*(2), 195–201.

Näätänen, R. (1992). *Attention and Brain Function.* Hillsdale: Lawrence Erlbaum Associates.

Naqvi, N. H., Rudrauf, D., Damasio, H., & Bechara, A. (2007). Damage to the insula disrupts addiction to cigarette smoking. *Science, 315*(5811), 531–534.

Neisser, U., & Harsch, N. (1992). Phantom flashbulbs: False recollections of hearing the news about challenger. In E. Winograd & U. Neisser (Eds), *Affect and Accuracy in Recall: Studies of "Flashbulb" Memories, Vol. 4,* 9–31. New York: Cambridge University Press.

Németh, G., Hegedüs, K., & Molnâr, L. (1988). Akinetic mutism associated with bicingular lesions: Clinicopathological and functional anatomical correlates. *European Archives of Psychiatry and Clinical Neuroscience, 237*(4), 218–222.

Newman, A. J., Ullman, M. T., Pancheva, R., Waligura, D. L., & Neville, H. J. (2007). An ERP study of regular and irregular English past tense inflection. *NeuroImage, 34*(1), 435–445.

Nieuwenhuys, R., Voogd, J., & Van Huijzen, C. (1988). *The Human Central Nervous System: A Synopsis and Atlas.* Berlin: Springer.nigg.

Nigg, J. T., Swanson, J. M., & Hinshaw, S. P. (1997). Covert visual spatial attention in boys with attention deficit hyperactivity disorder: Lateral effects, methylphenidate response and results for parents. *Neuropsychologia, 35*(2), 165–176.

Nishimoto, S., Vu, A. T., Naselaris, T., Benjamini, Y., Yu, B., & Gallant, J. L. (2011). Reconstructing visual experiences from brain activity evoked by natural movies. *Current Biology, 21,* 1641–1646.

Nobre, A. C., Allison, T., & McCarthy, G. (1994). Word recognition in the human inferior temporal lobe. *Nature, 372*(6503), 260–263.

Norman, K. A., Polyn, S. M., Detre, G. J., & Haxby, J. V. (2006). Beyond mind-reading: Multi-voxel pattern analysis of fMRI data. *Trends in Cognitive Sciences, 10*(9), 424–430.

Nyberg, L., Habib, R., McIntosh, A. R., & Tulving, E. (2000). Reactivation of encoding-related brain activity during memory retrieval. *Proceedings of the National Academy of Sciences USA, 97*(20), 11120–11124.

O'Carroll, R. E., Drysdale, E., Cahill, L., Shajahan, P., & Ebmeier, K. P. (1999). Memory for emotional material: A comparison of central versus peripheral beta blockade. *Journal of Psychopharmacology, 13*(1), 32–39.

O'Craven, K. M., Downing, P. E., & Kanwisher, N. (1999). fMRI evidence for objects as the units of attentional selection. *Nature, 401*(6753), 584.

O'Shea, J., Muggleton, N. G., Cowey, A., & Walsh, V. (2004). Timing of target discrimination in human frontal eye fields. *Journal of Cognitive Neuroscience, 16*(6), 1060–1067.

Oberman, L. M., Hubbard, E. M., McCleery, J. P., Altschuler, E. L., Ramachandran, V. S., & Pineda, J. A. (2005). EEG evidence for mirror neuron dysfunction in autism spectrum disorders. *Cognitive Brain Research, 24*(2), 190–198.

Ogawa, S., Lee, T., Kay, A., & Tank, D. (1990). Brain magnetic resonance imaging with contrast dependent on blood oxygenation. *Proceedings of the National Academy of Sciences of America, 87*(24), 9868–9872.

Olesen, P. J., Westerberg, H., & Klingberg, T. (2004). Increased prefrontal and parietal activity after training of working memory. *Nature Neuroscience, 7*(1), 75.

Oosterlaan, J., Logan, G. D., & Sergeant, J. A. (1998). Response inhibition in AD/HD, CD, comorbid AD/HD+CD, anxious, and control children: A meta-analysis of studies with the stop task. *Journal of Child Psychology and Psychiatry, 39*(3), 411–425.

Osipova, D., Hermes, D., & Jensen, O. (2008). Gamma power is phase-locked to posterior alpha activity. *PLoS ONE, 3*(12), e3990.

Overtoom, C. C. E., Bekker, E. M., van der Molen, M. W., Verbaten, M. N., Kooij, J. J. S., Buitelaar, J. K., et al. (2009). Methylphenidate restores link between stop-signal sensory impact and successful stopping in adults with attention-deficit/hyperactivity disorder. *Biological Psychiatry, 65*(7), 614–619.

Paller, K. A. (1990). Recall and stem-completion priming have different electrophysiological correlates and are modified differentially by directed forgetting. *Journal of Experimental Psychology: Learning, Memory, and Cognition, 16*(6), 1021–1032.

Parasuraman, R., Greenwood, P. M., Haxby, J. V., & Grady, C. L. (1992). Visuospatial attention in dementia of the Alzheimer type. *Brain, 115*(3), 711–733.

Pardo, J. V., Pardo, P. J., Janer, K. W., & Raichle, M. E. (1990). The anterior cingulate cortex mediates processing selection in the Stroop attentional conflict paradigm. *Proceedings of the National Academy of Science USA, 87*, 256–259.

Parton, A., Malhotra, P., & Husain, M. (2004). Hemispatial neglect. *Journal of Neurology, Neurosurgery & Psychiatry, 75*(1), 13–21.

Pascual-Marqui, R., Michel, C., & Lehmann, D. (1994). Low resolution electromagnetic tomography: A new method for localizing electrical activity in the brain. *International Journal of Psychophysiology, 18*, 49–65.

Pazo-Alvarez, P., Amenedo, E., Lorenzo-Lopez, L., & Cadaveira, F. (2004). Effects of stimulus location on automatic detection of changes in motion direction in the human brain. *Neuroscience Letters, 371*(2–3), 111–116.

Penke, M., Janssen, U., & Krause, M. (1999). The representation of inflectional morphology: Evidence from Broca's aphasia. *Brain and Language, 68*(1–2), 225–232.

Perlstein, W. M., Dixit, N. K., Carter, C. S., Noll, D. C., & Cohen, J. D. (2003). Prefrontal cortex dysfunction mediates deficits in working memory and prepotent responding in schizophrenia. *Biological Psychiatry, 53*(1), 25–38.

Pessoa, L. (2010). Emotion and cognition and the amygdala: From "what is it?" to "what's to be done?" *Neuropsychologia, 48*(12), 3416–3429.

Pessoa, L., McKenna, M., Gutierrez, E., & Ungerleider, L. G. (2002). Neural processing of emotional faces requires attention. *Proceedings of the National Academy of Sciences USA, 99*(17), 11458–11463.

Petersen, S. E., Fox, P. T., Posner, M. I., Mintun, M., & Raichle, M. E. (1989). Positron emission tomographic studies of the processing of single words. *Journal of Cognitive Neuroscience, 1*(2), 153–170.

Piazza, M., Pinel, P., Le Bihan, D., & Dehaene, S. (2007). A magnitude code common to numerosities and number symbols in human intraparietal cortex. *Neuron, 53*(2), 293.

Pliszka, S. R., Liotti, M., Bailey, B. Y., Perez, I. R., Glahn, D., & Semrud-Clikeman, M. (2007). Electrophysiological effects of stimulant treatment on inhibitory control in children with attention-deficit/hyperactivity disorder. *Journal of Child and Adolescent Psychopharmacology, 17* (3), 356–366.

Poldrack, R. A., Wagner, A. D., Prull, M. W., Desmond, J. E., Glover, G. H., & Gabrieli, J. D. E. (1999). Functional specialization for semantic and phonological processing in the left inferior prefrontal cortex. *NeuroImage, 10*(1), 15–35.

Posner, M., & Raichle, M. (1994). *Images of Mind.* New York: Scientifc American Library.

Posner, M., Sandson, J., Dhawan, M., & Shulman, G. (1989). Is word recognition automatic? A cognitive-anatomical approach. *Journal of Cognitive Neuroscience, 1*(1), 50–60.

Posner, M. I., & Dehaene, S. (1994). Attentional networks. *Trends in Neurosciences, 17*(2), 75–79.

Posner, M. I., & Petersen, S. E. (1990). The attention system of the human brain. *Annual Review of Neuroscience, 13*, 25–42.

Posner, M. I., Snyder, C. R., & Davidson, B. J. (1980). Attention and the detection signals. *Journal of Experimental Psychology, 109*, 160–174.

Posner, M. I., Walker, J. A., Friedrich, F. J., & Rafal, R. D. (1984). Effects of parietal injury on covert orienting of attention. *The Journal of Neuroscience, 4*(7), 1863–1874.

Price, C. J., Winterburn, D., Giraud, A. L., Moore, C. J., & Noppeney, U. (2003). Cortical localisation of the visual and auditory word form areas: A reconsideration of the evidence. *Brain and Language, 86*(2), 272–286.

Proctor, R.W., & Reeve, T.G. (1985). Compatibility effects in the assignment of symbolic stimuli to discrete finger responses. *Journal of Experimental Psychology: Human Perception and Performance, 11*(5), 623–639.

Pujol, J., Soriano-Mas, C., Alonso, P., Cardoner, N., Menchon, J. M., Deus, J., *et al.* (2004). Mapping structural brain alterations in obsessive-compulsive disorder. *Archives of General Psychiatry, 61*(7), 720–730.

Purves, D., Augustine, G. J., Fitzpatrick, D., Katz, L. C., LaMantia, A. S., McNamara, J. O., *et al.* (2001). *Neuroscience.* Sunderland: Sinauer.

Raichle, M. E. (2010). Two views of brain function. *Trends in Cognitive Sciences, 14*(4), 180–190.

Raos, V., Umilta, M.-A., Murata, A., Fogassi, L., & Gallese, V. (2006). Functional properties of grasping-related neurons in the ventral premotor area F5 of the Macaque monkey. *Journal of Neurophysiology, 95*(2), 709–729.

Raymond, J. E., Shapiro, K. L., & Arnell, K. M. (1992). Temporary suppression of visual processing in an RSVP task: An attentional blink? *Journal of Experimental Psychology: Human Perception and Performance, 18*(3), 849.

Redgrave, P., & Gurney, K. (2006). The short-latency dopamine signal: A role in discovering novel actions? *Nature Reviews Neuroscience, 7*(12), 967–975.

Rees, G., Frith, C. D., & Lavie, N. (1997). Modulating irrelevant motion perception by varying attentional load in an unrelated task. *Science, 278*(5343), 1616–1619.

Ressler, K. J., & Mayberg, H. S. (2007). Targeting abnormal neural circuits in mood and anxiety disorders: From the laboratory to the clinic. *Nature Neuroscience, 10*(9), 1116–1124.

Ressler, K. J., Rothbaum, B. O., Tannenbaum, L., Anderson, P., Graap, K., Zimand, E., *et al.* (2004). Cognitive enhancers as adjuncts to psychotherapy: Use of D-cycloserine in phobic individuals to facilitate extinction of fear. *Archives of General Psychiatry, 61*(11), 1136–1144.

Riba, J., Rodríguez-Fornells, A., Urbano, G., Morte, A., Antonijoan, R., & Barbanoj, M. (2001). Differential effects of alprazolam on the baseline and fear-potentiated startle reflex in humans: A dose-response study. *Psychopharmacology, 157*, 358–367.

Ridderinkhof, K. R., de Vlugt, Y., Bramlage, A., Spaan, M., Elton, M., Snel, J., *et al.* (2002). Alcohol consumption impairs detection of performance errors in mediofrontal cortex. *Science, 298*(5601), 2209–2211.

Riedel, W., Hogervorst, E., Leboux, R., Verhey, F., Van Praag, H., & Jolles, J. (1995). Caffeine attenuates scopolamine-induced memory impairment in humans. *Psychopharmacology, 122*, 158–168.

Rimmele, U., Domes, G., Mathiak, K., & Hautzinger, M. (2003). Cortisol has different effects on human memory for emotional and neutral stimuli. *Neuroreport, 19*, 2485–2488.

Rizzolatti, G., Riggio, L., Dascola, I., & Umilta, C. (1987). Reorienting attention across the horizontal and vertical meridians: Evidence in favor of a premotor theory of attention. *Neuropsychologia, 25*(1A), 31–40.

Robbins, T. W. (2000). Chemical neuromodulation of frontal-executive functions in humans and other animals. *Experimental Brain Research, 133*(1), 130–138.

Rodriguez-Fornells, A., Kofidis, C., & Münte, T. F. (2004). An electrophysiological study of errorless learning. *Cognitive Brain Research, 19*(2), 160–173.

Roelfsema, P. R., Lamme, V. A., & Spekreijse, H. (1998). Object-based attention in the primary visual cortex of the macaque monkey. *Nature, 395*(6700), 376–381.

Rogalsky, C., & Hickok, G. (2011). The role of Broca's area in sentence comprehension. *Journal of Cognitive Neuroscience, 23*(7), 1664–1680.

Roland, P. E., Larsen, B., Lassen, N. A., & Skinhoj, E. (1980). Supplementary motor area and other cortical areas in organization of voluntary movements in man. *Journal of Neurophysiology, 43*(1), 118–136.

Rosenbaum, R. S., Gao, F., Richards, B., Black, S. E., & Moscovitch, M. (2005). "Where to?" remote memory for spatial relations and landmark identity in former taxi drivers with Alzheimer's disease and encephalitis. *Journal of Cognitive Neuroscience, 17*, 446–462.

Rounis, E., Yarrow, K., & Rothwell, J. C. (2007). Effects of RTMS conditioning over the fronto-parietal network on motor versus visual attention. *Journal of Cognitive Neuroscience, 19*(3), 513–524.

Rubia, K., Smith, A. B., Brammer, M. J., Toone, B., & Taylor, E. (2005). Abnormal brain activation during inhibition and error detection in medication-naive adolescents with ADHD. *American Journal of Psychiatry, 162*(6), 1067–1075.

Rushworth, M. F. S., Ellison, A., & Walsh, V. (2001a). Complementary localization and lateralization of orienting and motor attention. *Nature Neuroscience, 4*(6), 656–661.

Rushworth, M. F. S., Paus, T., & Sipila, P.K. (2001b). Attention systems and the organization of the human parietal cortex. *The Journal of Neuroscience, 21*, 5262–5271.

Rushworth, M. F. S., Krams, M., & Passingham, R. E. (2001c). The attentional role of the left parietal cortex: The distinct lateralization and localization of motor attention in the human brain. *Journal of Cognitive Neuroscience, 13*(5), 698–710.

Sanders, A.F. (1990). Issues and trends in the debate on discrete vs. continuous processing of information. *Acta Psychologica, 74*, 123–167.

Sanfey, A. G., Rilling, J. K., Aronson, J. A., Nystrom, L. E., & Cohen, J. D. (2003). The neural basis of economic decision-making in the ultimatum game. *Science, 300*(5626), 1755–1758.

Santhanam, G., Ryu, S. I., Yu, B. M., Afshar, A., & Shenoy, K. V. (2006). A high-performance brain-computer interface. *Nature, 442*(7099), 195–198.

Santos, N. S., Kuzmanovic, B., David, N., Rotarska-Jagiela, A., Eickhoff, S. B., Shah, J. N., *et al.* (2010). Animated brain: A functional neuroimaging study on animacy experience. *NeuroImage, 53*(1), 291–302.

Sarkey, S., Azcoitia, I., Garcia-Segura, L. M., Garcia-Ovejero, D., & DonCarlos, L. L. (2008). Classical androgen receptors in non-classical sites in the brain. *Hormones and Behavior, 53*(5), 753–764.

Scheres, A., Oosterlaan, J., Swanson, J., Morein-Zamir, S., Meiran, N., Schut, H., *et al.* (2003). The effect of methylphenidate on three forms of response inhibition in boys with AD/HD. *Journal of Abnormal Child Psychology, 31*(1), 105–120.

Scherg, M., & Von Cramon, D. Y. (1985). A new interpretation of the generators of BAEP waves I–V: Results of a spatio-temporal dipole model. *Electroencephalography and Clinical Neurophysiology, 62*, 290–299.

Schultz, W. (2000). Multiple reward signals in the brain. *Nature Reviews Neuroscience, 1*(3), 199–207.

Schultz, W., Dayan, P., & Montague, P. R. (1997a). A neural substrate of prediction and reward. *Science, 275*, 1593–1599.

Schultz, W., Dayan, P., & Montague, P. R. (1997b). A neural substrate of prediction and reward. *Science, 275*(5306), 1593–1599.

Schupp, H. T., Junghöfer, M., Weike, A. I., & Hamm, A. O. (2003). Emotional facilitation of sensory processing in the visual cortex. *Psychological Science, 14*(1), 7–13.

Schutter, D. J. L. G., Leitner, C., Kenemans, J. L., & van Honk, J. (2006). Electrophysiological correlates of cortico-subcortical interaction: A cross-frequency spectral EEG analysis. *Clinical Neurophysiology, 117*(2), 381–387.

Schutter, D. J. L. G., & van Honk, J. (2005). Electrophysiological ratio markers for the balance between reward and punishment. *Cognitive Brain Research, 24*(3), 685–690.

Seitz, A., & Watanabe, T. (2005). A unified model for perceptual learning. *Trends in Cognitive Sciences, 9*(7), 329.

Seymour, B., Daw, N., Dayan, P., Singer, T., & Dolan, R. (2007). Differential encoding of losses and gains in the human striatum. *The Journal of Neuroscience, 27*(18), 4826–4831.

Siegert, R. J., Taylor, K. D., Weatherall, M., & Abernethy, D. A. (2006). Is implicit sequence learning impaired in Parkinson's disease? A meta-analysis. *Neuropsychology, 20*(4), 490–495.

Siero, J., Petridou, N., Hoogduin, H., Luijten, P., & Ramsey, N. O. (2011). Cortical depth-dependent temporal dynamics of the BOLD response in the human brain. *Journal of Cerebral Blood Flow and Metabolism, 31*, 1999–2008.

Sigman, M., & Gilbert, C. D. (2000). Learning to find a shape. *Nature Neuroscience, 3*(3), 264–269.

Silvanto, J., Lavie, N., & Walsh, V. (2006). Stimulation of the human frontal eye fields modulates sensitivity of extrastriate visual cortex. *Journal of Neurophysiology, 96*(2), 941–945.

Skinner, J. E., & Yingling, C. D. (1976). Regulation of slow potential shifts in nucleus reticularis thalami by the mesencephalic reticular formation and the frontal granular cortex. *Electroencephalography and Clinical Neurophysiology, 40*(3), 288.

Slagter, H. A., Kok, A., Mol, N., & Kenemans, J. L. (2005). Spatio-temporal dynamics of top-down control: Directing attention to location and/or color as revealed by ERPS and source modeling. *Cognitive Brain Research, 22*(3), 333–348.

Smith, E.E., Jonides, J., Marshuetz, C., & Koeppe, R.A. (1998). Components of verbal working memory: Evidence from neuro-imaging. *Proceedings of the National Academy of Sciences, 95*, 876–882.

Snyder, S. M., & Hall, J. R. (2006). A meta-analysis of quantitative EEG power associated with attention-deficit hyperactivity disorder. *Journal of Clinical Neurophysiology, 23*, 441–456.

Sokolov, E. N. (1963). Higher nervous functions: The orienting reflex. *Annual Review of Physiology, 25*(1), 545–580.

Sommer, M. A., & Wurtz, R. H. (2006). Influence of the thalamus on spatial visual processing in frontal cortex. *Nature, 444*(7117), 374–377.

Sonnby–Borgström, M. (2002). Automatic mimicry reactions as related to differences in emotional empathy. *Scandinavian Journal of Psychology, 43*(5), 433–443.

Soon, C. S., Brass, M., Heinze, H.-J., & Haynes, J.-D. (2008). Unconscious determinants of free decisions in the human brain. *Nature Neuroscience, 11*(5), 543–545.

Speer, N. K., Reynolds, J. R., Swallow, K. M., & Zacks, J. M. (2009). Reading stories activates neural representations of visual and motor experiences. *Psychological Science, 20*(8), 989–999.

Spencer, T., Wilens, T., Biederman, J., Faraone, S. V., Ablon, J. S., & Lapey, K. (1995). A double-blind, crossover comparison of methylphenidate and placebo in adults with childhood-onset attention-deficit hyperactivity disorder. *Archives of General Psychiatry, 52*(6), 434–443.

Sperry, R. (1950). Neural basis of the spontaneous optokinetic response produced by visual inversion. *Journal of Comparative and Physiological Psychology, 43*, 482–489.

Spitzer, H., Desimone, R., & Moran, J. (1988). Increased attention enhances both behavioral and neuronal performance. *Science, 240*(4850), 338.

Springer, U. S., Rosas, A., McGetrick, J., & Bowers, D. (2007). Differences in startle reactivity during the perception of angry and fearful faces. *Emotion, 7*(3), 516–525.

Squire, L. R. (2009). The legacy of patient H.M. for neuroscience. *Neuron, 61*(1), 6–9.

Stahl, S. M. (2008). *Essential Psychopharmacology: Neuroscientific Basis and Practical Applications.* Cambridge: Cambridge University Press.

Stark, R., Zimmermann, M., Kagerer, S., Schienle, A., Walter, B., Weygandt, M., *et al.* (2007). Hemodynamic brain correlates of disgust and fear ratings. *NeuroImage, 37*(2), 663–673.

Steele, C. J., & Penhune, V. B. (2010). Specific increases within global decreases: A functional magnetic resonance imaging investigation of five days of motor sequence learning. *The Journal of Neuroscience, 30*(24), 8332–8341.

Sternberg, S. (1969). The discovery of processing stages: Extensions of Donders' method. *Acta Psychologica, 30*, 276–315.

Sterpenich, V., D'Argembeau, A., Desseilles, M., Balteau, E., Albouy, G., Vandewalle, G., *et al*. (2006). The locus ceruleus is involved in the successful retrieval of emotional memories in humans. *The Journal of Neuroscience, 26*(28), 7416–7423.

Stillman, R., Jones, R., Moore, D., Walker, J., & Welm, S. (1993). Improved performance 4 hours after cocaine. *Psychopharmacology, 110*(4), 415–420.

Strack, F., Martin, L. L., & Stepper, S. (1988). Inhibiting and facilitating conditions of the human smile: A nonobtrusive test of the facial feedback hypothesis. *Journal of Personality and Social Psychology, 54*(5), 768–777.

Strange, B. A., & Dolan, R. J. (2004). Î²-adrenergic modulation of emotional memory-evoked human amygdala and hippocampal responses. *Proceedings of the National Academy of Sciences USA, 101*(31), 11454–11458.

Stroobant, N., & Vingerhoets, G. (2000). Transcranial doppler ultrasonography monitoring of cerebral hemodynamics during performance of cognitive tasks. A review. *Neuropsychological Review, 10*, 213–231.

Stroop, J. R. (1935). Studies of interference in serial verbal reactions. *Journal of Experimental Psychology, 18*, 643–662.

Supèr, H., van der Togt, C., Spekreijse, H., & Lamme, V. A. F. (2004). Correspondence of presaccadic activity in the monkey primary visual cortex with saccadic eye movements. *Proceedings of the National Academy of Sciences, 101*(9), 3230–3235.

Talarico, J. M., & Rubin, D. C. (2003). Confidence, not consistency, characterizes flashbulb memories. *Psychological Science (Wiley-Blackwell), 14*(5), 455–461.

Tamietto, M., Geminiani, G., Genero, R., & de Gelder, B. (2007). Seeing fearful body language overcomes attentional deficits in patients with neglect. *Journal of Cognitive Neuroscience, 19*(3), 445–454.

Taylor, J. G., & Fragopanagos, N. F. (2005). The interaction of attention and emotion. *Neural Networks, 18*(4), 353–369.

Thach, W. T., Mink, J. W., Goodkin, H. P., & Keating, J. G. (2000). Combining versus gating motor programs: Differential roles for cerebellum and basal ganglia? In M. S. Gazzaniga (Ed.), *Cognitive Neuroscience: A Reader*. Malden, MA: Blackwell Publishers Inc.

Thompson-Schill, S. L., D'Esposito, M., & Kan, I. P. (1999). Effects of repetition and competition on activity in left prefrontal cortex during word generation. *Neuron, 23*(3), 513–522.

Thompson, R. F., & Spencer, W. A. (1966). Habituation: A model phenomenon for the study of neuronal substrates of behavior. *Psychological Review, 73*(1), 16.

Thompson, R. F., & Steinmetz, J. E. (2009). The role of the cerebellum in classical conditioning of discrete behavioral responses. *Neuroscience, 162*(3), 732–755.

Thut, G., Hauert, C.-A., Viviani, P., Morand, S., Spinelli, L., Blanke, O., *et al*. (2000). Internally driven v. externally cued movement selection: A study on the timing of brain activity. *Cognitive Brain Research, 9*(3), 261–269.

Tognoli, E., Lagarde, J., DeGuzman, G. C., & Kelso, J. A. S. (2007). The phi complex as a neuromarker of human social coordination. *Proceedings of the National Academy of Sciences USA, 104*(19), 8190–8195.

Toichi, M., & Kamio, Y., (2002). Long-term memory and levels-of-processing in autism. *Neuropsychologia, 40*, 964–969.

Tsushima, Y., Sasaki, Y., & Watanabe, T. (2006). Greater disruption due to failure of inhibitory control on an ambiguous distractor. *Science, 314*(5806), 1786–1788.

Turetsky, B. I., Calkins, M. E., Light, G. A., Olincy, A., Radant, A. D., & Swerdlow, N. R. (2007). Neurophysiological endophenotypes of schizophrenia: The viability of selected candidate measures. *Schizophrenia Bulletin, 33*(1), 69–94.

Turner, D. C., Blackwell, A. D., Dowson, J. H., McLean, A., & Sahakian, B. J. (2005). Neurocognitive effects of methylphenidate in adult attention-deficit/hyperactivity disorder. *Psychopharmacology (Berl), 178*(2–3), 286–295.

Ullman, M. T. (2001). A neurocognitive perspective on language: The declarative/procedural model. *Nature Reviews Neuroscience, 2*(10), 717–726.

Ullman, M. T., Corkin, S., Coppola, M., Hickok, G., Growdon, J. H., Koroshetz, W. J., *et al.* (1997). A neural dissociation within language: Evidence that the mental dictionary is part of declarative memory, and that grammatical rules are processed by the procedural system. *Journal of Cognitive Neuroscience, 9*(2), 266–276.

Ullman, M. T., Pancheva, R., Love, T., Yee, E., Swinney, D., & Hickok, G. (2005). Neural correlates of lexicon and grammar: Evidence from the production, reading, and judgment of inflection in aphasia. *Brain and Language, 93*(2), 185–238.

Umeno, M. M., & Goldberg, M. E. (1997). Spatial processing in the monkey frontal eye field. I: Predictive visual responses. *Journal of Neurophysiology, 78*(3), 1373–1383.

Ungerleider, L. G., & Haxby, J. V. (1994). 'What' and 'where' in the human brain. *Current Opinion in Neurobiology, 4*(2), 157–165.

Vakalopoulos, C. (2006). Neuropharmacology of cognition and memory: A unifying theory of neuromodulator imbalance in psychiatry and amnesia. *Medical Hypotheses, 66*(2), 394–431.

Valera, E. M., Faraone, S. V., Murray, K. E., & Seidman, L. J. (2007). Meta-analysis of structural imaging findings in attention-deficit/hyperactivity disorder. *Biological Psychiatry, 61*(12), 1361.

van den Heuvel, M. P., Mandl, R. C., Stam, C. J., Kahn, R. S., & Hulshoff Pol, H. E. (2010). Aberrant frontal and temporal complex network structure in schizophrenia: A graph theoretical analysis. *Journal of Neuroscience, 30*(47), 15915–15926.

van den Wildenberg, W. P. M., van Boxtel, G. J. M., van der Molen, M. W., Bosch, D. A., Speelman, J. D., & Brunia, C. H. M. (2006). Stimulation of the subthalamic region facilitates the selection and inhibition of motor responses in Parkinson's disease. *Journal of Cognitive Neuroscience, 18*(4), 626–636.

Van der Heijden, A. H. C. (1992). *Selective attention in vision.* London: Routledge.

van der Lubbe, R. H. J., Neggers, S. F. W., Verleger, R., & Kenemans, J. L. (2006). Spatiotemporal overlap between brain activation related to saccade preparation and attentional orienting. *Brain Research, 1072*(1), 133–152.

van Honk, J., Harmon-Jones, E., Morgan, B. E., & Schutter, D. J. L. G. (2010). Socially explosive minds: The triple imbalance hypothesis of reactive aggression. *Journal of Personality, 78*(1), 67–94.

van Honk, J., Hermans, E. J., d'Alfonso, A. A. L., Schutter, D. J. L. G., van Doornen, L., & de Haan, E. H. F. (2002a). A left-prefrontal lateralized, sympathetic mechanism directs attention towards social threat in humans: Evidence from repetitive transcranial magnetic stimulation. *Neuroscience Letters, 319*(2), 99–102.

van Honk, J., Schutter, D. J., d'Alfonso, A. A., Kessels, R. P., & de Haan, E. H. (2002b). 1 Hz RTMS over the right prefrontal cortex reduces vigilant attention to unmasked but not to masked fearful faces. *Biological Psychiatry, 52*(4), 312–317.

van Minnen, A., Hoogduin, K. A. L., Keijsers, G. P. J., Hellenbrand, I., & Hendriks, G.-J. (2003). Treatment of trichotillomania with behavioral therapy or fluoxetine: A randomized, waiting-list controlled study. *Archives of General Psychiatry, 60*(5), 517–522.

van Schie, H. T., Mars, R. B., Coles, M. G. H., & Bekkering, H. (2004). Modulation of activity in medial frontal and motor cortices during error observation. *Nature Neuroscience, 7*(5), 549–554.

van Stegeren, A. H., Everaerd, W., Cahill, L., McGaugh, J. L., & Gooren, L. J. G. (1998). Memory for emotional events: Differential effects of centrally versus peripherally acting β-blocking agents. *Psychopharmacology, 138*(3), 305–310.

van Veen, V., & Carter, C. S. (2002). The timing of action-monitoring processes in the anterior cingulate cortex. *Journal of Cognitive Neuroscience, 14*(4), 593–602.

van Velzen, J., & Eimer, M. (2003). Early posterior erp components do not reflect the control of attentional shifts toward expected peripheral events. *Psychophysiology, 40*(5), 827–831.

Veldhuijzen, D. S., Kenemans, J. L., de Bruin, C. M., Olivier, B., & Volkerts, E. R. (2006). Pain and attention: Attentional disruption or distraction? *The Journal of Pain, 7*(1), 11–20.

Veldhuizen, M. G., Bender, G., Constable, R. T., & Small, D. M. (2007). Trying to detect taste in a taste-less solution: Modulation of early gustatory cortex by attention to taste. *Chemical Senses, 32*(6), 569–581.

Verwey, W. B., & Eikelboom, T. (2003). Evidence for lasting sequence segmentation in the discrete sequence-production task. *Journal of Motor Behavior, 35*(2), 171–181.

Villringer, A., Planck, J., Hock, C., Schleinkofer, L., & Dirnagl, U. (1993). Near infrared spectroscopy (NIRS): A new tool to study hemodynamic changes during activation of brain function in human adults. *Neuroscience Letters, 154*(1–2), 101–104.

Vollstädt-Klein, S., Wichert, S., Rabinstein, J., Bühler, M., Klein, O., Ende, G., *et al.* (2010). Initial, habitual and compulsive alcohol use is characterized by a shift of cue processing from ventral to dorsal striatum. *Addiction, 105*, 1741–1749.

Wagner, A. D., Koutstaal, W., & Schacter, D. L. (1999). When encodong yields remembering: Insights from event-related neuroimaging. *Philosophical Transactions of the Royal Society B: Biological Sciences, 354*(1387), 1307–1324.

Wagner, A. D., Schacter, D. L., Rotte, M., Koutstaal, W., Maril, A., Dale, A. M., *et al.* (1998). Building memories: Remembering and forgetting of verbal experiences as predicted by brain activity. *Science, 281*(5380), 1188–1191.

Weissman, D. H., Woldorff, M. G., Hazlett, C. J., & Mangun, G. R. (2002). Effects of practice on executive control investigated with fMRI. *Brain Research Cognitive Brain Research, 15*(1), 47–60.

West, R. (2003). Neural correlates of cognitive control and conflict detection in the Stroop and digit-location tasks. *Neuropsychologia, 41*(8), 1122–1135.

Wheeler, M. E., Petersen, S. E., & Buckner, R. L. (2000). Memory's echo: Vivid remembering reactivates sensory-specific cortex. *Proceedings of the National Academy of Sciences USA, 97*(20), 11125.

Wheeler, M. E., Shulman, G. L., Buckner, R. L., Miezin, F. M., Velanova, K., & Petersen, S. E. (2006). Evidence for separate perceptual reactivation and search processes during remembering. *Cerebral Cortex, 16*(7), 949–959.

Whiteside, S. P., Port, J. D., & Abramowitz, J. S. (2004). A meta-analysis of functional neuroimaging in obsessive-compulsive disorder. *Psychiatry Research: Neuroimaging, 132*(1), 69–79.

Willems, R. M., Hagoort, P., & Casasanto, D. (2010). Body-specific representations of action verbs. *Psychological Science, 21*(1), 67–74.

Willemssen, R., Müller, T., Schwarz, M., Falkenstein, M., & Beste, C. (2009). Response monitoring in de novo patients with Parkinson's disease. *PLoS ONE, 4*(3), e4898.

Wilson, B. A., Baddeley, A., Evans, J., & Shiel, A. (1994). Errorless learning in the rehabilitation of memory impaired people. *Neuropsychological Rehabilitation: An International Journal, 4*(3), 307–326.

Witte, E. A., Davidson, M. C., & Marrocco, R. T. (1997). Effects of altering brain cholinergic activity on covert orienting of attention: Comparison of monkey and human performance. *Psychopharmacology (Berl), 132*(4), 324–334.

Woldorff, M. G. (1993). Distortion of ERP averages due to overlap from temporally adjacent ERPs: Analysis and correction. *Psychophysiology, 30*(1), 98–119.

Woldorff, M. G., Gallen, C. C., Hampson, S. A., Hillyard, S. A., Pantev, C., Sobel, D., *et al.* (1993). Modulation of early sensory processing in human auditory cortex during auditory selective attention. *Proceedings of the National Academy of Sciences USA, 90*(18), 8722–8726.

Woldorff, M. G., & Hillyard, S. A. (1991). Modulation of early auditory processing during selective listening to rapidly presented tones. *Electroencephalography and Clinical Neurophysiology, 79*(3), 170–191.

Wolf, O. T. (2009). Stress and memory in humans: Twelve years of progress? *Brain Research, 1293*, 142–154.

Wood, N., & Cowan, N. (1995). The cocktail party phenomenon revisited: How frequent are attention shifts to one's name in an irrelevant auditory channel? *Journal of Experimental Psychology: Learning, Memory, and Cognition, 21*(1), 255.

Woods, D. L., Hillyard, S. A., & Hansen, J. C. (1984). Event-related brain potentials reveal similar attentional mechanisms during selective listening and shadowing. *Journal of Experimental Psychology: Human Perception and Performance, 10*(6), 761–777.

Wright, M. J., Burns, R. J., Geffen, G. M., & Geffen, L. B. (1990). Covert orientation of visual attention in Parkinson's disease: An impairment in the maintenance of attention. *Neuropsychologia, 28*(2), 151–159.

Yu-Feng, Z., Yong, H., Chao-Zhe, Z., Qing-Jiu, C., Man-Qiu, S., Meng, L., *et al.* (2007). Altered baseline brain activity in children with ADHD revealed by resting-state functional MRI. *Brain and Development, 29*(2), 83.

Zohar, J., Juven-Wetzler, A., Myers, V., & Fostick, L. (2008). Post-traumatic stress disorder: Facts and fiction. *Current opinion in psychiatry, 21*, 74–77.

Zorzi, M., Priftis, K., & Umilta, C. (2002). Brain damage: Neglect disrupts the mental number line. *Nature, 417*(6885), 138–139.

Index